IIC STUDIES

Studies in Industrial Property and Copyright Law

Christopher Heath and Anselm Kamperman
Sanders (editors)

New Frontiers of Intellectual Property Law
IP and Cultural Heritage – Geographical Indications –
Enforcement – Overprotection

INSTITUTE OF EUROPEAN STUDIES OF MACAU
澳 門 歐 洲 研 究 學 會
INSTITUTO DE ESTUDOS EUROPEUS DE MACAU

Universiteit Maastricht

·HART·
PUBLISHING

OXFORD AND PORTLAND, OREGON
2005

Hart Publishing
Oxford and Portland, Oregon

Published in North America (US and Canada) by
Hart Publishing c/o
International Specialized Book Services
5804 NE Hassalo Street
Portland, Oregon
97213-3644
USA

Hart Publishing is a specialist legal publisher based in Oxford,
England.
To order further copies of this book or to request a list of other
publications please write to:

Hart Publishing, Salter's Boatyard, Folly Bridge,
Abingdon Road, Oxford OX1 4LB
Telephone: +44 (0)1865 245533 or Fax: +44 (0)1865 794882
e-mail: mail@hartpub.co.uk
WEBSITE: http//www.hartpub.co.uk

British Library Cataloguing in Publication Data
Data Available
ISBN 1–84113–571–2 (paperback)

Typeset by Hope Services (Abingdon) Ltd.
Printed and bound in Great Britain on acid-free paper by
Page Bros (Norwich) Ltd

Studies in Industrial Property and Copyright Law

Volume 25

·H A R T·
PUBLISHING

OXFORD AND PORTLAND, OREGON
2005

Published by the Max Planck Institute for Foreign and
International Patent, Copyright and Competition Law, Munich

Editors

Professor Dr Josef Drexl
Professor Dr Reto Hilty
Professor Dr h.c. Joseph Strauss

Contents

Part 1 – IP Cultural Heritage

1 Back to the Future: Intellectual Property Rights and the Modernisation of Traditional Chinese Medicine   Bryan Bachner . .1

Introduction

Part 2 – Geographical Indications

Preface

The editors hereby present papers of the third and fourth IP conference organised by the Macau Institute of European Studies (IEEM) on intellectual property law and the economic challenges for Asia.

The objective of the conferences is to provide up-to-date information on developments in global intellectual property law and policy and their impact on regional economic and cultural development. The current volume deals with the rapid development in industrial property law, especially in areas that in the past have not featured prominently. The difficult balance between broad intellectual property protection and possible limitations was already addressed in the past volume. In this volume it is addressed from the angle of multiple and overprotection of IP rights that forms Part 3 of the book. The first two parts cover the protection of subject matters that are relative newcomers to the field of international intellectual property: cultural heritage and geographical indications. In both cases, the angle of public interest is arguably stronger than in traditional fields of intellectual property law and is thus broadly explored. Cultural heritage and geographical indications may deserve as much proprietary protection as they deserve protection against private misappropriation by third parties. And in contrast to traditional intellectual property rights, protection with the aim of preservation may be as important as protection with the aim of commercial exploitation. Finally, issues of enforcement have become a major point of interest after the substantive intellectual property rules were put in place. Particular emphasis is given to enforcement systems in Asia, and to the subject matter of criminal enforcement that in many parts of the world is considered an important tool of effective protection.

The success of the first five IEEM intellectual property law seminars have turned the venue into an annual event that since the year 2004 has been coupled with the intellectual property law summer school. The seminar in 2005 will look at the implications of free trade agreements for the international framework of intellectual property law, a topic of particular interest to the Asian region.

The editors would specifically like to thank Mr. Gonçalo Cabral, who has been instrumental in organising both the IEEM annual seminars and the intellectual property summer school, and to José Luís de Sales Marques, President of the IEEM, for his continuing support for both venues. Finally, the seminars would not have happened without the tireless commitment of Bentham Fong and the other staff members of IEEM in Macao, just as the publications would not have been possible without Erma Becker from the Max Planck Institute who competently handled the manuscripts.

Christopher Heath and Anselm Kamperman Sanders

List of Contributors

Christoph Antons, Ref. jur. (Rhineland Palatinate), Ass. jur. (Bavaria), Dr. jur. (Amsterdam), is Professor of Comparative Law, Faculty of Law and Director, Centre for Law and Sustainable Development in Asia, University of Wollongong, Australia. He is an adjunct fellow of the Queen Mary Intellectual Property Research Institute at the University of London and a QEII Fellow of the Australian Research Council.
He can be reached by e-mail at cantons@uow.edu.au.

Bryan Bachner is an Associate Professor of Law at the City University of Hong Kong. He received his J.D. Degree from American University's Washington College of Law in the United States and his Ph.D from Wuhan University in China. The current focus of his teaching and scholarship is intellectual property rights and environmental law.
He can be reached by e-mail at b.bachner@cityu.edu.hk.

Giovanni Casucci, attorney-at-law, is Head of the IP Department of Clifford Chance, Milan, and Director of the Master Program Industrial Property Management at the Polytechnic School of Engineering in Milan. He is the author of various publications on industrial property and a frequent lecturer at national and international conferences and seminars. Dr. Casucci completed a "Study on protection and defence of intellectual property rights for the textile and clothing industry" for the Far East countries organised by the European Commission, 1997.
He can be reached by e-mail at giovanni.casucci@cliffordchance.com.

António Corte-Real studied at the Law Faculty of the Lisbon University and graduated in European Studies from the Catholic University of Lisbon. He has worked in Lisbon as a consultant, attorney and litigator specialising in intellectual property and advertising law. He is a senior partner with the firm Simões, Garcia, Corte-Real & Associados of Lisbon and a legal advisor of ICAP, Portuguese Association for Advertising Self-Regulation. He is co-author of the *Guide to European Trademark Law & Litigation* (Sweet & Maxwell), *World Intellectual Property Rights and Remedies* (Oceana Public) and has written several IP related articles and conferences. He is a member of the Law and Harmonization Committees of the European Communities Trademark Association.
He can be reached by e-mail at sgcr@jrs.jazznet.pt.

Earl Gray is a partner and head of intellectual property at top tier New Zealand commercial law firm, Simpson Grierson. He studied at the Universities of Otago and Cambridge, and returned to New Zealand to re-join Simpson Grierson in 1995. Earl is current chair of the Intellectual Property Practice Group of Lex Mundi, the world's leading association of independent law firms, and is the New Zealand representative on the Asia-Pacific Subcommittee of the International Amicus Committee of the International Trademark Association. He is a co-author of the Butterworths New Zealand loose-leaf, *Copyright & Design* and a co-author of Brookers *A Guide to E-Commerce Law in New Zealand*.
He can be contacted by e-mail at earl.gray@simpsongrierson.com.

Christopher Heath studied at the Universities of Konstanz, Edinburgh and the LSE. He lived and worked in Japan for three years, and since 1992 has headed the Asian Department of the Max Planck Institute for Patent Law in Munich. Christopher Heath is the editor of the Max Planck Institute's Asian Intellectual Property Series published by Kluwer Law International.
He can be reached by e-mail at chh@ip.mpg.de.

Thomas Heide obtained his Ph.D from Cambridge University, where his topic dealt with copyright law and its interface with online contracts and technological protection measures. He is currently practising as an IP and competition lawyer at London firm SJ Berwin.
He can be reached by e-mail at thomas.heide@sjberwin.com.

Stephen Hubicki is a Research Fellow at the Australian Centre for Intellectual Property in Agriculture at the T.C. Beirne School of Law at the University of Queensland in Brisbane, Australia. He holds a Bachelor of Science and a Bachelor of Laws with Honours, both from Griffith University. His primary pedagogic and research interest is the patenting of chemical and biological inventions. He is currently an investigator in an Australian Research Council Discovery Project, "Gene Patents in Australia: Options for Reform".
He can be reached by e-mail at s.hubicki@griffith.edu.au

Anselm Kamperman Sanders Ph.D (Lond.), is Professor in European and International Intellectual Property Law at Maastricht University, The Netherlands. He was Marie Curie Research Fellow at Queen Mary and Westfield College, University of London. He has held a research grant from the VSB fund and a Chevening Scholarship. Further research, teaching and advisory affiliations comprise the International Institute of Infonomics, the ETH in Zürich, Switzerland and the Institute of European Studies of Macau SAR, China. In 2003 he was adjunct professor at the Queensland University of Technology, Brisbane, Australia. He is the author of *Unfair Competition Law, The Protection of Intellectual and Industrial Creativity* (1997,

Oxford, Clarendon Press) and his editorial and advisory board memberships comprise the Maastricht Journal of European and Comparative Law and the Intellectual Property Quarterly.

He can be reached by e-mail at A.KampermanSanders@pr.unimaas.nl.

Gabriela Kennedy is a partner of Lovells in Hong Kong practising in the Intellectual Property and TMT Group. She handles all aspects of intellectual property work including enforcement, licensing and registration work. She has handled a number of high profile cases in Hong Kong including a copyright case that went to the Court of Final Appeal in 1997. Her practice also includes all aspects of information technology, e-commerce and telecommunications work. Gabriela has written extensively on issues concerning e-commerce, intellectual property, information technology and telecommunications law for various publications. She is a member of the editorial board of the Computer Law and Security Report and was the Hong Kong editorial adviser of the now defunct IP Asia.

She can be reached by e-mail at gabriela.kennedy@lovells.com.

Lu Guoqiang is a Senior Judge and Vice Preisdent of Shanghai's Intermediate People's Court. In the past, Judge Lu served at the Shanghai High People's Court (1987-1994) and as Chief Judge of the Intellectual Property Tribunal of the High Court (1994-2001). Judge Lu holds an LL.B. from Shanghai Fudan University and an LL.M. from the Shanghai Academy of Social Sciences Law Institute. He was a visiting scholar at Harvard Law School, the University of British Columbia and the Max Planck Institute for Patent Law in Germany. Judge Lu is a prolific writer, mostly on issues of intellectual property law.

He can be reached by e-mail at gqlu8@yahoo.com.cn.

Sibylle Schlatter, attorney-at-law, is a senior researcher specialised in copyright and competition law and head of the Latin America Department at the Max Planck Institute for Intellectual Property, Competition and Tax Law in Munich. In addition, she serves as Africa co-editor of the Institute's English-language publication, IIC. She also acts as an independent consultant for several development/technical assistance projects of the World Bank, EU and GTZ, *inter alia*, for issues dealing with copyright law and the system of collective administration in a number of Asian and African countries.

She can be reached by e-mail at sibylle.schlatter@ip.mpg.de.

Brad Sherman is Professor of Law at the T.C. Beirne School, University of Queensland, Brisbane, Australia and is Director of the Australian Centre for Intellectual Property in Agriculture. Previously he worked at Griffith University, the London School of Economics and Emmanuel College, Cambridge.

He can be reached by e-mail at b.sherman@uq.edu.au.

Dieter Stauder began his career at the University of Munich and as a member of the Max Planck Institute for Foreign and International Patent, Copyright and Competition Law. Since 1992, he has been Director of the International Section of the "Centre d'études internationales de la propriété industrielle" (CEIPI) in Strasbourg, associate professor of the University Robert Schuman and member of the European Patent Office in Munich. His main task has been the teaching and training of prospective European patent attorneys. He has written extensively on industrial property law, and most recently was co-editor and co-author of a commentary on the European Patent Convention, "Singer/Stauder" (2003). Many of his writings draw on empiric research and comparative analysis. His particular interests are questions of jurisdiction, litigation and infringement of IPR.

He can be reached by e-mail at dstauder@epo.org.

Gregor Urbas, BA/LLB(Hons), Ph.D(ANU), Legal Practitioner (ACT), is a Lecturer in the Law Faculty of the Australian National University (ANU) teaching criminal law, evidence and intellectual property. Previously he worked in the Sophisticated Crime and Regulation Program of the Australian Institute of Criminology (AIC) and at IP Australia. He is the author of *Public Enforcement of Intellectual Property Rights* (AIC, 2000) and *Cyber Crime Legislation in the Asia-Pacific Region* (AIC / Hong Kong University, 2001), a co-author (with Russell Smith) of *Controlling Fraud on the Internet: A CAPA Perspective* (Report for the Confederation of Asian and Pacific Accountants), and (with Russell Smith and Peter Grabosky) a new book *Cyber Criminals on Trial* (Cambridge University Press, 2004).

He can be reached by e-mail at Gregor.Urbas@anu.edu.au.

Henry Wheare is a partner in and head of the intellectual property group of Lovells in Hong Kong. He has practised for over 25 years in all areas of intellectual property, information technology and telecommunications law. He also advises on competition law, licensing, branding and import and export requirements. He has given numerous presentations at international conferences and has widely published on intellectual property, the Internet and telecommunications law.

He can be reached by e-mail at henry.wheare@lovells.com

1
Back to the Future: Intellectual Property Rights and the Modernisation of Traditional Chinese Medicine

BRYAN BACHNER

A. Introduction

Honest opinions are consumed like good medicines that taste bitter.[1]

This Chinese proverb provides an appropriate starting point for an essay sceptical of conventional claims that modern approaches to intellectual property rights present the most effective methods to promote innovation and growth in the field of biotechnology, as it relates, in particular, to traditional ecological knowledge (TEK). This paper examines the processes that govern the control, use and treatment of Traditional Chinese Medicine (TCM) as a case study to evaluate the impact that the application of intellectual property rights has on TEK. The wealth of literature that examines the effect of intellectual property rights on TEK today and the relative absence of any similar consideration on TCM, perhaps the most globally relevant, culturally important, commercially valuable and medically significant resource, underlines the pertinence of such a study.

It is conventional to think that traditional medicines, particularly those created hundreds, if not thousands of years ago, should not be patentable. Contemporary intellectual property law embraces the ideas that, in terms of property rights, an old thing should be ignored while a new thing should be rewarded. The aim of this paper is to show that such a way of thinking not only relegates important cultural and scientific information and their custodians to the social margins, but it also imposes an unfair and uneconomical proprietary regime upon traditional resources.

A fundamental presumption of this study is that the modern conceptualisation of intellectual property rights, where it is understood that innovation depends upon absolute commercial control over newly invented products, is mistaken. In making this argument it will be shown that, historically, the dynamic evolution of TCM over the last 5,000 years did not depend upon an exclusive property rights regime; to the contrary, the most fertile and dynamic period of TCM development was "regulated" under the traditional legal regime, that, in effect, respected some private control while not

---

[1] Anonymous Chinese proverb.

preventing collaboration and a "natural evolution"[2] of the traditional knowledge. It is interesting to note that this so-called feudal system of traditional rights perhaps may be most favourably compared to what modern commentators would refer to as an "open source" approach to technology. Regrettably, with China's enthusiastic incorporation of the conventional intellectual property rights regime as embodied in the World Trade Organization's Agreement on Trade Related Aspects of Intellectual Property Rights (TRIPS Agreement), China's present approach is to disregard the domestic environment that historically has facilitated the evolution of her rich traditional knowledge and to overlook China's claim to rights of TCM in the global economy.

It is alarming that, despite the best intentions to preserve and protect traditional resources in China, lawmakers are contributing to its demise.[3] Part of the problem is the lack of realisation that intellectual property rights affect not only the motivation to create, but also may adversely impact the conservation of fundamental resources.[4] Lawmakers either do not appreciate or are not interested in the relevance of how the assignment of property rights impact the complex process of creativity and ignore this factor when devising criteria for the decision-making process to grant patents.

The main objective of this chapter is to respond to a yawning gap in the literature dealing with intellectual property rights regimes in China available to protect the important national heritage known as Traditional Chinese Medicine. It examines both historical and modern times. Its more specific aim is to explain those legal classifications under the intellectual property rights regime and how this legislation ignores its cultural and biological impact of the intellectual property rights regime. As a result, the law is con-

---

[2] Despite the powerful corporate message that innovation depends upon the assignment of exclusive property rights to firms that will assure their return on research and development (PHRMA, www.phrma.org. viewed on 3 May 2004.), innovation's basis is a far murkier concept. E.O. Wilson describes natural evolution as "guided by no vision, bound to no distant purpose." Edward Wilson, The Diversity of Life (Cambridge: Belknap Press of Harvard University Press, 1992) 80. Often scientific inspiration may derive from an accidental occurrence where inventors come up with an idea in conversation or two chemical components are mixed together. Without doubt, innovation depends upon the ability to improve upon what is already available. My point is that the creative spark is not necessarily driven by an economic incentive only and that a law that assumes this may be undermining the innovation it intends to promote. See generally, Tom Standage, The Victorian Internet (London: Wiedenfeld & Nicolson, 1998) (a remarkable story about the happenstance evolution of the telegraph), and Julie Fenster, Ether Day (New York: Harper Collins, 2001) (an important story about the invention of ether as a modern day anaesthetic).

[3] See generally, Zheng Chengsi, "Two Different Categories of Intellectual Property Rights", 12(70) Intellectual Property (2002) 2 (in Chinese only).

[4] See Timothy Swanson, "Conclusion: Tragedy of the Commons" in: Timothy Swanson (ed.), The Economics of Environmental Degradation (Cheltenham UK: Edward Elgar, 1996) 177.

tributing to the decline of an industry it was designed to advance. In order to correct this legislative deficit, lawmakers must re-conceptualise their views of intellectual property to account for not only commercial but also cultural-ecological concerns. The arguments set forward will compare the old intellectual property regime concerning traditional resources in China with the new one, explaining that it is no coincidence that for over 5,000 years, during feudal times, the evolution of China's traditional knowledge advanced dynamically, while in the last 50 years it has been in considerable decline.

The first period generally covers feudal times and the principle evolution, over 5,000 years, of Traditional Chinese Medicine. This period will be referred to here loosely as the "Open Source" period because it did not involve pro-active governmental policies to assign proprietary control over resources, but relied on collaboration and a more flexible system of trade secrets. The second period covers modern China and is dealt with in two parts. The first includes the greater era of the modern Chinese state from 1949 to approximately the start of the implementation of the "Open Door" Policy towards the end of the 1980s. It was during this period that the government actively participated in the TCM industry by appropriating the principle products and processes and publishing them for public consumption, with little heed for any proprietary control. This will be referred to here as the "Open Secret" phase. The second part extends from the start of the "Open Door" Policy until today. Shifting gears, the government has largely converted its intellectual property regime to converge with foreign principles of intellectual property rights and its approach to TCM changed in parallel. This phase will be called the "Closed Secret" period.

B. "Open Sources":[5] Feudal Times

Western legal scholars have created the perception that the concept of proprietary control over traditional knowledge in China was non-existent. They

---

[5] My apologies to the Open Source Initiative, a group with a political position regarding the promotion of innovation in software. According to their website, a one paragraph definition of their credo is: "Open source promotes software reliability and quality by supporting independent peer review and rapid evolution of source code. To be OSI certified, the software must be distributed under a license that guarantees the right to read, redistribute, modify, and use the software freely." Open Source Initiative, http://www.opensource.org/advocacy/faq.php, viewed on 3 May 2004. The Open Source Initiative is a faction that had separated from the Free Software Foundation, a group that believes that software should be guided by principles of freedom rather than price. According to their views, users of software should be free to run the program for any purpose, to study and adapt the program, redistribute copies to neighbours and improve the program: Free Software Foundation, http://www.gnu.org/fsf/fsf.html, viewed on 3 May 2004. While the views in this chapter more accurately concur with principles in the Free Software Movement, the author has adopted the "open source" terminology because it more closely captures the meaning in the English-language sense, as opposed to the software politics sense.

have subsequently used this "lack of intellectual property rights" argument to explain why China's early technological advancement fell into decline.[6] This is one explanation for a complex problem. TCM, amongst a host of other cultural and scientific creations, evolved under a non-state, non-monopoly based intellectual property regime. It is therefore worthwhile re-examining the intellectual property regime that existed during feudal times to see whether there are any lessons that can be applied to modern times.

The field of medical anthropology concerning traditional Chinese medicine is at an early stage of development and therefore it would be premature for anyone to arrive at general conclusions about the creative processes concerning technology generally[7] and TCM in particular.[8] There is enough research available, however, to identify some areas of the special intellectual property regime that existed then that may provide us some clues as to the reasons for the success of the TCM development. The story that is beginning to materialise is that a combination of non-state measures existed that would on the one hand ensure control by the practitioner-inventor, while on the other hand, encourage, if not allow, collaboration amongst different practitioner-inventors. The bottom line is that the state played no role in intervening and preventing a third party from researching and improving upon someone else's creation.

In early China, traditional healers would use a variety of non-governmental intellectual property modes to transmit secret knowledge that would assure the healer's control over that traditional knowledge, a reflection also of the Confucian respect for precedent and the past.[9] Masters of Chinese medical knowledge would only choose disciples who were of the right character and temperament. The method of transmission involved daily meditation and exercise designed exclusively by the Master. Learning the medical formulas through imitation of Daoist signs and incantations further limited access of third parties to the formulas. More secrecy was therefore assured on the basis that the acquisition of the secret knowledge was often an uncertain experience as it transpired after mindless verbal repetitions and physical exercise.

Only the correctly pronounced words held the power and only the Master could teach the appropriate pronunciation that would offer the relevant medical knowledge. Hsu concludes that the control of pronunciation led to the legitimisation of those in power, control over the distribution of

[6] Alford, To Steal A Book is an Elegant Offence: Intellectual Property Law in Chinese Civilization (Stanford: Stanford University Press, 1995).

[7] See generally, Robert Temple, The Genius of China: 3000 Years of Science, Discovery and Invention (London: Prion Books, 1998).

[8] See generally, Joseph Needham and Lu Gwei-Djen, Science and Civilization in China: Biology and Biological Technology (Cambridge: Cambridge University Press, 2000).

[9] Elisabeth Hsu, The Transmission of Chinese Medicine (New York: Cambridge University Press, 1995) 25.

knowledge and the exclusion of any critical assessment of the virtue of the pronunciation of the words.[10] Because the master controls the words, he can control the lineage of power and is free to innovate as he sees fit.

This non-governmental intellectual property is common amongst indigenous communities. Modern scholars point out however that the secrecy was not necessarily grounded on conventional trade secret principles. As Suchman writes,

"Rather than being too weak, the non-governmental intellectual property rights embodied in magic may actually be *too strong*, protecting existing technologies even to the point of denying crucial information to would-be inventors. Innovators have a strong interest in protecting their own ideas, but they have little or no interest in encouraging subsequent, potentially competing innovation by others. As a result, although the incentives for innovation may be fairly high, the raw material for innovation–technological know-how – either is closely guarded by established [traditional practitioners] or is rendered unintelligible by metaphysical obfuscation . . ."[11]

This form of control over information was not meant to induce change, but to preserve stability within the community and its economy.

Typically a western observer would look at such a system with jaundiced eyes. It is important, however, to keep in mind that the social priorities of indigenous inventors and their consumers were not necessarily the same bailiwick, namely, innovation. For the traditional society,

"[I]nnovation imposes substantial dangers . . . characterized by high information costs, minimal record keeping and subsistence economies. A subsistence economy can rarely afford to embrace a new technology that disrupts the social order or that interferes, even temporarily, with established modes of production. The intellectual property structures associated with [traditional knowledge] reduce these risks substantially. Shaman-priesthoods, in particular, foster high barriers to lay innovation and offer strong incentives for the most creative and persuasive members of society to uphold technologies that have withstood the test of time. Further such [traditional knowledge using] collectivities restrict creative activity to a relatively small and socially isolated subgroup, buffering the society's core technology from unproven techniques."[12]

Suchman concludes that an ideology that promotes "innovation" and "change" may not necessarily be valuable for all communities. He suggests that legal frameworks that allowed traditional societies to survive as traditional societies were those with the least dynamic potential, and therefore greatest stability.

One must keep in mind, however, that this prioritisation for stability and economies is only one side of the traditional resource coin. Beside social

---

[10] Id. at 51.
[11] Mark Suchman, "Invention and Ritual: Notes on the Interrelation of Magic and Intellectual Property in Preliterate Societies", 89 Columbia Law Review (1989) 1264.
[12] Id.

security, traditional communities were confronting the conventional pressures that arise from natural evolution. How to ensure that there was enough of a beneficent plant or animal species to continue to manufacture a medicine? How to incorporate new plant or animal species into their traditional medicines? How to create new medical remedies to deal with new diseases? How to borrow effective remedies from other practitioners or regions?

Innovation in traditional Chinese medicine during feudal times was less dependent upon proprietary control and more attributable to local concerns, geographical exigencies, political influences, the informal trade secret protection that arose from cultural rituals associated with the medicine, and perhaps most importantly, collaboration amongst other doctors.[13] As Hanson explains, the process of creativity in the discipline of traditional medicine is neither a divine inspiration nor a journey toward truth. "By producing medical texts, sharing experience, and consolidating support from members of the local elite, groups of practitioners form a consensus on new theories, diagnostic methods, and drug therapies."[14] For instance, in the late 19th century in Suzhou, medical doctors transformed and enhanced the canonical texts of universalised codes of Chinese medicines by articulating that specific geographical locales required distinct therapeutic interventions.[15]

While providing just a sketch of the medical anthropology concerning traditional Chinese medicine, this outline highlights some important aesthetic principles that help explain the evolution of TCM during feudal times. It is essential to ensure that the inventors are within an environment where their experimental work is not only protected against unwarranted exploitation and interruption but also available for collaborative investigation and research with relevant partners. In other words, the evolution of traditional Chinese medicine in feudal times appears to have thrived under an intellectual property regime that did not assign exclusive commercial property rights to the basic chemical components of a particular medicine. It is essential to understand that while a variety of non-state trade secret measures existed to protect the practitioner's control over the applied knowledge for a medicine, a considerable amount of sharing and collaboration with regard to the elemental components and formulas helped to promote the further development of the TCM.

In light of the modern evolution of patent law, in particular with regard to the TRIPS Agreement, this feudal, but certainly not futile, principle of collaboration would be near impossible to draft and legislate. The question that arises, however, is where TRIPS disavows the approach, is the approach

---

[13] Marta Hanson, "Robust Northerners and Delicate Southerners" in: Innovation in Chinese Medicine (Elizabeth Hsu ed.) (New York: Cambridge University Press, 2001) 266.
[14] Id.
[15] Id.

necessarily wrong? One must look to the present-day high-technology industry,[16] where intriguingly similar intellectual property approaches have been applied, for the answer. The end of the 20th century has been marked by dramatic developments in the biotechnology and computer industry; one can argue that the most valuable works in these fields have evolved under an "open source" approach somewhat similar to the TCM industry in feudal times.

For instance, the Human Genome Project managed to identify and publish the genetic code for human life, a fundamental set of data necessary for the invention of medicines and other resources that will have an unfathomably positive impact on humanity for years to come. This landmark work was produced without reliance on conventional intellectual property rights. To the contrary, the discoverers of the human genome were inspired by the recognition that progress depends upon collaboration first and commercial gain second. The creative process they recognised depends as much upon the capital necessary to build labs, purchase equipment and hire scientists as it does the cooperation and free-thinking amongst inventors to work through challenges as they crop up in the discovery process without the substantial limitations which intellectual property rights bring about. It is worth repeating the words of Sir John Sulston, the former Director of the Sanger Centre who led the British arm of the international team responsible for the Human Genome Project. He wrote:

"A patent . . . does not give you literal ownership of a gene, but it does specifically give you the right to prevent others from using that gene for any commercial purpose. It seems to me that your fencing off of a gene should be confined strictly to an application that you are working on – to an inventive step. I, or someone else, may want to work on an alternative application, and so need to have access to the gene as well. I can't go away and invent a human gene. So all the discovered part of genes – the sequence, the functions, everything – needs to be kept pre-competitive and free of property rights. After all, part of the point of the patent system is to stimulate competition. Anyone who wants to make a better mousetrap has to invent around existing mousetrap patents. You can't invent around a discovery; you can only invent around other inventions. . . . The most valuable applications for a gene are often far down the line from the first, easy, ones, so this is not just a matter of principle but has extremely importance consequences."[17]

---

[16] See also the free software movement and its successful application to the evolution of the GNU/Linux software model. The free software movement advocates a model of intellectual property rights where a software user is free to run, copy, distribute, study, change and improve the software. The basic presumption is that innovation and improvement to existing software depends upon the ability of users to access the basic information, which includes the source code. Users should be free to redistribute copies, either with or without modifications, either gratis or by charging a fee for distribution, to <u>anyone, anywhere</u>. Being free to do these things means (among other things) that you do not have to ask or pay for permission. GNU Project, http://www.gnu.org/philosophy/free-sw.html, viewed on 28 April 2004. See supra fn. 5.

[17] John Sulston/Georgina Ferry, The Common Thread (Washington DC: Joseph Henry Press, 2002) 267–268.

The important point made by Sulston is that research depends upon accessibility to information and the assignment of monopolies to genetic components as well as their application in medical terms is excessive because it will retard future research of these genetic components. Sustern recognises that those who "invent" valuable applications of genetic resources merit a patent in that application, but the base resources should not be fenced off from the public domain.

Although more medical anthropological research on traditional Chinese medicine needs to be done, one can conclude that, similar to the precepts underlying the Human Genome Project, traditional medical practitioners in China embraced, if not intentionally, at least accidentally, the importance of sharing information in the public domain, while recognising, under the cover of social stability, the right of an inventor to enjoy the benefits arising from his own invention. It is therefore feasible to argue, in light of the successful parallel development of biotechnology in both feudal and modern times under "open source" regimes, that the intellectual property rights model advocated by current TRIPS standards, where economic incentives and monopolistic property rights are seen as a prerequisite to invention, does not have a monopoly on the paradigm for innovation.

C. Modern Times

It is regrettable to note that despite its flourishing development during feudal times, the evolution of traditional Chinese medicine in modern times is facing a crisis. Although, today, the commercial value of traditional Chinese medicine expands exponentially, the traditional development of this medicine and its biological components has been halted and in some instances actually reversed.

The manufacture and distribution of TCM is emerging as a significant sector in the modern Chinese and global economy.[18] In 1996 the production of TCM in the Mainland topped US$3.7 billion with 13 of the 50 TCM pharmaceutical firms publicly traded and 14 firms state-owned.[19] TCM use in Japan by medical practitioners increased by over 110% between 1983 and 1989; sales in herbal supplements and medicine in Japan was over US$5 billion in 1996.[20] By 1997, TCM use in the United States was growing at a rate of about 15% per year, with sales in total nutritional products involving herbs hitting US$17 billion in 1995.[21] Europe also has increasingly turned to TCM, though at a slower clip, with a 10% growth rate per year.[22]

---

[18] See generally, Siobhan Farrell, "Green Balancing Act", South China Morning Post, 25 March 2002, Business Section, 2.

[19] Kerry ten Kate/Sarah Laird, The Commercial Use of Biodiversity: Access to Genetic Resources and Benefit-Sharing (London: Earthscan, 1999) 80.

[20] Id.

[21] Id.

[22] Id.

Although global demand for the products and processes of TCM grows, the traditional knowledge and biological resources that form the basis of TCM is being depleted. While Chinese traditional medical practitioners have historically relied on over 5,000 different plant species to create their medicine, it does not appear that present and future generations will have a similar richness of resources.[23] The Chinese Academy of Science states that:

"Today . . . the extinction is greater than evolution of new species. Due to human interference as well as loss of natural habitat, biological resources are being exhausted at an alarming speed. It is reported that two species of birds become extinct every three years and, by the year 2000, this could reach the level of one species every year. It is estimated that by the end of this century, there will be 50 or 60 thousand plant species becoming threatened in various degrees, and at present the extinction of plant species goes at the rate of one species every day worldwide. In that case, half or one million species of animals and plants may become extinct within next two decades."[24]

The CAS recognises that human activity is the main impetus for the acceleration of biodiversity decline in modern times and that, therefore, good conservation policy depends upon coming to terms with humanity's intervention. They continue:

"The present few million species are the modern-day survivors of several billion species that have ever existed. Past extinction occurred by natural processes but today human interference is responsible for rapid extinction of species. Scientists have conducted a series of surveys on biotic and natural resources, accumulating valuable materials. A rough estimation shows that in China about 398 vertebrate species are endangered amounting to 7.7% of the total vertebrate. In plants, the rare and endangered species are as follows: Bryophytes 28, Pteridophytes 80, Gymnospermae 75, Angiospermae 836, in total 1,019 species, amounting to 3.5% of the higher plants."[25]

This information published by the Chinese Academy of Sciences, through a project of cooperation with the United Nations Development Programme and the United Nations Environmental Programme, shores up the position that the existing models of exploitation of biological resources are not working effectively in China and that alternative models need to be considered.

Despite the considerable economic, cultural and ecological stakes and the significant political opportunity to lead Asia and the developing world toward a progressive regulatory position, China's approach to intellectual property and traditional ecological knowledge has evolved slowly and

---

[23] Worldwatch Institute: www.worldwatch.org/register/give.cgi?file=EWP148, viewed on 11 July 2002.

[24] Chinese Academy of Science: www.bpsp-neca.brim.ac.cn/books/bdinchn/3.html, viewed on 11 July 2002.

[25] Id.

Bryan Bachner

cautiously.[26] The Xinhua News Agency recently reported that during a
conference sponsored by the Chinese Pharmaceutical Association, a member of the Chinese Academy of Engineering complained that China still does
not recognise the importance of herbal medicines and natural remedies as
precursors to new medicines.[27] The lack of appropriate intellectual property
protection had been identified as a principal reason for the absence of traditional and local pharmaceutical innovation, the lack of a vital TCM industry,
as well as the multi-national and domestic pharmaceutical firms' appropriation of what has long been a local TCM industry. While China has taken
important steps toward effective protection of pharmaceuticals through the
establishment of a dynamic intellectual property rights regime,[28] It would be

---

[26] Officially China takes a proactive stance toward the protection of the cultural properties, including traditional medicine, of the 55 ethnic minorities within its sovereignty.
According to the White Paper, Progress in China's Human Rights Cause in 2000:

> "The Chinese government sets store by protecting and developing the traditional
> cultures of ethnic minorities, and respects their folkways and customs in such aspects
> as diet, marriage, funeral, festival celebration and religious belief. In February 2000,
> the Ministry of Culture and State Commission of Ethnic Affairs jointly promulgated
> the 'Proposals on Further Strengthening Ethnic Minority-related Cultural Work',
> stressing the need to protect the unique traditional cultures and rich cultural heritages
> of all the ethnic minorities and set up ethnic minority cultural and ecological preser-
> vation zones where possible, at the same time demanding that the Han-inhabited
> eastern developed regions increase their assistance to the minority-inhabited western
> regions in their projects for cultural development. To date, 24 art universities and
> colleges across the country have opened classes especially for training artists of minor-
> ity origin, and all the colleges for ethnic minorities and some middle schools and col-
> leges in autonomous areas have also offered special courses of study on minority
> literature, music, dance and fine arts. Since the 1990s, the central and local budgets
> have earmarked special subsides and funds for building, extending or repairing a
> number of libraries, cultural centers, cultural clubs, museums, cinemas and theaters.
> In recent years, the central and Tibetan regional governments have spent nearly 300
> million yuan to repair and protect the Potala Palace, Sakya Monastery, Jokhang
> Temple and Drepung Monastery, the Guge Kingdom ruins in Ngari, and other
> important cultural and historical sites. At present, there are over 50 Tibetan studies
> institutes nationwide with over 2,000 researchers, and more than 10 Tibetological
> periodicals in the Tibetan, Chinese and English languages. The first four Tibetan-
> language volumes of the Tibetan epic King Gesar, the highest achievement of ancient
> Tibetan culture, have been published. The College of Tibetan Medicine, the biggest
> and most authoritative of its kind in China, has trained over 650 undergraduate
> students and students of junior college level and 10 master's degree students."

An important area of research would be to evaluate the extent to which such forms of
state patronage impact the evolution of the traditional knowledge. White Paper:
www.china.org.cn/e-white/2000renquan/a-7.htm, viewed on 22 July 2002.
[27] See Xinhua News Agency, http://www.china.org.cn/english/scitech/56896.htm,
viewed on 9 February 2004.
[28] Qu Weijun, "The Protection of Intellectual Property Rights of Traditional
Medicine in China", paper presented in The Asia Pacific Traditional Medicine
Conference, article on file with the author.

an exaggeration to profess that China has created an operative IPR system that is able to manage optimally the complex nature of traditional ecological knowledge.

Modern Chinese IPR jurisprudence from 1949 can be divided into two periods. The first extends from 1949 to the late 1980s and accounts largely for the treatment of TCM under Chairman Mao's influence. The second extends from the late 1980s until today and includes the greater part of the legal and economic reform period.

I. "Open Secrets": 1949 to the late 1980s

The socialist economic principles originally espoused by Chairman Mao vested all property rights in the state and the masses. Chairman Mao, formerly a librarian, while acknowledging the importance of developing culture, revealed a marked departure from western visions of the creative process. He stated:

> "[O]ur purpose is to ensure that literature and art fit well into the whole revolutionary machine as a component part, that they operate as a powerful weapon for uniting and educating the people and for attacking and destroying the enemy, and that they help the people fight the enemy with one heart and one mind."[29]

Early Chinese socialism did not permit the privatisation of creative works. From 1949 until the early 1960's, in addition to regular salaries, the Chinese government offered minimal rewards to individual authors as compensation for their literary works.[30]

The economic and cultural leaders of the Cultural Revolution of the 1960s and 1970s, however, reversed the meagre individualistic recognition that had existed within the law and implemented an extremist form of socialist ideology embodying collectivist virtues.[31] One significant campaign emerging from the Cultural Revolution involved the criticism and jailing of intellectuals, writers, artists and painters.[32] The radical legal position of the Cultural Revolution denied not only the individual's contribution to the work, but also the collaborative nature of the authorship. The notion that the state not only inspired but merited all credit for creative works is perhaps best captured in the oft-quoted Cultural Revolution maxim: "Is it necessary for a steel worker to put his name on a steel ingot which he produces in the course of his duty? If not, why should a member of the intelligentsia enjoy the privilege of lending his name to his intellectual product?"

---

[29] Quotations from Chairman Mao (1967) 173.

[30] Bryan Bachner, "Intellectual Property Law" in: Introduction to Chinese Law (Hong Kong: Sweet & Maxwell, 1997) 441–443.

[31] Roderick MacFarquhar, The Origins of the Cultural Revolution (New York: Columbia University Press, 1974).

[32] To Steal a Book, supra fn. 6 at 63.

With the end of the Cultural Revolution and the advent of market reform in the late 1970s, an expectation arose, particularly among foreign investors looking to the Chinese market, that intellectual property rights would be respected and enforced. This expectation, however, proved, at an early stage of reform at least, to be overly optimistic.[33] Peter Yu explains that in response to centuries of colonial exploitation, many Chinese policy makers were suspicious of the movement to recognise intellectual property rights for individual copyright holders, particularly because there was little belief that it might benefit indigenous copyright holders. He writes:

"[M]any Chinese believed it was *right* to freely reproduce or to tolerate the unauthorized reproduction of foreign works that would help strengthen the country. Some of them also believed that copying was needed, or even necessary, for China to catch up with Western developed countries."[34]

Instead of a knee-jerk absorption of foreign copyright viewpoints, intellectual property rights debate during the early part of reform included important discourse of nation-building, indigenous cultural development, independence and self-sustenance.

The governmental treatment of TCM during this same period appears to have been influenced by the similar public concerns about indigenous development. Chinese academia published comprehensive volumes setting out the research results of much scientific study concerning the identification of drugs and components necessary for TCM.[35] These governmental publications include: the 1979 *Chinese Materia Medica*, describing about 1,000 drug recipes; 1977 *Encyclopedia of Chinese Materia Medica*, including over 5,760 drug formulas; 1982 *Colour Atlas of Chinese Herbal Drugs*, providing over 5,000 drug products; 1988 *New Compendium of Chinese Materia Medica*, identifying over 6,000 medicinal plants; and the 1988 *Colour Album of Chinese Herbal Medicines*, offering 5,000 photos of Chinese herbal medicine. While this approach does perform the important service of making available to the public the base resources and other applications, by their formulas, to the author's knowledge the government has neither taken steps to identify the inventors of these historical formulas nor to define any rights these custodians might have over them.

It would be overly simplistic to contend that the government, through these publications, has appropriated the traditional resources of China's indigenous communities without any semblance of fairness. The Chinese

---

[33] To Steal a Book, supra fn. 6 at 63.

[34] Peter Yu, "Piracy, Prejudice and Perspectives: An Attempt to Use Shakespeare to Reconfigure the US–China Intellectual Property Debate", 19(1) Boston University International Law Journal (2001) 1.

[35] Xiao Pei-gen, "The Chinese Approach to Medicinal Plants – Their Utilization and Conservation" in: Akerele/Heywood/Synge (eds.), Conservation of Medicinal Plants (Cambridge, Cambridge University Press, 1991) 306.

government has in fact taken a patronage approach toward traditional medicines and has invested considerable sums of money into the development of scientific institutions to preserve and develop this knowledge. The underlying problem with this approach is the lack of any rights for past indigenous contributions to traditional medicine and, due to the lack of legal capacity, future innovators. This example of the publication highlights one of the prime weaknesses of an intellectual property regime that does not respect past traditional innovations: Why would a traditional medical practitioner with a potentially valuable traditional medicine have an interest in making it available to any firm, if the original inventor has no claim over its use? Not only that, but such policy would, of course, serve to discourage the development of the indigenous industry and encourage its cultural demise.

This examination of the "open secret" phase indicates that lawmakers seemed to believe that the publication of the TCM and its placement in the public domain was in fact a public service for not only scientific but also cultural ends. It is questionable, however, whether such an approach actually served either end. Policy makers must keep in mind that the fact that patent law was not enforced in imperial times, does not necessarily mean that traditional Chinese medicine was part of the public domain. In fact, traditional practitioners maintained complex community-based rules that served to ensure proprietary and cultural protection of the formulas.[36] This process has included, amongst other things, the development of a bond between master and disciple, an assessment of character, the repetition and recitation of Daoist incantations and a process of dissemination of secrets from families, societies and individuals.[37] Such traditional customary rules protected the proprietary rights of the TCM makers, provided for a system of innovation and conservation that assured the long-term development of the medicine, supported a system that provided a living for the practitioners and a framework that ensured the conservation of the medical materials and their optimal use. While the public dissemination of TCM marked the early part of China's governmental treatment of traditional knowledge, this approach has considerably changed. It is to that period of history that we turn to next.

II. "Closed Secrets": The Reform Period

Following the Cultural Revolution and the onset of the "Open Door" Policy in 1978, Chinese lawmakers began to re-think governance strategies over traditional knowledge. While the new approach recognised property rights over traditional knowledge, the common thread throughout the diverse new IP laws that cover TCM, is the notion that only the inventors of new applications of TCM will be recognised and that such IPR over these

---

[36] Elizabeth Hsu, The Transmission of Chinese Medicine, (Cambridge: Cambridge University Press, 1999) 21–57
[37] See supra fns. 9–15 and accompanying text.

traditional resources would include not only the original inventor's traditional knowledge but also the genetic resources that constitute the invention. Intellectual property rights for traditional ecological knowledge in modern China is based on ten areas of legal protection: first, the Constitution; second, the ratification of relevant international law; third, the 1984 Patent Act as amended in 1992 and 2000; fourth, the 1992 Decree on the Protection of Traditional Chinese Medicines; fifth, trade secrets protection provided by the Unfair Competition Act; sixth, the Law on Pharmaceutical Regulation; seventh, Regulations on Plant Varieties; eighth, the Trade Mark Act; ninth, biotechnology laws; and tenth, copyright law.

1. The Constitution

The Constitution provides the basis for the evolution of intellectual property rights for Chinese Traditional Medicine.[38] Article 13 affords protection to intellectual property generally. According to Art. 20, the state must encourage the development of the natural and social sciences through the dissemination of scientific and technical knowledge as well as rewarding achievements in scientific research, including technological discoveries and inventions. Article 21 then emphasises how the state must promote the development of medical and health facilities including Chinese medicine.

2. International Law

On 10 December 2001, the Ministerial Conference of the World Trade Organization agreed to terms that allowed China to accede to the Marrakesh Agreement and conclude what had been, in effect, a 23 year process of reshaping her domestic economic regime.[39] The purpose of this reform was to ensure that China was in compliance with WTO rules, a precondition necessary to rejoin a group whose founding 1947 General Agreement on Tariffs and Trade she had originally signed.[40] With specific regard to intellectual property rights, it is useful to review the Report of the Working Party on China's Accession to the WTO (Report).[41] Under its conventional interpretation of international law, China automatically incorporates any ratified international agreement into its domestic jurisprudence. As a result of China's willingness to convey to a sceptical world a commitment to enforce WTO law and to clarify any potential domestic misinterpretations, China decided to incorporate the Agreement by enacting new domestic legislation.

---

[38] The Constitution of the People's Republic of China 2004.

[39] James Feinerman, "Chinese Law Relating to Foreign Investment and Trade: The Decade of Reform in Retrospect", in: China's Economic Dilemmas in the 1990s: The Problems of Reforms, Modernization, and Interdependence, The Joint Economic Committee, Congress of The United States (ed.) (New York: M.E. Sharpe, 1992) 828.

[40] US Government, International Trade Administration: www.mac.doc.gov/China/ProtocolandDecision.pdf, viewed on 11 July 2002.

[41] US Government, International Trade Administration: www.mac.doc.gov/China/WPReport11-10-01.pdf, viewed on 11 July 2002.

A key policy objective of the TRIPS Agreement is the notion that each member must ensure the promotion and protection of the commercial rights of intellectual property holders.[42] China had been moving towards the achievement of this goal through the reform of her patent law system since the Open Door Policy began in 1978. The amendments made by China noted in the Report highlight the narrow commercial concerns of the Ministerial Conference. Professor Zheng Chengsi, the pre-eminent intellectual property rights expert of China, emphasises that China had no choice but to strengthen its intellectual property system and comply with the WTO standards.[43] As the Chinese representative emphasised, "China had made the protection of intellectual property rights an essential component of its reform and opening-up policy and socialist legal construction."[44] The avowed objective of China's intellectual property legislation is to comply with "world dimension and world standards".[45] The report, in fact, describes a litany of statutory change describing how China had, in effect, commoditised her intellectual property system. For instance, the 1992 and 2000 amendments extended patent rights to include the prevention of the making, using, selling, offering for sale or importing of patented products or products deriving from patented processes without permission of the patent holder. Also the 1992 patent law amendments broadened its coverage to food, beverages, flavourings, pharmaceuticals and materials made by chemical methods. It also limited patent exclusions to scientific discoveries, rules and methods of intellectual activities, diagnostic and therapeutic methods for the treatment of diseases, animal and plant varieties as well as materials obtained by the change of nucleus.[46]

The WTO approach, however, does not adequately consider its impact on TEK. Despite paragraph 19 of the Doha Declaration[47] as well as a variety

---

[42] See generally, Peter Gerhart, "Special Introduction: Reflections: Beyond Compliance Theory–TRIPS as a Substantive Issue", 32 Case Western Reserve Journal of International Law (Summer, 2000) 357.

[43] Zheng Chengsi, "TRIPS Agreement and IP Protection in China", 9 Duke Journal of Comparative and International Law (2000) 219.

[44] Id. at 49.

[45] Id.

[46] Id. at 57.

[47] Paragraph 19 states: "We instruct the Council for TRIPS, in pursuing its work programme including under the review of Article 27.3(b), the review of the implementation of the TRIPS Agreement under Article 71.1 and the work foreseen pursuant to paragraph 12 of this declaration, to examine, inter alia, the relationship between the TRIPS Agreement and the Convention on Biological Diversity, the protection of traditional knowledge and folklore, and other relevant new developments raised by members pursuant to Article 71.1. In undertaking this work, the TRIPS Council shall be guided by the objectives and principles set out in Articles 7 and 8 of the TRIPS Agreement and shall take fully into account the development dimension." World Trade Organization, http://www.wto.org/english/thewto_e/minist_e/min01_e/mindecl_e.htm, viewed on 3 May 2004.

of meetings and discussion papers[48] examining how traditional knowledge relates to Art. 27.3b and the patentability of plants and animals, the WTO conceptualisation of IPR still favours an inventors-based approach to commercialising traditional knowledge. In the absence of limited monopoly rights over an innovation, the inventor will have no material incentive to research and develop new ideas. An economic problem arises, however, when the inventor is granted excessive monopoly rights because the creative process depends as much on material incentives as it does on accessibility to raw information upon which innovations may be made.[49] Another public aspect of the problem is the extent to which the benefits of invention should be extended to traditional custodians of biological resources upon which modern inventions are based. This has obvious implications for the preservation of cultural and biological diversity.[50] As one commentator points out:

"The TRIPS Agreement is also bad for the South for ecological and environmental reasons. By allowing monopolistic control of life forms, the TRIPS Agreement has serious ramifications for biodiversity conservation and the environment. The most significant ecological impacts of TRIPS relate to changes in the ecology of species interactions that will occur as a result of commercial releases of patented and genetically engineered organisms. Other impacts include: 1) The spread of monocultures as corporations with IPRs attempt to maximize returns on investments by increasing market shares; 2) An increase in chemical pollution as biotechnology patents create an impetus for genetically engineered crops resistant to herbicides and pesticides [like Monsanto's Round-Up ready crops] 3) New risks of biological pollution as patented genetically engineered organisms are released into the environment; 4)An undermining of the ethics of conservation as the intrinsic value of species is replaced by an instrumental value associated with intellectual property rights and 5).The undermining of traditional rights of local communities to biodiversity and, hence, a weakening of their capacity to conserve biodiversity."[51]

Although aware of the adverse domestic and cultural implications, lawmakers, perhaps more attentive to concerns of foreign investors than local interests, determined that the WTO approach was sound.

China's appreciation of and resignation to the local problems with governance over TEK is apparent in China's two national reports concerning compliance with the Convention on Biological Diversity (CBD). The first

---

[48] World Trade Organization, http://www.wto.org/english/tratop_e/trips_e/art27_3b_e.htm, viewed on 3 May 2004.

[49] See generally, Nuno Pires de Carvalho, "Requiring Disclosure of the Origin of Genetic Resources and Prior Informed Consent in Patent Applications Without Infringing The TRIPS Agreement: The Problem and The Solution", 2 Washington University Journal of Law & Policy (2000) 371.

[50] See Muria Kruger, "Harmonizing TRIPs and the CBD: A Proposal from India", 10 Minnesota Journal of Global Trade (Winter 2001) 169.

[51] Scott Holwick, "Developing Nations and the Agreement on Trade-Related Aspects of Intellectual Property Rights", Colorado Journal of International Law and Policy (1999) 49, 57–58.

report, issued by the National Environmental Protection Agency in December 1997, describes a governance strategy that separates conservation from commercial policy, revealing a lack of recognition of the extent to which commercial policy actually impacts conservation of TEK.[52] In 1958, the State Council had issued declarations concerning the protection of wild flora used for traditional medicine and the development of state-sponsored specially protected habitats for the cultivation of the plants. In July 1983 a leading group of relevant organisations, including the State Pharmaceutical Administration, the Ministry of Health and the Ministry of Forests, initiated a nationwide survey of all Chinese herbal sources, ostensibly to facilitate the development of a strategic industrial plan.

The final report identified 12,807 Chinese herbal plant sources, which included 383 families, 2,309 genera, 11,146 species. They also identified 1,581 species of herbal animals (sic), which included 395 families and 862 genera as well as 80 species of herbal minerals (sic). Needless to say the compilation of such a range of information is essential for the coordination of an appropriate biological diversity strategy. The use of the information, however, was not limited to research for the formulation of a government policy: much of the data was published in a series of books[53] for purposes of "research, education, production, business and decision-making concerning (agricultural and animal) husbandry." Additionally the government had established a public "data bank" for the storage of 360 of the species identified in the study.[54] The omission of any discussion concerning the

---

[52] CBD: www.biodiv.org/doc/world/cn/cn-nr-01-en.pdf, viewed on 12 July 2002.

[53] The titles included: "Chinese Herbal Resources", "A Summary Record of Chinese Herbal Resources", "Regional Distribution of Chinese Herbs", "Common Chinese Herbs", "Atlas of Chinese Herbal Resources" and "Local Medicine and Prescriptions".

[54] One may speculate that the proprietary nature of cultural knowledge was side-stepped due to the fact that the intellectual property protection of traditional information had yet to be adapted to a market economy still struggling to transform itself from a socialist model of state ownership. While China has recognised the economic importance of indigenous communities, the extent to which they will be able to control their own economic development is complicated by issues related to poverty and the Constitution. China, however, has taken significant steps toward the recognition of the rights of these local communities to control and trade their own cultural properties should they choose to. According to the Information Office of the State Council, as of December 2000:

"The state adopts preferential policies toward ethnic trade. For instance, since 1963 it has adopted a threefold policy in this regard. This ensures a portion of reserved profits, self-owned capital and price subsidies for minority peoples. To respect the folkways, customs and religious beliefs of ethnic minorities and satisfy their needs for special articles of daily use, the state guarantees the production of more than 4,000 varieties of ethnic articles, which fall into 16 categories, such as garments, shoes, hats, furniture, silks and satins, foodstuff, production tools, handicrafts, ornaments and musical instruments. It has also extended some preferential policies, such as setting up special production bases, giving priority to the guarantee of production capital

intellectual property rights of the species suggests that they were characterised as common property available for free use without recognition of prior agricultural, medicinal or cultural contributions.[55]

In 1991, the State Pharmaceutical Administration formulated an "industrial" policy for the development of traditional Chinese medicine. Chinese medicine remained a national priority and would receive support through the agricultural, science and technology sectors. Rather than utilizing a privitisation regime, it appears that China's initial approach was to encourage the development of TCM through state patronage in the form of financial support or property rights. There was recognition that the industrialisation of Chinese medicine should account for the need to conserve biological resources. When discussing the problems associated with the sustainable utilisation of traditional medicine, the report emphasises how the state is struggling to invest in the biotechnology necessary to study the relevant biological resources, to cope with competitive market demands for the raw materials necessary for Chinese medicine and to respond to a critical international community that does not understand the cultural aspects of Chinese medicine.[56] With regard to an action plan to further the development of Chinese medicine, the report indicates plans to set up seed nursery

---

and the supply of raw and processed materials, reduction of and exemption from taxes, low-interest loans, transportation subsidies, etc.

"Since 1991, in light of the new situation of reform and opening-up, the state has made appropriate readjustments in the preferential policies concerning ethnic trade and the production of ethnic articles for daily use. During the Eighth Five-Year Plan period (1991–1995), the state offered preferential treatment to commercial, supply and marketing and pharmaceuticals enterprises and more than 2,300 designated enterprises for producing ethnic articles for daily use in the 426 designated ethnic trade counties in terms of credits, investment, taxation and the supply of commodities, and offered special discount-interest loans for the construction of an ethnic trade network, and the technological transformation of designated enterprises for producing ethnic articles for daily use. As part of a new package of preferential policies offered for the same purpose by the state in June 1997, the People's Bank of China will offer 100 million yuan in a discount-interest loan a year during the Ninth Five-Year Plan period (1996–2000) for the construction of an ethnic trade network and the technological transformation of the designated enterprises for producing ethnic articles for daily use, and the state-owned ethnic trade enterprises and grass-roots supply and marketing cooperatives below the county level (excluding the county) shall be exempt from value-added tax."

State Council: www.china.com.cn/e-white/4/4.4.htm, viewed on 12 July 2002.

[55] Chetan Gulati, "The "Tragedy of the Commons" in: Plant Genetic Resources: The Need for a New International Regime Centered Around an International Biotechnology Patent Office", 4 Yale Human Rights & Development Law Journal (2001) 63.

[56] For a discussion by WWF-Target, the prominent non-governmental organisation, dealing with these issues, please see www.traffic.org/briefings/tcm.html, viewed on 12 July 2002. For a local programme designed to respond to the critique, see www.sedac.ciesin.org/china/policy/acca21/218-3.html, viewed on 12 July 2002.

bases modelled after the existing germplasm banks from the protected herbal areas, to improve the existing germplasm banks, to promote artificial breeding and generally encourage the use of biotechnology for the development of Chinese medicines.

The second report on the CBD issued by the State Environmental Protection Administration in September 2001 is substantially different from the first report in that it recognises that rights in traditional ecological knowledge will contribute towards the protection and promotion of important ecological, economic and cultural values.[57] It states:

> "China is a civilized old country with a long history, and has accumulated rich traditional knowledge, innovations and practices in its thousands of years of agricultural production. China also has multiple nationalities. Even in today's civilized world, many farmers living in remote mountainous areas, especially the minorities, still inherit, use and develop the traditional knowledge and practices that are beneficial to the conservation and sustainable use of the biological diversity. The Chinese government attaches great importance to the maintaining and use of the traditional knowledge, innovations and practices, and stresses the equitable sharing of the benefit from the traditional knowledge, initiatives and practices.
>
> "China is a country with multiple nationalities. The people of these nationalities have accumulated very rich traditional knowledge in their long-term practice of production and living. The Chinese government fully respects and protects the traditional knowledge. However, the resources available for meeting the obligations and recommendations made on this Article [of the CBD] are limited due to the lack of policies and mechanism for sharing the benefits from the traditional knowledge, innovations and practices as well as the limitation of the financial capacity of the country."[58]

The report suggests that a primary reason that the recognition of these values in practice remains problematic is the lack of state resources to protect them.

The report goes on to say that the existing intellectual property system does not protect traditional knowledge. It specifically recognizes that farmers rights in floral species that the farmer has cultivated are non-existent because, according to Chinese policy, they are presently part of the national common heritage and freely accessible. China's perception of the problem is sobering:

> "Although some progress has been made in the conservation of traditional knowledge in China, the traditional knowledge, innovations and practices are scattered greatly among local people and have not been better summed up. Along with the process of modernization, the eminent national traditional cultures are dying away gradually. There is inadequate awareness on the conservation of traditional knowledge, and the national policies, strategies and legislation in this field are still very weak. The mechanism of equitable sharing of benefits from the utilization of traditional knowledge, innovations and practices has not been established. The national capacity and technologies for conservation of traditional knowledge are still weak."[59]

---

[57] CBD: www.biodiv.org/world/reports.asp?t=s, viewed on 12 July 2002.
[58] Id. at Report, 40.
[59] Id. at 45.

China's willingness to embrace the recognition of the innovative conceptualisations of intellectual property that will allow for equitable sharing of
benefits, when legitimate innovative or practical contributions have been
made to an intellectual property, offers one cause for cautious optimism. An
analysis of the existing intellectual property law relating to traditional knowledge, in particular that patent law, suggests that the enshrinement of such a
policy would need, at least, a major change in the current IP policy.

3. Patent Law

Patents are intended to provide incentives to inventors to invent by rewarding their investment of time, intellect and money into the creation of a
novel, useful invention. The reward provides to the inventor a private
property right that gives him the exclusive right to exploit the invention for
a limited period. At the same time, it is meant to encourage innovation by
placing the design of the invention in the public domain for scrutiny by other
inventors.

On 12 March 1984 the Sixth National People's Congress enacted China's
modern patent law. The State Council accepted the implementing regulations on 19 January 1985. In order to comply with new international
rules specified in the TRIPS Agreement, the 1984 Patent Act was modified
in.[60] Before 1992, China had exempted pharmaceutical products from
intellectual property protection.[61] It was the 1992 modification to the Patent
Act that saw the first inclusion of any pharmaceutical products as subject
matter for patent protection in China.[62] The law drafters were responding to
considerable domestic and international pressure to align with TRIPS
principles and thereby encourage foreign and local investment in pharma-

---

[60] Lin Jianjun/Yang Jinqi, "Several Issues Relating to the Implementation of the
Revised Patent Law", 4 China Patents and Trademarks (Hong Kong: China Patent
Agents, 2001) 15. Additionally, the government has taken a number of steps to strengthen
the enforcement measures. In June 2001, China revised its Implementing Regulations of
the Patent Law. On 1 February 2003, The State Council revised the rules concerning
international patent applications in China through the "Decision by the State Council on
Revision of the Implementing Regulation of the Patent Law". The Supreme People's
Court, in June 2001, adopted "Several Provisions of the Supreme People's Court for the
Application of Law to Stopping Infringement of Patent Right before Instituting Legal
Proceedings" as well as "Several Provisions of the Supreme People's Court on Issues
Relating to Application of Law to Adjudication of Patent Law Disputes".

[61] Prior to 1992, pharmaceutical patents were not protected under the patent law. As a
result, foreign pharmaceutical firms pressured the government to provide them some legal
protection. The government therefore enacted Rules for the Administrative Protection
for Pharmaceutical Drugs to protect drugs that had been patented abroad, but could not
be patented in China. Zhang Qinkui, "Revision of the Legislation for IPR Protection
over Pharmaceutical Drugs is Urgently Required", (2002) Patent Law Studies.

[62] See generally, Zheng Chengsi, "The Trips Agreement and Intellectual Property
Protection in China", 9 Duke Journal of Comparative and International Law (Fall 1998)
219.

ceutical enterprises.[63] This is illustrated by examining how the law defines subject matter, ownership rights and patentability.

a) Subject matter

The Chinese Patent Act is the most popular legal measure used to seek protection for Chinese traditional medicine.[64] After the enactment of the new Patent Act in 1992, which included the protection of pharmaceutical drugs, the number of patent applications for traditional Chinese medicine increased dramatically.[65] The year before the new law, only 500 patent applications for TCM had been received; by the year 2001, 3,000 applications had been made.

The scope of protection for TCM under the Patent Act is considerable. Medical products, including new compounds and their products, useful extracts from TCM, novel products which modify TCM and products which improve TCM are all patentable. Processes for the manufacturing of TCM products, novel or improved methods for manufacturing the TCM and special breeding or manufacturing processes for TCM are also patentable. It does not matter whether the product is known or new, any proven new use is patentable. For TCM the most popular application is for the protection of a new use of a drug; in other words, even if a drug has been in use for many years, a newly discovered use is patentable.

Feng highlights that new pharmaceutical uses for known chemical substances are continuously being discovered.[66] The known substance, because it is part of the state of the art, is not patentable; however, the new application of the known chemical substance is. This innovative process and any resulting new product may be patented. The law, however, does not clarify whether the patent will then prohibit others from using that same known chemical substance to investigate whether other applications exist.[67] Neither does the law account for whether contributions by prior "inventors" should be accounted for, despite the obligation to establish novelty before granting a patent.[68] For instance, in the case of TCM, it is obvious that enterprises that discover a "new" application for an old TCM may modify the prior

---

[63] Assafa Endeshaw, "A Critical Assessment of the U.S.–China Conflict on Intellectual Property", 6 Albany Law Journal of Science & Technology (1996) 295.

[64] See generally, Zheng Yongfeng, "An Overview of Applications for Patents for Traditional Chinese Medicine and the Examination Practice", 4(67) China Patents and Trademarks (October 2001) 23.

[65] Qu Weijun, "The Intellectual Property Rights and Protection of Traditional Medicine in China", paper presented at APEC Symposium on Traditional Medicine (Hong Kong) 19–22 March 2002.

[66] Peter Feng, Intellectual Property in China, (Hong Kong: Sweet & Maxwell Asia, 2003) 212–213.

[67] See supra fn. 17 and accompanying text.

[68] See, e.g. Marcia Ellen DeGeer, "Biopiracy: The Appropriation of Indigenous Peoples' Cultural Knowledge", 9 New Eng. J. Int'l & Comp. L. (2003) 9.

unpatentable TCM only marginally, but still be awarded full benefits for the use of that TCM.

b) Ownership

The ownership of a patent right in China belongs to the inventor, unless that property right is assigned to another party. The inventor, according to Sec. 12 of the 2001 Patent Act Implementing Regulations, is the party that creatively contributed to the substantive features of the invention.[69] Organisers, financial sponsors, administrative heads or assistants who have not provided "creative" input are not eligible to enjoy the moral or material benefits to be derived from the work unless they:

(1) did the overall design and came up with (but not necessarily accomplished) the technical solution satisfying the patent requirement of novelty, inventiveness and practical applicability;
(2) played a "key and guiding role" in solving crucial technical problems of the patentable technical solution; or
(3) had been in charge of the project throughout the invention period and made "creative contributions" to crucial technical features.

For the purposes of this paper, though, it is important to note how the regulatory language clearly limits the status of inventor to those who make a "creative" contribution. The emerging interpretation of "creativity" in the courts seems to limit it to the person that discovers a new application or improves in some way an older work. For instance, the courts have affirmed that the inventor who learned the secret art of incense manufacture, a process kept private by the family for centuries, could not receive a patent for this process. The justification was that not the applicant, but the ancestors of the family were actually the inventors; however, since they were no longer among the living, they could not receive property rights. Improvements on the process by inventors outside the family, however, were deemed patentable.[70]

As Feng points out, patents are not an effective means for custodians of traditional products to assure they will continue to benefit from the use of their work. Securing the patent for a family's traditional commodity that may have been kept secret may be bad business for the family, because in return for putting the invention into the public domain, they would receive a patent limited only to a technological improvement over the original product. In the meantime, all newcomers would have access to the principle composition of the product. This is clearly an incentive to simply keep the process a family secret. But even this is not an effective solution. The

---

[69] See, e.g. Marcia Ellen DeGeer, "Biopiracy: The Appropriation of Indigenous Peoples' Cultural Knowledge", 9 New Eng. J. Int'l & Comp. L. (2003) at 201.

[70] *Zeng Fenying v. Zeng Changyuan* (1993), Nanning Intermediate Court, Guangxi, as cited in Feng at 192.

problem with this is that a larger firm will be able to reverse engineer, reveal the components of the product, improve it and perhaps claim a patent on the innovation. The family will more likely than not have no legal claim to the exploitation of this innovation. The absence of material benefit to inventors of traditional technologies appears then to serve as a disincentive for them to explore their marketability, thereby denying to the public potentially valuable commodities. Likewise, where the traditional inventors have no civil claim against persons that appropriate their original technologies or a means to share the benefits of its exploitation, the further development and sustainability of these traditional cultures and resources is at risk.

c) Patentability

Patentability sets out the criterion to determine whether an invention merits being assigned individual property rights. The test is important because it formalises the characteristics of the invention that the state deems valuable by rewarding inventors for achieving these characteristics in the invention. Article 22 states that a patent will only be granted to inventions that show novelty and inventiveness and have practical or industrial applicability.[71]

The purpose of the novelty standard is to assure that an application is new and not already part of the public domain. Novelty can be lost through a conference speech, media presentation or advertisement. If the product is publicly used in China, which means that the device is used, sold or displayed prior to the material date, novelty may not be claimed. Novelty for TCM will be determined on the basis of the principle of "present identical specification". This means that where an identical specification is available to the public prior to the filing of the application, the application will be ruled not novel and therefore not patentable.

Inventiveness means that the invention under application is not obvious to a person skilled in the art. It should embody substantive features and represent notable progress in comparison to the state of the art. Under Chinese law, inventiveness for pharmaceutical products means that the product composition is newly made and a novel active ingredient (i.e. herbal medicine) has been included.[72] Alternatively, a medicine is inventive if by varying its existing compounds new indications, greater effectiveness or fewer side effects occur. Inventiveness of method is established where the novel method of production shows benefits, such as a higher yield, cost reduction, increased purity of the extract or decreased side effects of the product.

---

[71] Flora Wang, "An Overview of the Development of China's Patent System", in: Mark Cohen/Elizabeth Bang/Stephanie Mitchell (eds.), Chinese Intellectual Property: Law and Practice (Boston: Kluwer Law International, 1999) 14.

[72] World Health Organization: www.who.int/medicines/library/trm/who-edm-trm-2001-1/who-edm-trm-2001-1.doc, viewed on 4 August 2002.

Other issues include: Does the invention solve long-standing technical problems? Does it break new ground that enables similar products to appear on the market? Is it commercially successful? Should the contribution of the original inventor or past custodians of a traditional invention be recognised? Where a Chinese doctor or modern family's ancestors had invented a TCM that was useful for the village, it is unlikely that such a discovery would measure up to the standard of commercial success. In such a case, should the firm that discovered the mass appeal of a drug be the only party to enjoy its benefits, particularly where another party had discovered its curative power?

The final criterion is practical applicability, and for TCM this means that it has a medical use. In China this means that the product must not only be capable of being "manufactured and used" but also of producing "positive effects". Such positive effects could be measured according to social, economic or technical standards. This standard is broader than the international standard of "industrial applicability" and allows for consideration of environmental factors that might serve to undermine an application. It also usefully provides flexibility for the examination authorities to consider the detrimental impact that limited ownership rights might have on the environment and the sustainability of the TCM industry.

Sec. 25 of the Patent Act expressly stipulates that methods for diagnosis or treatment of diseases are not patentable. Much TCM is a composition based upon a doctor's assessment of a patient's physical or psychological situation. Such an assessment will not be considered patentable because it is a method of diagnosis or a specific treatment of a disease. Patentability for TCM depends upon a proven industrial application . Feng describes the industrial application test as an assessment as to whether the TCM compound is applied for preparation of a pharmaceutical product. Where a TCM product would have an industrial application of specific pharmaceutical value, it would be patentable. A TCM that is only used for the treatment of a disease, however, would not be patentable because there is no industrial use, merely a curative one.

Dr Zhang Yongfeng of the State Intellectual Property Office identifies a number of challenges facing the patent protection of TCM. He writes:

- Patent rights are granted for a period of 20 years, but the time taken for filing and examining the patent application and development of the invention takes 2–5 years. This period of time is not deducted from the validity period of the patent, resulting in lost time for which no compensation is given.
- Inventors are reluctant to disclose their technology before patents are granted, but such disclosures is required for publication 18 months after the date of filing of the application.
- It is usually difficult for patent applicants to describe the constitution of a traditional medicine clearly, because most of the time traditional

medicine is a mixture of many unknown substances, so it is also difficult for the judge to determine whether an infringement has taken place between the patented drugs and the suspected products.[73]

Other more practical problems arise with the application of patent law to TCM.

Some commentators have argued that a problem may arise where TCM compositions are filled at a pharmacy. Although most TCM compositions are not generally patentable, where a patent has been granted to a new industrial process for making a traditional TCM composition, some perceive that filling a prescription at a pharmacy or producing that drug at the pharmacy may be an infringement. It seems, however, that this may not be the case.[74] Sec. 11(1) Patent Act states that the scope of protection for a process patent is the process plus the product directly obtained from the process, and therefore can only cover any new industrial process and the product directly derived from this application. Because the traditionally made TCM would not be manufactured in accordance with this new industrial process, it appears unlikely that any traditional production of a TCM by a Chinese pharmacy would create any civil liability.

Foreign policy makers argue that China must enact and enforce a stricter patent law. This is certainly important to reward local inventors and to provide adequate protection for foreign investors to encourage them to export and license their products. The question remains, however, whether the strict application of patent law for indigenous products such as TCM is appropriate. Important questions arise such as whether the cultural contribution of the original TCM practitioners should be recognised by law? Does the absence of recognition discourage individuals from entering the TCM industry? Would its recognition encourage it? What about foreign uses of indigenous TCM products? Should foreign multinationals be obliged to recognise through some sort of royalty or licence the contribution made by the original inventors of the TCM or at least the nation where it was developed? Where a nation receives such compensation what is the optimal way to distribute the funds raised?

4. Regulations on the Protection of TCM

Where the patent law does not provide adequate protection for TCM, China has sought to create a *sui generis* regulatory framework that does.[75] On 14 October 1992 the State Council promulgated the most important of these regulations in the form of the Decree 106 entitled Regulations on Protection of Traditional Medicine. The purpose of the law was to raise the quality of all

---

[73] World Health Organization: www.who.int/medicines/library/trm/who-edm-trm-2001-1/who-edm-trm-2001-1.doc, viewed on 4 August 2002.

[74] The author would like to thank Jiang Qinfeng for bringing this to his attention.

[75] See generally, Zhang Qingkui, "On the IP Protection of Medicine In China", 12(68) Intellectual Property (March 2002) 15 (in Chinese).

varieties of TCM, protect the legal rights and interests of enterprises manufacturing TCM and to promote the development of the activities related to TCM.
The law does not provide protection to inventors of TCM applying for patent
protection. Health departments are responsible for administering the law.

The regulations stipulate that there are two grades of varieties protected.
Any traditional medicine that complies with one of the following may apply
for Grade one protection. They must: (1) have special therapeutic results for
a given disease; (2) be prepared with natural medicinal herbs covered by
Grade one protection; or (3) be applicable to the prevention and treatment
of certain specific diseases. Grade two application may be made for varieties
that include one of the following conditions: (1) they conform with the
stipulations mentioned above but are removed from Grade one protection;
(2) they have noticeable therapeutic results for a given disease; or (3) they are
extracted and/or specially prepared with its effective ingredient from natural
medicinal herbs. The vagueness of the terms of approval provides considerable discretion to the relevant health department to determine awards.

Only enterprises that are engaged in the preparation of traditional Chinese
medicines are permitted to apply for protection of conforming products; it is
unclear whether non-enterprises including individuals may apply. The
relevant health departments must seek advice from the National Committee
on the Assessment of the Protected Traditional Chinese Medicinal Products
for an assessment on the viability of the applications. Membership on the
committee is limited to experts of TCM in areas of clinical activities, scientific research, laboratory experiments, administration and management.
After consultation with this committee, the health administrative department will decide whether to grant the "Certificate of Variety of Traditional
Chinese Medicine Under Protection", and if protection is granted must
publish designated papers to provide notice to the public.

Grade one protection may last either 10, 20 or 30 years. Grade two
protection lasts for 7 years. The ingredients, formulae and the technical
know-how regarding its preparation shall remain a secret for the protection
period. No government body or any other individual or enterprise given
access to the TCM's details may make it public. Any transmission of this
privileged information to areas outside the country must be done in conformity with security regulations. Extensions of protection may be applied for,
but will not be longer than the original term of grant. Where a conflict exists
between two enterprises claiming to have invented the TCM, a drug control
institution will be appointed to investigate and determine whether a new
certificate should be issued and whether the previous approval should be
withdrawn. According to the principle of compulsory licensing, the state has
the right to replicate a TCM after providing reasonable compensation where
it is deemed necessary. Section 20 requires that all enterprises involved in the
preparation of TCM improve their working conditions and raise the quality
of their products. The relevant health department will consider overseas
applications for registration.

The problem with this *sui generis* law is that it is not entirely clear where the patent law starts and these regulations begin. The regulation does not specify the protective scope of the TCM approved by the Health Department,[76] nor does it clarify how to enforce the law once the intellectual property protection is approved. This includes a lack of consideration of the authority to enforce the law as well as measures such as powers of seizure, fines and interrogation. Finally, like the Patent Act, these regulations are silent with regard to the recognition of the cultural contributions of the product.

5. *Trade Secrets*

In addition to protection under the Patent Act and the Regulations on the Protection of Traditional Chinese Medicine, inventors of TCM may find protection under the 1993 Unfair Competition Law (UCA). Under this law a trade secret is defined as any technological or business information for which the party has adopted measures to keep the information secret, has a practical use and is economically valuable. In cases where inventors do not wish to disclose their formula in the public domain as required under the patent law or find it prohibitive in terms of time and money to apply for protection under the Regulations, the UCA may provide trade secret protection. According to Qu Weijun of the State Intellectual Property Office, the ingredients of the TCM, the manufacturing technique and process may be protected as either technological or business information. The UCA was intended to serve as a contingency where the intellectual property rules were not effective[77] and the formalised the good faith principles embodied in the General Principles of the Civil Code.

In 1985 the State Council recognised the notion that technology was a transferable commodity. Know-how, under the Regulations on Administration of Technology Import Contracts of 1985, was undisclosed technical knowledge, not yet protectable under industrial property law, for manufacture, application, product designs, technological process, formulae, quality control or management.[78] The UCA stretched that definition to include information (1) undisclosed to the public and guarded by the proprietor who has taken adequate measures to keep it from disclosure; (2) capable of producing economic benefits or commercial advantage; and (3) for industrial or commercial application (in order to exclude theories or ideas). Feng acknowledges that trade secrets may include technology, processes and formulas on the basis of good faith competition. A proprietor under the UCA would include the person in possession of the proprietary information. The law requires that the proprietor must have taken all reasonable measures to prevent others from taking the proprietary information by ordinary means.

---

[76] The author would like to thank Jiang Qinfeng for bringing this to his attention.
[77] Feng at 385–387.
[78] Id.

The effectiveness of the trade secrets law however is limited.[79] Section 2(2) specifies that the law only governs unfair competition committed by operators. Section 2(3) defines operators as those legal persons, economic organisations and individuals involved in the production of goods or other related profit-making services. The actual custodians of the trade secrets of TCM normally include natural persons, families or communities that are not necessarily official legal or profit-making entities.

Criminal liability for violation of trade secrets exists, but it should be noted that the UCA itself does not provide for criminal sanctions against infringement of the trade secrets provisions. Criminal liability for the violation of trade secrets arises from the new Criminal Code. It stipulates that only a breach of the UCA's trade secret law that gives rise to the owner's heavy economic losses will be deemed a criminal act.

6.   *Law on the Administration of Pharmaceuticals*

The 1984 Law on the Administration of Pharmaceuticals, as amended in 2001, and its companion implementing Measures of the Law on the Administration of Pharmaceuticals, are the main laws in China that regulate the administration and supervision, manufacture, distribution and preparation of pharmaceuticals, including TCM, on the Mainland.[80] The State Drug Administration, having taken over the portfolios of the Ministry of Public Health, the State Drug Administration Bureau and the State Administration of Chinese Traditional Medicines in 1998, is the principal institutional authority. Under the Foreign Investment Industrial Guidance Catalogue issued by the then State Planning Commission, the manufacture of certain TCM's falls within restricted categories for foreign investment. In August 2002, the State Council issued the "Implementing Regulation on the Law of Pharmaceutical Administration".

These categories include medicines listed as natural resources protected by the state or medicinal foods or products prepared by means of secret Chinese recipes. Such "protection" for traditional Chinese medicine, may actually deter traditional medicine holders from seeking intellectual property protection on the grounds that in order to receive "protection, they would first have to disseminate their secret formula to the public"![81] Supplemental to any patent law protection, the State Drug Administration has the discretion to issue to an approved TCM a licence arising from the 1999 Measures Concerning the Protection of New Pharmaceutical Products. The term of protection for this certificate is normally between six and 12 years. Until

---

[79] The author would like to express thanks to Jiang Qinfeng for bringing this to his attention. In 1995, the State Administration for Industry and Commerce promulgated "Several Provisions on Prohibition of Infringement of the Anti-Unfair Competition Law".

[80] Catherine Guo, "The Legal and Regulatory Framework for the Chinese Traditional Medicine Industry in China", Hong Kong Lawyer (June 2001) 35, 36–37.

[81] See supra fns. 35–36 and accompanying text.

now, according to Catherine Guo, foreign investment and participation in the local manufacturing or distribution of TCM's has been substantially restricted, but it is anticipated that with China's accession to WTO, foreign investors will be able to take part in the TCM industry.[82] As China's domestic market for TCM opens to foreign investors and overseas demand for TCM expands, China must come to terms with the extent of protection that will be afforded to traditional knowledge holders; the urgency, relevance and importance of the problem is highlighted by the example of a Japanese company that patented a Chinese traditional cloisonné production method. While the Japanese company was able to dominate the global market for the product, the traditional inventors of the system not only lost their own market share, but because China did not afford them intellectual property rights in traditional methods, the traditional holders lost control and use over their own invention.[83]

7. *Plant Variety Regulations*

China has recently acceded to the Food and Agricultural Organization's International Undertaking on Plant Genetic Resources (UPOV) 1978 Act. In light of this international obligation, the State Council promulgated the 1997 Regulations on the Protection of New Varieties of Plants. The rules are intended to establish and protect property rights in new plant varieties to provide incentives to the agriculture and forestry industry to breed new plants. The rights of variety rights holders extend to preventing others from producing or selling any of the protected breeding material and from using the protected breed repeatedly.[84] Exception to this exclusive right is provided when the protected variety is being used for scientific research activities or when peasants are using the protected variety for their own breeding material.

Commentators have argued that China's plant variety regulations fall short of those of developed countries. They argue that China should adopt the UPOV Act 1991. This act expands treaty protection to plant genera. It also broadens the scope of protection entitled to breeders. In the absence of such coverage, commentators argue that the incentive for national manufacturers to breed plant varieties and for foreign enterprises to license new plant varieties to China will decline.[85] This approach, however, has been criticised on the ground that it falsely assumes that plant genetic resources are part of

---

[82] See supra fn. 80 at 38.

[83] China Daily, http://english.peopledaily.com.cn/200104/12/eng20010412_67507.html, viewed on 4 October 2002.

[84] Compare: Neil Hamilton, "Legal Issues Shaping Society's Acceptance of Biotechnology and Genetically Modified Organisms", 6 Drake Journal of Agricultural Law (Spring 2001) 81.

[85] Lester Ross/Libin Zhang, "Agricultural Development and Intellectual Property Protection For Plant Varieties: China Joins the UPOV", 17 University of California Pacific Basin Law Journal (Fall, 1999 / Spring, 2000) 226.

the public domain and therefore free to be privatised through the assignment of intellectual property rights. This divergent view is based on the notion that the state, local or indigenous bodies may have cultural or legal proprietary claims over plant genetic resources. Before adopting standards equal to other developed countries, China needs to think carefully about how its plant genetic resources, the source of much TCM, should be used.

8. Trade Marks

The 1982 Trade Mark Act, as amended in 1993 and 2001, can also bring indirect proprietary protection to the trade mark registrant of a traditional Chinese medicine.[86] The purpose of the Chinese trade mark law is to encourage industrial productivity, ensure the quality of the product and protect the reputation of the trader by prohibiting unauthorised uses of the trade mark.[87] It does so by preventing third parties from using a similar sign that will likely confuse consumers. To receive protection, a trade mark must be registered under the Trade Mark Act. The only unregistered trade marks that will receive protection in China are well-known trade marks. All pharmaceutical firms must seek trade mark registration for their products, including traditional Chinese medicines.[88] The trade mark is valid for ten years and is subject to unlimited renewal.

The present trade mark laws afford protection to "well-known" trade marks and "geographical representations". This source of civil claim will prove quite helpful to proprietors of traditional Chinese medicine. With regard to "well-known" trade marks, firms with nationally and internationally famous marks representing high quality products and service that have failed to register on the Mainland will have recourse should another firm surreptitiously register the "well-known" mark in China without permission. Likewise, because the potency of a traditional Chinese medicine often depends upon its environment, climate, water quality, sunlight, soil, etc., its place of origin carries with it considerable value. A mark's geographic origin will be protected where considerable goodwill and reputation has been built up. It is a historical convention that Chinese medicines adopt the name of the geographic region where the plant was cultivated. The "geographical representation" protection will prevent applicants from claiming unauthorised or inaccurate geographical origins in their name.

---

[86] Trade Mark Act of the People's Republic of China, Sec. 38. Since 2001, the State Council and the Supreme People's Court have established rules that have further enhanced protection of trade marks. In August of 2002, the State Council revised the Implementing Regulations. In 2002, there were three Supreme People's Court decisions that clarified procedural matters for the application of the law.

[87] Qu Weijun, "The Intellectual Property Rights and Protection of Traditional Medicine in China", paper presented at APEC Symposium on Traditional Medicine (Hong Kong) 19–22 March 2002.

[88] See generally, Fu Gang, "View on the Trade Mark Protection of Traditional Chinese Medicine", 12(69) Intellectual Property (2002) 28 (in Chinese).

While the advent of well-known trade marks and geographic representations does provide ample opportunity for legal protection of traditional knowledge,[89] the institutionalisation of trade marks also creates obstacles. First, indigenous custodians of traditional medicine in China, simply by virtue of the fact that they live in isolated areas, may not be aware of the availability of trade mark protection. Without an application, third parties are free to apply and seek proprietary rights over the mark. Second, even if a traditional medicine holder knows of trade mark protection, the costs for the application and its defence may be prohibitive.

9. Biotechnology

In contrast to the evolution of intellectual property law concerning biotechnology internationally,[90] China's development is at a relatively early stage,[91] giving one cause for cautious optimism that it may be able to incorporate the recognition of traditional ecological knowledge over the coming years. With regard to intellectual property rights over genetic resources,[92] some progress has already been made. State Council Order No. 36 enacted the new human Gene IPR rules of China on 10 June 1998.[93] The law is intended to protect the intellectual property rights of local and foreign partners through an open negotiation of use and access rights and thereby prevent the unfair exploitation of China's genetic resources.[94]

Otherwise, Chinese intellectual property jurisprudence largely follows western notions of patent protection for biotechnology.[95] Section 25(4) Patent Act stipulates that patent rights for animal and plant varieties are prohibited. According to the Director General of the Chemical Department of the Patent Office of the State Intellectual Property Office, in accordance

---

[89] David Downes, "How Intellectual Property Could Be a Tool to Protect Traditional Knowledge", 25 Columbia Journal of Environmental Law (2000) 253, 281.

[90] Sean Murphy, "Biotechnology and International Law", 42 Harvard International Law Journal (Winter 2001) 47.

[91] See generally, Zhang Qingkui, "Patent Protection for Biological Inventions In China" 4(63) China Patents and Trademarks (October 2000) 24.

[92] Carrie Smith, " Patenting Life: The Potential and the Pitfalls of Using the WTO to Globalize Intellectual Property Rights", 26 North Carolina Journal of International Law & Commercial Regulation (Fall 2000) 143.

[93] See, e.g. J.M. Spectar, "Patent Necessity: Intellectual Property Dilemmas in the Biotech Domain & Treatment Equity for Developing Countries", 24 Houston Journal of International Law (Winter 2002) 227.

[94] According to media reports, the policy responded the threat posed by multi-national pharmaceutical firms that could exploit the Chinese gene pool. The Beijing Youth Weekly reported that "if China does not get its own patents, then in the next century China's biotechnology industry . . . will be like 'The Admiral of the Northern Fleet who saw all his ships capsize and sink beneath the waves'. Unless we spend a large sum of money to buy patents from other people, we will have no right to manufacture these living organisms and pharmaceuticals."

[95] Zhang Qingkui, "Patent Protection for Biological Inventions in China", 4 China Patents and Trademarks (2000) 24, 25.

with *Chakrabarty*,[96] Sec. 25(1) Patent Act prevents the patenting of natural micro-organisms and genetic substances but allows for the patenting of "technically treated" micro-organisms including bacteria, fungi, actinomyces, viruses, cell lines, plasmids, protozoans and algae. In 2001, the State Intellectual Property Office clarified the extent to which genes could be considered as patentable subject matter. The office explained that:

"The gene or its DNA extracts existing in its natural state discovered by someone are mere discoveries and shall not be the subject of patent right. However, if a gene or DNA extract, for the first time, is separated or extracted from nature, of which the sequence of the base group remains unknown in the prior art and can accurately be characterized, and its susceptible to application in industry, that gene or DNA extract per se and the process to obtain it may be patented."[97]

It also appears that biological products from microorganisms, metabolite of microorganisms, animal toxins, human or animal blood or tissue for the prevention, diagnosis or treatment of diseases is patentable.

It would appear then that the commercialisation of traditional ecological knowledge without the recognition of the indigenous contributors would be the next logical step. Western observers are already encouraging China to adopt western methods of traditional knowledge resource exploitation.

"For the most part, China has been able to control the foreign manipulation of traditional Chinese herbs by either forming joint ventures or contracting for a share of the profits derived from foreign biomedical enterprises. Once the industry has a few years to grow, China may be able to exclusively transform materials from their natural habitat into new pharmaceuticals without the need for any foreign control. If China can amass enough capital, establish strong research teams, and produce qualified economists, the only remaining foreign component that is required to construct biopharmaceuticals is high tech machinery."[98]

Their advice, however well-intentioned in terms of encouraging the development of the biotechnology industry, fails to account for the impact which the absence of recognition of traditional ecological knowledge will have on the long-term development of biological resources.

10. Copyright

Both patent law and copyright have similar functions and regulatory frameworks. They both create property rights in intellectual creations. The goal of both is to promote creativity. In comparison to the regulation of traditional ecological knowledge already discussed, an analysis of the copyright law of China, by analogy, will provide valuable insights into the extensive transplantation of individualism into the Chinese intellectual property rights system.

---

[96] *Diamond v. Chakrabarty*, 447 US 303 (1980).
[97] Chapter 10, Section 7.1.2.2, Guidelines for Examination (2001).
[98] Leslie Cataldo, "A Dynasty Weaned From Biotechnology: The Emerging Face Of China", 26 Syracuse Journal of International Law and Commerce (Fall 1998) 151, 161.

The copyright protection of traditional indigenous works, known as works of folklore in China, illustrates China's preference for an author-centred copyright law. Authorship for traditional works is not easy to define, particularly in terms of modern copyright law, because they may be indigenous expressions with uncertain historical origins that may be composed under a collective process of creativity or further classified by sacred characteristics. While the Chinese government's policy is to preserve the cultural heritage of its ethnic minorities, such traditional expressions are presently treated as if they were part of the public domain, subject to new administrative regulations promised under Sec. 6 Copyright Act. Collators of the work are entitled to copyright in their collection, while not even the paternity of the original authors is protected by law.[99] One scholar suggests that the establishment of a competent authority to represent the interests of the folkloric works, in line with Art. 15(4) Berne Convention would be the equivalent of imposing a politically incorrect tax on the trade and consumption of folkloric works.[100] Such an analysis, however, circumvents the issue that the absence of moral and material recognition of indigenous rights in traditional expression may have on the development of the Chinese ethnic groups and on the conservation of the cultural heritage itself.[101]

A recent December 2003 decision of the Beijing Superior People's Court, on appeal from the Beijing Intermediate People's Court, however, indicates that the recognition of traditional resource rights in intellectual property rights is entering the public dialogue.[102] It further shows that lawmakers recognise the importance of preserving cultural heritage, despite considerable commercial pressures. The dispute arose as a result of a claim by the singer Guo Song that she was the copyright owner of a traditional folk song of the ethnic Hezhe minority from the Hezhe Sipai village. Guo Song claimed during a CCTV broadcast and in writing on the VCD of the Folk Song Festival where she sang the song, that she was the copyright owner of the song. An expert group, designated by the court, determined that the melody style of Guo Song's version was similar to several traditional Hezhe folk songs. The local government of the Hezhe minority sued on the minority's behalf. Although the court ruled that Guo Song's version was not a new

---

[99]   According to the CTR, however, the collator must recognise the contribution of the original source and compensate the provider of the data.

[100]   Feng at 159–160.

[101]   A particularly interesting decision cited by Feng is the *Wang Luobin* case. In this case, a collator of traditional songs from northwest and central China, transferred copyright in the traditional songs to a Taiwanese publisher. According to Feng, the National Copyright Administration approved of the permanent assignment of copyright to the third party. Feng at 160–161.

[102]   The decision and subsequent analysis derives from a Mainland newspaper account of the decision. Beijing Times, 20 December 2003. http://www.bjt.net.cn/news.asp?newsid=46159., viewed on 9 January 2004.

composition, any productions of the song should carry the notice that it is adapted from the folk music of the Hezhe ethnic minority.[103]

The decision raises important issues with regard to the protection of traditional resources in China. First, the plaintiff claimed that the local government had no standing to represent the ethnic minority; the court dismissed this allegation on the basis that the minority had settled in their jurisdiction, that in fact they had no choice about their settlement area and that the local government had an obligation and right to protect the cultural heritage of the ethnic group. Second, the plaintiff claimed that because the folk song was part of the public domain and authored collectively, no copyright in the original authors could arise. The court held that Guo Song had adapted the song and, due to the fact that adaptations are not permissible without the consent of the author, the court implied that the Hezhe ethnic minority was the original author of the work. The fact that the only remedy authorised was the requirement that the Hezhe minority be acknowledged as the author of the work and that the modest legal fees of the local government be paid, shows that the court must have calculated that such an unauthorised adaptation was not a full infringement.

D. Conclusion

Contrary to the general perception that Mainland China has not established intellectual property rights over TCM, this paper has tried to show that China has taken strides toward the protection of local traditional knowledge. A patchwork of laws exists that seek to formalise a business model of TCM that does not include the inventors of the traditional knowledge in the first place. A further conclusion drawn is that the emergence of intellectual property rights for traditional knowledge in China follows global trends. It has largely incorporated an author/inventor-centred approach, and tends to over-protect the new owners of the resources and under-protect the true inventors of these precious resources. In effect, the true inventors of TCM have no claim to any right in their inventions.[104]

Although in the short term, this approach may attract further foreign investment into the Mainland, one may suggest that the price of this achievement is too high. It not only marginalises local and indigenous cultural and scientific industry, it simply disregards the social and ecological value of preserving Chinese traditional knowledge. In order to ensure the sustainable use of biological diversity on the Mainland, it is therefore essential that a

---

[103] See the case report and comment by Bryan Bachner, in 35 IIC [2004], forthcoming. See also Shi Gu, "Case Analysis: Dispute Over Copyright in Wusuli Rivery Chantey", China Law (April 2004) 109–117.

[104] See generally, Joseph Henry Vogel, Genes for Sale: Privitisation as a Conservation Policy (New York: Oxford University Press, 1994).

reconceptualisation of the intellectual property rights, particularly as they relate to traditional ecological knowledge, be undertaken. This reconceptualisation should balance the interests between the modern and traditional custodians of traditional knowledge. While any dilution of existing standards of intellectual property rights will lead to a hue and cry from owners that the incentive to invent will likewise be diluted, 5,000 years of evidence of the flourishing of TCM in China should reinforce the notion that state's enforcement of exclusive property rights is not the only way to encourage innovation and sustainability.

At the end of the day, this paper has investigated how to use rules to formulate rights that will create optimal uses for the development of traditional ecological knowledge on the Chinese Mainland. Modern conceptualisations of intellectual property rights, as we have seen, are principally and comprehensively based upon the interests of inventors and owners. Under such a closed system, the law fences off the natural resources and their new uses from public access by allowing the inventor or right owner to exploit his invention through a near absolute monopoly. Does the articulation of property rights that are primarily concerned with the prevention of unauthorised uses of the basic components of TCM advance its development? Does the enactment of IPR that overlook either economic or moral rights for the true inventor of a TCM actually contribute to the innovation and invention of TCM? At best, the answer is unclear as no empirical evidence to the author's knowledge exists to support the notion that the establishment of commercial rights over TCM will encourage improvement of TCM. At worst, we have the historical evidence set out in this paper, that only an open system has been shown to create an environment where the development of TCM can thrive.

In addition to the absence of any substantiation that enhanced commercialisation will improve the process of innovation in the field of TCM, there are arguments, which bear reciting in brief, that such an approach will adversely impact innovation in the TCM industry. First, an intellectual property regime that grants a patent over a TCM to a pharmaceutical firm will provide an incentive to the firm to prevent "third parties" from using that TCM in any form that does not meet the patent's own commercial interests; "third parties" would normally include the traditional practitioner or the indigenous community that had originally invented the TCM and remains the traditional custodian over it. The best possible outcome of such a regulatory approach is the curtailing of further invention by the traditional practitioner. Second, the complex nature of the patenting regime would necessarily increase the price of the TCM on the conventional market, particularly in comparison to the normal price of the traditional industry; accessibility to important and affordable medicines will be held back from not only from consumers but also, in cases where the pharmaceutical firm is based in a developed country, developing countries. Third, the intensive capitalisation involved in the manufacture and distribution of a marketable drug normally means that pharmaceutical firms will only invest in research for "winning" drugs; such a business model does not encourage investment in the bio-cultural diversity of traditional medicines, and thereby limits the evolution of newer traditional medicines. Fourth, the lack of any recognition of property rights deriving from the inventive contributors of the traditional medicine means that anyone may pirate the invention, domestically or internationally, and the state will do nothing to prevent it; likewise, the state, by ignoring the value of traditional resources, allows foreign parties to expropriate China's own cultural heritage for free.

The modern trend for the development of intellectual property rights on the Mainland, with particular reference to its treatment of traditional Chinese medicine, is to provide to "inventors" comprehensive proprietary control over the biological resource and its application. This process of commodifying valuable traditional knowledge and preventing not only the traditional practitioners but also other pharmaceutical researchers from accessing and evaluating potentially new and beneficial applications serves to undermine the ultimate goal of the intellectual property system: innovation. The conceptualisation of current intellectual property rights has actually taken a step backward in that its monopolisation of the culture of improvement has calcified, rather then enhanced the process of innovation. It seems that the modern regime has much to learn from its traditional forebears.

2
Traditional Knowledge and Intellectual Property Rights in Australia and Southeast Asia

CHRISTOPH ANTONS[1]

A. International Efforts to Harmonise Legal Approaches to Folklore and Traditional Knowledge Protection

This paper will present a short survey of various approaches to traditional knowledge and folklore protection in Australia and Southeast Asia. It seems that both the terminology used in the debate about traditional knowledge and folklore and the legal solutions envisaged are very diverse. Over the last decade there has been an explosion of international declarations and organisations advocating internationally harmonised notions of rights to culture, often on behalf of indigenous minorities or other local communities. This often leads to what Cowan, Dembour and Wilson[2] have called "strategic essentialism". The term refers to the attempts by activists from or working on behalf of communities to define unanimous or seemingly unanimous demands with regard to culture and rights and to make them fit into the categories of national or international legal regimes. The authors assume that "we need to be more cognisant of the role played by law in essentialising categories and fixing identities, as a concomitant of its task of developing general principles to include, ideally, all possible cases."[3] In other words, litigants in cases involving indigenous rights legislation might be forced to adopt a notion of culture as static and inflexible[4] and "as a preexisting given . . . rather than as something creatively reworked during struggles to actualise rights."[5] As a result, the international concepts of community rights to culture and heritage in the form of traditional

---

[1] The author's research into traditional knowledge protection and intellectual property in Australia and Southeast Asia is currently supported by a Queen Elizabeth II fellowship of the Australian Research Council (ARC).

[2] J.K. Cowan/M.B. Dembour/R.A. Wilson, "Introduction", in: J.K. Cowan/ M.B. Dembour/R.A. Wilson, *Culture and Rights: Anthropological Perspectives*, Cambridge University Press 2001, 10–11.

[3] *Ibid.*, 21.

[4] S.E. Merry, "Changing Rights, Changing Culture", in: J.K. Cowan, M.B. Dembour and R.A. Wilson (above note 2), 39.

[5] J.K. Cowan/M.B. Dembour/R.A. Wilson, "Introduction" (above note 2), 19.

knowledge or folklore protection begin to look more unified than they actually are.[6]

This presentation aims to demonstrate the diversity of the approaches. It shows how much of the debate originated in settler colonies with significant indigenous minorities such as Australia. However, if one moves to Asia, there is a different understanding as to who may be bearing rights to folklore and traditional knowledge. There is still little recognition of indigenous minorities and instead Asian governments push at international conventions and in national legislation for the rights of farmers, herbalists and other "local communities". Much of the current discussion tends to blur this distinction and one finds publications discussing the rights of Thai farmers, Korean shamans or Indian Ayurvedic healers together with Aboriginal or North American Indian minorities. The attempt to harmonise the various approaches has also shifted the terminology from "folklore" to "traditional knowledge" based on the holistic understanding of the material by some of the communities involved in the international debate. In line with the author's current ARC funded research project, Southeast Asian examples for this paper will be drawn mainly from Indonesia and the Philippines, with occasional reference to Thailand.

B. The Diversity of Approaches: Folklore and Traditional Knowledge Protection in Australia, the Philippines, Thailand and Indonesia

The discussion about aspects of traditional knowledge has a fairly long tradition in Australia, yet it is relatively new to Southeast Asia. There are several reasons for this, which have to do with the differences in approach between Australia on the one hand and Southeast Asian nations on the other. The first reason is that the term was for a long time used more or less simultaneously with the term "indigenous knowledge". Writers from countries with significant and officially recognised indigenous minorities such as Australia or Canada dominated the international debate, in part also because they published their case materials and articles in English. However, as Kingsbury has shown,[7] the concept of "indigenous peoples" is problematic in Asian countries. It is particularly problematic in Southeast Asia where colonial legacy has created a multiethnic society with various waves of migration bringing in ethnic minorities from India, the Arab peninsula and from

---

    [6] For a sceptical assessment of the role of intellectual property in protecting indigenous culture see also M.F. Brown, "Can culture be copyrighted?", *Current Anthropology*, Vol. 39 No. 2, 193; M.F. Brown, *Who owns native culture?*, Harvard University Press, Cambridge/Mass.-London, 2003.

    [7] B. Kingsbury, "The Applicability of the International Legal Concept of "Indigenous Peoples" in Asia", in: J.R. Bauer/D.A. Bell, *The East Asian Challenge for Human Rights*, Cambridge University Press 1999.

China. As a consequence, the term "indigenous" is understood in Indonesia or Malaysia as referring to a person who is ethnic Malay and literally translated as "son of the soil" (*"pribumi"* or *"bumiputra"*) as opposed to "alien" minorities of Chinese and Indian descent. Descendants from even earlier waves of migration to Southeast Asia, who can be found, for example, in the interior of Borneo or on the Mentawai islands off the coast of West Sumatra, were until recently referred to in Indonesia as *"suku bangsa terasing"*, remote or secluded living ethnic groups. To recognise these groups as bearers of particular rights is more difficult to argue in densely populated post-colonial Asia than in settler colonies such as Australia, where recognition of Aboriginal rights is often regarded as recognition of past injustices and as an important component of the reconciliation process.

There is, however, little conformity in this regard in Southeast Asia. On the one hand, there is some recognition of indigenous peoples in the Malaysian Constitution[8] and the Philippines has enacted an Act to recognise, protect and promote the rights of indigenous cultural communities/indigenous people.[9] The Philippines is an interesting case study, because its different approach to the issue has its historical roots in the US administration during the first half of the 20th century.[10] At the time, the Americans established a Bureau of Non-Christian Tribes and applied policies similar to those for American Indians,[11] hence the similarities of the Philippines in this respect with the Anglo-Saxon settler colonies. On the other hand, countries such as Thailand recognise the hill tribes of North and Northwest Thailand as ethnic groups but have made it plain to the United Nations that such groups "are not considered to be minorities or indigenous peoples but as Thais who are able to enjoy fundamental rights . . . as any other Thai citizen."[12] As a consequence, the amended Thai Constitution of 1997 in Art. 46 protects "traditional communities", who are given the right ". . . to conserve or restore their customs, local knowledge, arts or good culture of their community and of the nation and participate in the management, maintenance, preservation and exploitation of natural resources and the environment in a balanced fashion and persistently. . . ."[13] Similarly, the Indonesian Constitution of 1945, amended four times between 1999 and 2002, declares

---

    [8] R. Bulan, "Native Status under the Law", in: Wu Min Aun (ed.), *Public Law in Contemporary Malaysia*, Longman, Petaling Jaya 1999, 259; S. Gray, "Skeletal Principles in Malaysia's Common Law Cupboard: The Future of Indigenous Native Title in Malaysian Common Law", in: LAWASIA Journal 2002, 101.

    [9] Republic Act No. 8371 of 1997.

    [10] For a recent collection with comparative essays on US rule in the Philippines see J. Go/A.L. Foster (eds.), *The American Colonial State in the Philippines: Global Perspectives*, Duke University Press, Durham and London 2003.

    [11] Kingsbury (above note 7), 353.

    [12] See the statement of the Government of Thailand of 12 May 1992, cited in Kingsbury (above note 7), 357.

    [13] Cf. Section 46 of the Constitution of the Kingdom of Thailand of 1997.

in Art. 18B(2) that the state "recognises and respects adat law communities along with their traditional rights". A concept from the Arabic language, *adat* is widely used in communities all over Indonesia and usually translated as custom. Yet, as von Benda-Beckmann has pointed out, it has a wider meaning in Indonesian society covering originally both the supernatural and the secular social reality.[14] It was treated and developed as a legal system by the Dutch colonial government and since then refers to forms which are enforceable and have legal consequences.[15] Distinct from the situation in Thailand, however, such recognition of customary rights occurs only "as long as these remain in existence and are in accordance with the societal development and the principles of the Unitary State of the Republic of Indonesia, which are regulated by law." Furthermore, Art. 28I in the new Chapter XA on "Human Rights" maintains that "the cultural identities and rights of traditional communities shall be respected", but again adding the qualification that this has to happen "in accordance with contemporary development and civilisation."

A second reason is the newness of the term "traditional knowledge" as opposed to the still better known term "folklore". Traditional knowledge, as it is now defined by WIPO, includes "tradition based literary, artistic and scientific works, performances, inventions, scientific discoveries, designs, marks, names and symbols, undisclosed information and all other tradition-based innovations and creations resulting from intellectual activity in the industrial, scientific, literary or artistic field." This is a working definition used in a WIPO report of 2001 on the intellectual property needs and expectations of traditional knowledge holders.[16] The report was the result of several fact-finding missions that took WIPO delegations to countries on four continents. Australia was included in the fact-finding mission to the South Pacific and roundtable discussions were held in 1998 in both Darwin and Sydney. It is obvious from the definition of traditional knowledge that the definition is written by people concerned with intellectual property law. At the same time, however, the definition crosses the entire range of intellectual property rights. It makes no distinction between copyrights, patents, trade marks or other forms of intellectual property. The definition does, however, distinguish intellectual property related forms of traditional knowledge from other forms of real or moveable property and from heritage protection in a broader sense.

As Michael Blakeney has pointed out, the shift away from the term "folklore" occurred after it was criticised for its eurocentric content and lack

---

[14] F. von Benda-Beckmann, *Property in Social Continuity: Continuity and Change in the Maintenance of Property Relationships Through Time in Minangkabau, West Sumatra*, Martinus Nijhoff, The Hague 1979, 113–114

[15] *Ibid.*, 116–118

[16] World Intellectual Property Organization, *Intellectual Property Needs and Expectations of Traditional Knowledge Holders – WIPO Report on Fact-finding Missions on Intellectual Property and Traditional Knowledge*, Geneva 2001, 25.

of capability to express the holistic conception of many non-Western communities with regards to knowledge and the transmission of knowledge. The term folklore was regarded as giving the impression of dealing with static rather than evolving traditions and it gave the communities an inferior status in comparison with the dominant culture.[17] The view of indigenous Australian representatives was prominent in this criticism. In her report "Our Culture: Our Future", written in 1998 for the Aboriginal and Torres Straits Islander Commission (ATSIC), Terri Janke preferred to use the term "indigenous cultural and intellectual property rights" introduced a few years earlier by Ms. Erica Daes, the Special Rapporteur of the UN Sub-Commission on Prevention of Discrimination and Protection of Minorities.[18]

The WIPO definition is narrower than the definition of "indigenous cultural and intellectual property" used in the report drafted by Terri Janke. This report's definition includes indigenous ancestral remains, sacred indigenous sites, so-called "cultural environment resources" such as minerals and species and even languages as far as they are relevant for "cultural identity, knowledge, skill and the teaching of culture".[19] On the other hand, the WIPO definition is much wider than the previously predominant term of "folklore", which clearly focused on copyright related artistic expressions such as handicrafts, dances and music.[20] WIPO has illustrated the new approach with a picture of overlapping circles.[21] The WIPO term is, therefore, narrower than heritage, but wider than both "expressions of folklore" and "indigenous knowledge", because the material in question may be produced by indigenous people, but that is not necessarily the case.

In view of the reluctance of developing countries of Southeast Asia to provide special protection for indigenous peoples, it comes as no surprise that the term "indigenous knowledge" has not found much acceptance in this part of the world. The Philippines is again a notable exception here. In the Indigenous Peoples Rights Act of 1997, it recognises "community intellectual rights" and "rights to indigenous knowledge systems" of indigenous cultural communities and indigenous peoples. "Indigenous societies" are also mentioned as potential beneficiaries in the Traditional and Alternative Medicine Act of 1997[22] and Executive Order No. 247 of 1995 and the

---

[17] M. Blakeney, "The Protection of Traditional Knowledge under Intellectual Property Law", [2000] E.I.P.R. 251.

[18] T. Janke, *Our Culture: Our Future – Report on Australian Indigenous Cultural and Intellectual Property Rights*, Michael Frankel & Company, Sydney 1998.

[19] T. Janke, 11–12.

[20] See WIPO (above, note 16), 22. In 1982, WIPO and UNESCO drafted the Model Provisions for National Laws on the Protection of Folklore Against Illicit Exploitation and other Prejudicial Actions.

[21] *Ibid.*, 26.

[22] Republic Act No. 8423.

implementing rules and regulations for this order of 1996[23] speak again of indigenous cultural communities and indigenous peoples.

Thailand's Plant Varieties Protection Act of 1999 allows for the registration of local plant varieties by "local communities". The Act on the Protection and Promotion of Thai Traditional Medicine of 1999 distinguishes between medicinal formulas that are in the public domain and other that may be privately owned or become the property of the state. The latter occurs when the formula is of significant benefit or has special medical value and has been declared as such by the Ministry of Health.[24] The special mentioning of "local communities" as rights holders is a consequence of the amendment of the Thai Constitution in 1997 and the granting of rights to "traditional communities" that was mentioned earlier.

While Thailand allows for appropriation of forms of traditional knowledge only in the field of traditional medicine, Indonesia provides for the strongest centralised role of the state of the countries surveyed here. It speaks of "folklore" and of "products of the culture of the people" in the Copyright Act and stipulates that the state holds the copyright with regards to this material. In fact, while many countries have recently shifted from using the term "folklore" to "traditional knowledge", Indonesia has gone the opposite way, at least in its legislation. The term "folklore" has been newly introduced into the Copyright Act of 2002, whereas the previous Act spoke only of the "products of popular culture". According to the Plant Varieties Act, local varieties that are "property of the public" are controlled by the state.

A third reason for the differences in approach has to do with culture and with customary law. Cultural taboos and customary law prohibitions dealing with traditional knowledge material are strong in relatively isolated indigenous communities. In such communities, traditional knowledge material is often regarded as secret and sacred, because it plays a vital role in the survival of the community. It is linked to animist practices and religion and as long as local belief systems remain sufficiently strong, it is possible for local elders, headmen and practitioners of traditional forms of medicines to enforce the taboos. However, in the setting of the larger society of a nation state, where the majority of the people adheres to mainstream religions such as Islam, Buddhism or Christianity, taboos based on customary law lose their power and can no longer be enforced. The question of recognition of such customary enforcement depends then on how much scope the nation state and the majority or majorities are prepared to grant to indigenous customary law. Here, we can perceive again a distinction between the policies of the various countries in this survey. In Australia, customary law is still strong in Aboriginal communities in the northern part of the country. It is only in

---

[23] Department Administrative Order No. 96-20.

[24] J. Kuanpoth/G. Dutfield/O. Luanratana, *Devising New Kinds of International and National Systems for the Protection of Traditional Medicine* (draft report for the WHO, on file with the author), 83–86.

recent years that it has gained recognition as part of the national legal system, but Aboriginal communities are in a fairly strong bargaining position here due to the international attention paid to the issue and the necessity for a settler society to find ways for reconciliation.

In the Philippines, the recognition of indigenous customary rights has improved with the acceptance of the international concept of "indigenous peoples" by the government.[25] In Thailand, there is practical assistance for the "hill-tribe" people of North and Northwest Thailand, but apparently so far little recognition of their customary law.[26] The Thai Ministry of Foreign Affairs has pointed out that it is committed to capacity building programs for "local community and grassroots people in rural areas".[27] In addition, the amended Thai Constitution now gives "traditional communities" the right "to conserve or restore their customs" but the precise meaning of this right is yet to be established. In Indonesia, customary law or *hukum adat* is officially recognised as part of the legal system. It is important, however, to distinguish between what has been termed as "remote living communities" and the much larger communities of Javanese, Sundanese, Balinese, etc., that together form Indonesia. Mystical practices certainly play a great role in Java, for example, but the Javanese are little acquainted with the idea that knowledge should be sacred and secret. In an interesting study carried out in 1997 and 1998 for her PhD thesis, Cita Citrawinda Priapantja surveyed the attitudes of sellers of traditional *jamu* (herbal medicine) and of traditional Chinese medicine in the area of Metropolitan Jakarta and in Semarang and Yogyakarta in Central Java.[28] She found that especially the sellers of *jamu gendong* (literally: carried *jamu*, sold by street peddlers and carried in a bottle on their backs) in Jakarta were poor migrant women from central Java for whom the traditional Javanese values of village cooperation (*gotong royong*) and harmony *(rukun)* were more important than business competition or the secrecy of their formulas.[29] As far as artistic expressions are concerned, the anthropologist Koentjaraningrat has pointed out that in Javanese religious symbolism, ceremonies play a very important role to give magical power to artistic items. The Javanese dagger (*kris*) for example becomes magical only through ritual and only in relation to a particular person.[30] There is,

---

[25] Kingsbury (above note 7), 353–354.

[26] Kingsbury (above note 7), 356. See also the website of the Statement of the South-East Asia Indigenous and Tribal Peoples Consultation Workshop of the Asia Partnership for Human Development at http://www.pphd.or.th/southeast_RP.html.

[27] See the website of the Ministry of Foreign Affairs, Kingdom of Thailand at http://www.mfa.go.th/web/24.php.

[28] C.C. Priapantja, *Budaya Hukum Indonesia menghadapi Globalisasi: Perlindungan Rahasia Dagang di Bidang Farmasi* (Indonesian Legal Culture Facing Globalisation: The Protection of Trade Secrets in the Field of Pharmaceuticals), Chandra Pertama, Jakarta 1999.

[29] C.C. Priapantja (above note 28), 299–307.

[30] Koentjaraningrat, *Javanese Culture*, Oxford University Press, Singapore 1985, 343–345, 414–415.

therefore, no particular reason why such an item without spiritual energy may not be produced as folklore for the tourist market.

C. The National Approaches in Detail

I. Australia

In Australia, the issue of folklore protection has attracted the attention of policy makers for many years. A working party to examine the issue was formed as early as 1974 and in 1981, the Department of Home Affairs and Environment published a "Report of the Working Party on the Protection of Aboriginal Folklore", which recommended the adoption of an Aboriginal Folklore Act and the establishment of a Folklore Commission. However, the model law did not provide for indigenous ownership of the material.[31] It was soon superseded by judicial developments when the High Court overturned the doctrine of *terra nullius* that had declared Australia as uninhabited at the time of settlement in *Mabo and Others v. Queensland* [No. 2]. However, *Mabo* concerned the recognition of native title to land, but left open the question of a more general recognition of Aboriginal customary law. Shortly after the *Mabo* decision, the High Court refused to recognise customary criminal law in *Walker v. New South Wales* ((1994–95) 182 CLR 45, at 49–50).[32] Academic commentators attempted to extend native title to land to intellectual property based on the holistic understanding of Aboriginal people of the connection between songs or stories about land and the knowledge transmitted in those stories. However, so far these attempts have not been successful. In *John Bulun Bulun & Anor v. R & T Textiles Pty. Ltd.* (1082 FCA (1998)), Justice von Doussa pointed out that the assumption of communal ownership to a copyrighted work would involve the creation of rights not otherwise recognised by the Australian legal system.

Instead of communal ownership, Justice von Doussa in an important *obiter* remark was prepared to recognise a fiduciary obligation of an Aboriginal artist as the individual holder of the copyright to preserve the religious and ritual significance of a work that made use of traditional symbols. By using the equitable concept of the fiduciary obligation, the judge placed the Aboriginal artist in a similar position vis-à-vis his/her community as a trustee towards a beneficiary.[33] It seems that the possibilities of the law of equity in common law countries with regards to folklore and traditional knowledge protection are yet to be fully explored. Unconscionable conduct and undue

---

[31] T. Janke (above note 18), 299–300.

[32] Extract reprinted in H. McRae/G. Nettheim/L. Beacroft, *Indigenous Legal Issues: Commentary and Materials*, 2nd ed., LBC Information Services 1997, 126.

[33] See also the more general assumption of a fiduciary relationship in Canada between the state and its indigenous population in *R v. Sparrow* (70 DLR (4th) 385 (1990)), as cited in P. Parkinson (ed.), *The Principles of Equity*, LBC Information Services, Sydney 1996, 360.

influence are further doctrines that the courts might turn to in cases involving traditional knowledge of indigenous communities. Finally, there is the doctrine of confidential information that could help to counter the common attempt to use indigenous or local knowledge as a springboard for the development of new products without compensating the holders of that knowledge. Traditional knowledge, however, is often used by a fairly large number of people, making it difficult to impose an obligation of confidentiality on all of them to prevent the secret from leaking out. There is also the possibility that the confidential information approach backfires, for example, if the knowledge is discovered from outside the community through independent research or anthropological observation. In this case, communities might have an interest in arguing that the material has been published and is in the public domain.

Apart from these approaches using doctrines of the law of equity, there is, of course, the much discussed contractual approach to conclude benefit sharing agreements with indigenous communities. These agreements usually restrict the assertion of intellectual property rights and they require and facilitate the sharing of the benefits resulting from the use of traditional knowledge. A draft set of regulations dealing with these issues is currently in preparation for inclusion in the Environment Protection and Biodiversity Conservation Act.

II. The Philippines

In the Philippines, the rights of "indigenous cultural communities" to the preservation and development of their cultures, traditions and institutions has found expression in the Constitution and in four further pieces of legislation:

- The Indigenous Peoples Rights Act of 1997
- The Traditional and Alternative Medicine Act of 1997
- Executive Order No. 247 of 1995 prescribing guidelines and establishing a regulatory framework for the prospecting of biological and genetic resources, their by-products and derivatives, for scientific and commercial purposes and for other purposes
- Department Administrative Order No. 96-20 on implementing rules and regulations on the prospecting of biological and genetic resources

Section 32 of the Indigenous Peoples Rights Acts guarantees "community intellectual rights", whereas Sec. 34 recognises "Rights to Indigenous Knowledge Systems and Practices". It encourages the state to take "special measures to control, develop and protect their sciences, technologies and cultural manifestations". Access to biological and genetic resources needs the prior informed consent obtained in accordance with the customary laws of the communities (Sec. 35). Rights to "sustainable agro-technical development" are recognised in Sec. 36 and there is a definition of "sustainable traditional resource rights" in Sec. 3 o. According to Kingsbury,[34] somewhat more than 10 percent of the Filipino population may be referred to as belonging to "indigenous cultural communities" and, as a consequence, the concept is well established in political life in the Philippines. Nevertheless, even in the Philippines there are ambiguities as to who precisely is "indigenous". Section 3 h. defines "indigenous cultural communities/indigenous peoples" as "a group of people or homogenous societies identified by self-ascription and ascription by others, who have continuously lived as organised community on communally bounded and defined territory, and who have, under claims of ownership since time immemorial, occupied, possessed and utilised such territories, sharing common bonds of language, customs, traditions and other distinctive cultural traits, or who have, through resistance to political, social and cultural inroads of colonisation, non-indigenous religions and culture, become historically differentiated from the rest of the Filipinos." While this sounds like a classical definition of "indigenous peoples", the same section continues then as follows: "Indigenous cultural communities/indigenous peoples shall likewise include peoples who are regarded as indigenous on account of their descent from the populations which inhabited the country at the time of conquest or colonisation, or at the time of inroads of non-indigenous religions and cultures, or the establishment of the present state boundaries, who retain some or all of their own social, economic, cultural and political institutions, but who may have been displaced from their traditional domains or who may have resettled outside their ancestral domains." This second part of the definition can in fact be stretched to include any Filipinos of Malay descent claiming to retain "some" of the pre-colonial social, economic, cultural or political institutions. Presumably such a claim would be very hard to disprove.[35]

The Indigenous Peoples Rights Act creates a powerful National Commission on Indigenous Peoples (NCIP) appointed by the President and acting under the Office of the President to formulate and implement policies, plans and programs under the legislation (Sec. 3 k.). The NCIP has a legal affairs office, which at the same time decides legal disputes by applying customary law where local dispute resolution mechanisms have failed. Further appeals, however, go to the state courts. Indigenous customary law is recognised, but only "as may be compatible with the national legal system and with internationally recognised human rights."

---

[34] Above note 7, 353–354.
[35] Interestingly, the earlier Implementing Rules and Regulations on the Prospecting of Biological and Genetic Resources in Department Administrative order No. 96-20 of 1996 of the Department of Environment and Natural Resources did not yet contain the second, broader part of the definition. However, the Indigenous Peoples Rights Act of 1997 must be seen as overriding the earlier implementing order.

The earlier Executive Order No. 247 with the official content of "prescribing guidelines and establishing a regulatory framework for the prospecting of biological and genetic resources, their by-products and derivatives, for scientific and commercial purposes, and for other purposes" and the Department Administrative Order No. 96-20 of 1996 of the Department of Environment and Natural Resources on the subject of "Implementing rules and regulations on the prospecting of biological and genetic resources" establish the framework for bioprospecting and for benefit sharing agreements. The Preamble of Executive Order No. 247 mentions the aim of the state "to identify and recognise the rights of indigenous cultural communities and other Philippine communities to their traditional knowledge and practices." Section 1 of the Department Administrative Order refers to relevant sections in the Philippines Constitution and to the Preamble of the UN Convention on Biological Diversity. The orders distinguish between academic and commercial research agreements, create mechanisms for prior informed consent and prescribe minimum terms and conditions for research agreements. As for "traditional use", as defined in Department Administrative Order No. 96-20, this is "the customary utilisation of biological and genetic resources by the local community and indigenous people in accordance with written or unwritten rules, usages, customs and practices traditionally observed, accepted and recognised by them." Again, the definition used in various parts of the legislation widens the scope of the beneficiaries of the legislation from indigenous people to "local communities" such as farming communities and other bearers of traditional knowledge. The legislation creates an Inter-Agency Committee on Biological and Genetic Resources with members from various government departments, the science community, the National Museum, an NGO and a "People's Organisation" with membership drawn from indigenous cultural communities/indigenous peoples.

Finally, there is the Traditional and Alternative Medicine Act (TAMA) of 1997. It protects and promotes "traditional medicine" defined as "the sum of total knowledge, skills and practice on health care, not necessarily explicable in the context of modern, scientific philosophical framework, but recognised by the people to help maintain and improve their health towards the wholeness of their being the community and society, and their interrelations based on culture, history, heritage and consciousness." While the Act speaks of the protection of "indigenous and natural health resources", it is less clear than in the case of bioprospecting that this refers to "indigenous cultural communities/indigenous peoples" as they are defined in the Indigenous Peoples Rights Acts. The guiding principles of the legislation in Sec. 2 require the state to "seek a legally workable basis by which indigenous societies would own their knowledge of traditional medicine" and refers to benefit sharing agreements if such knowledge is used by "outsiders". However, the holders of this traditional medicinal knowledge according to the legislation are "traditional healers" defined as "the relatively old, highly respected people with a profound knowledge of traditional remedies". This seems to refer to Filipino traditional healers in general and, thus, is not confined to "indigenous people". A further indication in that direction is that, different from the bioprospecting legislation, the Board of Trustees of the newly formed Philippine Institute of Traditional and Alternative Heath Care includes again representatives from various government departments, environmental sector organisations in addition to medical practitioners and a food industry representative. The holders of traditional medicinal knowledge, however, are only represented by a single traditional and alternative health care practitioner. It seems, therefore, that traditional medicine is not limited to "indigenous medicine", but wider and more in accordance with "alternative medicine" as in many Western countries.

III. Indonesia

Indonesia protects forms of traditional knowledge in the Copyright Act of 2002 and in the Plant Variety Protection Act of 2000. The Term "traditional knowledge" (*pengetahuan tradisional*), however, while part of the Indonesian intellectual property vocabulary by now and used on various websites, appears nowhere in the legislation. Instead, the Copyright Act of 2002 returns in fact in Sec. 10 to the older term of "folklore" which has now been added to the previously used "products of the culture of the people" (*hasil kebudayaan rakyat*). Section 10(2) explains that such folklore is common property held by the state and gives as examples "stories, tales, fairy tales, legends, chronicles, songs, handicrafts, choreographies, dances, calligraphies and other works of art". Arguably, the common understanding of folklore does not normally extend to works of choreography and calligraphy, which would have individual character, so what is meant here are apparently "choreographies" for traditional forms of dance, etc.

The folklore provision of Sec. 10 is part of the Indonesian copyright legislation since the enactment of the first Copyright Act in 1982. It raised concerns at the time that the state wanted to appropriate forms of local culture and that this would lead to restrictions for communities to freely exercise their local culture. According to Ajip Rosidi,[36] this finally led to a compromise that found expression in Sec. 10(3) that the state would hold the copyright to such works only "with regards to foreign countries", so that Indonesians themselves would be free to use this material. This has now also entered the new Copyright Act of 2002 and Sec. 10(3) in its current wording provides that non-Indonesians will need to obtain a licence from a relevant institution to publish or multiply any of the "works" as defined in Sec. 10(2). According to the explanatory memorandum to the new Act, the provision aims to prevent the monopolisation and commercialisation as well

---

[36] A. Rosidi, *Undang-Undang Hak Cipta – Pandangan Seorang Awam* (The Copyright Act – A layman's perspective), Jakarta 1984, 79–80.

as potentially damaging acts for Indonesian cultural values by foreign parties without the approval of the Indonesian state as the copyright holder.

Academic commentators have pointed out that the legislation leaves many crucial issues unresolved, such as who will distinguish between modern and traditional forms of, for example, handicrafts, songs or dances, who will collect and distribute the royalties and what will be the manner of distribution.[37] It has also been pointed out that the restriction for foreigners to use the material can easily be circumvented by incorporating a (foreign-owned) Indonesian company that would not fall under the restrictions of Sec. 10.[38] Finally, the legislation tries to create a national approach to material that must be regarded as an expression of local identity. Not surprisingly, the explanatory memorandum stresses the national aspect of preventing appropriation by foreigners, but it fails to mention the local character of the material. For example, would a Balinese artist who has acquired Australian citizenship have to apply for a licence of the Indonesian government to use cultural expressions from his home village?[39] The centralisation that is attempted by Sec. 10 Copyright Act is quite clearly difficult to reconcile with the Indonesian decentralisation policy that attempts to give greater autonomy and decision making powers to the provinces and that has found expression in the provisions of Chapter VI of the amended Constitution. Instead, it is closer to the approach in Art. 33(2) of the Constitution, which has not been amended and maintains that "sectors of production which are important for the state and for the living of the people are controlled by the state." A further provision of relevance in this context is to be found in Chapter XIII of the Constitution dealing with Education. Article 32 (1) stipulates that "the state shall advance the national culture of Indonesia among the civilisations of the world by assuring the freedom of society to preserve and develop cultural values."

It is perhaps for all these reasons that the Government Regulation to implement the provision required in Sec. 10(4) has not been issued in the 22 years since the first Copyright Act came into force. Rather surprisingly, the approach has nevertheless found its way again into the new copyright legislation of 2002. Academic commentators in Indonesia doubt whether the provision will ever become operative and prefer a *sui generis* legislation for the issue.

As a further interesting aspect of the debate in Indonesia, there is at least one stream of thought among academic commentators that, apparently

---

[37] C. Antons, *Intellectual Property Law in Indonesia*, Kluwer Law International, London 2000, 88.

[38] A. Sardjono, "Perlindungan Folklore: Apakah Rezim Hak Cipta Memadai?" (The Protection of Folklore: Is the Copyright Regime Sufficient?), in: *Jurnal Hukum Internasional*, Vol. 1 No. 1, 2003, 124–137.

[39] C. Antons, "Law and Development Thinking after the Asian Crisis of 1997", in: *Forum of International Development*, Vol. 20 No. 12, 2001, 219–220.

inspired by anthropological explanations, regards the term "folklore" as wider than the term "traditional knowledge".[40] This is clearly different from the current WIPO working definition and shows an understanding that puts a lot of emphasis on the oral and artistic transmission of the knowledge. The second piece of legislation of some relevance for traditional knowledge protection is the Plant Varieties Act of 2000. It protects in Sec. 7(1) "local varieties owned by the public that are controlled by the State."

D. Conclusion

The case studies from Australia and Southeast Asia show that there are significant differences in the way the debate about forms of traditional knowledge and intellectual property rights is conducted in various countries. It is most intensive in the settler colonies of Australia, Canada, the US, New Zealand and Latin America, where it appears as a debate between a non-indigenous majority and an indigenous minority about the right to self-determination, facilitated by the fact that traditional knowledge is often regarded as more or less exclusively held by the indigenous minority. In the developing countries of Southeast Asia, on the other hand, much of traditional knowledge is not confined to indigenous minorities but held by traditional healers or farming communities that can be termed "local" but are not necessarily "indigenous". Because of the size and the spread of the communities and because of the importance of the issue for the national development efforts, we find the state (the national government) slipping into the role of the negotiator for those communities vis-à-vis foreign parties. As a result, the distinction between "indigenous", "local" and "national" interests is blurred.

At a conceptual level, indigenous communities with strong concepts of taboos related to secret and sacred expressions and a lack of distinction between artistic expressions and knowledge of scientific relevance prefer the wider term "traditional knowledge" to "folklore". But again, this term is not universally understood as representing a wider concept. Many local communities in Asia do not share the same kind of taboos regarding secrecy and do not use artistic expressions to communicate knowledge of scientific value, so that a clearer distinction between "traditional knowledge" related to medicine, food production or the environment and "folklore" related to artistic expressions is in fact possible.

The comparison shows how different national governments and communities in the South Pacific region try to adapt local culture to national or international legal concepts. While benefit sharing agreements, in particular with regards to bioprospecting, are widely promoted, few countries have attempted to grant intellectual property rights to forms of traditional know-

---

[40] A. Sardjono, above note 38.

ledge. Where such attempts have been made as in the Indonesian Copyright Act, the Thai Traditional Medicine Act or the Thai Plant Varieties Act, the rights are usually exercised by the state on behalf of local communities or simply not yet implemented. This demonstrates the continuing incompatibilities of traditional knowledge and intellectual property. It is further interesting to note that WIPO in its more recent documents seems to be moving away from the holistic notion of traditional knowledge adopted in its 2001 report. The Secretariat in a document prepared for the Intergovernmental Committee on Intellectual Property and Genetic Resources, Traditional Knowledge and Folklore acknowledges that "some national and regional instruments aim to protect both expressions of folklore/traditional cultural expressions and traditional knowledge together". It continues, however that "in line with the practice of this committee, this document deals specifically with the protection of traditional knowledge in the strict sense." Earlier in the same document, traditional knowledge in the strict sense was defined as "technical traditional knowledge".[41] It must be concluded, therefore, that it remains difficult for intellectual property law at an international stage to discard the distinction between folklore on the one hand and other forms of traditional knowledge on the other, and instead to adopt the holistic concepts advocated by the representatives of indigenous groups.

---

[41] See WIPO/GRTKF/IC/6/4 of 12 December 2003, Intergovernmental Committee on Intellectual Property and Genetic Resources, Traditional Knowledge and Folklore, Sixth Session, Geneva, 15–19 March 2004 – Traditional Knowledge: Policy and Legal Options, 5.

3
Copyright Collecting Societies in Developing Countries: Possibilities and Dangers

SIBYLLE E. SCHLATTER

A. Introduction

I. The Role of the Arts in Developing Countries

In developing countries the arts play a larger and different role than in industrialised countries. This applies in particular to those categories of art which do not require incorporation into a tangible medium to be perceived by an audience. Therefore it is without question that music is one of the most important means to express the genuine culture of all ethnic groups. Music contributes to the national/ethnical self-identity and, along with dance, has an integrative effect as it usually involves group members performing together. Sociologically and politically music serves as a stabilising parameter within the group. Outside the original community it can assist in creating confidence, understanding and even friendship among ethnic groups which may otherwise be prone to conflict because of fear of the unknown. Music and dance are the two art forms which are most suitable for overcoming such fears, as in contrast to literature or the fine arts neither translation nor transportation of materialised objects are necessary for their dissemination beyond the national borders.

On the other hand, particularly in the case of music, cultural heritage and contemporary music can also be seen as commercial products. As such they may be of considerable economic value, contributing to the national economy of a developing country, in particular if two prerequisites are alternatively or preferably simultaneously fulfilled: The first is that the music meets the consumer taste and market needs of the ethnic group, and that there is sufficient economic/financial potential to develop a market for this music within the community; this was the case, for example, in Nashville, Tennessee, a poor region which developed into the wealthy centre of American folk and country music. The second condition is that even beyond ethnic and national borders such music, in its original or adapted form, meets consumer taste and has adequate access to regional and international markets.

II. International Distribution of Traditional Music

The above requirements are met, for example, by the music of a number of African countries. All over black Africa music plays a central role in daily life of the indigenous populations in villages in remote areas as well as in the growing cities. In particular in West Africa, traditional music has experienced an extraordinary international development, even though unintentionally, coming as it did to the Americas with the African slaves and blending with other styles, for example, with the British and French music of the Mississippi Delta or with Salsa, Merengue, Tango and other sounds common in Latin America and the Caribbean. During the last two decades, this adapted music has returned to its roots, where it now influences traditional and modern African music. This is at least one of the reasons given by experts as to why contemporary African music gained in attraction within the continent and abroad. In West Africa during the last ten years the music market has developed to an amazing extent, considering the low average income of the population. And according to expert opinion, there still is a large market potential due to the growing regional and international demand for African music.

On the other hand, it is a well-known fact that Latin American dance music has conquered Northern America and Europe, and even traditional songs of the Andean Indios have found favour amongst a small circle of international connoisseurs.

III. The Role of Collecting Societies

Most traditional music is not protected by copyright law, be it because an individual author cannot be identified or be it because the protection period has lapsed. It is well known that particularly in developing and threshold countries,[1] and on a regional[2] and to some extent international[3] level, attempts have been made to have ethnic communities from where the music originates benefit from acts of commercial exploitation. In other cases of original or adopted works of traditional or modern music, there can be no doubt as to the author or existing copyright protection. In both cases, the international dimension of marketing such music no longer allows the individual or collective authors to control the exploitation of their works. They will thus have to rely on the services of a collecting society that represents their interests, collectively administers their rights, collects the dues and transfers them to the authors. Already the national distribution of such requires properly functioning collecting societies as well as the enactment and correct application of modern laws containing rules for copyright con-

---

[1] A number of domestic copyright laws expressly provide for a protection for expressions of folklore, partly under a *sui generis* regime (e.g. Sec. 5 Cameroonian Copyright Act, Sec. 28 Nigerian Copyright Act, Art. 83 Paraguayan Copyright Act), partly – but mistakenly – as copyrighted works (e.g. Art. 1 No. 13 Senegalese Copyright Act).

[2] See, e.g. Treaty of Bangui on the West African intellectual property organization, Annex VII, Title II, chapter I.

[3] Only indirect protection is provided in the WPPT, protecting the performers of folklore; WIPO has established the Intergovernmental Committee on Intellectual Property and Genetic Resources, Traditional Knowledge and Folklore, for first results of their sessions see the reports at www.wipo.int.

tracts and enforcement, which prohibit extortionist practices[4] and secure an adequate remuneration to authors and performers.

While industrialised nations can look back to a tradition of collecting societies of one hundred years, in developing countries a system of collective administration of rights has been virtually unknown as recently as 20 years ago and in some cases still is. In the age of globalisation, this sometimes leads to bizarre results when it comes to the commercial exploitation of protected works, as the following example will demonstrate: Since about the mid-20th century, national collecting societies have entered into bilateral agreements with their counterparts abroad in order to represent the interests of foreign authors and artists, and to have the interests of their members equally represented abroad. Such a network exists for developed countries at least amongst the members of CISAC.[5] This organisation is not a supra-national collecting society, but rather an important umbrella organisation for national collecting societies with the aim of promoting co-operation amongst the approximately 200 collecting societies that are members. These societies are based in more than 100 nations, some of them developing countries. The collecting societies from developed countries thus effectively represent and license the world repertoire within their territory. Accordingly, they receive the royalties for acts of exploitation also on behalf of foreign authors and performing artists, yet forward them only in part. The sometimes incomprehensible reason for this is the alleged absence of a functioning collecting society in the home country of the respective author or artist.[6] This practice appears to be in conformity with CISAC's rules and is even more depressing from the point of view of development policies when taking into account that after a couple of years such royalties are deemed non-distributable and will thus be used for other purposes, such as the promotion of culture in the respective developed country.

On the other hand, one should not ignore that within the last two decades collecting societies set up in Africa as well as in South America have

---

[4] An extreme example of these so-called "buy-out contracts" is the South African Zulu hunting song, "The Lion Sleeps Tonight", adapted and amended by the tribesman Salomon Linda, that became famous worldwide as of 1950 in many different forms, e.g. as a US country song, a New Zealand military march, the British Soccer World Cup jingle, and as TV commercial and film music. Singers and musicians as well as the music industry have made a fortune with this song, and according to estimates have reaped in royalties and related revenues of US$ 10 to 20 million. However, Linda received just one pound in cash and a menial job at the record company to which he had totally transferred the copyright in his creation according to South African copyright law.

[5] The Confédération Internationale des Sociétés d'Auteurs et Compositeurs founded in Paris in 1926.

[6] To give an example: Inquiries of the journalist Jay Rutledge confirmed that the German collecting society GEMA, even two years after the song "Jalgaty" by the Senegalese hip-hop band Pee Froiss was broadcast by the Bayerischer Rundfunk and Westdeutscher Rundfunk, had not paid any royalties to the Senegalese collecting society BSDA that was founded 20 years ago, arguing that GEMA and BSDA did not have a reciprocity or cooperation agreement.

demonstrated certain structural and functional shortcomings which have resulted in authors and performing artists not receiving proper compensation. The issues mentioned below are based on the author's mixed experiences with collecting societies both in Africa and in South America. The following remarks might serve to avoid future mistakes in founding new or restructuring existing collecting societies, and in regulating their activities. They are also meant to give suggestions to legislatures on how to avoid certain pitfalls so as to ensure the proper functioning of a collective administration of rights.

B. Basic Questions on the Structure of a Collecting Society

In theory, there is no need for an explicit legal basis for setting up a collecting society, as shown by the examples of Europe and the US in the first half of the 20th century, where collecting societies were exclusively set up as private legal entities. Yet since a collecting society usually enjoys a monopoly over the exploitation of a certain category of rights (which in the interests of the licensees regarding a transparent and simple acquisition of exploitation rights should be the case), the state, within the framework of its economic control function, is obliged to exercise anti-trust oversight over these societies. State control may result in an undesirable dependence on day-to-day politics or arbitrary interference in the organisation of a collecting society or its ongoing activities, though. This is particularly so in developing countries, as anti-trust law is frequently only inadequately codified or not suited to this type of activity that cannot be compared to the activities of producing or trading enterprises. It is thus highly recommendable to enact specific rules on the structure, the minimum contents of statutes or articles of incorporation, the scope of business of collecting societies and their control by their members and the state. For the sake of clarity and easy comprehension also for lay persons, such legal rules should be laid down as a separate chapter in the national copyright laws. In so doing the legislature has to decide the following basic issues, *inter alia*:

I. Legal Nature of Collecting Societies

With the exception of the communist and socialist countries,[7] European, American and Asian collecting societies have been organised as private legal entities. By contrast, in Africa these institutions have partly been set up as public entities. Both structures have advantages and disadvantages, some of which shall be explained in the following.

1. *Collecting societies as public institutions*

The fact that collecting societies in communist countries have been organised as public entities, frequently as state copyright administrations, agencies

---

[7] E.g. in Cuba, Vietnam and China. In the former Eastern Bloc countries, almost all collecting societies have been privatised.

or offices or parts thereof, was a consequence of the copyright systems that provided for a transfer of all exploitation rights to the state. The exercise of such rights was thus the task of the collecting societies under the tutelage of the Ministry of Culture, while the author at most had a right for a "modest but continuing remuneration and the honour".[8] The exploitation of a work would normally require its registration with the copyright administration. Undoubtedly, the function of such publicly organised collecting societies was political censorship rather than adequate administration and protection of copyrights, which is obvious in light of the predominantly remuneration-free use of works by, e.g., a state-owned broadcasting organisation or other governmental organisers of cultural events.

It is not clear to what extent this motive was of relevance when the first African collecting society was founded in Senegal still under the influence of French colonial rule. But in the first 20 years of its existence, the shortcomings of a collecting society as a state-owned institution have become clear: The Chairman and Board of Directors are nominated by the Minister of Culture or with his consent. These ministers have changed frequently[9] and also have to oversee other important fields such as communications. Due to their lack of specialised knowledge prior to being nominated, they hardly have any possibilities of independently selecting the personnel of a collecting society. The Minister is also responsible for controlling the operation of the collecting societies, including their annual budget figures, yet is unlikely to act meaningfully due to a lack of time to gain specialised knowledge of the subject matter.[10] The levies collected, e.g. for music, for many years were surprisingly modest, given the size of the music market and the frequency of musical broadcasts: Neither private nor public broadcasting organisations had been seriously asked (i.e. by threatening court sanctions) to pay royalties for broadcasting licences. This had gone unnoticed for many years even by members of the advisory board who had no specialised knowledge whatsoever and were in part illiterate.

From this and other examples in other countries, the following pitfalls of state-owned collecting societies can be summarised:

(1) As collecting societies can only represent the private interests of right owners (copyright and neighbouring rights) conflicts of private and public interest become inevitable, especially when state-owned

---

[8] So verbatim a Vietnamese composer, who in the mid-1990s lamented that the economic opening of the country meant a discontinuation of state payments, although state organised concerts and broadcasts were continued.

[9] Between 2001 and 2004 seven different ministers were in office.

[10] The Advisory Board highlighted vaguenesses in the balance for the year 2002 and referred this to the competent minister. Until today, the open questions have not been clarified, yet the distribution of royalties to the right owners were made on the basis of that balance. The Senegalese law does not provide for any consequences in cases of unclear or incorrect accounting, a feature it shares with other countries with state-owned collecting societies.

licensees are requested to pay royalties (e.g. broadcasting organisations, schools, theatres and other organisers of events).

(2) There is a certain danger that collecting societies take on tasks alien to
their duties (e.g. censorship, assistance in the drafting of laws when
there are no other copyright specialists in the country, representation
of the country before the WIPO and other copyright institutions on
a regional or international level). In such case, the right owners
finance these activities, as the costs of administration incurred by
the collecting societies would be deducted from the receipts to be
distributed to right owners.

(3) The financial activities of the collecting societies are less open to
scrutiny, and therefore irregularities are often not subject to sanctions.[11]

(4) Right owners have no sufficient means of controlling the administration in general, e.g. the determination of royalty tariffs and distribution schemes, the annual accounting and individual payments. There
is no judicial control and right owners have no remedies to sue against
the above-mentioned irregularities, or omissions, etc.

(5) Where the state, instead of the members of the collecting society, is
empowered to choose the board of directors or the advisory board,
criteria other than professional competence may play a role.[12]

Due to all these weaknesses, collecting societies which are state-owned or by
some other means governmentally controlled are not recommendable, as
experience of the past decades, particularly in Eastern Europe and Africa, has
shown. Insufficient control to some extent has fostered failed investments,
nepotism and corruption at the expense of copyright owners and performing artists without sufficient political clout to enforce their justified interests.
Also the opinion voiced by the WIPO advisors, in the past responsible
for setting up collecting societies in developing countries, that only public
institutions would be in a position to enforce the payment of royalties by
broadcasting organisations (the most important source of receipts for newly
set up collecting societies) has proved fallacious. Rather, the situation only
changed once the artists became active themselves by way of publicity
campaigns in their struggle against music piracy and for a better system of
collective administration of their rights.

2. Privately structured organisations

Many of the above-mentioned dangers or pitfalls can be avoided when
collecting societies are privately organised. First of all, a private organisation
is a voluntary union of persons with comparable interests based on contractual agreements. Furthermore, the principle of self-administration of

---

[11] E.g. when a copyright-related trip of the competent minister is organised and paid
by the collecting society.
[12] It was a well known practice, in particular in socialist countries, that merited party
members were rewarded with the well-paid position of director of a collecting society.

members or partners is assured by democratically elected representatives on the board (board of directors, advisory board or other organs, special committees, e.g. in order to classify works or decide on social issues), by way of participation in basic questions of the activity (e.g. royalty tariffs, distribution plans, approval of the annual budget) and by way of thorough financial control (auditing committees, external audits by independent firms, right of members to inspect the books, etc.). The basic pillars of a collecting society should already be laid down by the legislature as necessary contents of statutes, the articles of incorporation or contract.[13] However, also privately structured collecting societies have shown weaknesses as will be shown in the following together with the measures to avoid such pitfalls:

(1) Especially in the beginning, privately organised collecting societies only represent a small percentage of right owners due to a limited participation in the foundation. The founding members will thus be privileged. This can be balanced by legal requirements of a minimum number of members or a minimum percentage of national right owners that have to be represented for business activities to start. In addition, the society's obligation also to administer the rights of non-members may be stipulated. These rules should be drawn up on the legal assumption that the collecting society represents all national right owners irrespective of their membership. This would prevent work users (and foreign collecting societies) from refusing to pay royalties based on the argument that the relevant right owner is not a member.

(2) Collecting societies could become vehicles for the self-enrichment of their directors and other administrators, so that the royalties collected would primarily serve to finance the salaries and often extravagant lifestyles of these employees. Countermeasures would be legal provisions limiting the maximum administrative costs for collecting societies. These should not exceed 20 % (for young societies 30 %) of the income as suggested by the CISAC rules.[14]

(3) Exaggerated business expenses (e.g. for company cars,[15] business travels,[16] representation costs[17] or service personnel[18]) might diminish the receipts to be distributed. This could be countered by an

---

[13] For this and other details, see below III.

[14] They are not compulsory, and can be characterised as non-binding recommendations.

[15] The possibilities of fraud have no limits in this case and range from reimbursement for predominantly private trips to fabricated claims for repair costs for accidents that have not actually occurred and where the garage pockets half for falsifying the bill. The only remedy against this would be a proportional contribution of the user to the costs.

[16] E.g. first class flights, five star hotels, in combination with private holiday trips, shopping instead of business activities.

[17] E.g. a dinner for private friends being called a business dinner, a birthday party being dubbed an anniversary celebration of the society.

[18] In particular, the use of service personnel for private purposes, such as for the transport of family members, for private gardening or private correspondence.

exact auditing by an internal auditing committee and/or (e.g. on request of the members or a public control body) an additional external audit by an independent auditor.

(4) Even against blatant infringements of rights, no action or only selective action will be taken, often in connection with bribery. To prevent such favouritism, the law should stipulate the appointment of at least two directors controlling each other, and a competent and well-informed control body, i.e. advisory board (whose members can be re-elected[19] due to the time it takes to obtain the necessary knowledge). Functioning laws against corruption are a must as well.

(5) At times, representatives of the collecting society, in particular royalty controllers in remote provinces (in developing countries such outposts are necessary due to bad road conditions and high travel costs) pocket bribe money instead of collecting royalties for performances in discos, bars and concerts. Since a round-the-clock control of this outpost personnel is too expensive, senior members of the society domiciled there should be empowered to exercise controls on a rotating system (in order to make bribery too expensive). In any case, the law should stipulate a double royalty where the use of works is not notified prior to the event or public performance.

(6) Against the purchase of votes in order to influence ballots at the general assembly, a restriction on representing other members and exercising their voting right would be of help, e.g. providing that only a small number of absent members can be represented.

(7) A threatening domination by right owners that are also work users and therefore potential licensees may be countered by a law that would distinguish between full and associate members with and without voting rights.

3. *Privately organised collecting societies under state control*

It goes without saying that some of the pitfalls mentioned in connection with privately organised collecting societies also apply to state-owned institutions, e.g. preferential treatment or bribery. However, a comparison shows that a functioning self control could prevent many of these deficiencies in the first place. For state-owned institutions, self control is absent and other means usually not effective, as even in developed democracies it is difficult to get the decisions of state authorities overturned by the judiciary. This applies even more to developing countries where public law is usually less developed and hardly applied or enforced in favour of the citizen. Furthermore,

---

[19] Advisory boards are often composed of creative or performing artists who are knowledgeable in their field but require specific know-how for the work of collecting societies. There are examples where directors tried to get rid of members of the advisory board who critically examined their activities by proposing changes in the society's statutes and introducing a clause that prohibits the re-election of advisory board members.

where the state and its organs do not function properly or are corrupt, the affected citizens will rarely have legal redress. Thus, for the basic question of how to organise collecting societies, the balance is heavily tipped towards privately owned collecting societies.

National company law must decide which form of organisation is most suitable. Since collecting societies already as a matter of course must be profit oriented for the benefit of their members, a non-profit association or trust may be unsuitable under many national laws. In such case it is advisable to find a form of organisation where the institution's existence and operation is unaffected by changes in membership. This may make it recommendable to set up an association, cooperative society or other form of corporation which is a legal entity rather than a civil law association or other form of non-trading partnership. Of importance for the choice would also be the national tax law: The often high taxation rate for companies would run counter to the purpose of collecting societies which is to have a maximum of the collected receipts available to the right owners. In addition, the individual taxation for the authors or artists may be relatively little, depending on their total income.[20] The best solution would be a tax exemption for collecting societies under domestic law. A possible abuse of such preferential treatment should be countered by restricting the collecting society's activities. Collecting societies should only be entitled to administer and enforce the rights of authors and neighbouring right holders and to defend their interests; they would be prohibited from performing any other business activities. Furthermore, an obligation of the collecting society to inform the fiscal authorities about the amount paid to each right owner could be stipulated. This would enable them to impose the correct amount of taxes due on the individual artist.

The self-administration and self control of a collecting society should be complemented by state control in order to avoid any abuse vis-à-vis individual members, non-members, or work users. Such control should not be limited to providing a functioning judicial system to rely on in cases of conflict with collecting societies. Instead, state control should start by making governmental authorisation prerequisite for the collecting society's commencement of operation. And state control should continue until the society's business activities cease. Details will be subsequently elaborated under V.

II. Which Rights Should Be Enforced Through a Collecting Society?

1. Permitting one or more collecting societies

In industrialised countries and some threshold countries as well, there are typically several collecting societies that either only take care of certain

---

[20] In order to promote the arts, many countries have introduced a preferential lower taxation of income resulting directly from artistic activities.

exploitation rights (e.g. reproduction and distribution rights on the one side, performance, broadcast and other rights of use in intangible form on the other) or of all rights but limited to certain types of works (e.g. music, film, fine arts, literature, software) or neighbouring rights (of performing artists, broadcasters, database producers etc). Neither practice can be recommended for developing countries, as a multitude of collecting societies necessarily leads to a multiplication of the administrative costs, resulting in the distribution of the total receipts being unnecessarily diminished.

Of course, in the course of time it may become necessary to establish additional collecting societies, e.g. in cases of strong market development or unbridgeable internal differences between the different groups of right owners. For that reason, copyright laws should not limit the number of collecting societies per se to one, but rather link the authorisation of additional ones to the proof of actual demand (preferably only several years after the first collecting society has been set up). However, it should be specified by law that only one collecting society should be entitled to enforce one type of work or neighbouring right (monopoly for certain categories of works). It would be less commendable to divide collecting societies by certain types of exploitation rights, as the types of use tend to multiply through the invention of new technologies more often than the categories of protected works or performances.

The fear often voiced by painters and performing artists that they are not adequately represented if there is only one collecting society may be countered by law or the statutes of association that provide for an adequate participation and representation of all right owners in the organs or boards of the collecting society, or a balancing of the different categories of rights for the casting of votes in the general assembly.

2. Exercise of all or only specific economic rights

In industrialised countries often only the mere claims for remuneration and the exclusive exploitation rights concerning the uncontrolled mass use of copyrights by, e.g. broadcast, non-live performances and rentals, are exercised by collecting societies, while copyright owners and performing artists normally conclude their own agreements with publishers, phonogram and film producers, theatres and other organisers of live performances. In developing countries, laws or statutes of association often entrust the administration of all economic rights and sometimes even of moral rights to collecting societies, a practice sometimes justified by the inexperience of artists in commercial matters or bargaining with users, or even by the illiteracy of some artists. The results of past campaigns and only rudimentary training programmes for musicians in the course of World Bank and Ford Foundation projects in Africa in the last couple of years have manifested that such generalisations are often groundless and that at least in the field of music, dance, film and literature, creators in the age of radio, television and the Internet are no longer so inexperienced as to justify such a drastic limitation of their contractual freedom.

Thus, the exercise of rights by collecting societies should basically be limited to those forms of use that right owners cannot individually control, i.e. mass use, secondary use and mere rights of remuneration (e.g. levies for public lending, private copying and reprography, etc.). Alternatively, there could be a rule whereby all rights would be exercised by collecting societies, that in turn would be obliged to inform the right owner prior to certain kinds of licensing agreements and to retransfer the respective exploitation right to the right owner so that he himself (possibly on more favourable terms) could conclude an agreement with the user (such is, e.g., the case in Germany for film rights). As a general rule, moral rights should not be transferred or entrusted to collecting societies, as it should be the right and the task of the author to exercise such rights and to determine where action should be taken against infringements.

C. Minimum Contents of the Articles of Incorporation or Statutes of Association

Apart from the general national rules of company law, the following aspects should definitely be considered in the statutes of association of a collecting society. In order to avoid clauses that are detrimental to the interests of right owners or unclear, it is recommended that the minimum contents of the statutes should be prescribed by law as a prerequisite for the governmental authorisation mentioned above permitting a collecting society's activities:

(1) The legal form of the collecting society should be stipulated by law, preferably as an incorporated association or a similar legal entity. The same applies to its business operations which should be restricted to the administration of copyright and neighbouring rights.[21]

(2) This purpose of incorporation (including an obligation of the association to represent all right owners concerned, including non members and to conclude licensing contracts with all interested potential licensees), and the voluntary restraint of other economic activities is to be identified.

(3) As a minimum, a collecting society should stipulate rules for the assembly of members, the board of directors (ideally several, but not necessarily full time), one member of which should be a lawyer or judge, an advisory board to control the board of directors consisting of representatives from all different branches of arts and neighbouring rights concerned, and finally an audit committee.

(4) Full and associated members with and without voting rights should be defined,[22] just as the requirements of membership (e.g. an annual minimum income from artistic activities).

---

[21] See above II.1.c).
[22] See above II.1.b) No.7 and II.2.a) at the end.

(5) The financial participation of right owners who are not members must be guaranteed in the same manner as that of foreign right owners to the extent that reciprocal agreements with the relevant domestic collecting societies exist.[23]

(6) The fair determination of the royalty and levy tariffs for all administered rights and remuneration claims and for all forms of exploitation or use has to be ascertained. The participation of associations of work users, producers, etc. in this procedure must be guaranteed, and the state must be given the possibility of control in order to prevent the abuse of the collecting society's branch monopoly.[24]

(7) Work users must be obliged to notify the collecting society in advance of any planned use of a copyrighted work, protected performances, etc., as otherwise the collecting society may be entitled to collect a double royalty (the latter must be stipulated by law).

(8) Fair procedures must be guaranteed when the distribution of the royalties to the right owners is determined by way of a distribution scheme.

(9) The kind of administrative costs to be deducted from the distribution is to be defined. Their amount should be limited to 20% of the receipts (30% during the first five business years), expenses for cultural and social purposes to another 10%.

(10) Details for the accounting, in particular concerning the annual report and balance sheet, the deadline for their preparation and their examination by the audit committee should be stipulated, as well as the general assembly's approval of the audited annual report and balance sheet. On request of a member or the supervising authorities, an additional independent accountant should be called upon.[25]

(11) The basics of individual settlement of accounts and payment to the individual right owners should be determined (deadlines, inspection of books and records, possibilities of appeal in cases of differences).

D. Further Rules on the Organisation, Activity, Membership, and Users

The above rules are basic clauses that should be the minimum contents of the statutes required for obtaining the governmental authorisation for the collecting society's economic activities. These minimum rules should be contained in the domestic Copyright Act. The statutes of the association may be supplemented by further provisions. Alternatively, supplementary details

---

[23] See above I.3.

[24] For details see V below.

[25] In order to avoid abuse and additional costs to be borne by the right owners, additional accounting controls should be paid by the collecting societies or the responsible directors when irregularities are discovered, otherwise by the person making the request.

could be regulated in separate internal organisation rules. The advantage of the latter is the fact they may be amended by simple majority of the general assembly and would not require a qualified majority as is often the case for an amendment of the statutes. Internal organisation rules in the case of collecting societies would typically contain the following specifications:

(1) Acceptance and exclusion of members and suspension of memberships should be issues decided by the advisory board with an internal appeal to the general assembly.

(2) Forms for applying for membership and for the administration of rights should be determined by the advisory board at the request of the board of directors with the approval of the general assembly. The same applies to forms for registration of works and for global, group and individual licensing agreements.

(3) A member should be obliged to register his current (and, where permissible by law, future) works with the collecting society, and to transfer or entrust the exploitation of rights and claims for remuneration to the collecting society for collective administration.

(4) The collecting society is obliged to do its best to ensure the proper administration of these rights and to conclude contracts with users at adequate conditions and with the obligation of equal treatment and uniform tariffs in comparable situations.

(5) Royalty and levy tariffs should be determined by the advisory board after hearings of the user associations. They must be subsequently confirmed by the general assembly. The same applies to distribution schemes. In both cases, an appeal should be brought before a special court (see below V).

(6) An internal committee on classification and identification manned with specialists and appointed by the advisory board with the approval of the general assembly should decide on the classification of works in the relevant categories (e.g. original works, adaptations, classical or modern music). Appeals against such a decision should be made before the court, as above.

(7) Similarly appointed committees on culture and social issues should decide on subsidies, grants, scholarships or other measures of promoting culture and supporting needy artists proposed by the advisory board.[26] No appeals would be possible here, yet the audit committee should be able to conduct an investigation on possible abuses.

---

[26] E.g. awards or scholarships of young artists, but not regular or continuing payments to "artists having contributed to the glory of their country", in other words, artists who are already well-established and may have a sufficient income of their own, such as the poet and former President of Senegal, who has been subsidised by the Senegalese collecting society BSDA for a number of years. Awards of honour for a specific work or the complete oeuvre of a great artist are of course another cup of tea.

(8) To the extent that there is a health insurance or pension scheme for artists, the relevant contribution for this should already be deducted from the amount of remuneration to be paid to the right owners.

(9) Other details for the modes of payment would be, e.g., cash payments if no bank account exists, putting monies in trust for artists whose whereabouts are unknown, who have died without known heirs, or advance payments. Taxes should not be withheld from the due payment of remuneration to the right owners, however.[27]

(10) For disputes between the collecting society and its members, other right owners and licensees or other work users, the advisory board should decide in first instance with a further appeal to the special court mentioned below V.

(11) Besides the organs already mentioned, the organisation scheme of a collecting society should feature the individual departments within the central organisation (secretary to director, accounting, external control, TV and radio monitoring,[28] registry, sale of identification means to be attached to copies in order to prove payment of licences,[29] etc.) as well as the number, place and size of outposts.

E. State Control and Legal Remedies in the Case of Conflicts

As mentioned above,[30] state control over private collecting societies should be twofold, consisting of a governmental authorisation system on the one side and the state's participation in conflict settlement on the other. In both cases governmental agencies such as trade supervisory or anti-trust administration and the ordinary courts appear unsuitable to exercise such state control due to their lack of detailed knowledge about the specific questions connected with copyright law and the collective administration of rights.

With respect to the first, many countries have established a special authorisation board as a separate body or subsection of the ministries of culture or justice. Wherever such institution is placed, it has to be ensured that the members of this board are independent from day-to-day politics and from

---

[27] This is a usual practise of state-owned institutions, yet misguided since the tax is based on a fixed percentage of the remuneration that some artists with relatively low incomes may not have to pay in the first place. See also above II.1.c).

[28] Ideally, broadcasts should be recorded around the clock with a sample monitoring. Otherwise, a broadcaster could announce the frequent broadcast of songs by a crony of the responsible program director, but instead play the well-known songs of other composers.

[29] This does not concern the technical copy-protection measures or electronic rights management information mentioned in Arts. 11, 12 WCT and Arts. 18, 29 WPPT, but rather watermarks, holograms, and other signs on commercial phonograms or audiovisual carriers in order to combat piracy: Their absence can serve as a *prima facie* evidence of pirated copies and would allow the sequestration of such copies.

[30] See II.1.c).

changes of ministers and their lead personnel. The institution should employ persons familiar with anti-trust, copyright and company law and micro-economy with the focus on accounting in order to properly examine the statutes of the association and other documents which the society should present to prove that it is able to fulfil the goal of collective administration. The details of the authorisation procedure should be stipulated in the Copyright Act, including delays for the presentation of supplementary means of proof, notifications thereof and of decisions, appeals against them, etc.[31]

All national laws providing a system of private collecting societies contain regulations on state control over the continuous business activity of a collecting society, including the possibility to revoke the operating authorisation in the case of grave and repeated contravention against obligations despite warnings. Of course, the authorisation board should also be competent for this procedure. The legislature has to decide whether the board should only act on request of an affected party or *ex officio*. However, it is recommended to provide the board with a right to information about the running business[32] and an inspection right in case of severe doubts about the society's fair business practice. Such a provision would best enable the board to determine the facts justifying the termination of business of a collecting society. It can be assumed that the TRIPS enforcement rules also apply to the state control of copyright collecting societies. Therefore, an appeal against final decisions of the authorisation board to the courts should be stipulated according to Art. 41.4 TRIPS.

This also applies where the mechanisms of internal control of the collecting society's operating and the internal procedures of conflict settlement are inadequate to guarantee the rights of members, other right owners, licensees and other work users. In this case the law must allow for the possibility of launching an appeal in court or a comparable institution. Since the most varied kinds of disputes may arise, ranging from copyright law, general contract law and company law to anti-trust law, different courts may have jurisdiction and be required to gain expertise in this difficult subject matter. Considering that there are hardly any specialised attorneys or judges in developing countries, it has to be strongly advocated that ordinary courts be excluded by law from hearing these cases and that instead civil courts specialised in copyright law be established with exclusive jurisdiction. Such courts should be set up

---

[31] Because experience shows that inactivity of such authorities can be used to prevent or considerably delay the operating of a functioning system of collective administration.

[32] The society should be obliged to provide the board with its royalty and levy tariffs, distribution schemes, protocols of general assembly and advisory board meetings. The authorisation board should have the right to participate in both, but without a claim of "honorarium" or reimbursement of expenses to be borne by the right owners, as is the case in some developing countries, because this activity pertains to the state's public functions financed by tax revenues of all citizens.

for all copyright disputes in order to ensure an efficient enforcement of rights as mandated by Part III of the TRIPS Agreement.

Another possibility would be to set up a special arbitration board under the umbrella of the ministry of justice or culture. The authorisation board mentioned above should not be involved in these cases already for reasons of constitutional law, because it is part of the state's executive power and lacks judicial independence. Besides, its duties should be limited to the overall control exercised by authorising and prohibiting the business activity. Arguments against an independent arbitration board are a possible dependence on day-to-day politics and the disadvantages of rapidly rotating personnel. Furthermore, taking into account that the final decisions of an arbitration board must also be subject to appeals to the court, this system would make procedures of conflict settlement perhaps "unnecessarily complicated" and probably even "costly, or entail unreasonable time-limits or unwarranted delays", to use the wording of Art. 41.2 TRIPS. Therefore, setting up a specialised court seems the preferable option. The issue is not only one of developing countries: Also a number of industrialised countries have established special courts or special divisions within civil courts, while others have set up mediation or arbitration boards outside the national court system. In Germany, both systems exist, which proves too difficult and complicated to be recommended to developing countries. Here, the British system of a copyright tribunal competent for all kinds of cases mentioned above is more adequate.

A special court should deal with the following issues:

(1) Possible appeals against the internal decisions mentioned under (3) above and (IV) that concern measures of the collecting societies against individual members, right owners, licensees and users.
(2) Appeals against internal decisions concerning groups of members, etc., particularly royalty tariffs and distribution schemes.
(3) The decision on employing an external independent accountant in cases of reasonable doubts against the correctness of annual report and balance sheet.
(4) Conflicts between the collecting society and its organs for failure to comply with their duties.
(5) Anti-trust control of the activities of collecting societies, including appeals against decisions of the authorisation board.

It has been pointed out already under above II. 1. a) that a functioning system of state and court control would no longer make it necessary or useful to apply the principles of general anti-trust law in cases of a possible abuse of a dominant position where the collecting society holds a monopolistic position. The experiences in European countries such as Germany or Great Britain, often over decades, have shown that such a specific control is far more efficient. Therefore, the application of general anti-trust law should be expressly excluded.

Of course, details of all legal rules mentioned above must be made in accordance with the existing domestic law (e.g. civil and public procedure law and the general principles of substantive law). Particularly in developing countries, an often uncoordinated legislative procedure does not always comply with these requirements. In view of the latter, and taking into account the difficulty involved in arousing the interest of domestic politicians in issues related to the protection of creative artists and creativity as such, it must be said that the above-mentioned proposals are currently still far from reality. However, they may serve as a reminder for future action. Yet it should not be forgotten that even the best laws and statutes can only provide a basis for setting up a collecting society. Whether such society is actually working and fulfilling its function very much depends on the technical knowledge and integrity of its organs and other personnel, apart from the active involvement and cooperation of each individual author and performing artist, independent of his or her education, training and business experience.

4
Maori Culture and Trade Mark Law in New Zealand

EARL GRAY

A. Introduction

New Zealand's Trade Marks Act 2002 came into force on 10 August 2002. At a substantive level, the 2002 Act would appear to change little from the 1953 Act in terms of traditional words and images – it merely replaces a prohibition on registration of "scandalous"[1] material with a prohibition on registration of material which is likely to offend a significant section of the community.

However, the Act goes further in terms of message and process:

a) it specifically designates Maori as a significant section of the community[2] (which in general would have gone without saying);
b) it sets up a statutory Maori Advisory Committee[3] to assess applications which appear to contain Maori words and images.

In the author's view, this is a limited but calculated step towards recognition of Maori Intellectual Property in New Zealand. There is much more to come, but the detail remains unformulated or buried in the depths of Government policy development (or both).

This paper gives overview of some of the issues surrounding the registration of Maori words and images under the new Trade Marks Act 2002, including:

a) the Maori world view and the concepts of traditional knowledge and treasures;
b) Maori concerns with current intellectual property law;
c) Maori aims for protecting traditional knowledge and treasures with systems of intellectual property;
d) the Trade Marks Act 2002 and traditional words and images as trade marks;
e) some examples of Maori traditional knowledge and treasures as trade marks;
f) other tools for protecting Maori intellectual property rights; and
g) the future – where are we headed?

---

[1] Trade Marks Act 1953, section 16(1).
[2] Trade Marks Act 2002, section 17 (text attached as appendix 1 to this paper).
[3] Ibid., sections 177–180 (text attached as appendix 1 to this paper).

To better understand Maori views on intellectual property it is necessary to give a brief outline of Maori beliefs and the Maori "world view".

B. Background[4]

I. History of Settlement

New Zealand's first inhabitants were the Maori. There are many versions, theories and accounts of where the Maori people originated from, but it cannot be disputed that the Maori, at some point, crossed the Pacific Ocean and settled in New Zealand. Archaeological evidence suggests that a Maori population may have been established in New Zealand as early as A.D. 700.

The Dutch navigator Abel Tasman is credited with the European discovery of New Zealand in 1642. However, Tasman did not stay in New Zealand as he became disillusioned by the trading prospects. In 1769 the British explorer James Cook circumnavigated New Zealand. Spanish, French and other British explorers followed. When the British established a penal colony in New South Wales (Australia) in 1788, New Zealand experienced more contact with the outside world. Traders realising the commercial value of flax, seals, whales and timber called at New Zealand ports. As trade and settlement increased, New Zealand became increasingly under the influence of Britain. Lawlessness among European settlers, inter-tribal fighting, ad hoc colonisation, and land speculation all resulted from increased European contact. By the early 1800s there was a feeling not only that the Maori were being exploited, but that law and order needed to be established to curb the unsavoury elements that were developing in New Zealand.

II. The Treaty of Waitangi

On 6 February 1840 the Treaty of Waitangi was signed. This document is often cited as the founding document of New Zealand. The document purported to cede sovereignty over New Zealand to the English Crown in return for protection for Maori people and their way of life. The Treaty was signed by representatives of the Maori and of Queen Victoria. However, there are two versions of the Treaty, one in English and one in Maori, and these versions conflict. This conflict, and the argument over which version should prevail is, to this day, at the heart of many Treaty claims.

In the context of Intellectual Property, Articles 1 and 2 of the Treaty are important. In Article 1 of the English version, the Chiefs and Tribes ceded their "sovereignty" to Queen Victoria. But Article 1 of the Maori version

---

    [4] The author is grateful to Spencer Webster of Simpson Grierson's Maori Business Unit, of Ngai Te Rangi, Ngapuhi and Ngati Wai iwi, for his review and suggestions for this and other sections of this paper.

refers to a grant of kawanatanga (governorship).[5] Similar interpretational issues exist in Article 2. The English version of Article 2 reads as follows:

"Her Majesty the Queen of England confirms and guarantees to the Chiefs and Tribes of New Zealand and to the respective families and individuals thereof the full exclusive and undisturbed possession of their Lands and Estates, Forests, Fisheries and other properties which they may collectively or individually possess so long as it is their wish and desire to retain the same in their possession."

In the Maori version Article 2 guarantees the "tino rangatiratanga" of the Maori over "taonga". Article 2 of the Maori version has been interpreted as meaning that the Chiefs and Tribes of New Zealand would retain their "chiefly authority" to manage their own affairs in relation to their lands, "treasures", and people.

"Taonga" roughly translates to treasures, but includes language, cultural heritage and things that would be classified as intellectual property.

III. Maori World View

At the heart of many of the concerns Maori have with New Zealand's current intellectual property system is the Maori world view. This view is central to Maori customs and culture.

The Maori culture can be defined as an animist culture. Animists believe all things, living or not living, are interconnected. Maori culture therefore accords Whakapapa (genealogy) to all things.[6] This world view is not unique to Maori, but Maori have their own creation story and traditions.

The basis for the Maori world view starts with the legend of creation. In the beginning there was Papatuanuku (the earth mother) and Ranginui (the sky father). They were joined together, and accordingly their children lived in the darkness between them. Then one of the children, Tane Mahuta, separated his parents. From these two parents come all creation – their children are the atua (gods). For example, Tane Mahuta is god of the forests and Tangaroa is god of the sea. Humankind was the creation of Tane. Thus humankind can trace its ancestry back to the land. In this way, Maori have a direct genealogical connection to the land and sea, and all its inhabitants (whakapapa).

Like most other indigenous traditional peoples, Maori have a unique relationship with their natural world; they view themselves as part of and not dominant over their natural flora and fauna. Maori lack an identifiable legal system. Their society is regulated by customs and traditions (tikanga), and their genealogy (whakapapa). Whakapapa is an organising principle which

---

[5] Much of the discussion in this and the following section on the Maori world view is gleaned from M. Solomon, "Intellectual Property Rights and Indigenous Peoples' Rights and Obligations", http://www.inmotionmagazine.com/ra01/ms2.html.
[6] C. James, "Labour's Cultural Challenge – the taniwha term", *The New Zealand Herald,* 7 January 2003.

provides that the world and all that is within it is connected through a web of physical and spiritual relationships.

The ideas of reciprocity and balance are fundamental to Maori culture. All things are connected to everything else, and the balance between these things must be maintained. Maori believe themselves to be "kaitiaki" or guardians, having the role of maintaining or redressing that balance and looking after the earth and all that is on it.

In order for Maori to survive and prosper from the land and the sea, they first had to show respect to their deities. Respect was shown by taking care of their environment. This is known as "kaitiakitanga", which requires Maori to undertake a type of caretaker role in relation to natural resources. For example, it was commonplace for a rahui (ban) to be imposed to allow resources to replenish in times when they were scarce. Resources under rahui could not simply be taken for individual or even the collective good when the need arose. Instead, blessings had to be given and permission sought from the Gods beforehand. This is because Maori view all things on Earth, whether animate or inanimate, as having a life force (mauri) and a spirit (wairua) of their own; in that respect they are regarded as being sacred (tapu).

In summary, the Maori relationship with the land was a reciprocal one; their caretaker roles were balanced against their right to use and exploit resources for their own purposes.

IV. Concepts of Matauranga Maori and Taonga (traditional knowledge and treasures)

Maui Solomon, a Maori barrister, defines Matauranga Maori as traditional knowledge of the natural world. According to Moana Jackson, a Maori commentator, Maori cultural and intellectual property can best be defined as "'taonga tuku iho' (precious things) which explain and make sense of the Maori world, the things which that world gives to nurture and protect its people, things which give spiritual or artistic expression to the Maori sense of being".[7]

Traditional Maori knowledge includes (in general) the art of moko (Maori tattooing), genealogy, Maori legends, songs, art, carvings in wood, bone, and greenstone, and the practice of medicine and religion.[8] It was never in the best interests of society for such knowledge to die with the person holding it.[9] Traditional Maori society did not benefit when Matauranga Maori was monopolised by one person from one generation either.[10] Rather, "ownership" was communal, in that it was held by the

---

    [7] M. Jackson, "Defining Intellectual Property: A Paper prepared for the World Indigenous Conference on Intellectual Property", Mataatua, New Zealand, March 1992.
    [8] B. Garrity, "Conflict Between Maori and Western Concepts of Intellectual Property", (1999) 8 Auckland U L Rev 1203.
    [9] Ibid., 1204.
    [10] Ibid.

tribe/sub-tribe/family structural framework, and was passed down from generation to generation eternally.[11]

V. Maori Concept of Property and Rights/Differences from the "European" View and Intellectual Property Systems

For a number of reasons the Maori definition of cultural and intellectual property does not fit well within Western intellectual property law. European intellectual property law is largely concerned with ownership, duration, and fixation. These concepts are not aligned with Maori concepts of property and rights, and the nature of Maori society.

First, Maori lived in a very community-based society. Roles and responsibilities, as well as benefits, were shared among the iwi or whanau. Thus, there is a sense of communal, not private, ownership of tangible and intangible property. This sense of community ownership does not fit within Western notions of individual property ownership. Further, the concept is not really community "ownership" as such, but kaitakitanga or a caretaker role.

Another feature of Maori society is that traditions, stories and customs were passed down orally from generation to generation. Again, this does not translate well into Western property laws. It is therefore hard to establish essential features of Western intellectual property law, for example ownership, duration and fixation.

Kaitiakitanga (the caretaker role) extended to the protection of "traditional Maori knowledge". The term "intellectual property'" is not itself recognised in Maori terminology. There are two reasons why this is so. First, the term "intellectual property" generally connotes "intellectual creations or ideas" held by "individuals". As discussed earlier, Maori society was communal. Any "intellectual creations or ideas" are held by the society as a whole. Secondly, in Maori society there was no differentiation between intellectual property and cultural property (which has been interpreted to mean "physical evidence of a certain stage of a culture's development, such as works of art or archaeological and historical objects").[12]

So the term "traditional Maori knowledge" (or Matauranga Maori) is more apt than the term "intellectual property".

The divide between Western views on intellectual property and the corresponding views of the Maori is patently clear; the West believe in "private property rights" whereas the Maori treat such things as a communal right, which has and always will remain in the hands of the community.

---

[11] Ibid., 1205.
[12] See, for example, Ministry of Commerce, Intellectual Property Law Reform Bill: Maori Consultation Paper (1994) 5, B. Garrity, "Conflict Between Maori and Western Concepts of Intellectual Property", (1999) 8 Auckland U L Rev 1200.

C. Maori Concerns with Intellectual Property

I. No Adequate Protection for Maori Traditional Knowledge and Treasures

Maori have long been concerned at the lack of legislative recognition of their cultural property under existing legislation. This concern is held by many indigenous peoples.

The protections available for intellectual property in New Zealand are many and varied, and are provided for by statute and common law. The protections span patents, copyright, passing off, confidential information, and designs. In New Zealand there are six statutes which give protection to intellectual property: the Trade Marks Act 2002, the Copyright Act 1994, the Patents Act 1953, the Designs Act 1953, the Plant Variety Rights Act 1987 and the Layout Designs Act 1994. These Acts "protect" most aspects of intellectual property. They do so by giving the holder of the right "powerful property based remedies within the protection period".[13] However, for a variety of reasons each of these regimes fail to protect Maori traditional knowledge and treasures. The next section of this paper will discuss why copyright and patents fail to protect Maori interests. Trade mark protection will be considered in more depth later in the paper.

1. Copyright

The Copyright Act 1994 provides protection for "original works".[14] Under this Act, a person is afforded rights in a work (copyright) to the exclusion of others. "Works" covered by the Act include, amongst others, literary and dramatic works, films, and typographical arrangements of published editions.[15] Rights in a work include copying, performing, and broadcasting.[16] Generally, copyright begins at the end of the calendar year in which a work is made and lasts for the life of the author plus 50 years.

There are no specific provisions in the Act to deal with rights in traditional Maori works. The Copyright Act is founded entirely upon Western notions of intellectual property. Consequently it does not offer much to those seeking to preserve or protect the special characteristics of Matauranga Maori.

Generally, problems with copyright law include:

(i)   It does not protect ideas themselves, but only the expression of those ideas. As mentioned earlier, traditional Maori knowledge is passed on orally, and thus has no physical expression to which copyright can be attached.

---

[13] S. Frankel/G. McLay, *Intellectual Property in New Zealand*, 2002, Wellington, LexisNexis Butterworths, 19.

[14] Copyright Act 1994, s14.

[15] Copyright Act 1994, s14.

[16] Copyright Act 1994, s16(1).

(ii)   Copyright is only for a limited duration. After the expiry of the copyright period, the work is considered to be in the public domain and available for exploitation by anyone. This does not help Maori protect their work.

(iii) In general, copyright laws only recognise identifiable authors.[17] Copyright law is unable to accommodate communal ownership, or at least the concept does not fit easily.[18]

2. Patents

The Patents Act 1953 protects "any manner of new manufacture".[19] The grant of a patent provides the patent owner with a right to exclude others from making, using, or selling the patented invention. Under the Patents Act 1953, this right lasts 20 years from the date when the patent was issued (back-dated to the date of application).[20]

Similar to copyright, there is no specific protection for Maori cultural property, and there are many reasons why Maori cultural property cannot avail itself of patent protection. The main reasons patent protection is not applicable are:

(i)   Patents are only for a limited duration (usually 20 years). After that the invention is considered to be in the public domain. Patents, therefore, do not provide long term protection for traditional Maori knowledge.

(ii)   The invention or process patented must be novel or inventive. Because most traditional Maori knowledge has been around for generations, it can no longer be considered novel or inventive.

(iii) Community ownership does not fit well with New Zealand's patent law. Maui Solomon summarises this as follows: "because of the intergenerational nature of Maori knowledge and communal belief systems, it is virtually impossible for Maori to identify one individual inventor; moreover, such a notion is antithetical to Maori culture."[21]

(iv)   Obtaining a patent is a costly process and, when this is coupled with the limited duration of protection, patents are seen not to be the best protection for traditional Maori knowledge.

Maori medicines and knowledge regarding the healing properties of plants is one area where commentators believe patent-type protection would be

---

[17] For the limited provisions dealing with works of unidentified authorship, see Copyright Act 1994, ss7, 22(3) and 97(6).

[18] The concept of joint ownership is recognised in the Copyright Act 1994, ss8, 18(3), 18(4) and 22(6) but only to the effect that the joint owners are tenants in common of the private property asset.

[19] Patents Act 1953, s2(1).

[20] Patents Act 1953, s30(3).

[21] M. Solomon, *Maori Cultural and Intellectual Property Rights* Speech notes for Institute for International Research Conference, Auckland, 24–25 February 1997, 12.

particularly useful, as they have been successfully exploited by non-Maori. Posey and Dutfield estimate that in 1990, US$50 billion was generated from pharmaceutical products derived from indigenous knowledge and a similar amount in relation to pesticide and herbicide products, but only, 0.001% was "returned" to indigenous cultures or traditional communities from whence the knowledge originated.[22]

3. International Recognition

Maori are not alone in their concern for the protection for their traditional knowledge and treasures. Over the last few decades there has been growing international recognition of the need to protect the traditional cultural knowledge of indigenous peoples around the world. New Zealand has played a major role in the international arena on this issue. Examples where New Zealand has made a significant contribution include:

(i)   The Convention on Biological Diversity

The Convention on Biological Diversity of 1992 recognises that cultural diversity is fundamental to the maintenance of biological diversity. Article 8(j) talks about respecting, preserving and maintaining traditional knowledge as it relates to sustainable use of biological diversity and that this must be done with the "approval and involvement of the holders of such knowledge".[23]

However, Maori commentators believe that these "worthy sentiments" are overridden by the caveat that each contracting country is only obliged to respect and maintain such knowledge "as far as possible and appropriate" to their own country's circumstances.[24]

(ii) The WIPO Intergovernmental Committee on Intellectual Property and Genetic Resources, Traditional Knowledge and Folklore

The fourth session of this committee was held in Geneva from 9–17 December 2002, where the committee listened to presentations from various countries, including New Zealand, on the protection in their respective countries for indigenous rights in traditional knowledge.[25]

While recognising the rights of indigenous peoples, these conventions have no binding power. They have, though, increased international awareness and put pressure on nations to rethink mechanisms for the protection of traditional knowledge.

---

[22] D. Posey/G. Dutfield, Traditional resource rights: international instruments for protection and compensation for indigenous peoples and local communities, 1996, Switzerland, IUCN – The World Conservation Union.

[23] See www.biodiv.org/convention/articles.asp.

[24] Solomon, see above note 21.

[25] See www.wipo.int/documents/en/meetings/2002/igc.

II. Conflict with Exclusivity Granted by IP Rights

As discussed earlier, one of the fundamental conflicts with Western intellectual property laws is that they are based on the idea of exclusivity. Intellectual property laws work by granting some form of exclusivity of use to those who qualify for protection.

This is in direct contrast to Maori society, which is founded on the assumption that knowledge will be passed down from generation to generation, so as to benefit society for long periods of time. In general, Maori do not wish to ensure that no one can use their knowledge, only that it is used appropriately. For this reason the exclusivity granted by Western intellectual property rights does not help Maori to protect their knowledge. There is no "owner" (in the private property sense) of Maori traditional knowledge, and Maori do not want to see knowledge and other treasures in the hands of only a few, which is the type of protection Western intellectual property laws offer.

By granting "ownership" to individuals, trade marks and other Western intellectual property rights are seen as being an "appropriation" of part of Maori culture or heritage.

There are a number of examples, many recent, where attempts have been made to register Maori words and imagery as trade marks, or Maori words and imagery have been used in a way which at least some Maori perceive as inappropriate. Many of these recent cases have been high profile and have caused a great deal of debate and concern among Maori.

1. *Air New Zealand: The Koru*

The koru (or fern device) has been identified as the emblem of Air New Zealand since 1973. It has even been registered by Air New Zealand as a trade mark. One Maori commentator has argued that this is "the most obvious example" of how a Maori symbol is being used in a modern-day context without the permission of Maori.[26]

In 1998, in a bid to be more sensitive to cultural concerns, Air NZ removed its famous koru symbol from areas where it was likely to be offensive, particularly areas where it could be walked on or sat on (such as carpets and upholstery).

---

[26] J. Weir, "'Culturally Sensitive' Air NZ Removes Koru Symbol", The Dominion INL, 28 March 1998.

2. Maori head and moko for foodstuffs

For Maori, it is offensive to use a representation of a head, which is tapu, in relation to food, which is noa (common). However, New Zealand trade mark no. 19115 depicted a Maori man's moko-ed (tattooed) head in relation to preserved meat. This mark only lapsed in 1999.

3. Canterbury rugby boots

Clothing manufacturer Canterbury International Ltd proposed to introduce a range of rugby boots with names such as "Rangatira" and "Moko".[27]

The New Zealand report to the WIPO Intergovernmental Committee listed this as an example of inappropriate use of Maori words and symbols.

"The first example raised . . . related to the use of Maori names such as 'Rangatira', 'Moko' and 'Tane-Toa' by a major New Zealand apparel company, on rugby football boots. The manufacturer, Canterbury New Zealand, had not sought trade mark protection for these names. The submitter argued that the use of such sacred names was very offensive, and noted, for example that Tane was one of the creator gods in Maori belief. The submitter suggested that Christian people might be "similarly outraged" if rugby football boots bearing the name "Jesus Christ" were produced."[28]

4. Robbie Williams' Moko

The art of traditional Maori tattoo, moko, is also a topic for debate, with some Maori finding some modern uses inappropriate or offensive. An example is performer Robbie Williams' prominent moko inspired tattoo. There is, though, some difference among Maori as to whether, if properly managed, this sort of prominence is positive for Maori culture in modern times. As well as concern over possibly inappropriate use, there was also concern over non-Maori tattooists performing the tattoo without the proper ceremony.

---

[27] J. Milne, "Maori seek Trademarks Protection", The Dominion, 2 November 2001.

[28] WIPO. Report of the Intergovernmental Committee on Intellectual Property and Genetic Resources, Traditional Knowledge and Folklore, Fourth Session, Geneva, 9–17 December 2002, Annex II, page 5.

This was also listed as an example in the New Zealand report to the WIPO Intergovernmental Committee. The report stated: [29]

"Ta Moko, the art of Maori tattoo, is a process of carving deep grooves and colouring the skin for family and personal identification. Certain people were entitled to wear moko for particular reasons such as rank, status, achievements, membership and also life history. As tattooing involved marking the face and the shedding of blood, it was highly tapu or sacred and the process was associated with extensive ritual and regulations. While in contemporary society, the practice of ta moko is not as prevalent as in traditional times, the norms governing this art form still exist. Given these restrictions, it causes offence when it takes place outside of these parameters, particularly when sacred images are used in an inappropriate context."

5. Sony PlayStation 2 Game

In May 2003, it was brought to world attention that Sony had drawn extensively on Maori culture and imagery for the PlayStation 2 game "The Mask of Kri", including moko and taiaha (traditional weapons).

6. Moko Restaurant

Dutch restaurateur, Casper Reijnders, runs an upmarket Amsterdam restaurant named Moko. The restaurant serves New Zealand and Australian-inspired food and uses the image of a blonde Dutch woman with a modernistic "moko" on her face.[30]

7. Taiwan honey producer: Manuka

A Taiwanese honey-producer has registered the name Manuka as a trade mark in Taiwan for honey. Whilst there were initial fears that the registered proprietor could sue any New Zealand exporter of honey to Taiwan where the description "manuka honey" was used, this fear has been assuaged by the fact that the registration is in the Taiwanese language and is not immediately apparent as the word manuka.

---

[29] Ibid., 6.
[30] J. Milne, "Maori Outrage at Dutch Café's 'Abuse' of Moko", The Dominion, INL, 2002.

8. *Spice Girls: haka*

The Maori haka (commonly interpreted to mean war dance, but may also be used generically to describe all forms of Maori dance and performance) has also been at issue. The English pop band the Spice Girls came under criticism in 1997 when they performed the haka on stage. While Maori opinion was mixed on whether the band's actions were positive, negative or irrelevant, the common feeling was one of annoyance that Maori opinion and guidance had not even been sought.

9. *Lego: "Bionicle" toy range*

Danish toymaker, Lego, began marketing a range of toys, with characters whose names were derived from Maori culture. The "Bionicle" range included mythical inhabitants from the island Mata Nui; the "Tohunga", and the "Toa" warriors. There was concern amongst Maori that the names had important meanings behind them, yet they were being inappropriately and incorrectly communicated to the consumer market.

Maori lawyer, Maui Solomon, wrote to Lego to "complain about the use of more than 10 Maori words to name the Bionicle toys. They included spiritual people called Tohunga (Maori for priest), face masks called Konohi (face), a stone warrior called Pohatu (stone) and a tunnelling character called Whenua (earth)".[31]

As a result, Lego agreed to discontinue the range of toys, and entered talks with Maori to develop a code of conduct in relation to use of traditional knowledge in the manufacture of toys.

The willingness of Lego to respond to complaints shows how much international recognition is growing. However the issue is still controversial. Even in New Zealand there is still debate about the need to protect some forms of traditional Maori knowledge. A 2001 article in the Timaru Herald regarding the Lego saga stated (with some confusion about intellectual property rights):

> ". . . no one 'owns' words like priest, stone, face, and earth, the Maori translations of which were being used by Lego . . . Lego was trying to place a copyright on the words, but only as they related to the naming of toys. That seems reasonable."[32]

III. No Control Over the Use of Maori Intellectual Property

Maori have been outspoken about their view that Western intellectual property laws fail to protect traditional Maori knowledge and treasures. Perhaps the most important objection by Maori people to New Zealand's intellectual property legislation is that, from the Maori point of view, it contravenes Article 2 of the Treaty of Waitangi. This is highlighted in both the Mataatua

---

[31] "Lego agrees to stop Maori-name toys", The Christchurch Press, 31 October 2001.
[32] Editorial, "What's in a word", Timaru Herald, INL, 5 November 2001,

Declaration and the Wai 262 claim before the Waitangi Tribunal, which will be discussed later.

"Maori concerns have been summarised in the Mataatua Declaration on Cultural and Intellectual Property of Indigenous Peoples. This Declaration resulted from a hui/workshop in New Zealand's Bay of Plenty in June 1993 attended by over 150 delegates from 14 countries."

"The following are the central themes of the Mataatua Declaration:

- Indigenous peoples are the guardians of their customary knowledge and have the right to protect and control dissemination of that knowledge.
- Existing protection mechanisms are insufficient for the protection of indigenous peoples' intellectual and cultural property rights.
- States should develop (in full co-operation with indigenous peoples) an additional intellectual and cultural property rights regime incorporating certain specified matters.
- Commercialisation of any traditional plants and medicines of indigenous peoples must be managed by the indigenous peoples who have inherited such knowledge.
- Indigenous peoples should define for themselves their own intellectual and cultural property.
- Indigenous peoples should develop codes of ethics to be observed by "external users" (for example, other hapu and iwi, as well as governmental and non-governmental agencies)."[33]

IV. Wai 262

The Wai 262 claim stems from interpretation of guarantees under the Treaty of Waitangi.

Wai 262 is a claim lodged with the Waitangi Tribunal by representatives of six iwi (Ngati Kuri, Ngati Wai, Te Rarawa, Ngati Porou, Ngati Kahungunu and Ngati Koata). The claim generally asserts exclusive and comprehensive rights to flora, fauna, cultural knowledge and property as taonga protected by article 2 of the Treaty of Waitangi.

The claim was lodged in 1991 and hearings began in 1998. However the hearing of evidence is not yet complete and, following the filing of the Crown's Statement of Response on 28 June 2002, the Tribunal has indicated that all remaining Wai 262 hearings will be put on hold for a period to allow the Tribunal to complete a Statement of Issues based on the Statements of Claim and the Crown's Statement of Response.

The four statements of claim set out four categories of traditional knowledge/intellectual property:[34]

---

[33] <http://www.med.govt.nz/buslt/int_prop/info-sheets/wai-262.html>; See also <http://www.waitangi-tribunal.govt.nz/research/wai262/>.
[34] Ibid.

(i) "Matauranga Maori (traditional knowledge) – concerning the retention and protection of knowledge concerning nga toi Maori (arts),
     whakairo (carving), history, oral tradition, Waiata, te reo Maori, and
     rongoa Maori (Maori medicine and healing). The claimants' concern
     is about the protection and retention of such knowledge. They note
     that traditional knowledge systems are being increasingly targeted
     internationally.

(ii) Maori cultural property (manifestation of matauranga maori) – as
     affected by the failure of legislation and policies to protect existing
     Maori collective ownership of cultural taonga and to protect against
     exploitation and misappropriation of cultural taonga, for example
     traditional artefacts, carvings, mokomokai (preserved heads).

(iii) Maori intellectual and cultural property rights – as affected by New
     Zealand's intellectual property legislation, international obligations
     and proposed law reforms. Issues include the patenting of life form
     inventions, the inappropriate registration of trade marks based on
     Maori text and imagery, and the unsuitable nature of intellectual
     property rights for the protection of both Maori traditional knowledge and cultural property.

(iv) Environmental, resource and conservation management – including
     concerns about bio-prospecting and access to indigenous flora and
     fauna, biotechnological developments involving indigenous genetic
     material, ownership claims to resources and species, and iwi-Maori
     participation in decision making on these matters."

The claim was described in the 2002 WIPO session as follows:

"The Wai 262 claim is an extremely broad Treaty claim. . . . The intellectual property issues
raised by the Wai 262 claim are twofold. First, the perceived adverse effects intellectual property rights can have on traditional knowledge and associated cultural property and biological
resources. The key concern here is the granting of intellectual property rights to third parties
for creations or inventions based on traditional knowledge or practices (where there is no
originality or novelty) and the resulting commercialisation that occurs in some cases. The
inappropriate use and registration of trade marks containing Maori text and imagery is an
example of this. The claimants are also concerned about the patenting of life-form inventions.

Secondly, the claimants are concerned about the inability of Maori to obtain or use intellectual property rights to enable them to protect or commercially exploit (where appropriate) their
traditional knowledge, cultural property and biological resources."[35]

Maui Solomon has summarised the intellectual property related part of the
claim as follows:

"In essence the Wai 262 claim seeks to give Maori the ability to define for themselves the
parameters of their cultural and intellectual property rights and to control how those rights are
developed."[36]

---

[35] WIPO Report, note 28, Annex II, page 8.
[36] Solomon, above note 21, 6.

D. Maori Aims

I. A Tikanga Maori (Customary) System to Govern Maori IP?

As already discussed, many of the concerns Maori have with the current intellectual property system stem from the Maori world view. Whereas Western views on intellectual property believe in "private property rights", Maori treat their taonga as a communal right, which has and always will remain in the hands of the community. The exclusivity granted by Western intellectual property rights is not seen to help Maori to protect their knowledge. Consequently, it is critically important to some Maori that any remedies are built on a foundation of tikanga Maori or customary values. That means viewing any system of protection from a Maori cultural viewpoint, as opposed to something imposed from the outside. A Tikanga Maori Framework of Protection (TMFP) has been suggested by Maui Solomon.

Careful consideration is being given to what such a system may look like, how it would be structured and how it would operate. There is no one consistent Maori view, except perhaps that such a system must be owned and controlled by Maori and not simply another Crown agency set up by statute with members appointed by the Crown.

Maui Solomon has suggested that a TMFP should have some or all of the following features: "the system be developed by Maori; the system be based in tikanga Maori; reflecting Maori cultural values and ethos; inherent in this system will be the acknowledgement, protection and promotion of rights and obligations to manage, utilise and protect resources in accordance with Maori cultural values and preferences; flexibility will be very important".

How such a framework could be mandated by Maori would be a vital and challenging ingredient. The TMFP might merely act as a referral body to iwi (tribes), hapu (sub tribes), whanau (families) or individuals. Once it is determined which level of Maori decision-making should be involved, the relevant issue would be appropriately advanced. For example, where it was obvious that certain issues affected only a particular tribe, the issue would be immediately referred to that tribe to deal with. The TMFP would act to assist Maori in the formulation of policies to assist them in their role as kaitiaki (guardian) of their various taonga (treasured things).

II. The Maori Trade Marks Focus Group

In 1994 the Ministry of Commerce established the Maori Trade Marks Focus Group comprising Maori with experience in issues associated with the registration of trade marks containing Maori words or symbols. The objectives of the Maori Trade Marks Focus Group were to:

(i) identify and define issues concerning the registration of trade marks involving Maori words, symbols, sounds or smells; and

(ii) identify issues or develop proposals for the Ministry of Economic
      Development to consider in relation to the registration of trade marks
      involving Maori words, symbols, sounds or smells which may be
      offensive.

The Focus Group considered the major issue to be that the protection
available to Maori cultural and intellectual property is limited because it
often falls outside the protection provided under the conventional system of
intellectual property rights.

The Focus Group began by considering whether, for a start, Maori words,
symbols, sounds or smells should be able to be registered as trade marks at all.
After considerable difficulty, the Focus Group proposed that such trade
marks should be able to be registered for the following reasons:

(i)   Registration of Maori words, symbols, sounds or smells allows for
      recognition in New Zealand of aspects of Maori culture.
(ii) The Trade Marks Act is a mechanism which can be used to protect
      Maori cultural and intellectual property. It provides an opportunity
      for addressing the issue of cultural inappropriateness.
(iii) If Maori words, symbols, sounds or smells are unable to be registered,
      then Maori will also be excluded from registering them.
(iv) Trade marks benefit New Zealand industry.

However, despite showing a willingness to allow Maori words, symbols,
sounds or smells to be registered, the Focus Group recommended that applicants should be able to:

(i)   provide clear evidence of the origin of the trade mark;
(ii) show in some way that the relevant iwi, hapu or whanau had given
      permission to the applicant to use the mark; and
(iii) show that the appropriate source had been identified.

Accordingly, the Focus Group suggested that any person who could show
that he/she had permission or had identified the appropriate source for the
use of a Maori word, symbol, sound or smell in the proposed trade mark,
should be able to make an application for the mark to be registered. The
Focus Group further recommended that it somehow be required that the use
of any proposed trade mark incorporating a Maori element should also be
culturally appropriate.

The Focus Group considered that the best option for implementing these
recommendations was to put in place an effective process to ensure that
applications are properly assessed. Under the Trade Marks Act 2002 this
process has been acknowledged in the form of the Maori Trade Marks
Advisory Committee, but the Act only goes a certain way to implementing
the Focus Group's proposals.

E. Trade Marks Act 2002 – Traditional Words/Images as Trade Marks

I. Section 17

This Act was enacted after significant consultation with and input from Maori groups, particularly the Maori Trade Marks Focus Group. There is now a specific process for marks based on Maori text or imagery. Section 17 of the Act prohibits the registration of trade marks if they *"would be likely to offend a significant section of the community, including Maori"*.[37]

In order to establish whether a mark is derivative of a Maori sign and whether it is culturally offensive, section 177 of the Act allows the Commissioner of Trade Marks to appoint a Maori Trade Marks Advisory Committee to assess these questions. Five people were appointed as the members of the Maori Trade Marks Advisory Committee on 23 October 2003.[38]

In accordance with the Act, the members of the Committee are statutorily required to have knowledge of te ao Maori (Maori world view) and tikanga Maori. Other desirable attributes include having an understanding of and experience in te reo Maori (the Maori language) and Matauranga Maori, as well as business and/or legal expertise and strong Maori networks. Members are appointed by the Commissioner for a period of up to three years, with provision for reappointment.[39]

The key rationale for establishing the Advisory Committee is to minimise the risk that the Crown may inadvertently register Maori text or imagery as a trade mark, where registration or use of the trade mark is likely to cause offence to Maori.[40]

There is also a retrospective element to the new legislation. An already registered trade mark can be revoked if it is found that it was offensive in terms of section 17 at the time of registration.[41]

Therefore, the new Trade Marks Act has put in place some protection for Maori marks.

---

[37] Trade Marks Act 2002, s17(1)(b)(ii).

[38] For the Ministry of Economic Development's summary of these appointees see <http://www.iponz.govt.nz/pls/web/dbssiten.main> (attached as appendix 2 to this paper).

[39] Trade Marks Act 2002, ss177–180.

[40] Ministry of Economic Development, "Maori Trade Marks Advisory Committee: background information", <http://www.med.govt.nz/buslt/int_prop/mtmac/background.html>.

[41] Trade Marks Act 2002, s73 (invalidity) and s208 (transitional provision).

II. How Different Is This to What Was in Place Before?

Section 16(1) of the Trade Marks Act 1953 provided:

> "It shall not be lawful to register as a trade mark or part of a trade mark any scandalous matter or any matter the use of which would be likely to deceive or cause confusion or would be contrary to law or morality or would otherwise be disentitled to protection in a Court of justice."

There were limited cases in New Zealand where a trade mark had been deemed unregistrable on the grounds that it was "scandalous" or "contrary to morality".[42] Consequently, under the 1953 Act it was not necessarily clear whether the "scandalous" and "contrary to morality" ground of objection referred solely to matters of morality, or could also include cultural offensiveness.

From a cultural point of view, there may be some marks which should not be registered for any goods or services. An example may be TAPU (sacred). Perhaps MANA could also be in this category.

In this sense, the 2002 Act has probably broadened the grounds on which a mark can be refused registration. Further, cultural offensiveness can be seen in some respects as a more concrete term as most cultures have words or actions that are clearly regarded as offensive, whereas morality is a highly personal matter, with many differing opinions. Additionally, the potential for subjective or discretionary assessments is largely removed as the Commissioner must in the case of Maori words or images defer to those with expertise in determining "offensiveness", in this case the Advisory Committee.

III. Criteria/Process – Delays and Costs of This New Procedure?

There were some initial views that the new procedure will cause unnecessary cost and delay to those trying to register trade marks. Currently, all trade mark applications containing Maori text or imagery go through a three step process.[43]

1. Step One

All trade mark applications received by the New Zealand Intellectual Property Office (IPONZ) are assessed to determine whether they may contain, or be derived from, Maori text or imagery. Within five days, applications identified as potentially containing Maori text or imagery will be

---

[42] See, e.g., application for BULLSHIT by Red Bull GmbH 2001/33 19-Jul-01 (rejected by the Commissioner of Trade Marks) compare New Zealand trade mark registration no. 308977 BUGGER and device by Robert Van Huesen (accepted by the Commissioner of Trade Marks).

[43] For the process and other background, see <http://www.iponz.govt.nz/pls/web/dbsiten.main>. An IPONZ flow diagram of the process is attached as appendix 3 to this paper.

forwarded (on behalf of the Commissioner) to the Advisory Committee. IPONZ will issue a Partial Compliance Report informing the applicant that the mark has been referred to the Advisory Committee.

2. *Step Two*

If the Advisory Committee determines that the trade mark does contain Maori text or imagery, the applicant is advised that the Commissioner is seeking the advice of experts (the Advisory Committee) to determine whether the mark is likely to be offensive to Maori.

To ensure there are no undue delays to registration, individual Committee members will be required to advise the Commissioner within two weeks of the outcome of their "preliminary consideration". If individual members are confident that the registration of the trade mark will not cause offence to Maori, IPONZ will advise the applicant accordingly, and the application will then proceed through the usual process of trade mark examination.

3. *Step Three*

If individual committee members have initial concerns (or the trade mark is filed shortly before a Committee meeting), the Committee will meet to consider the application and determine whether the trade mark is:

(i) Not offensive to Maori;
(ii) Not likely to be offensive to Maori;
(iii) Likely to be offensive to Maori; or
(iv) Offensive to Maori.

Alternatively, the Committee may advise that further information is required before a determination can be made. In such a case the Committee must advise the Commissioner of this, together with the nature of the further information required. The Commissioner will consider the Committee's advice in such cases and determine whether to advise the applicant to obtain this additional information.

The advice of the Committee is not binding on the Commissioner. The Commissioner will consider the advice taking into account all relevant factors affecting registrability and may come to a determination on the eligibility of an application that is different to the advice received from the Committee.

IV. Experience to Date

The Trade Marks Act 2002 came into force on 10 August 2003. It is expected that the Advisory Committee will meet every two months. As at 31 January 2004, it had met twice, with another meeting scheduled for March 2004. Some 180 marks had been considered by the Committee by 31 January 2004. Only one mark has been found to be offensive or likely to be offensive to Maori. Approximately 20 were awaiting consideration by the Committee.

The Committee looks at both the mark and the goods or services for which it is applied. Thus an application for a potentially sacred (tapu) mark, such a MANA, would not be accepted for goods or services which are common (noa) such as food.

IPONZ, on the recommendation of the Committee, referred the applicant for the one "rejected" application to an appropriate Maori body (or runanga) to consult. The Committee, though, has concerns about this part of the process and is reviewing its procedures on this point. In particular, the Committee believes that the onus should be on the applicant to identify those with whom the applicant should consult about the mark.

On its face, this process and the experience appears to indicate that the Advisory Committee system works, but it is early days.

V. A Limited Step

There has already been some criticism of this process from Maori. Maori argue it may not go far enough in protecting Matauranga Maori from appropriation by unauthorised people.

A key point is that the legislation does not attempt to deal with unregistered use of Maori words and images. It is only when a trade mark application is filed, which would give a statutory monopoly, that the Act operates. Further, once a mark has been registered, there is no control over future unpredicted uses which may be offensive to Maori.

Some commentators argue that even Maori should be prevented from registering such trade marks, as once a trade mark is registered, it could be assigned to anyone else, including non-Maori. This, however, is not the approach taken by the Advisory Committee to date.

Those issues are for the future. The step taken by the 2002 Act is a significant, but very limited, step towards recognition of Maori words and images.

VI. What Are "Maori Words and Images"?

There is no exclusive definition in the 2002 Act of what constitutes "Maori words and imagery". However, IPONZ had been consulting a third party for advice in relation to Maori trade marks even before the 2002 Act came into force, and had been referring any words which appeared to be of Maori origin and any stylisation that had Maori "influences". What could be considered "Maori words and images" is therefore wide-ranging and undefined.

The actual origin of the mark in question may be irrelevant. It is the potential offensiveness to Maori (or any other significant section of the community) which is relevant. For example, an applicant has applied to register a name of Italian origin, but the word looks potentially Maori so the application has been referred to the Advisory Committee.

The wording of section 17 states that marks are prohibited from being registered if they *"would be likely to offend a significant section of the community, including Maori"*. While Maori have been particularly included, potentially any culture (or other "section") could object to the registration of a trade mark on the basis that it offends a significant section of the community. However, "significant" is undefined. If a culture other than Maori lodged an objection to a trade mark, debate could arise as to whether their culture is a significant section of the New Zealand community. It does appear, however, that the word "significant" has been included so as to avoid a situation where very small groups could object to a trade mark on the basis of offensiveness.

Even within Maori a question may arise as to when a group of Maori is significant enough to be relevant. Can it apply to as small a group as a whanau (family)?

VII. "Maori Words and Images" Not Automatically Prevented from Registration

Maori words and images are not automatically prevented from registration. Provided that the Advisory Committee and the Commissioner are satisfied that use of the mark for the specified goods or services will not offend Maori, the word and/or image is registrable for those goods or services.

This raises the issue of how far protection of Maori words should go. Words of any language are available to be trademarked by anybody, as long as they are not descriptive of the goods or services. Why should Maori words be different? Will Maori culture be more effectively preserved by preventing people from using Maori words and/or images?[44]

F. Other Tools Available for Indigenous IP Rights

There is a certain amount of agreement that there are opportunities presented by the main forms of intellectual property protection that have not yet been fully investigated.[45]

At a general level, there is also opportunity for the development of sui generis protection for aspects of traditional knowledge rights, such as a

---

[44] Some Maori marks could fall foul of traditional grounds to reject trade mark applications, such as that the mark is descriptive, laudatory or such a general word as to be incapable of distinguishing the applicant's goods or services. Section 17 gives effect to a different world view – i.e.: that marks may be rejected because they offend against culture.

[45] *Detailed Report on Access and Benefit-Sharing* <http://www.biodiv.org/doc/world/nz/nz-nr-abs-en.doc>.

tikanga Maori system. Further, within New Zealand protection of traditional knowledge rights can be promoted through treaty settlements on a
tribe-by-tribe basis. They can also be protected through changes in
Government policy, such as the requirements in the Trade Marks Act 2002
and the proposal for the Patents Act requiring consultation with Maori over
certain issues. While the traditional application of Western intellectual property law may have failed to adequately protect Maori cultural and intellectual
property, modifications to and consultation on these schemes can make
meaningful changes.

A positive initiative in the Trade Mark area is the establishment of the Toi
Iho certification mark, a mark which operates like New Zealand's
well-known woolmark. The Toi Iho mark that has been registered by
Creative NZ, a Government body, with the intention of later transferring it
to a Maori-run body. A similar mark has been established in Australia. The
Toi Iho mark designates authentic Maori work and can be licensed by people
and companies which satisfy the criteria.

There are two other marks associated with the Toi Iho mark. One designates
a mainly Maori work and the other designates a Maori co-production. The
idea behind these marks is to stop cheap and offensive rip-offs of Maori art
and culture.

"The Maori Made Mark (Toi Iho) is another mechanism developed in response to concerns
raised by Maori about the protection of traditional cultural expressions, including the mis-use
of Maori concepts, styles and imagery and the lack of commercial returns accruing to Maori.
The mark is considered by many as an interim means of providing limited protection to Maori
traditional and cultural expressions, by decreasing the market for copy-cat works produced by
non-Maori.

The Maori Made Mark, developed by the Maori Arts Board (Te Waka Toi) of the Arts
Council of New Zealand (Creative New Zealand), is a registered trade mark and a mark of
authenticity used to promote and sell authentic, quality Maori arts and crafts. The mark
indicates to consumers that the creator of the works is of Maori descent and produces work of a
particular quality."[46]

---

[46] WIPO Report, note 28, Annex II, page 16. (on WIPO website at
<http://www.wipo.org/news/en/>.).

G. Future – Where Are We Headed?

New Zealand is making some progress in the arena of indigenous peoples' intellectual property rights. The Ministry of Economic Development is mapping out a studied programme to address the issue (or issues). There is a clear need for international reflection and coordination. Like all cultural issues, the question can be particularly emotive, and can be characterised by ignorant and knee-jerk responses. Examples of the Ministry of Economic Development's inclusion of Matauranga Maori and taonga in reviews of intellectual property legislation include the March 2002 Discussion Paper on the Plant Variety Rights Act 1987[47] and the June 2003 Discussion Paper on the Patents Act 1953.[48] The, still distant, recommendations of the Waitangi Tribunal in the Wai 262 claim are likely to herald an era in which Maori concerns over Matauranga Maori and taonga enter a new level of public importance. Government responses to these recommendations, and which recommendations are implemented, will be fascinating to watch.

The changes in New Zealand's Trade Marks Act 2002 are on their face limited, but provide a clear message that New Zealand is prepared to tackle these issues in a measured and sensitive way. It is (currently at least) a matter of small steps.

Glossary of Maori words/terms

Atua	gods
Haka	traditional term for Maori chant with dance/ actions
Hapu	subdivision of a tribe, or a sub tribe
Iwi	tribe
Kaitiaki	guardians
Kaitiakitanga	Maori caretaker role in relation to natural resources
Kanohi	face
Kawana	governor
Koru	fern
Mana	authority or influence
Matauranga Maori	traditional Maori knowledge
Mauri	life force
Moko	Maori tattooing
Mokomokai	preserved heads
Nga toi	arts
Noa	opposite of tapu, and includes the concept of common

---

[47] <http://www.med.govt.nz/buslt/int_prop/plantvarietyreview/discussion/index.html>.
[48] <http://www.med.govt.nz/buslt/int_prop/pharmaceutical/discussion/index.html>.

Papatuanuku	the earth mother
Pohatu	stone
Rahui	ban
Rangatira	chief
Ranginui	the sky father
Rongoa	medicine and healing
Runanga	"trustee" group
Taiaha	traditional weapon
Tane Mahuta	god of the forests
Tangaroa	god of the sea
Taonga	treasures or precious things (includes language, cultural heritage, etc.)
Taonga tuku iho	treasures/precious things handed down from ancestors Tapu sacred
Te reo Maori	the Maori language
Tikanga	customs and traditions
Tino rangatiratanga	chiefly authority
Tohunga	priest
Waiata	song
Wairua	spirit
Whakairo	carving
Whakapapa	genealogy
Whanau	family
Whenua	earth

Appendix 1

17. Absolute grounds for not registering trade mark: general –
    (1) The Commissioner must not do any of the following things:
        (a) register as a trade mark or part of a trade mark any matter the use of which would be likely to deceive or cause confusion:
        (b) register a trade mark or part of a trade mark if –
            (i) its use is contrary to New Zealand law or would otherwise be disentitled to protection in any court:
            (ii) the Commissioner considers that its use or registration would be likely to offend a significant section of the community, including Maori:
            (iii) the application for the registration of the trade mark is made in bad faith.
    (2) Despite subsection (1)(b)(i), the Commissioner may register a trade mark even if use of the trade mark is restricted or prohibited under the Smoke-free Environments Act 1990.
Cf 1953 No 66 s 16

Subpart 2 – Advisory committee

177 Advisory committee
    (1) The Commissioner must appoint an advisory committee.
    (2) The Commissioner may alter the advisory committee.

178 Function of advisory committee
    The function of the advisory committee is to advise the Commissioner whether the proposed use or registration of a trade mark that is, or appears to be, derivative of a Maori sign,

including text and imagery, is, or is likely to be, offensive to Maori.

179 Membership of advisory committee

(1) The Commissioner may, at any time, appoint or discharge a member of the advisory committee and, if the Commissioner thinks fit, appoint another member in a discharged member's place.

(2) A person must not be appointed as a member of the advisory committee unless, in the opinion of the Commissioner, the person is qualified for appointment, having regard to that person's knowledge of te ao Maori (Maori worldview) and tikanga Maori (Maori protocol and culture).

(3) A member of the advisory committee may resign office by notice in writing to the Commissioner.

180 Advisory committee may regulate own procedure

Subject to any direction given by the Commissioner, the advisory committee may regulate its own procedure.

Appendix 2

Mâori Trade Marks Advisory Committee

The members of the Mâori Trade Marks Advisory Committee established under the Trade Marks Act 2002 have now been appointed by the Commissioner of Trade Marks, and will shortly commence meetings to consider trade mark applications referred to them.

The function of the Committee is to advise the Commissioner as to whether the proposed use or registration of a trade mark that is, or appears to be, derivative of a Mâori sign, including text and imagery, is, or is likely to be, offensive to Mâori.

- Ms Karen Te O Kahurangi Waaka was part of the Mâori Advisory Committee to the Ministry of Commerce facilitating the Trade Marks Discussion in 1995 and 1996. Karen also has extensive experience in Mâori Tourism. Karen will sit as Chair of the Committee.
- Dr Deidre Brown is Senior Lecturer in Fine Arts and Art History at the University of Canterbury School of Fine Arts in Christchurch. Her specialist areas are Mâori art and architecture, and Mâori and technology. Deidre is widely published and has lectured internationally on the topics of Mâori art and iconography.
- Mr Pare Keiha is Dean of the Faculty of Mâori Development at the Auckland University of Technology. Pare has had extensive experience as a Director and brings business experience, broad Mâori networks and commercial and legal knowledge to the Committee.
- Mr Mauriora Kingi is Director of Kaupapa Mâori at the Rotorua District Council. He has advised many government agencies, Ministers and dignitaries on tikanga Mâori, protocol and etiquette. Mauriora has 10 years experience in local government. He has advised ministries such as, Te Puni Kokiri, Health, Environment, Internal Affairs, Conservation, Courts and the NZ Toursim Board. He has been Aide de comp for Governor Generals, Prime Ministers and Ministers of the Crown.
- Ms Tui Te Hau has previously been New Zealand Trade Commissioner to Melbourne. Tui brings international commercial experience to the Committee and has previously advised businesses on issues such as entering international markets, and brand marketing.

Appendix 3

Māori Advisory Committee Process Diagram

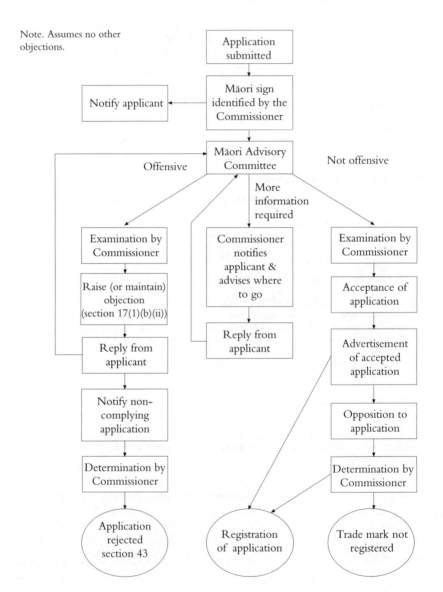

5
Geographical Indications: International, Bilateral and Regional Agreements

CHRISTOPHER HEATH

A. Introduction

The protection of geographical indications started with the protection against misleading use. In order to determine what exactly is misleading, the principles under trade mark law may serve as a useful guideline. However, some differences should be noted. For one, trade mark protection for geographical indications is not only denied in cases of misleading, but also in cases of descriptive use. This is understandable, as a descriptive trade mark cannot confer an origin. On the other hand, the use (rather than registration) of a descriptive indication does not cause confusion nor is it misleading in any way. Further, trade mark law is not only concerned with actual, but also with potential conflicts. Registration can be denied not only if the place is currently not associated with certain goods or services, but also if this could be the case in the future. Finally, public interest might require denying proprietary protection by registration for one single enterprise, where (non-misleading) use in commerce is completely permissible. In fact, the argument that registration of a geographical indication should be denied because other undertakings might have a legitimate interest in using this indication already presumes that such use by other undertakings is lawful.

B. International Agreements

I. The Paris Convention 1883

The concept of preventing misconceptions in trade was adopted by the Paris Convention and the Madrid Arrangement.

The Paris Convention, already in its original version of 1883, listed geographical indications as one form of industrial property to be protected. This at least ensured that the principle of national treatment specified in Art. 2 Paris Convention would apply. A definition of a geographical indication was not provided, although Art. 1 refers to "indications of source or appellations of origin", thereby indicating a broad definition of the subject matter. The protection provided for in Art. 10 is rather odd. While in the course of negotiations, an absolute prohibition of false indications of origin was proposed, this met with opposition. It was subsequently changed to cases where the false indication of origin was used as a trade name of a fictitious character or used with fraudulent intention.[1] Art. 10 reads as follows:

"The provisions of the preceding article shall be applicable to any product bearing falsely as an indication of origin the name of a locality or of a determined country, when the indication is joined to a fictitious commercial name or a name borrowed with fraudulent intention.

There shall be in any case recognised as an interested party, whether it be a natural or juristic person, any producer, manufacturer or trader of such product either in the locality falsely indicated as place of origin or in the region where such locality is situated or in the country falsely indicated."

A case that might clarify this obscure wording could be the use of "Swiss Chalet" for chocolate manufactured in England. Such use was ultimately found impermissible by the English Appeal Court, yet based on (proprietary) interests of Swiss chocolate manufacturers.[2] But Art. 10 Paris Convention is confined to "false" indications, not "misleading" ones. The sanctions provided in Art. 9 include seizure upon importation, prohibition of importation, or seizure within the country. These remedies have not proved very efficient.[3]

II. The Madrid Arrangement 1891

No sooner had the Paris Convention came into force, attempts were made to strengthen the protection of geographical indications. Amendments of Art. 10 at the Rome Conference in 1886 were never ratified by the member states, and only concerned minor clarifications. Further reaching were the proposals made at the Madrid Conference 1890. A number of countries were determined to conclude a separate arrangement for protecting indications of origin beyond what was stipulated in Art. 10 Paris Convention. Varying proposals were tabled. One of these sought to clarify that indications which had become generic or descriptive should be excluded from protection. Portugal wanted the opposite: in cases where the reputation of an indication was based on the special conditions of soil and climate, any imitation should be prohibited, even though the indication had become generic. The French proposal sought to limit this provision to products of the vine. While the mechanisms for enforcement were basically those as provided for in Art. 9 Paris Convention, the Madrid Arrangement Concerning the Prevention of False or Misleading Indications of Source 1890 went beyond the Paris Convention in one important respect: Although indications were excluded from the Arrangement that in the domestic context were deemed descriptive or generic, no such exclusion was to be applied to appellations of wine and

---

[1] The history is provided by Ladas, Patents, Trademarks and Related Rights, Cambridge, Mass. 1975, 1577/1578.

[2] *Chocosuisse v. Cadbury*, English Court of Appeal, [1999] R.P.C. 826.

[3] Albrecht Krieger, Der internationale Schutz von geographischen Bezeichnungen aus deutscher Sicht, GRUR Int. 1984, 71, 72.

wine-related products. The difference is important because it demonstrates how the Madrid Arrangement serves as the bridge between the Paris Convention, with its recognition of geographical indications without proprietary protection, and the Lisbon Arrangement, that is solely based on the concept of proprietary rights for appellations of origin.

Both the Paris Convention (at the Hague Conference in 1925) and the Madrid Arrangement (at the Revision Conference in London 1934) were complemented by provisions to repress acts of unfair competition. The Hague Revision Conference with its Art. 10bis introduced protection against passing-off into the Convention, and the London Revision Conference 1934 rendered the Madrid Arrangement not only applicable to "false" indications, but also "misleading" ones. The structure of the Madrid Arrangement (with a membership of 33 states as of 2004) is thus as follows:

(1) All goods bearing false or deceptive indications related to a member state of the Arrangement shall be seized upon importation;
(2) Each country is free to refuse protection for those indications that have become generic or descriptive for certain types of goods in that particular country;
(3) The above rule (2) does not apply for indications relating to wine or wine products. These have to be protected as indications of origin although the general public might regard them as generic or descriptive.

The Arrangement also protects against the use of false or misleading "indirect" indications,[4] or false or misleading indications with such additions as "system", "type", or the like.[5]

Whether or not an indication is generic has to be decided by "the tribunals of each country", Art. 4 Madrid Arrangement. This was considered to be a significant weakness of the Arrangement in general:

"The position under which the tribunal of any country may decide that an appellation of origin has become generic creates insecurity and also contradiction. An appellation of origin protected by legislation or jurisprudence in a certain country may not be used by producers or manufacturers of such country and yet may be used freely by producers or manufacturers in a contracting country. Be this as it may, it has proved impossible to change the first portion of Art. 4 at successive conferences of revision (reference omitted). Instead, an effort has been made to enlarge the exception contained in the latter portion of Art. 4."[6]

---

[4] An example would be the decision of the Japanese Patent Office to refuse registration of the mark "Loreley" for wine products which bore no relation to Germany: Japanese Patent Office, 23 October 1991, 24 IIC 409 [1993].

[5] In almost all bilateral agreements on the protection of geographical indications, provisions can be found indicating that "diluting" an indication by additions such as "type", "method", etc., is not permissible.

[6] Ladas, Patents, Trademarks and Related Rights, Cambridge, Mass. 1975, 1589.

The latter portion of Art. 4 provides an exception to the above rule: "however, the regional appellations of origin of wine products are not included in the reservation specified by this article." In other words, wine products can never be declared generic by "the tribunals of each country".

"At various congresses of the international association (footnote omitted) and at the Washington Conference of Revision (reference omitted), it had already been proposed that the appellations of origin of all products which derive their national qualities from the soil and climate be exempted from the rule of Art. 4. It was also proposed that each of the contracting countries should give notice to the others, through the agency of the International Bureau, of the applications which it regards as such . . . Two of the countries, whose accession to the Arrangement through this amendment was sought, responded differently. Austria then would have acceded, because its own indications of origin, 'Pilsen' and 'Budweis', would have always been protected . . . At the Conference of the Hague a similar proposal of the International Bureau did not fare any better. Four delegations opposed the further extension to the exception. They also opposed a Czechoslovakian proposal that the appellations of beer and mineral waters be treated like those concerning products of the vine. The obligatory character of definitions of appellations of origin communicated through the agency of the International Bureau by the country of origin was also objected to."[7]

The above attempts to revise the Madrid Arrangement already clarify the motives for concluding the subsequent Lisbon Agreement:

(1) To prevent the tribunals of any member state from holding an indication generic. In other words, no indication of origin should be exempt from protection because it is considered generic.
(2) To set up a system whereby protection was not decided by the member whose indication was the object of a dispute, but by the member from which the indication originated.

Both conditions are vital for understanding the Lisbon Agreement, as both limit the competence of national courts. National courts ("tribunals") should neither be entitled to hold an indication generic, nor should they be entitled to question the validity of an indication once that indication has been protected in the country of origin, communicated to the International Bureau and examined by the other countries.

III. The Versailles Peace Treaty 1919

The first agreement where such absolute form of protection was put to practice was the treaty of Versailles, which in Art. 275 obliged Germany, Austria, Hungary and Bulgaria:

"On condition of reciprocal treatment on the part of the Allied and Associated powers, to give binding force to the law or decisions of the country to which a regional appellation of products of the vine belongs. The tribunals are no longer free to decide that a regional appellation of spirits, for instance the name 'Cognac', is a generic or descriptive term, if by the law of the

---

[7] Ladas, Patents, Trademarks and Related Rights, Cambridge, Mass. 1975, 1592/1593.

country of origin (in the instance cited, France), or by its court's decisions, the appellation in question is a true appellation of origin belonging to the products of a specified region."[8]

With the attempts to revise the Madrid Arrangement and the Versailles Treaty, the protection of geographical indications was carried far out of the ambit of the concept of misconception and already some way towards absolute proprietary protection. Such absolute proprietary protection is also sought by bilateral treaties for protecting geographical indications.

IV. The Lisbon Agreement for the Protection of Appellations of Origin 1958

1. In General

The foregoing explanations on the regime for protecting geographical indications under the Paris Convention, the Madrid Arrangement and bilateral agreements are not only informative, but are essential for an understanding of the Lisbon Agreement. In particular, shortcomings of the preceding agreements and the attempts to remedy such perceived shortcomings give a clearer idea of the Lisbon Agreement and its interpretation.

The Lisbon Agreement came into force in 1966 with the original member states of Cuba, Czechoslovakia, France, Haiti, Israel, Mexico and Portugal. Subsequently, the following countries acceded to the Agreement: Hungary (1967), Italy (1968), Algeria (1972), Tunisia (1973), Bulgaria (1975), Burkina Faso (1975), Gabun (1975), Togo (1975), Congo (1977), the Czech Republic and Slovakia (1993), Costa Rica (1997), and Yugoslavia (1999). In total, the Agreement has a membership of 19 countries.

2. Outline of the Agreement

The Lisbon Agreement is meant to give better protection than the aforementioned agreements. But it is limited in its application to appellations of origin that are more narrowly defined than geographical indications in general. According to Art. 2 Lisbon Agreement, protection is granted to a "geographical name of a country, region or locality, which serves to designate a product originating therein, whose quality and characteristics are due exclusively or essentially to the geographical environment, including natural and human factors."

This excludes all geographical indications for industrial products from protection. On the other hand, a distinction is no longer made between wine products and other agricultural products, as was the case in the Madrid Arrangement. At the same conference in Lisbon 1958, enhanced protection was also afforded against the misleading use of geographical indications in general. The Paris Convention was amended by adding subsection 3 to Art. 10bis(3) in order to prohibit the use of misleading indications in commerce. The Madrid Arrangement was amplified in that not only false but also mis-

---

8 Ladas, Patents, Trademarks and Related Rights, Cambridge, Mass. 1975, 1597.

leading indications were included. Thereby, enhanced protection was also granted to geographical indications in general, even if only indirectly.

But while for indications of origin in general, protection under the Paris Convention and the Madrid Arrangement was only afforded under the general rules of unfair competition law, the protection under the Lisbon Agreement was of proprietary nature and works as follows:

"Every member state of the Paris Convention that also adheres to the agreement undertakes to protect in its own territory all appellations of origin of other member states for those products registered on the express condition that protection is also afforded in the home countries. The expression 'qualified' means that the right of an appellation of origin first of all needs to be recognised in the country of origin. The agreement thereby imposes on all member states a uniform set of rules, yet without separating this from national rules . . . Registration of an appellation of origin under the agreement can only be demanded by the country of origin. . . . Protection must thus be granted against all attacks of the exclusive rights given to those entitled to use the appellation, be it against the unlawful use . . ., be it against the fraudulent imitation of an appellation."[9]

The Lisbon Agreement thus regulates three particular issues: the procedure for obtaining protection, the rights conferred, and the conflict between marks and appellations of origin.

The Lisbon Agreement is complemented by the Regulations under the Lisbon Agreements that were last amended as of 1 April 2002.

The Lisbon Agreement, the Regulations and all working group sessions are in the French language only.

3. Statistics

Table 1   Appellations of origin registered under the Lisbon Agreement arranged by country of origin*

Country of origin of the AO	Number of registrations	Per cent of registrations	Accumulated number of registrations	Per cent of accumulated registrations
France	508	66,3	508	66,3
Czech Rep.	73	9,5	581	75,8
Bulgaria	49	6,4	630	82,2
Slovak Rep.	38	5,0	668	87,2
Hungary	28	3,7	696	90,9
Italy	26	3,4	722	94,3
Cuba	18	2,3	740	96,6
Algeria	7	0,9	747	97,5
Tunisia	7	0,9	754	98,4
Portugal	6	0,8	760	99,2
Mexico	5	0,7	765	99,9
Israel	1	0,1	766	100,0
TOTAL	**766**	**100**	**766**	**100,0**

Source: WIPO statistics on appellations of origin under the Lisbon Agreement.
* Countries that have not yet requested registration of appellations of origin are omitted in this Table.

[9] Actes de la Conference du Lisbonne 1958, Geneva 1963, 814/815.

Table 2 Protected products under the Lisbon Agreement

Product	Number of registrations	Per cent of registrations	Accumulated registrations	Per cent of accumulated registrations
Wines	470	61.4	470	61.4
Spirits	73	9.5	543	70.9
Agricultural products	51	6,7	594	77.6
Cheeses	50	6.5	644	84.1
Ornamental products	33	4.3	677	88.4
Tobacco and cigarettes	33	4.3	710	92.7
Miscellaneous	25	3.3	735	96.0
Mineral water	17	2.2	752	98.2
Beer and malt	14	1.8	764	100.0
	766	**100**	**766**	**100.0**

Source: WIPO statistics on appellations of origin under the Lisbon Agreement.

It is noticeable that certain countries only acceded to the Agreement in order to have specific products protected. This was, e.g. the case for Israel that acceded in order to receive protection for the "Jaffa" oranges. In the case of Cuba, all indications concern tobacco and cigarettes. And in the case of the Czech Republic, the special interest was the registration of mineral waters and beer.

4. Registration Procedure

a) In general

The registration procedure is regulated in great detail in Art. 5, the fundamental provision of the agreement. An application can only be made by a member state of the agreement, not by any individual or organisation:

> "It is indeed for each contracting country to decide, on grounds specific to it, which national authorities are to be involved in the application of the provisions of the Lisbon system. The experience of the International Bureau is that there are generally a number of such authorities. In France, for example, the authority in power to request an international registration under the Lisbon Agreement is the General Director for Competition, Consumers and Prevention of Fraud (DGCCRF), whereas the authority competent to receive notifications from the International Bureau is the National Institute of Industrial Property (INPI) and the authority able to grant to third parties established on its territory a maximum period of two years in accordance with Article 5(6) is the National Institute of Appellations of Origin (INAO)."[10]

---

[10] Mentioned in the WIPO document, LI-GT/1/2 of 10 May 2000, working group on the modification of the regulations under the Lisbon Agreement for the Protection of Appellations of Origin and Their International Registration.

The application by a member state has to be addressed to the International Bureau of the World Intellectual Property Organisation (WIPO) in Geneva and meet with certain formality requirements. The application has to specify the applying country, the application date, who is entitled to use the appellation, the product and product classification for which the appellation is used, the area of production and the provisions or decisions on which domestic registration is based. The application is then published by the International Bureau, and the other member states are duly notified of the application. The question to what extent other member states could refuse the appellation in their respective countries was intensely discussed in the sessions chaired by the Italian *Tullio Ascarelli*. While some countries, France and Italy in particular, wanted the right of refusal to be limited to certain conditions, e.g., the fact that the appellation had become generic in a country, the original proposal had not envisaged this, and ultimately, no such limitation was introduced. Therefore, all member states under the agreement have a right to refuse to protect another country's appellation of origin, yet are obliged to give specific reasons for such rejection. The country of origin has a right to judicial or administrative review of such decision. A rejection, however, is limited by two conditions. First, it can only be declared by "the administrations" of the receiving country, not by any court of law. Second, the rejection can only be declared within one year from the date of notification. In the latter respect, Art. 5(4) is very clear:

"Such declaration (of protection) can no longer be opposed by the administrations of the member states after the expiration of one year from [the receipt of the notification of registration]."

It is thus very clear that in the absence of a notification to the contrary, an appellation of origin duly registered with the International Bureau is afforded protection in all other member states without any limitations. And if an appellation afforded protection in the other member states has already been used by third parties in a member state prior to the date of international registration, the administration in this member state has the possibility of granting these third parties a period of up to two years to discontinue use, Art. 5(6).

WIPO mentions the following regarding refusals:

"Sixty-two refusals of protection, concerning 51 international registrations, have been entered in the national register. The grounds most frequently given for refusal by the authorities of the contracting countries are that the appellation of origin for which registration is sought conflicts with an earlier mark that is protected in the country concerned."[11]

b) Detailed contents of registration

In the course of the Lisbon Agreement's functioning, a number of differences in the practice of registration have emerged. This is so because the

---

[11] WIPO document LI-GT/1/2 of 10 May 2000.

Regulations are to some extent vague, and also because the WIPO's bureau does not regard itself competent to interpret these Regulations in any meaningful way. The following issues were brought to the attention of the member states in the course of the re-negotiation of the Regulations in 2000–2001.

(1) The indication as such

Although a definition of "appellation of origin" is given in Art. 2 as the geographical name of a country, region, or locality, which serves to designate a product originating therein, the question has emerged to what extent the application as such may also contain equivalent translations in other languages. An example for this would be the Budweiser indication. Here, the following four indications have been registered together with the translation:

(1) "CESKOBUDEJOVICKE PIVO /BUDWEISER BIER/BIERE DE CESKE BUDEJOVICE/BUDWEIS BEER"; (No. 49)
(2) "BUDEJOVICKE PIVO-BUDVAR/BUDWEISER BIER-BUDVAR/BIERE DE · BUDWEIS-BUDVAR/ BUDWEIS BEER-BUDVAR"; (No. 50)
(3) "BUDEJOVICKY BUDVAR/BUDWEISER BUDVAR"; (No. 51) and
(4) "BUDEJOVICKE PIVO/BUDWEISER BIER/BIERE DE BUDWEIS/BUDWEIS BEER"; (No. 52)

WIPO mentions that,

"Requesting authorities frequently give the name of the appellation of origin in the national language together with its translation into a certain number of other languages. The practice . . . seems pointless, however, in view of Article 3 of the Lisbon Agreement which stipulates that 'protection shall be ensured against any usurpation or imitation, even if (. . .) the appellation is used in translated form (. . .)." In other words, Article 3 of the Agreement means that an appellation of origin contained in an international registration is protected against any use in translation, even if that translation is not referred to in the international registration. Consequently, it is suggested that it should only be possible for the indication of the appellation of origin, as referred to in Rule 1(2)(iv) of the Regulations to be provided in the official language or languages of the country of origin. Nevertheless, it is undeniable that the translation of the name of the appellation of origin may constitute useful information for users of the Lisbon system and for third parties in general, particularly where the translation differs considerably from one language to another. In order to maintain such information in the framework of an international registration, the Regulations could provide the possibility for requesting authorities to furnish one or more translations of the appellation of origin, not as part of the indication of the appellation of origin as referred to in Rule 1(2)(iv), but as additional (optional) information. Such translations would appear under a separate heading on the application form. They would in no way be checked by the International Bureau."[12]

---

[12] WIPO document LI-GT/1/2 of 10 May 2000.

This suggestion has been taken up by the Regulation that in Rule 5 now distinguishes between mandatory contents (subsection (2)) and optional contents (subsection (3)). Under the mandatory contents, (iii) now mentions "the appellation of origin for which registration is sought, in the official language of the country of origin or, where the country of origin has more than one official language, in one or more of those official languages." Under subsection (3)(ii), it is optional to furnish "one or more translations of the appellation of origin, in as many languages as the competent authority of the country or origin wishes."

(2) Entities entitled to use the appellation

The Lisbon Agreement as such in Art. 5(1) mentions that "The registration of appellations of origin shall be effected . . . in the name of any natural persons or legal entities, public or private, having, according to their national legislation, the right to use such appellations." According to the opinion of the Milan Appeal Court in the Budweiser case,[13] this requires an indication of all the owners by name. In the case at issue, reference was made to "those organisations that in the region are engaged in the production of the products mentioned." No specific names of producers were given, however. Art. 5(1) Lisbon Agreement has to be read together with Art. 5(4) of the old Regulations. This provision requires a new international registration for "modifications relating to the country of origin, the owners, the appellation of origin or the product to which it applies." The practical consequence of the court's opinion would be that, e.g. in the case of Chianti, the complete name register of all owners of vineyards in that region had to be supplied for the appellation. This could be well over 500. Any change in ownership of even one of these vineyards, according to the Milan Court, would mean a complete re-registration of the appellation according to Art. 5(4) Regulations. This is neither practical nor could it have been the intention of the Agreement. The purpose of the Agreement was to ensure that those entitled to production were *identifiable* rather than *identified*. This has now been clarified by the Regulations and was already raised as an issue during the session of the working group:

> "The owner or owners of the right to use may be indicated in two ways only: either indication by name or a generic or collective indication. Where there are a number of owners of the right to use, it would not seem feasible to give a list of the names of the owners in the framework of the administration of the Lisbon system, since there may exist thousands of users of an appellation of origin (that is the case, for example, of the wine appellation of origin "Bordeaux") and Rule 5(4) requires, as it is apparently worded, that any modification relating to owners necessitates a new international registration. It may also be noted that the 'Council established by the Lisbon Agreement' (whose functions have been exercised by the Lisbon Union Assembly since the entry into force of the Stockholm Act) unanimously agree at its 5th session on

---

[13] Milan Appeal Court, 1 December 2000, 350 Rivista di Diritto Industriale, II, 112.

September 26, 1970, that, with regard to the designation of the owners of the right in an appellation of origin, it was not necessary that they be identified by name, but it was sufficient, following the practice already adopted by several offices, that the circle of owners be clearly specified . . . Except for the very marginal cases where there is a single user identified by name, the practice adopted currently by all the requesting authorities is to identify the owners of the right to use in a collective manner ('producers or groups of producers entitled to use the appellation of origin', 'association of producers entitled to use the appellation of origin', 'association for the defence of the appellation of origin', 'organisations which, in the region concerned, are engaged in the production of the product referred to', 'syndicates', 'product control association' or 'government'). It would thus seem that the owners of the right to use indicated in the application for international registration by the requesting authorities are those economic operators, whether public or private, to whom their domestic legislation has given the prerogative of authorising or designating those persons entitled to affix the appellation of origin concerned on the product concerned, and/or to verify that such persons comply with the applicable conditions of production, or any natural or legal person who complies with the conditions for protection as defined by the applicable texts."

Accordingly, the new Rule 5(2)(ii) now requires indication of "the holder or holders of the right to use the appellation of origin, designated collectively or, where collective designation is not possible, by name. Also the rules for modification have significantly changed, as is explained below.

5. Scope of Protection

Scope and contents of such right are regulated in Arts. 3, 5(6) and 6.

a) Variations and translations

Art. 3 provides that protection is not only afforded to the appellation as such, but also against the use of translations, or the use of the appellation in combination with additions such as "type", "manner", "imitation", or the like. It is interesting to note that the Czechoslovakian delegation was particularly interested in having the appellation "Pils" also protected against variations such as "Pilsner" or "Pilsen", and was assured that the provision did indeed extend to such variance.[14] Now that under the 2002 rules variants or translations can no longer be registered as such, it is necessary to address the problem to what extent they might be protected nonetheless. In several cases the issue of what can be considered a translation has come up. In the Portuguese Budweiser case, the Supreme Court held as follows:

". . . This can be understood to the effect that each location may be called by more than one name, without this necessarily meaning that they are synonyms. One should, for example, call attention to the Ilhas Malvinas or the Falklands, respectively. To say that one geographical designation is a translation of another designation of the same region can mean nothing less than they are treated as synonymous expressions. What is of interest here is to take into account that

---

[14] Actes de Lisbonne 1958, 834.

the expressions simply designate the same region, or that some of these expressions may now no longer be officially used."[15]

Again in a Budweiser case, the New Zealand Court of Appeal reached the opposite conclusion:

> "Contrary to claims throughout the evidence that 'Budweiser' is a translation of Budejovicky, it is not. It is another name for the same place used by people who speak a different language. It is no more a translation than Aotearoa is a translation of New Zealand."[16]

The view taken by the New Zealand Appeal Court is perhaps a misunderstanding on what is meant by translation. The Falklands are no more or no less a translation of the Malvinas than Aotearoa is of New Zealand. Yet a translation is exactly meant to confer the same meaning into another language, and this is exactly what these different expressions do. Linguistically speaking, the German Neuseeland might be a translation of "New Zealand", while Aix-en-Chapelle is not a translation of the German town of Aachen. Rather, Aachen is a vulgarisation of Aix. And St. Petersburg is definitely not a translation of Leningrad (nor vice versa), yet there should be little doubt that protection should apply to both, and due regard should be taken of the right owner's interest to use the name that in the language of the public of a certain area is the more common one.

b) Appellations deemed generic

No less important is the provision of Art. 6 that takes Art. 4 Madrid Arrangement one step further. Not only wine products, but all appellations of origin duly registered with the International Bureau and not opposed within one year "may not be considered having become generic for as long as they are protected as an appellation of origin in the country of origin". The Protocols of the Lisbon Agreement give the following explanation for this provision:

> "The General Assembly holds it necessary to regulate this case explicitly. After all, there could be opportunities where member states might wish to find exceptions to this fundamental rule that an appellation of origin once registered could never again be considered as generic".[17]

In other words, because member states could be tempted to regard appellations of origin as generic even after the one year period for objection has expired, Art. 6 had to be drafted in the most explicit terms possible. In this respect, attention should be drawn to an Italian Supreme Court decision that had to interpret this provision.[18] The case concerned the appellation

---

[15] Portuguese Supreme Court, 23 January 2001, 34 IIC 682, 683 (2003) – "Budweiser III".

[16] New Zealand High Court, *Anheuser-Busch v. Budweiser Budvar National Corporation*, 19 September 2002, paragraph 16.

[17] Actes de Lisbonne 1958, 838.

[18] Italian Supreme Court, 3 April 1996, [1998] European Trademark Reports 169 – "Pilsen Urquell".

"Pilsen", registered as an international appellation of origin under the Lisbon Agreement on 22 November 1967 and published in March 1968. The exact appellation is "Plzen", and the given translations are "Pilsen Pils", "Pilsener", and "Pilsner". An Italian brewery had inserted the word "Pilsener" on its product labels, and was sued by the Czech undertaking Pilsener Urquell, an enterprise entitled to use the appellation of origin as specified under the Lisbon Agreement. While the Italian Supreme Court took note of Art. 6 Lisbon Agreement, it held the provision only as a presumption, not an unchallengeable right:

"The owner of such a right, while not being in possession of the unchallengeable right which the appellant claims (against the literal meaning of the words of the above-cited Article 6 of the agreement) can nonetheless rely, as a consequence of the registration, on a presumption of legitimacy in its use."

The Italian Supreme Court has reiterated this position in the Budweiser II decision:

"The registration in question, as the Supreme Court has already clarified (Case No. 10587 of 1996) can only consist of a presumption of the legitimacy of the use of such domination. However, the judge can overrule this presumption in favour of someone who has alleged and proven a better right. This is exactly what the courts have done from the first one onwards. Most importantly, the judge correctly has examined the question of the missing geographical link. . . . In fact, the lower court has clarified that the characteristics of the beer in question do no depend on natural factors or at least those linked to the geographical area of production, as it may well be produced elsewhere."[19]

This interpretation is open to question. In interpreting Art. 6 Lisbon Agreement, the comparison with Art. 4 Madrid Arrangement is of particular importance. Art. 4 Madrid Arrangement gives the domestic courts clear jurisdiction in deciding whether an appellation has become generic or not:

"The tribunals of each country have to decide which are the appellations that by reason of their generic character escape from the provisions of the present arrangement; however the regional appellations of origin of wine products are not included in the reservation specified by this article."

When considering that with Art. 6 the Lisbon Agreement meant to extend the unchallengeable nature of wine products as conferred under the Madrid Arrangement to all appellations of origin duly registered under the Lisbon Agreement, it becomes clear that Art. 6 Lisbon Agreement has to be interpreted literally: the agreement was concluded particularly because Art. 4 Madrid Arrangement was deemed unsatisfactory for products other than wine products. It was considered unsatisfactory because the tribunals of each country had the possibility of deciding whether an appellation had become generic or not. It was exactly these shortcomings that Art. 6 Lisbon

---

[19] Italian Supreme Court, 21 May 2002, 34 IIC 676 – "Budweiser III".

Agreement was meant to remedy. Thus, the Italian Supreme Court would be correct in its interpretation if the plaintiff had based its arguments on Art. 4 Madrid Arrangement. Under this provision, beer products are indeed subject to the scrutiny of domestic courts in determining to what extent the appellation has become generic. This line of argument, however, is not open when it comes to Art. 6 Lisbon Agreement. Here, protection is absolute, and domestic courts are in no position to merely regard registration as *prima facie* evidence. The Italian Supreme Court seems to make a distinction between whether the appellation of origin in question was already generic at the time of registration or has subsequently become so. Art. 6 Lisbon Agreement governs the case where the appellation has become generic subsequent to registration, by stipulating that no court has the power to hold so. But even if the appellation was considered generic in Italy at the time of international registration, this gives the court no jurisdiction over the case. Art. 5 Lisbon Agreement clearly states that only the "administrations" of each member state can reject an appellation of origin from another member state (e.g., because it is considered generic), and they can only do so within one year. Neither of these conditions was met in the Italian case. Nor is it possible to argue that the courts can exercise jurisdiction because the national administration only undertakes a registration without examination. While this may be so in some countries with respect to patents or trade marks (e.g., in Italy or France), the Lisbon Agreement clearly requires the national administration to undertake a substantive examination as to the registrability of the appellation of origin. Such examination has to be conducted within one year, and in the absence of any action taken by the national administration, no court can challenge the appellation after one year has elapsed. The Milan first instance court in the aforementioned Pilsen decision was thus correct in holding that use of the term "Pilsener" by a third party was an infringement of the appellation of origin "Pilsen". The issue of national jurisdiction over the invalidation of appellations registered under the Lisbon Agreement is further elaborated under 6(5) below.

c) Conflicts between an appellation and a trade mark

Finally, Art. 5(6) Lisbon Agreement addresses the conflict between a registered appellation of origin and third parties having used such appellation in one or more of the member states prior to such registration.

As mentioned above, this provision tries to resolve the conflict between a subsequently registered appellation of origin and a previously used trade mark which conflicts with the former. The user of such mark is required to cease such use once the conflicting appellation of origin is registered. The provision does not mention any cancellation of a registration, as the question of registration is not dealt with at all. It is therefore not easy to interpret what the provision of Art. 5(6) had in mind, in particular because the Conference protocols are silent on the matter. One could of course invoke none-use if the owner of a mark registered prior to the registration of a conflicting appellation of origin may no longer be entitled to the use of the mark. This train of thought encounters some difficulties, however. For one, it requires the Lisbon Agreement to be either directly applicable or to require a corresponding provision under national law. Direct applicability is already difficult to argue because of the somewhat ambiguous character of the provision as such. It reads:

"If an appellation which has been granted protection in a given country pursuant to notification of its international registration has already been used by third parties in that country from a date prior to such notification, the competent office of the said country shall have the right to grant to third parties a period not exceeding two years to terminate such use, on condition that it advises the International Bureau accordingly during the three months following the expiration of the period of one year provided for in paragraph (3) above".

The provision in fact does little to clarify the conflict between a mark and an appellation of origin, because it never refers to a registered mark, and it does not clearly indicate how to solve the conflict if the prior user has already obtained some protection due to such use. Ladas interprets the provision as follows:

"Persons who have been using an appellation of origin as a generic term may ask for a term of two years at the end of which they must discontinue such use. This tends to imply that if such private persons do not ask for the term of two years they would have to discontinue immediately any generic use of the appellation of origin. This result would not be consistent with the administration's right of refusal within one year. Certainly this does not apply in the case where the alleged appellation of origin does not comply with the definition of Art. 2 or in the case where such appellation infringes vested trade mark rights. Furthermore, in many countries a treaty itself cannot affect private rights, and in any case, it would be up to the courts rather than to the administration to resolve a conflict between the attempted international registration of an appellation of origin and pre-existing private rights."[20]

That Art. 5(6) did not envisage an expropriation of trade mark owners is also indicated by examining it in light of comparable provisions in EC Regulations. The EC Wine Regulation of 1989[21] solves the conflict in Art. 40(3) by granting the owner of registered marks that conflict with appellations of origin a grace period up to 31 December 2002. Only thereafter would further use be prohibited. However, even before this period, the trade mark owner cannot object to the use of the mark as an appellation of origin. Unlike the Lisbon Agreement, the conflict between a registered mark and a protected appellation of origin is directly regulated. The Regulation's preamble also leaves little doubt that in the end of the day, a conflicting trade mark has to be surrendered. This is different in the EC Regulation on Geographical Indications of Agricultural Products, etc. of

---

[20] Ladas, Patents, Trademarks and Related Rights, Cambridge, Mass. 1975, 1604/05.
[21] Regulation No. 2392/89 of 24 July 1989, EC O.J.L 232/13 of 9 August 1989.

1992[22] that in Art. 14(2) allows a continued use of a previously registered mark as long as there are no grounds for cancellation under the Trade Mark Directive.[23]

As a result, one can conclude that those entitled to use a registered appellation of origin may not be in a position to demand the expropriation of proprietary positions already achieved prior to the registration of the appellation. If at all, Art. 5(6) only requires third parties to cease the use of the appellation as a mark in cases where such use is not based on a proprietary right. On the other hand, the owner of a conflicting trade mark should not be in a position to request cessation of use of the appellation of origin, either. Art. 5(6) Lisbon Agreement makes clear that an appellation of origin takes precedence over the "simple" use of the appellation as a mark. It is no basis for requesting expropriation, yet if the wording is anything to go by, appellations of origin shall take precedence over marks. This would lead to the inevitable conclusion that the owner of a trade mark obtained prior to the registration of an appellation of origin may not invoke the trade mark right against use of the appellation of origin as an appellation of origin rather than a mark. This conclusion is also indicated by a comparison with the EC Regulation on Geographical Indications, and of the mechanism as provided in Art. 5 in general: if a registered appellation of origin conflicts with a prior trade mark, it is up to the administrative authorities to refuse protection, just as would be the case in systems where trade mark applications are substantially examined for conflicts with prior rights.

6. Judicial Review

This already leads to the last and perhaps least explored facet of the Lisbon Agreement: to what extent can the use of a registered appellation of origin be made subject to judicial review and scrutiny. Can the courts of other member states for an indeterminate period of time scrutinise the international registration of an appellation of origin and refuse protection if they believe that the appellation did not meet the requirements for registrability, has subsequently become generic, conflicts with other marks, etc.? The text of the agreement does not necessarily give a definite answer to this question. Rather, a solution must be based on the structure of the whole Agreement, the historical context between the Madrid Arrangement and the Lisbon Agreement, the Protocols of the Preparatory Conference of the Agreement and the revised Rules. In this respect the following should be distinguished:

(1) The question to what extent the courts can find that an internationally registered appellation of origin can become generic after registration has already been addressed above. A comparison between the corresponding provision of the Madrid Arrangement and Art. 6 Lisbon Agreement makes this unequivocally clear. While under the Madrid Arrangement, national

---

[22] Regulation No. 2081/92 of 14 July 1992, EC O.J.L 208/1 of 24 July 1992.
[23] Directive No. 89/104 of 21 December 1988, EC O.J.L 40/1 of 11 February 1989.

courts have the power to refuse protection to geographical indications if considered generic, the Arrangement makes an exemption in this respect for wine products. Already under the Madrid Arrangement, the courts may not hold geographical indications for wine products generic, regardless of public perception. The Lisbon Agreement carries this exemption further to all those appellations duly registered under the Lisbon Agreement. Thus, even though the public in a particular country might regard an appellation as a generic term, the courts of this country cannot deny protection to this appellation. Here, the concept of appellations of origin as proprietary rights clearly takes precedence over the concept of protection by way of unfair competition principles. Art. 6 Lisbon Agreement only concerns the case where appellations have become generic over time. If an appellation is considered generic from the beginning, the national authorities of that country must deny protection within one year. It is submitted that the courts are not empowered to subsequently invalidate an appellation due to its being generic. But see also below (5).

(2) It is equally clear that it is up to the courts to decide to what extent indications similar to those of the registered appellations of origin constitute an infringement under Art. 3 Lisbon Agreement. This is an issue that may well be raised in infringement procedures, and the courts are called upon to settle such matters.

(3) Art. 7 Lisbon Agreement obliges every member to protect an internationally registered geographical indication by domestic law as long as it is protected as an appellation of origin in the country where it originates. This provision seems to indicate that both the administration as well as the courts of any given member state are competent to inquire to what extent an internationally registered appellation is still protected in its country of origin. In doing so, the legal and factual situation in the country of origin rather than the country where the court or administration is situated would have to be examined.

(4) This leaves the question to what degree the courts in any given member state may determine not only if and to what extent the appellation of origin is still protected in its home country, but also whether the appellation of origin indeed satisfies the criteria set out under Art. 2 and thus qualifies as an appellation of origin under the agreement. That the courts can do so has been held by three decisions: by the Appeal Court Douai in 1976,[24] by the above-mentioned decision of the Lisbon District Court of 11 March 1995, and the decision of the Italian Supreme Court. That the courts cannot do so has been held by two decisions of the Israel Supreme Court,[25] the Bulgarian Supreme Court[26] and by two French

---

[24] Appeal Court Douai, 30 June 1976, Gazette du Palais 1976, 648 – "Pilsheim".

[25] Israel Supreme Court, 10 January 1990, 22 IIC 255 [1991] – "Budweiser"; Israel Supreme Court, 13 September 1992, 25 IIC 589 – "Budweiser II".

[26] Bulgarian Supreme Court, 7 January 2001, Civil Case 333/2000.

academics.[27] Other academics who have written on the Lisbon Agreement do not mention the problem at all.[28] Given the importance of this question, this is somewhat surprising.

The Appeal Court Douai was primarily concerned with the interpretation of Art. 5(6) Lisbon Agreement, the conflict between a registered appellation and a similar indication. However, the court made clear that it did not regard the registered appellation "Pilsen" as worthy of protection in view of its widely generic use. In his comment, Plaisant argues that this consideration is mistaken: "Rather, the legislature or the negotiators of the [Lisbon Agreement] had to reserve the rights of third parties that use an appellation of origin that may be generic but can be revived: the case is quite common for cheeses".[29] In fact, in the last twenty years the European legislature and negotiators have lobbied very hard for a re-transformation of generic indications back to appellations of origin. Not least the Italians are huge beneficiaries of these attempts, if one considers the success of EC negotiators in reestablishing the indication "Chianti" as one for wine originating in the Chianti region, even in those parts of the world where it was considered generic, e.g., Australia. The French court was thus incorrect in denying protection to the internationally registered appellation "Pilsen" merely because it might have been considered generic in France: The French administration did not refuse protection to the international appellation "Pils" within one year, thereby indicating that it was willing to accept "Pilsen" as a valid appellation of origin incontestable in court.

Both the Lisbon and Italian Supreme Courts denied protection to the appellation "Budweiser" because beer was not a product that could qualify for an appellation of origin. The Lisbon court in this respect merely states that "the expressions 'Budweiser' or 'Bud' do not consist of a geographic denomination of a region or locality that can be used to designate any good originating from that place . . . Accordingly, when the registrations of the appellations of origin . . . were granted to the defendant, something was registered that did not meet the minimum legal requirements to be protected

---

[27] Devlétian, case comment on Appeal Court Douai, 76 Revue internationale de la propriété industrielle 1976, 178 (RIPIA); Plaisant, case comment on Appeal Court Douai, Gazette du Palais 1977, 233.

[28] E.g. Vivez, L'arrangement de Lisbonne du 31 Octobre 1958, La Semaine Juridique (Doctrine) 2198 (1968); Ronga, L'arrangement de Lisbonne du 13 Octobre 1958, Revue Trimestrielle 1967, 425; Beier, Geographische Herkunftsbezeichnungen und Ursprungsangaben, GRUR Int. 1968, 69; Knaak, The protection of geographical indications according to the TRIPs Agreement, in: Beier/Schricker, From GATT to TRIPs, IIC Studies 18, Weinheim 1995; Escudero, International protection of geographical indications and developing countries, www.southcentre.org/publications; Faure, Le droit des appellations d'origine, Paris 1974; Plaisant/Auby, Le droit des appellations d'origine, Litect 1974; Bäumer, The international protection of geographical indications, WIPO publication Geneva 1992.

[29] Plaisant, Gazette du Palais 1977, 234.

as appellations of origin and consequently should never be registered as such . . ." The court does not examine the question to what extent it is entitled to decide this matter. The Appeal Court Milan declares that the appellations of origin "Budweiser" and "Bud" could not have been registered as they did not qualify as appellations of origin, and because the plaintiff A.B. (Anheuser-Busch) already enjoyed prior conflicting rights based on an unregistered, but well-known trade mark. While the court examines at length to what extent beer can qualify as an appellation of origin and why the circle of those entitled to use the appellation was amended at a certain time, it never questions its competence to deny protection to a valid appellation of origin. The one court that did examine this question at length was the Israel Supreme Court in the two above-mentioned decisions. Particularly because the Israeli decisions deal with the interpretation of the Lisbon Agreement at length do the decisions deserve some mention. The case arose because A.B. wanted to register its trade marks "Bud" and "Budweiser" in Israel, while also petitioning to cancel the internationally registered appellations of origin by B.B. (Budweiser Budvar) because it did not qualify as an appellation of origin. The registrar denied this request, while the Court of First Instance decided in favour of A.B., arguing that an internationally registered appellation of origin should not be treated different from an appellation of origin registered under the Israeli Appellations of Origin Act. The Supreme Court held in favour of B.B., because a foreign appellation of origin protected under the Lisbon Agreement received its validity not under the Israeli Appellations of Origin Act, but by virtue of protection in the country of origin.

"In this way, expression is given to the basic principle of the Lisbon Agreement, pursuant whereto once a foreign appellation is registered, 'it cannot be regarded in that country as if it were the name of a type, so long as it is protected as an appellation of origin in the country of origin' (section 6 of the Lisbon Agreement). This principle appears expressly in the Appellations of Origin Law, which provides that 'the validity of the registration of an appellation of origin which is made pursuant to a notice received pursuant to section 17 is the same as its validity in the country of origin'. It follows from this that if in the country of origin the law is – like the law in Israel – that after registration the appellation of origin may not be opposed on the ground that the registration from the start was not lawful, because the appellation is not an appellation of origin but a mark of provenance or type only, then also in Israel there is no longer any possibility of opposing the appellation of origin on this ground. In the appeal before us, the respondent has not claimed that the appellation of origin of the appellant is invalid in Czechoslovakia or that it may be opposed in Czechoslovakia on the ground that the registration thereof was at the outset unlawful because it is not an appellation of origin but a mark of provenance or type only, since it is clear that by way of direct opposition, the claim may not be raised before the Registrar that the registration of the foreign appellation should be struck out on the ground only that, at the time of registration thereof, it was not an appellation of origin. This result is called for by the policy upon which the Appellations of Origin Law and the Lisbon Agreement are based. This policy was the giving of comprehensive protection to a foreign appellation of origin and giving it the status in the foreign state which it enjoyed in the original state (see Tilmann, 'Die

Geographische Herkunftsangabe' 415 (1976)). Only if in the original state the appellation is no longer protected will it cease to be protected in the foreign state. In this matter, it is not made clear, either in the Appellations of Origin Law or in the Lisbon Agreement, whether the decision in the foreign country relating to the absence of protection in the original country must be based on the decision of the Registrar or the courts in the country of origin that the appellation is not protected therein (direct opposition in the country of origin) or whether it is sufficient that, in the opinion of the foreign state, there is a ground on the strength of which the appellation of origin may be deleted in the country of origin (indirect opposition in the foreign state). We have no need to resolve this question in the matter before us, because the claim that the appellation of origin of the appellant was not protected in the country of origin, because there is a ground for opposing the same in the country of origin, was not raised before us. Indeed, if the foreign appellation is protected in the country of origin, it must be protected also in the foreign country.

. . .

In my opinion, if it is not possible to oppose the actual validity of a registered appellation of origin directly before the Registrar, it is not possible to oppose the validity of the registered appellation of origin indirectly in the court. The Israeli legislature wished to protect a registered appellation of origin and opened the door to direct opposition thereof on limited grounds. I do not think that it left open the possibility of circumventing its will by way of indirect opposition and thus facilitating damage to the registered appellation of origin on additional grounds (see Benson, 'Toward a New Treaty for the Protection of Geographical Indications', 1987 Industrial Property 127, 133).

It should not be assumed that, in the case before us, that which cannot be obtained directly can be obtained indirectly. This matter is particularly prominent in the case of a foreign appellation of origin. The objective of the Appellations of Origin Law against the background of the Lisbon Agreement – was to give a foreign appellation in Israel the same degree of protection given to it in the country of origin. If we allow the courts in Israel to revoke a foreign appellation of origin protected in the country of origin, we shall deviate sharply from the purpose of the law and from Israel's international commitment. This purpose and commitment will be met if a court in Israel will only cancel a foreign appellation of origin or make a declaration as to the revocation thereof on those grounds upon which the Registrar himself could do so, that is to say, only if the foreign appellation of origin is not protected in the country of origin. Thus, we give protection in Israel to appellations of origin which arise outside Israel. Thus also, we ensure the protection outside Israel of Israeli appellations of origin.

24. The district court, as we have seen, reached the opposite conclusion. It seems to me that the mistake is to be found in the fact that it regarded the case before us as a case Which turned on a question of the jurisdiction of the civil court. As I have noted, the civil court has jurisdiction to consider the validity of the appellation of Origin. The question is not one of jurisdiction, but of a ground. The question is, on what grounds may the competent court invalidate an appellation of origin? The existence of general jurisdiction does not confer permission to invalidate appellations of origin on any ground whatsoever. . . . We have already indicated the clear policy of the legislature – following the Lisbon Agreement – to give protection in Israel to foreign appellations of origin to the same extent as that foreign appellation of origin is protected in the country of origin. The giving of the possibility to the court in Israel to decide that a foreign appellation of origin, valid in the country of origin, is not valid in Israel will be contrary to the policy of the legislature and the Lisbon Agreement, the

fulfilment of which is the objective which every commentator must gain in interpreting the Appellations of Origin Law."[30]

In a rehearing, the Supreme Court affirmed the aforementioned decision in the clearest of terms:

"1. In the Lisbon Agreement, the state of Israel assumed international obligations to the agreement's member states, so that one must assume that, when the appellations of origin law was enacted, the legislature sought to give validity to such obligations. Any legal interpretation must therefore be in accordance with the Lisbon Agreement.

2. It is the principle of the Lisbon Agreement that its members mutually recognize and honor the property rights reserved, provided that such rights have been recognized by the states and are duly registered. Such protection in favor of a foreign state is absolute and exclusive with the only exception provided for in Sec. 5 (3) of the agreement, which allows the declaration that a specific appellation of origin cannot be protected. The reasons for this can be that the alleged appellation is only an indication of provenance or that the person claiming protection is not entitled to use it.

3. The only reason to strike out the registration of a foreign appellation of origin is that the appellation is no longer protected in the country of origin or has ceased to be protected there."[31]

The plaintiff A.B. even had the temerity to petition the Israel Supreme Court a third time in the request for obtaining registration of the Budweiser mark. Unsurprisingly, it failed again.[32]

In other words, it is the clear position of the Israel Supreme Court that once the period of one year has elapsed from the international registration date, there are only limited grounds for challenging an international appellation of origin registered under the Lisbon Agreement. In effect, there is only one: that the appellation is no longer protected in the country of origin. No one can be heard with the argument that the appellation does not properly meet the requirements of Art. 2 (definition) or that it has become generic. These arguments cannot be raised in the other member states of the agreement, but only in the home country of the appellation. Only there can a challenge be raised to the effect that the appellation does not properly qualify as such, that it has become generic, or that those given the right to use the application are in fact incorrectly named.

A similar line of argument is taken by those academics who have dealt with the question. Thus, Plaisant writes: "Once an appellation is registered with WIPO and the country where protection is sought has not exercised its right to refuse protection within one year, it seems that no judge can subsequently do so".[33]

Finally, the Protocols on the Lisbon Agreement are equivocal on the question of judicial review. The only remark that can be found was made by

---

[30] Israel Supreme Court, 10 January 1990, 22 IIC 261–263 – "Budweiser".

[31] Israel Supreme Court, 13 December 1992, 25 IIC 589 [1994] – "Budweiser II".

[32] Reported in 28 IIC 596 [1997] – "Budweiser III".

[33] Plaisant, Gazette du Palais 1977, 234.

the delegation of Israel which insisted on a definition of appellations of origin in Art. 2 in order for such definition to be "invoked before the courts so that they should be able to decide if an appellation, although registered, would really qualify as an appellation of origin".[34] Even this statement does not clarify, however, which courts should be competent to decide. According to the view taken by the courts of Israel and the above-mentioned academic authors, most certainly the courts in the country of origin should be competent to decide if an appellation qualifies as such. There is no doubt that the lawfulness of the appellation "Budweiser" can be challenged before the Czech courts. However, it cannot be challenged before the courts in the other member states of the Lisbon Agreement. Only this interpretation is consistent with the combined efforts of the Paris Convention and the Lisbon Agreement towards an improved protection of appellations of origin. It is exactly the principle of incontestability that gives the Lisbon Agreement its true meaning and ensures that protection is indeed homogeneous in all member states and not gradually chipped away by the courts after the one-year opposition period has expired.

(5) The above analysis has shown that only the court of the country where the appellation has its origin can be entitled (under national law) to invalidate the appellation. It would be alien to the whole fabric and framework of the Lisbon Agreement to hold otherwise. Still, in the past the courts of two countries (Italy and Portugal) have ordered the invalidation of appellations of origin at least for their territory. Presumably due to pressure from these countries, the regulations under the Lisbon Agreement have been amended as of 1 April 2002 and now contain Rule 16 on invalidation. The relevant section reads:

> "(1) Where the effects of an international registration are invalidated in a contracting country and the invalidation is no longer subject to appeal, the invalidation shall be notified to the International Bureau by the competent authority of that contracting country."

The invalidation does not refer to a declaration of refusal or a judicial confirmation thereof, as in the latter respect Rules 9-11 apply. The *traveaux préparatoires* on this issue are relatively insubstantial, given the importance of this point. The WIPO report[35] simply states this:

> "(70) It has come to the knowledge of the International Bureau that a certain number of decisions rendered by the courts of contracting states (in particular Portugal and Italy) have been 'invalidated', for their territory, the effects of the registration of an international appellation of origin that was not the object of a refusal of protection under Art. 5.3. . . . (71) . . . It is certainly not up to the International Bureau of the WIPO to determine the correctness of the decisions

---

[34] Actes de Lisbonne 1958, 832.
[35] Questions for the Working Group on the Modification of the Regulations under the Lisbon Agreement for the Protection of Appellations of Origin and Their International Registration, Geneva, 10–13 July 2000, Document LI/GT/1/2 of 12 July 2000.

of administrative or judicial authorities of the member states of the Lisbon Agreement regarding their territory. Yet the International Bureau is not in a position to comply with such requests in the absence of any rule in the arrangement or in the rules that would allow to enter such a notification."

And subsequently, the following comment was made:

"(83) The Secretariat, while stressing that it was a controversial issue, said that the fact that a national administration could not issue a refusal of protection with respect to an international registration of an appellation of origin should not prevent the protection thus granted from being contested subsequently before a court (subject, in particular, to Article 6 of the Agreement, under which an appellation of origin accepted for protection in a country could not be held to have become generic in that country as long as it was protected as such in its country of origin). Consequently, machinery permitting the International Bureau to enter such invalidation in the International Register (particularly with a view to informing third parties) should be expressly provided for in the Regulations."

Also mentioned is the particular interest in this issue of the European Community Trade Mark Association, a particularly vested interest group when it comes to the conflict between trade mark and geographical indications. It is noteworthy that no country seems to have expressed any firm opinion on this point (France expressed reservations in the beginning), despite the fact that it is one of the core aspects of the Agreement.

V. The TRIPS Agreement

Unlike the above-mentioned agreements, the TRIPS Agreement comprises a relatively large membership and in the field of geographical indications had to accommodate the most diverse interests. Fault lines were in particular between European countries with a relatively strong tradition of protecting geographical indications, and New World countries such as the US and Australia, where a good number of (European) geographical indications have become or are considered generic. The TRIPS provisions Arts. 22–24 are thus largely the result of watered-down proposals from the European Union and Switzerland. In view of the different interests involved, the TRIPS provisions are highly convoluted, difficult to read and marked by far-reaching exemptions. Similar to the Madrid Arrangement, the TRIPs Agreement makes a distinction between ordinary indications and those used for wines and spirits. The latter enjoy increased protection under Art. 23. Art. 22(1) defines geographical indications as "indications which identify a good as originating in the territory of a member, or a region or locality in that territory, where a given quality, reputation or other characteristic of the good is essentially attributable to its geographical origin." This definition is much broader than the one used in the Lisbon Agreement and also applies to industrial or artisan products that enjoy a particular reputation due to manufacturing know-how, e.g., Meissen Porcelain, Salzburger Mozartkugeln or Sheffield Steel.

The following features of protection are noteworthy:

(1) Protection of geographical indications is non proprietary in principle and granted only against use "which misleads the public as to the geographical origin of the good". The perception of the general public in the country where protection is sought is thus relevant for protection. In this respect, protection follows the system introduced by the Madrid Arrangement. To the extent that the public in a certain country does regard a geographical indication as generic, no misconception can occur. Another ground for refusing protection would be the fact that the geographical indication is not protected as such in its home country, Art. 24(9).

(2) Protection beyond misconception or unfair competition is only granted to wines and spirits. Here, protection has to be granted even though this would not give rise to confusion. An exception to this provision is provided in Art. 24(4) for prior users in good faith, or in the absence of good faith for prior use of at least 10 years preceding the conclusion of the TRIPs Agreement.

(3) The TRIPs Agreement attaches considerable consideration to the problem of trade marks conflicting with geographical indications. According to Art. 22(3), trade marks which contain or consist of geographical indications, the use of which is misleading as to the true place of origin of the goods, have to be refused or invalidated. If use of the trade mark is for wines and spirits, the mark has to be refused or invalidated, even in the absence of misconception, Art. 23(2). Again, an exception is provided for trade marks that have been applied for or registered in good faith or have been acquired through use in good faith prior to the TRIPs Agreement taking effect, Art. 24(5). Member states may further limit requests for invalidation of a trade mark to a period of five years, provided registration has not been effected in bad faith, Art. 24(7).

(4) Finally, Art. 24(6) provides for the "Champagne" exception. Members are not obliged to protect a geographical indication (be it for wines or other goods) "for which the relevant indication is identical with the term customary in common language as the common name for such goods or services in the territory of that member." In other words, if Champagne is used as a generic term for sparkling wine in a member state, this member state is not obliged to protect Champagne as a geographical indication. Other examples might include "Pils" for a certain type of beer or "Dresdner Stollen" for a certain type of Christmas cake.

By and large, the TRIPs Agreement follows the principles and limits of protection laid down by the Madrid Arrangement: protection against misleading use and confined to indications that have not become generic. What goes beyond the Madrid Arrangement are the detailed rules on the conflict between trade marks and geographical indications, and the obligation "to enter into negotiations aimed at increasing the protection of individual geographical indications", including a general review after two years and further negotiations in the Council for Trade Related Aspects of Intellectual Property Rights (Arts. 23(4), 24(1), (2)).

After the conclusion of the TRIPs Agreement, a number of efforts have been made to expand protection for geographical indications:

The proposal tabled by the European Union centres around a register for geographical indications administered by the WTO Secretariat. Member states would be responsible for supplying geographical indications to the Secretariat, and protection would become automatic in other member states unless objections were raised within one year. The procedure thereby closely resembles the one under the Lisbon Agreement. Proposals by the U.S. and Japan also called for an international register, yet without any binding effect on WTO member states.[36]

Calls for an increased protection of geographical indications on an international level have also been voiced by the Czech Republic (better protection for beer),[37] Slovenia ("Lipizzaner Horses"), India ("Basmati Rice"), and Thailand ("Jasmine Rice").

As yet, no solution is in sight that would find a majority among WTO member states.

It should also be noted that geographical indications have now become part of the negotiations for a planned regional free trade agreement between the EU and the MERCOSUR.

C. Bilateral Treaties

It has been mentioned above that protection afforded to foreign appellations of origin, rather than being proprietary, was mainly afforded on the basis of unfair competition law. While this by and large proved satisfactory from the perspective of consumer protection, it helped very little against exploitation of reputation in the cast of well-known appellations such as "Champagne" and "Cognac". This was particularly vexing for France, as the main "offenders", particularly Austria, Germany and Italy, at that time were not members of the Madrid Arrangement. In fact, the wish to continue using Champagne and Cognac was one of the main reasons for Germany not acceding to the Madrid Agreement. Yet, fate was on the side of France when it could dictate a couple of provisions into the Versailles Agreement of 1919 (see above).

In subsequent bilateral treaties, <u>the principle was established that the law of the country of origin should govern the question of whether a designation was a true indication of origin belonging to the producers in a specified</u>

---

[36] Reported in World Intellectual Property Report May 2000, 157.
[37] Reported in World Intellectual Property Report, January 2000, 7.

region or whether it could be treated as generic or descriptive. Treaties were entered into between France and Finland, Norway, Czechoslovakia, Poland, Latvia and Belgium Luxembourg. A particular agreement with England was not so urgent because England was a party to the Madrid Arrangement. The French–Swiss Agreement of 1928 covered the two appellations "Cognac" and "Armagnac". The other country that France was particularly concerned about, Italy, acceded to the Madrid Arrangement in 1951. In addition, Italy joined the Lisbon Agreement in 1968, after having strengthened domestic protection for appellations of origin by means of legislation.

Under an exchange of letters between the French and U.S. authorities in December 1970 and January 1971, France agreed to prohibit the sale in France and export from France of products bearing the appellation "Bourbon" and "Bourbon Whisky" to designate any whisky or blend of whiskies unless made in the United States, and the U.S. agree to prohibit the use of the appellations "Cognac", "Armagnac" and "Calvados" for anything other than French products having the right to these appellations by virtue of French legislation.

In recent years, the EC has concluded a number of bilateral agreements on the protection of appellations of origin with, *inter alia*, Bulgaria, Hungary, Romania and Australia. An agreement with Austria became obsolete once Austria joined the European Community, and the same may well hold true for similar reasons in the future for the East European countries mentioned above. Outside Europe, the EC has concluded agreements with Morocco, Tunisia, and South Africa, apart from the one concluded with Australia.

The agreement with Australia is perhaps the most interesting from an international point of view, and shall be explained here in more detail.

The agreement was concluded in January 1994, although negotiations had been under way for a couple of years, and by 1994 Australia had already undertaken a number of measures to comply with the agreement's requirements.

The agreement is guided by the following principles:

(1) Reciprocal protection of geographical indications for wines;
(2) Protection is afforded reciprocally on condition that an indication is protected in its home country;
(3) The contracting parties shall prevent use of a traditional expression or geographical indication identifying wines for wines not originating in the place indicated by the geographical indication in question (Art. 6(1));
(4) Protection is also afforded against the expressions "kind", "type", "style", "imitation", "method", or the like;
(5) Trade marks identical with geographical indications for wines shall be refused registration or shall be prone to cancellation if used for wines not originating in the territory of such indication;

(6) The agreement envisages three different transitional periods to phase out certain indications used in Australia. The first period, ending on 31 December 1993, concerns Beaujolais, *inter alia*. The second transitional period, lasting until 31 December 1997 applies to Chianti, *inter alia*. The last transitional period not yet specified in the agreement concerns perhaps the most important geographical indications, namely Chablis, Champagne and Sherry.

The agreement follows the pattern already explained above for the European harmonisation process. As distinct from the Lisbon Agreement, both parties must agree in advance on a list of geographical indications mutually protected. Accordingly, subsequent opposition by private parties may not be raised, and the number of protected geographical indications may only be broadened by mutual consent and a subsequent amendment. Transitional periods facilitate the phasing out of indications incorrectly used by either member state.

It should be mentioned that Italy was a particular beneficiary of these bilateral agreements, since countries such as South Africa and Australia were obliged to cease use of the indication "Chianti", the value of which is of course very high in export trade.

Finally, a look at the actual workings of bilateral agreements in cases of legal conflicts may be useful at this stage. In fact, very few of these bilateral agreements have ever come before the courts. The European Court of Justice has held that bilateral agreements can exist alongside European legislation,[38] but no decision on the interpretation of a bilateral agreement was made in this decision. One case where a bilateral agreement was directly used as a basis of decision was the Swiss Budweiser case. The Swiss–Czech bilateral agreement on the protection of indications of origin, appellations of origin and other geographical indications concluded in 1973 and in force since 14 January 1976, obliges both contracting states to protect certain geographical indications listed in the appendices to the agreement. The Czech indications of origin listed there

"are exclusively reserved to Czech products and goods in the territory of Switzerland. In Switzerland, they may only be used in the same circumstances as Czechoslovakian law allows, with certain exceptions (Art. 2(1)(ii)). The same holds true for the use of Swiss indications of origin listed in Appendix A that are used in the territory of the former Czechoslovakia (Art. 3(1), (2)). This rule that is based on the principle of origin in the same manner as other bilateral agreements with Germany . . ., Spain . . ., France . . ., Hungary . . ., and Portugal . . ., guarantees equal protection of indications of origin of both sides in the respective territories (. . . Dutoit, Le nouveau droit suisse des indications de provenance et des appellations d'origine; ombres et lumière, ZSR 1993 I, 281) and leads in effect to a transfer of protection from the country of origin to the country where protection is sought (Jürg Simon, Die Ursprungsregeln im WTO-Recht, in: Baudenbacher, Aktuelle Probleme des Europäischen und Internationalen

---

[38] European Court of Justice, 10 November 1992, 25 IIC 73 – "Turron de Alicante".

Wirtschaftsrechts, I, 435; for the corresponding French–Swiss agreement, see the European Court's decision "Turrones de Alicante". . . . This leads to the consequence that the protection does not depend on the fact that also domestic circles view the geographical indication as such (so held for the bilateral agreements concluded by Germany, Baumbach/Hefermehl, Wettbewerbsrecht, 20 ed., 1998, § 3 Unfair Competition Prevention Act, marginal note 260). Thus, geographical indications are protected even though they may be unknown in the country where protection is sought and that therefore could not lead to any misconception among the public: the protection of those indications contained in the appendices does not require any danger of misconception (J. David Meisser, Herkunftsangaben und andere geographische Bezeichnungen, in: Schweizerisches Immaterialgüter- und Wettbewerbsrecht, III, 368. For one, the bilateral agreement shall prevent that those indications listed become generic terms or are used as imaginary indications (Urs Glaus, Die geographische Herkunftsangabe als Kennzeichen, Diss. Freiburg 1996, 131 . . .). And on the other hand, the agreement shall allow a redevelopment towards interpreting an indication as a protected indication of origin (see Lucas David, Basler Kommentar, Art. 47 Trade Mark Act, marginal note 19). This is consistent with the provisional rule under Art. 7(2). Here, some protection is afforded to proprietary rights that already exist . . .: Persons and undertakings that have already used a protected indication already at the time the agreement was signed, have the right of continued use for a period of six years from the date of enforcement. Further use is unlawful."[39]

The Swiss Supreme Court has thus identified two recurrent issues in the enforcement of bilateral agreements: first, geographical indications listed in these agreements may not be treated as generic indications despite the fact that they might be so regarded in the country where protection is sought. Second, the courts in the country where protection is sought are not allowed to deny protection for an indication that is validly listed in the agreement. The courts have to take the geographical indication at face value. Even though a geographical indication listed in the agreement may not qualify for protection as a geographical indication under the domestic laws of the country where protection is sought, this is immaterial. In such case, the indication is protected not on the basis of domestic law, but on the basis of the agreement. In other words, the indication is protected because it is listed in the agreement, regardless of whether it qualifies as an indication of origin in the country where protection is sought. Ultimately, this view was also shared by the Portuguese Supreme Court[40] which did not base the rejection of "Budweiser" application by A.B. on the Lisbon Agreement, but on the bilateral Portuguese–Czech agreement. Already previously, the Portuguese Supreme Court had rejected an application for the mark "König-Pilsener" on behalf of a German company based on the Portuguese–Czech treaty. This was despite the fact that in Portugal, Pilsener might be regarded as a generic indication, and Budweiser as coming from the United States. But that is exactly the mechanism of both bilateral agreements and the Lisbon Agreement, that the validity of an appellation is not examined for the

[39] Swiss Supreme Court, 15 February 1999, GRUR Int. 1999, 1072, 1073 – "BUD".
[40] Portuguese Supreme Court, 23 January 2001, 34 IIC 682 (2003) – "Budweiser III".

country where protection is sought, but based on the protection in the country of origin.

For the status of bilateral treaties under EU law, see below C.

D. Regional Agreements on Geographical Indications – Europe

I. Legislative Framework in General

European rules on geographical indications as of now only relate to agricultural products. This is largely due to the fact that the rules for protecting geographical indications were based on the common agricultural policy rather than the rules on harmonising internal trade. The first regulations were issued in the field of wines and spirits. These are:

Council Regulation 823/87 (for wines);[41] and
Council Regulation 1576/89 (for spirits).[42]

Subsequently, rules for the protection of mineral and spring waters were enacted:

Council Directive 80/777/EEC of 15 July 1980.

The most comprehensive rules on the protection of geographical indications outside the sphere of alcoholic drinks can be found in:

Council Regulation No. 2081/92 of 14 July 1992, as amended by
Council Regulation No. 692/2003 of 8 April 2003.[43]

As of now, there are no other intra-European rules on the protection of geographical indications. However, one should also note the provisions in the Trade Mark Directive and Regulation that contain rules on the registration of geographical indications as trade marks:

Art. 7(1)c) Trade Mark Regulation does not allow the registration of marks that exclusively consist of indications related to the geographical origin, and Art. 7(1)g) does not allow for registration of marks that may be misleading regarding the geographical origin.

Apart from that, the EC has concluded a number of bilateral agreements on the protection of wines and spirits, especially with Australia, South Africa, Bulgaria and Romania (see above).

---

[41] Council Regulation 823/87 of 16 March 1987, OJ L 84/24 of 1987.
[42] Council Regulation 1576/89 of 29 May 1989, OJ L 160/1 of 1989.
[43] Council Regulation 2081/92: OJ L 208 of 24 July 1992; Council Regulation 692/2003: OJ L 99/1 of 17 April 2003.

II. The Council Regulation 2081/92

1. Scope

The Regulation applies to

Geographical indications of agricultural products intended for human consumption with the exception of wines and spirits. Products that are covered by the Regulation are listed in Annexes I and II. The Annexes basically cover all kinds of foods, plus beverages such as beer, natural mineral waters (deleted from the Annex I by amendment in 2003), beverages made from plant extracts, and certain agricultural products such as hay, essential oils, wool or cork.

The Regulation distinguishes between designations of origin and geographical indications.

Designations of origin mean a specific place used to describe a product that:

a) originates in that region, and
b) derives its characteristics essentially or exclusively from this geographical environment.

Geographical indications need to fulfil the same requirements, but it is only necessary that they possess a specific quality, reputation or other characteristics attributable to that geographical origin.

Thus, designations of origin require a more intensive connection between quality and provenance, while geographical indications do not necessarily have to derive their qualities from the soil as such. Such a close connection between soil and quality would be particularly missing in the case of chocolates or sweets. These, after all, may enjoy a special reputation when produced at a certain location, but could, in theory, also be produced elsewhere in the same quality.

Eligible names are regions, specific places or countries. In certain circumstances, even non-geographical names may qualify for protection if they indicate a certain origin. The most important example in Europe would be "Feta" cheese, originating from Greece. There is no place called Feta.

2. Procedure for Protection

Protection is conditional to the registration of an indication in the European Register. Registration procedures are as follows:

(1) Specification
It is indispensable for protection that a geographical indication or designation of origin has a specification. the specification needs to contain the name of the product, its description, the definition of the geographical area, a description of the production method, a description of the link between product and geographical area, labelling details, and other requirements that might be stipulated in national law.

(2) Those entitled to apply
The application procedure is carried out in two stages. The first stage is the application before a designated national authority. The authority examines the application and if found sufficient passes it on to the Commission in Brussels. The national authorities as such are not entitled to request registration. Rather, only groups or associations may apply for such registration. When the Regulation was enacted, the German government passed on 900 indications to the Commission. These could not be properly processed because the applications came from the German authorities rather than associations dealing with the agricultural products.

(3) Further procedures
Once passed on to the Commission in Brussels, the latter shall verify whether the protection requirements are met. Thereupon, the registration shall be published. The publication is meant to present an opportunity for opposition. Up to the legislative changes in 2003, only other member states could object to the registration. Natural or legal persons of one of the member states could not directly object, but only express their concerns to the member state of residence that could then decide on how to proceed. In view of Art. 22 TRIPS Agreement, this right to object has now been broadened and allows natural or legal persons to file oppositions directly. Third countries or private parties from outside the area of the European Union may raise objections on the basis of reciprocity, i.e. that equivalent rights of opposition are granted to EU residents in that respective country.

(4) Generic names
Names that have become generic may not be registered. In order to determine to what extent a name has become generic, both the situation in the member state of origin as well as the other member states shall be taken into account. Friction over classification as generic has not been infrequent. The most prominent example is Feta cheese, that in the country of origin, Greece, indicates Greek origin and requires production with milk from goats and sheep, yet that in other countries is deemed a certain cheese type product. Already twice the Commission has held the indication to be not generic,[44] yet was once overturned by the European Court of Justice.[45] The second lawsuit is still pending.

3. Relationship to Trade Mark Law

A trade mark, whose application date is later than the registration of a geographical indication for the same or similar products, that may lead to

---

[44] First regulation on the protection of the indication "Feta" No. 1107/96 of 21 June 1996; second regulation No. 1829/2002 of 14 October 2002, O.J.L 277/10 of 15 October 2002.
[45] ECJ, 16 March 1999, Cases C–289/96, C–293/96, and C–299/96.

confusion or to the undue exploitation of the geographical indication's reputation shall be refused.

Art. 14.1(iii) extends this to trade marks that have not been registered at the time the geographical indication is published.

Far more difficult are cases where trade marks were registered prior to the registration of a geographical indication. The following situations can be distinguished.

Where the trade mark was registered in bad faith, it is prone to invalidation. What exactly is to be understood as bad faith has not yet been clarified. If bad faith means knowledge of a geographical location of that name, the provision would be very broad. If bad faith would be knowledge of the existence of an actual geographical indication for conflicting products, application would be more narrow.

If the trade mark was registered in good faith, Art. 14.2 seems to indicate a co-existence between the trade mark and the geographical indication, although the exact character of this co-existence is not clear.

Where the trade mark has become well-known for products that could also originate from the geographical place, the trade mark takes precedence, Art. 14.3. An example (although not European) could be "Tabasco". Although Tabasco is a Mexican province, the Tabasco sauce that is exported in many countries originates from the United States, and the name is used as a trade mark rather than an indication of origin.

It is not clear what should happen to trade marks that are well-known, yet that have been registered in bad faith.

4. Scope of Protection

The scope of protection is determined by Art. 13. Registered names shall be protected against commercial use of the name for identical or similar products, for other cases of false or misleading use, including translated versions of the name, and against use accompanied by expressions such as "style", "type", etc.

5. Enforcement

The enforcement of geographical indications protected under Regulation 2081/92 is left to the domestic laws of the member states. This is somewhat unfortunate as there are countries that have not enacted any specific provisions in this respect. Yet it is important to have clarification of who would be entitled to enforce an indication (only the association that obtained registration, each member of the association, or the state), and what remedies should be available against infringing acts.

a) Remedies against registration

Registration, as mentioned above, is a two-step procedure. First, registration has to be effected on a national level and, subsequently, at the European level. In both cases, third party interests can be affected. Competitors in certain regions might feel unjustly excluded by a narrow definition of a geographical area, other competitors may be interested in using the indication as a generic term, or else the registration may conflict with a registered trade mark. Remedies are different for the national and European phase.

Art. 5 of the Regulation concerns remedies at the national level. According to the ECJ,[46] national law has to provide remedies according to Arts. 6 and 13 European Convention on Human Rights. Not all member states provide such remedies, however. Germany at this stage does not. Not even the competent court has been established yet.[47]

On a European level, national member states can object to the registration. Under the amended regulation, also third parties can, yet on condition that they are not resident in the member state from which the geographical indication originates and that (where non-member states are concerned) reciprocity is assured. The latter requirement is doubtful in view of Art. 3(1) TRIPS Agreement (national treatment).

b) Remedies against refusal of registration

Remedies might also be sought where member states or the European Commission *refuse* registration and/or protection. According to Art. 12(1) Regulation 2081/92, also third country indications can be registered on condition of reciprocity. This raises the question of compatibility with TRIPS Art. 3(1), but also the question whether in the case of registration, sufficient protection has been provided by the registering states against conflicting interests (see above a)), especially in view of the fact that objections may not be heard from residents of the registering state.

Rather curiously, the Commission has sued Germany for insufficient protection of the indication "Parmesan" under Art. 226 EC Treaty (non-compliance with Treaty obligations).[48] Such a suit can only be successful where there is an actual duty to act. Yet, if geographical indications were regarded as purely private rights, why should there be an *ex officio* protection in the absence of any lawsuit that would claim infringement of the indication by third parties.

c) Scope of protection

The Regulation leaves the scope of protection fairly open. Protection is apparently only provided against the use of the indication on "products". This excludes services, yet does not necessarily limit the scope of protection

---

[46] European Court of Justice, decision of 6 December 2001, Case 269/99 – "Spreewälder Gurken".

[47] According to Administrative Court Berlin, 10 April 2003, the Administrative Courts are not competent to hear such cases. The court forwarded the case to the Federal Patent Court. The latter thus had to deal with the case, but in its decision of 2 June 2003 – "Thüringer Rostbratwurst" – thought the Administrative Courts should deal with the matter.

[48] The issue was reported in several newspapers on 13 April 2004, e.g. the Münchner Merkur.

to similar products, which may provide a scope of protection that is too broad particularly where no specific goodwill is attached to the indication.

d) Remedies against infringement

Art. 13 Regulation 2081/92 stipulates that member states should provide remedies in cases of infringement of an indication by third parties. This very rudimentary provision leaves much room for interpretation. It is not clear who should be the competent plaintiff in such case (each party entitled to use the indication, the registrant of the indication, national governments?), and says nothing about the remedies. The latter problem to some extent might be resolved by the new Enforcement Directive.[49] Yet it still remains an open question whether the remedies envisaged there are appropriate in the first place. Awarding a licensing fee as a way of damage calculation might be appropriate in cases where licences can be granted in the first place, that is, for intellectual property rights such as patents, trade marks or designs. Yet this is not the case for geographical indications. How, thus, should such a licensing fee be calculated? And, more broadly, who should be entitled to damages in the case of an infringement: the individual lawful user, the association or the state?

e) Defences against infringement

Not only the infringement claim and its remedies are unclear, but also the defences. One could think of both nullity and non-infringement. As to nullity, Art. 11a Regulation 2081/92 only allows the registrant to make such a request. A nullity suit can further be brought by any member state under Art. 230(2) EC Treaty. Individuals do not seem to be competent to raise a nullity suit under Art. 230(4) EC Treaty.[50] Where nullity is alleged, the tribunal deciding on infringement would thus have to refer the case to the ECJ under Art. 234 EC Treaty, if possible at all. Furthermore, it is doubtful to what extent the ECJ could decide about the most prominent reason for requesting nullity, that is, that the indication is considered generic. According to an opinion of the Advocate General, the European Court of Justice would not be competent to decide on this question, yet could only determine whether the Commission had considered all relevant aspects in this regard.[51]

f) Geographical indications as private or public rights?

The above-mentioned remedies leave serious doubts about the definition of geographical indications as private rights, as is supposed by the preamble of

---

[49] Directive on Enforcement of Intellectual Property Rights of 26 April 2004. The directive has to be implemented into national law within two years. On earlier drafts, see Cornish/Drexel/Hilty/Kur, Procedures and Remedies for Enforcing IPRs: The European Commission's Proposed Directive, 2003 EIPR 447.

[50] ECJ, 25 July 2002, Case C–50/00 – "UPA": but see also, Court of First Instance, 3 May 2002, Case T–177/01 – "Jégo".

[51] Attorney General Le'Ger in the case C/66/00, European Court of Justice, decision of 25 June 2002 – "Dante Bigi".

the TRIPS Agreement and the ECJ decision *Exportur*.[52] The fact that no licences can be granted for geographical indications, that there is supposed to be an obligation of member states to protect geographical indications even in the absence of a private infringement suit that geographical indications cannot be invalidated as ordinary intellectual property rights, and that some countries stress the public interest in combating infringement by criminal means (France in particular) point to the fact that geographical indications are as much public as private rights. It would thus be consequent to also allow the state to pursue infringement actions not only by criminal or administrative, but also by civil means.

III. Relationship Between European and National Protection

From the above definition of geographical indications protected under the Regulation 2081/92, it is clear that not all geographical indications can be protected under the Regulation. Rather only those indications are protectable that are not deemed generic within the Community as a whole and that can be described via a specification that has been explained above. Other, so-called "simple" geographical indications without such specification are not protectable at least under the Regulation. Such indications could be "Made in Germany", or "Thai Silk". In neither case is there a specific rule that would require certain quality standards to be adhered to that could be a basis of a specification. Such simple geographical indications can thus be protected under national law.

The same holds true for geographical indications protected under bilateral agreements at least between member states.[53] It is not yet clear if the same considerations also apply to indications that cannot be registered because they are deemed generic in a majority of member states, yet not in the country of origin. This could be the case for Feta cheese if the registration would be overturned by the European Court of Justice, or it could be the case for the Czech indication "Pilsen" that in most European countries is considered as a generic type of beer, yet that in the Czech Republic, Slovakia, Poland and Austria, is deemed an indication of origin.

The Commission seems to take the view that those indications that could be registered under the Regulation, but that have not been registered are no longer eligible for protection.[54] This at least was not the position of the Commission and member states when the Regulation was negotiated.[55]

[52] ECJ, 10 November 1992, 25 IIC 81 (1994) – "Exportur", and ECJ, 18 November 2003, Case C–216/01 – "Budvar".
[53] European Court of Justice, 10 November 1992, 25 IIC 73 – "Turron de Alicante".
[54] Communication by the European Commission of 9 October 1993, OJ C 273/4 of 9 October 1993 with the specific mention of mozzarella.
[55] Von Mühlendahl, Zeitschrift für Lebensmittelrecht 1993, 187, 196.

IV. Statistics

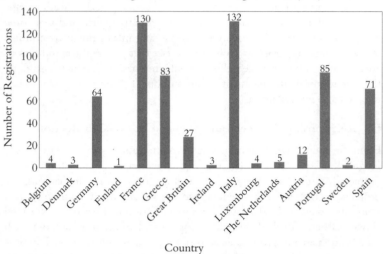

Regulation 2081/92: Registrations (626)

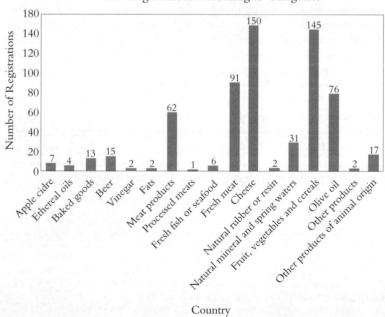

Regulation 2081/92:
626 Registrations According to Categories

6
Future Solutions for Protecting Geographical Indications Worldwide

ANSELM KAMPERMAN SANDERS

A. Introduction

European law and policies on geographical indications (GIs) have come into conflict with those of "New World" nations such as the US and Australia. This conflict has come to a head in two areas. First, the US and Australia have brought actions under the WTO dispute resolution mechanism claiming that the national treatment principle of the TRIPS Agreement is violated by the EU's legislation on GIs. Second, the US has taken the position in the TRIPS Council that the additional operation of the TRIPS Agreement in relation to wines and spirits ought not to be extended to other products, whereas the EU takes the position that a Multilateral Register in relation to agricultural products and handicrafts needs to be established.

In view of the 2004 WTO Ministerial Conference, this conflict profoundly dominates not only the TRIPS, but also the agricultural agenda.

This contribution aims at analysing the points of view underlying the two conflict areas, the future solutions for protecting GIs internationally, as well as alternatives to GI protection.

B. The Protection of Geographical Indications Prior to TRIPS

GIs may indicate a country, region, locality, city, or even an address from which a product or service emanates. Like a trade mark, a GI is a sign whose function[1] is to provide information and protect its owner. GIs indicate the precise geographical origin, and denote a quality or reputation that results from that place of origin of a product. The definition of what exactly constitutes a GI is not uniform. The Paris Convention[2] covers two notions of GIs: "indications of source or appellations of origin",[3] which are further defined

---

[1] On the functions of trade marks see Spyros M. Maniatis and Anselm Kamperman Sanders, "A Consumer Trade Mark: Protection based on Origin and Quality", [1993] 11 *EIPR* 406.

[2] Paris Convention for the Protection of Industrial Property of 20 March 1883, as revised at Brussels, 1900, Washington, 1911, The Hague, 1925, London, 1934, Lisbon, 1958, and Stockholm, 1967, and as amended on 2 October 1979.

[3] Art. 10 Paris Convention, on False indications of source of goods.

by the 1891 Madrid Agreement[4] and the Lisbon Agreement. It is of importance to realise that, the notion of "appellation" covers names, whereas "indication" also comprises drawings, photographs, national emblems, flags, or even symbolism.

The Madrid Agreement indicates that "indications of source" denote that a product or service originates from a certain area, country, region or locality. According to the Lisbon Agreement, an "appellation of origin" covers a "geographical name of a country, region, or locality, which serves to designate a product originating therein, the quality and characteristics of which are due exclusively or essentially to the geographical environment, including natural and human factors".[5] The European Court of Justice has defined the "indications of source" and "appellation of origin" in similar terms in the Exportur decision of 1992.[6]

Furthermore in the EC GIs are protected on the basis of Regulation 2081/92/EEC,[7] which offers protection to geographical indications of agricultural products and foodstuffs.[8] It employs other definitions. Whereas the definition of designation of origin[9] corresponds largely with those of the Lisbon Agreement, the definition of "geographical indication"[10] raises the threshold for appellations of origin.

---

[4] Madrid Agreement for the Repression of False or Deceptive Indications of Source on Goods of 14 April 1891, as revised at Washington 1911, The Hague, 1925, London, 1934, and Lisbon, 1958.

[5] Art. 2 Lisbon Agreement for the Protection of Appellations of Origin and their International Registration of 31 October 1958, as revised at Stockholm, 1967, and as amended on 28 September 1979.

[6] ECJ C–3/91 of 10 November, 1992.

[7] Council Regulation on the protection of geographical indications and designations of origin for agricultural products and foodstuffs (2081/92/EEC) No 2081/92 of 14 July 1992, as amended by Council Regulation 692/2003.

[8] B. O'Connor, "The Legal Protection of Geographical Indications" [2004] 1 *IPQ* 35.

[9] Regulation 2081/92/EEC Art. 2(2)(a) designation of origin: means the name of a region, a specific place or, in exceptional cases, a country, used to describe an agricultural product or a foodstuff:

– originating in that region, specific place or country, and
– the quality or characteristics of which are essentially or exclusively due to a particular geographical environment with its inherent natural and human factors, and the produFction, processing and preparation of which take place in the defined geographical area.

[10] Regulation 2081/92/EEC Art. 2(2)(b) geographical indication: means the name of a region, a specific place or, in exceptional cases, a country, used to describe an agricultural product or a foodstuff:

– originating in that region, specific place or country, and
– which possesses a specific quality, reputation or other characteristics attributable to that geographical origin and the production and/or processing and/or preparation of which take place in the defined geographical area.

C. The Protection of Geographical Indications Under TRIPS

The TRIPS Agreement of 1994 has yet another definition in Art. 22, which defines geographical indications as "indications which identify a good as originating in the territory of a Member, or locality in that territory, where a given quality, reputation or other characteristic of the good is essentially attributable to its geographic origin".

Although similar to the definition in Regulation 2081/92/EEC, the notion of "indication" is wider than that of "name", and its overall scope is somewhat wider.[11]

For the purpose of understanding the present stand-off in the TRIPS Council over the future protection of geographical indications, the diverging notions of what GIs are, and which level of protection ought to be offered accordingly.

Article 22(2) TRIPS provides:

"[i]n respect of geographical indications, Members shall provide the legal means for interested parties to prevent:

(a) the use of any means in the designation or presentation of a good that indicates or suggests that the good in question originates in a geographical area other than the true place of origin in a manner which misleads the public as to the geographical origin of the good;

(b) any use which constitutes an act of unfair competition within the meaning of Article 10bis of the Paris Convention (1967)."

Under Art. 23 GIs for wines and spirits are offered enhanced protection, which raises the threshold to situations where misuse would not cause the public to be misled. The enhanced protection is limited by the fact that such an indication should not have become generic, or registered as a trade mark.

At the heart of the conflict, however, lies the additional protection of geographical indications for wines and spirits[12] and the establishment of a multilateral system of notification and registration of geographical indications for wines and spirits. The obligation to engage in further negotiations to increase the protection of individual geographical indications under Art. 23[13] has furthermore increased tensions. The EU's position of GIs for the Cancun Ministerial Conference consisted of three steps for reform, that was seen by some, most notably the US and Australia, as three steps too many. The EU's objectives[14] can be summarised as follows:

---

[11] D.J. Gervais, *The TRIPS Agreement. Drafting History and Analysis* (1998, London, Sweet & Maxwell) at 123–5; T. Stewart, *The GATT Uruguay Round, A Negotiating History* (1993, Kluwer Law International) 2245–2313.

[12] Art. 23 TRIPS.

[13] Art. 24(1) TRIPS.

[14] For the EU proposal see WTO document IP/C/W/107/Rev.1, and for supportive statements see document TN/IP/W/3, signed by Bulgaria, Cyprus, the Czech Republic,

(1) Establishment of a multilateral register of GIs for wines and spirits, based on Art. 24(4) TRIPS and the Doha mandates;
(2) Extension of the current wines and spirits' protection to other goods, thus extending Art. 23 TRIPS protection and opening the multilateral register to all goods;
(3) Entry into market access negotiations based on Art. 24(1) to:
   (a) extend and register GIs;
   (b) table a list of EU names in the context of market access negotiations on agriculture; and
   (c) to do so in keeping with Art. 24 exceptions.

The second step has brought about a mixed reaction:[15] countries such as Bulgaria, China, the Czech Republic, the EU, Hungary, Liechtenstein, Kenya, Mauritius, Nigeria, Pakistan, the Slovak Republic, Slovenia, Sri Lanka, Switzerland, Thailand and Turkey favoured an extension, whereas others such as Japan, Chinese Taipei, and certain Southeast Asian countries as well as the US, Canada, Australia, New Zealand, Argentina and a number of other Latin American countries considered Art. 23 protection to be too high. It is clear from the positions that various members have taken that the difference of opinion on the protection of GIs does not coincide with the "Old World – New World" dichotomy. It is clear though that developing nations have more problems with the (EU required) third step in the EU approach, since the tie with agricultural negotiations is considered to be inappropriate.[16]

Generally, though, criticism of GI protection as pursued by the EU boils down to the notion that the benefits from such protection will accrue in European countries, that a register will place undue administrative burdens on developing countries, and that GI protection is bereft of incentive structures that underlie the patent, copyright and trade mark systems.[17]

---

the EU, Georgia, Hungary, Iceland, Malta, Mauritius, Moldova, Nigeria, Romania, the Slovak Republic, Slovenia, Sri Lanka, Switzerland and Turkey, available at the WTO website http://docsonline.wto.org.

[15] For a compilation of positions, see WTO documents TN/IP/W/7/Rev.1 and TN/IP/W/7/Rev.1/Corr.1, available at the WTO website http://docsonline.wto.org.

[16] See the joint paper, WTO documents N/IP/W/5 from Argentina, Australia, Canada, Chile, Colombia, Costa Rica, Dominican Republic, Ecuador, El Salvador, Guatemala, Honduras, Japan, Namibia, New Zealand, the Philippines, Chinese Taipei and the US, and TN/IP/W/6, available at the WTO website http://docsonline.wto.org.

[17] J. Hughes, "The Spirited Debate Over Geographic Indications" [unpublished, but made available at the eleventh Fordham Annual Conference on International Intellectual Property Law & Policy, 24–25 April 2003 and the Queen Mary Intellectual Property Research Institute and Fordham University Law School Dialogue on Geographical Indications, 21 November 2003] at 51.

D. GIs or Certification Marks

Many, but not all[18] of the nations opposing the EU's proposal offer protection by means of certification marks as an alternative to specific GI protection. Certification marks are a subset of trade marks capable of indicating that the goods or services on which they are used are certified by the proprietor of the mark in respect of geographical origin, material, method of manufacture of goods, standard of performance of services, quality, accuracy, or other characteristics. Typically an applicant for a certification mark must also supply a copy of the regulations governing the use of the mark, which must indicate: 1) who is authorised to use the mark, 2) the characteristics to be certified by the mark, 3) how the certifying body is to test those characteristics and supervise the use of the mark, 4) the fees (if any) to be paid in connection with the operation of the mark, and 5) the procedures for resolving disputes. Commonly, owners of certification marks do not themselves trade in the goods covered by the registration,[19] but set the terms under which producers may trade under the certification mark.[20]

A certification mark has the scope of protection on par with Art. 22(2) TRIPS Agreement and protects against deceptive use of the certification mark.[21]

---

[18] China amended its Trade Mark Law in 2002, making their certification and collective mark system similar to that of the US. See Chian Ling Li, "New Chinese Trademark Law", 143 *Trademark World* (2002) 37.

[19] N. Dawson, *Certification Trade Marks* (1988, London, IPP).

[20] Examples of certification marks registered in the US, but foreign to the US: "Banshu Somen" for noodles originating from Banshu in Japan (U.S. Trademark Registration No. 2,238,960); "Darjeeling" for tea, certifying that the tea contains at least 100% tea originating in the Darjeeling region in India and that the blend meets other specifications established by the certifier (U.S. Trademark Registration No. 2,685,923); "Jamaica Blue Mountain Coffee", certifying that the coffee in respect of which the mark is used is grown in the Blue Mountain Area of Jamaica by a person registered to grow coffee in that area pursuant to the coffee industry regulations 1953 of Jamaica (U.S. Trademark Registration No. 1,414,598); "Columbian" for coffee, certifying that the coffee was grown in the Republic of Columbia (U.S. Trademark Registration No. 1,160,492); "Parmigiano Reggiano" for cheese, as used by persons authorised by the certifier, certifies that the goods originate in the Parma–Reggio region of Italy, specifically the zone comprising the territory of the provinces Parma, Reggio Emilia, Modena and Mantua on the right bank of the river Po and Bologna on the left bank of the river Reno (U.S. Trademark Registration Nos. 1,754,410; 1,892,496; 1896,683; 2,320,595).

[21] See for example the US Lanham Act (15 U.S.C. § 1127) and the case of *Community of Roquefort v. William Faehndrich Inc.* United States Court of Appeals, Second Circuit 303 F.2d 497 (1962). "Roquefort" for cheese is the certification mark used on goods to indicate that they have been manufactured from sheep's milk only, and have been cured in the natural caves of the Community of Roquefort, Department of Aveyron, France (U.S. Trademark Registration No. 571,798).

The benefit of a system based on certification marks is that the existing national trade mark regime[22] can be relied upon for applications, registrations, oppositions, cancellations, adjudication and enforcement and would meet the requirement for national treatment and TRIPS enforcement requirements in tandem with the national trade mark regime. The disadvantage, however, is clear to see. Although such multiple registration may not be a problem for strong entities or regions which have considerable economic power,[23] the smaller the region or municipality, the greater the difficulty and cost of undertaking the task of registering in numerous countries. Whereas the criticism of the GI protection system is one of Eurocentricism, the criticism of of the certification mark system is one of Multinationalcentricism.

E. The Scope of Protection – Deceptive Use or "Expressive" Use

The scope of protection for GIs found in the TRIPS Agreement encompasses two levels, protecting them as indicators of consistent quality and an enhanced protection enabling product differentiation.

I. Integrity of Information

The prohibited acts described in Art. 22(2) TRIPS encompass misleading use of GIs "by any means in the designation or presentation of a good that indicated that the good in question originates in a geographical area other than the true place of origin" and acts of unfair competition as defined under Art. 10[bis] Paris Convention.[24] Article 22(4) extends this protection to the use

---

[22] See L. Bengedkey and C. Mead, "International Protection of Appellations of Origin and Other Geographical Designations of Regional Origin Under the Lanham Act", 82 *Trademark Reporter* 765 (1992); and L. Pollack, "Roquefort – An Example of Multiple Protection for a Designation of Regional Origin Under the Lanham Act", 52 *Trademark Reporter* 755 (1962); see also J. McCarthy, *McCarthy on Trademarks and Unfair Competition* (3d ed 1993) at 19.32.

[23] *Vide* Champagne or indeed Roquefort.

[24] Paris Convention, Art. 10[bis] – Unfair Competition reads:

> "(1) The countries of the Union are bound to assure to nationals of such countries effective protection against unfair competition.
> (2) Any act of competition contrary to honest practices in industrial or commercial matters constitutes an act of unfair competition.
> (3) The following in particular shall be prohibited:
> 1. all acts of such a nature as to create confusion by any means whatever with the establishment, the goods, or the industrial or commercial activities, of a competitor;
> 2. false allegations in the course of trade of such a nature as to discredit the establishment, the goods, or the industrial or commercial activities, of a competitor;
> 3. indications or allegations the use of which in the course of trade is liable to mislead the public as to the nature, the manufacturing process, the characteristics, the suitability for their purpose, or the quantity, of the goods."

of GIs that, although correct, do not correspond with the geographical indication commonly understood to produce the goods with the special qualities in question, or, which although factually correct, do not meet with consumer expectations as to origin and quality. Usually this situation arises in cases where the same name exists in different locations,[25] or when a description is used that is likely to confuse the consumer as to the geographical area from which the product is commonly understood to originate from, e.g.: "Parma cheese produced in America".

Article 22(2) not only covers misleading allusions to or connotations of origin by use of both words and graphics, but through Art. 10[bis] Paris Convention also the use of a GI on goods of low(er) quality emanating from the proper geographical area.

Article 22(2) protection is designed to ensure that the consumer receives accurate information that would enable him to differentiate between products emanating from the designated area and substitute products from outside this area.[26] As indicators of quality, GIs provide information that help consumers make choices and reduce risk. When the integrity of this information is tampered with so as to render it incomplete or deceptive, this can lead to market failure[27] and welfare loss. Articles 22(2) and 22(4) therefore also protect against allusions to a geographical indication or connotations in writing and device that distort reality.

II. Product Differentiation

Article 23 TRIPS is limited in application to wines and spirits, but offers a wider scope of protection. There is no need for the consumer to be misled or prove that certain behaviour constitutes an act of unfair competition. The burden of proof is not as high. For wines and spirits this additional protection translates into the possibility to protect GIs even when the consumer is not confused. A prohibition of use of expressions such as "kind", "type" or "style" in relation to a GI reflects that the purpose for the protection lies in the safeguarding of a particular production technique or product characteristic and

---

[25] The "Old World, New World" conflict comes into view once more. Many cities, towns, regions or localities were named after the places the new settlers came from. See L. Baeumer, "Protection of Geographical Indications under WIPO Treaties and Questions Concerning the Relationship between those Treaties and the TRIPS Agreement" in: *Symposium on the Protection of Geographical Indications in the Worldwide Context*, WIPO publication Nr. 760(E), (1999, Geneva, WIPO) at 17.

[26] See W. Cornish and J. Phillips, "The Economic Function of Trade Marks: An Analysis with Special Reference to Developing Countries", [1982] 13 *IIC* 41–64 at 43: "If he [the consumer] is interested in origin, it is normally because origin imports an expectation about some quality".

[27] See G. Akerlof, "The Market for 'Lemons'", 84 *Quarterly Journal of Economics* (1970) 488–500, who succinctly depicts the breakdown in the market when the consumer cannot trust the information about the product he wishes to purchase. The consumer will then prefer to buy goods of lower quality until – as in a vicious circle – the only goods available will be those of the lowest quality.

may even be used to protect a GI against the dilution of a reputation for superior quality. As such, Art. 23 protection may be used to facilitate product differentiation and would ideally enable producers in a designated geographical area to set higher prices, produce more, and preserve those traditional methods of production and levels of high quality that result from sustained investment, enable start-up industries to develop innovative production techniques, or enable producers to make the transformation from local to global markets.

Still, it is important to realise that there are limitations to Article 23 protection. Through Art. 24(4) existing use of a GI is preserved and generic terms are excluded from protection. Apart from formal limitations, there is also a real-life limitation in economic terms. For a GI to derive real benefit from this level of enhanced protection, investment in advertising and marketing is a must. Reputation needs time to develop.[28]

Even with these limitations, enhanced GI protection can enable nascent industries to obtain easy market access to world economies without the uncertainty of having to face copycats: "Indeed, the ease of entry by competitors (i.e., imitators or copycats) is normally judged to be an important indicator of how well markets function – the lower the barriers to entry, the better. Free entry makes the non-appropriability problem worse, and undercuts the incentive to invest in discovering what a country is good at producing'. [29] It is commonly accepted that intellectual and industrial property rights are decisive in the success of R&D-dependent industries. The same is true for developing nations that are still "learning" and are trying to find opportunities in the global marketplace.[30] In order to promote sustainable export trade based on GIs, building a reputation is a prerequisite. Trade barriers and protectionism are not desirable to bring about such economic development, as these measures do not discriminate between innovators and copycats.[31] Similarly export subsidies, now illegal under the WTO frame-

---

[28] R. Hausman and D. Rodrik, "Economic Development As Self-Discovery", *National Bureau of Economic Research* Working Paper 8952 (2002), available at http://ksghome.harvard.edu/~.drodrik.academic.ksg/papers.html, who emphasise that the key to economic development is learning what one is good at producing.

[29] Ibid. at 6.

[30] Ibid. at 32, where Hausman and Rodrik conclude that "laissez-faire leads to underprovision of innovation and governments need to play a dual role in fostering industrial growth and transformation".

[31] Ibid at 33 : "[T]emporary trade protection is far from an ideal instrument. It may increase expected profits of innovators, but it does so only for firms selling in the local market. Moreover, since it does not discriminate between innovators and copycats, it promotes early entry, thus lowering the expected payoff to innovation while inefficiently channeling resources to copycats. Moreover, as protection gets extended to intermediate goods, it will make downstream activities less competitive. As a consequence, innovation will tend to focus on domestic markets, instead of new export activities. Since domestic markets are small relative to world markets, the social returns to innovation will be likewise diminished. Hence, trade protection is not an efficient way of promoting self-discovery".

work, may stimulate better performance on world markets, but they do not foster innovation. Temporary public sector credit or guarantees through investment banks, specifically targeted at innovative initiatives, are mooted as a way to stimulate "self-discovery" and increase economic performance. The patent system is similarly recognised as a public policy instrument to foster R&D. The question is whether GI protection can be classified as a similar instrument, since Art. 23 protection may also function similar to trade protection mechanisms, such as tariffs, quotas or other trade barriers.[32] Therefore, the economic effects of GI protection and the appropriate scope of protection need to be considered with caution. Economic research suggests that GI protection may very well be used as a public policy instrument to foster development in superior production techniques and world market share. In a study on the economic effects of GI protection for the Tequila market, Hardwick and Kretschmer conclude that:

1. "The GI protection may help to create a virtual 'country' or 'regional' monopoly for a particular brand . . .;
2. The GI protection may help to create a segregated market, with the 'superior' GI-protected commodity in one part of the market, and 'inferior' lower-priced substitutes in another . . .; and
3. The GI protection may help to create a monopolistically competitive market of many brands, each with its own established reputation and GI protection, and each competing vigorously with the others for a share of the world market . . ."

III. Extension of Art. 23 TRIPS Protection to Products Other Than Wines and Spirits

When considering an extension of Art. 23 protection to products other than wines and spirits,[33] development economics should be a decisive factor in establishing the appropriate scope of protection. Most of the discussion has, however, gone another way. To advocates of extension, the special status offered to wines and spirits is simply not tenable. It is seen as a historical anomaly favouring producers of certain agricultural products who had the good fortune of being at the right place at the right time when international agreements were forged. Indeed of the Lisbon Agreement indications, 84% of the indications come from four product categories: wines (61.4%), spirits (9.5%), agricultural products (6.7%) and cheese (6.5%), with France accounting for 82% of the wine indications.[34] With Australia, South Africa,

[32] P. Hardwick and M. Kretschmer, "The Economics of Geographical Indications" (as yet unpublished).

[33] D. Rangnekar, *Geographical Indications, a review of proposals at the TRIPS Council: extending article 23 to products other than wines and spirits*. UNCTAD-ICTSD project on IPRs and Sustainable Development, Issue paper No. 4 (2003).

[34] S. Escudero, "International protection of geographical indications and developing countries. TRADE working papers no. 10, (2001, Geneva South Centre), available at: http://www.southcentre.org /publications/geoindication/toc.htm.

the US and South America also competing heavily in the world wine market, it is clear that the economic interests of "Old World" and "New World" producers are at the forefront of the discussion, overlooking the interests of developing nations with agricultural traditions, as well as developing nations with handicraft traditions that are trying to find their footing on the ladder of economic development that the WTO promises.

Another key word in this debate is "genericism". Whereas opponents of extended protection make the case that there is no economic data to suggest that Art. 22 protection is insufficient,[35] advocates of extended protection argue that many "once famous" GIs are now generic. Since Art. 22 does not prevent the use of a GI in translated form, accompanied by expressions like "such as", "type", "kind" or even "imitation", these GIs may be subject to dilution to the point where they become generic.[36] With the burden of proof on the right holder under Art. 22, the argument is that this allows for "wide juridical discretion leading to inconsistent decisions and legal uncertainty",[37] which undermines international trade. The counterargument is that this risk is overstated, because: "commercial experience clearly indicates that genuine, internationally recognised GIs will always command a premium on world markets. Indeed, far from detracting from the market value of a genuine GI, free and fair imitation of the product often enhances the intrinsic value (and premium) of the genuine GI."[38]

If this argument were to be raised in respect of trade-marked goods or any other intellectual property right, many would find the notion that grey-market goods or counterfeits enhance the value of the genuine product an anathema. It is true that in a perfectly transparent market the consumer benefits from enhanced choice and lower prices. It is, however, not the case that investment in the economic success of a GI in terms of advertising and marketing is safeguarded if imitations can be made.

The argument that imitation enhances the value of the genuine GI also denies proprietors of a nascent or local GI the possibility for development of the reputation through marketing, and the preservation or commercial articulation of local traditions. The fact is that a GI can function in the same way as any other intellectual property right to enable a right holder to achieve a return on investment free from copycats. This possibility should not be

---

[35] This discussion also concerns the Certification Mark as an alternative to GI protection. Whereas it is true that certification mark protection offers protection on par with Art. 22 TRIPS, there are other drawbacks to the certification mark regime as an international standard that seem to be obscured by this debate.

[36] See F. Schechter, "The Rational Basis for Trade Mark Protection", 40 *Harvard Law Review* (1927) 813. GIs that have suffered this fate: Arabica Coffee, Indiarubber, chinaware, Cheddar cheese, and kiwifruit.

[37] WTO document IP/C/W/247, para. 13, available at WTO website http://docsonline.wto.org.

[38] WTO document IP/C/W/289, at 5–6, available at WTO website http://docsonline.wto.org.

discarded because of the fear that, especially European, nations wish to reclaim words or (fallaciously) methods of production that settlers to new worlds bought with them.[39] This only muddles the debate over what is appropriate for world trade, economic development or even preservation of cultural diversity. The discussion on the extension of Art. 23 protection should therefore not focus on whether extension is justified, but on how it can be achieved in a balanced way. The creation of a multilateral register for GIs that is not polluted by generic GIs and which provides low-cost equal access for all members of the WTO should be the focus of discussion.

The sensitive area of genericism is, however, also overtaking the multilateral registry discussion, in the sense that many nations seeking GI protection face the fact that some countries without a strong GI tradition (most notably the US and Canada) already deem many GIs generic or semi-generic.[40] The pointed example of the market domination[41] since the introduction in 1994 of RiceTec's genetically engineered rice derived from Basmati rice, lines,[42] initially under descriptions such as "Texmati, Long Grain American Basmati Rice" illustrates the impact of a "free and fair imitation of the product" as opposed to that India and Pakistan's interest in Art. 23 protection. The only way forward appears to lie in WTO ministerial negotiations on which GIs that are in danger of becoming generic can be "reclaimed" and protected under Art. 23, and which are beyond redemption. The Czech Republic's quest to reclaim "Budweiser"[43] shows just how entrenched positions can be.

F. Lowering the Costs of the GI system

Whereas the patent regime is usually out of reach for innovative industries in developing countries, GI protection may not be. This requires a low-cost, easily accessible multilateral registry for GIs. In this respect the administrative burden on nations, especially developing ones, may be high in view of the enactment of new legislation and the fact that some WTO members seek to

---

[39] J. Hughes, "Surrendering Words to the EU" at 4: "Pursuant to the recent EU–South Africa trade treaty, South Africa had to surrender hundreds of European terms – the treaty annex reads like an atlas of quaint European villages and hamlets. The GI debate is one in which the EU continues to pursue a bureaucratic outlook that centralized control is better than markets in preserving traditional agriculture".

[40] J. Watal, *Intellectual Property Rights in the WTO and Developing Countries* (2001, The Hague, Kluwer Law International) at 273.

[41] US imports of Basmati rice from India and Pakistan fell from 22,449 metric tons in 2000 to 15,319 metric tons in 2002, see http://www.riceonline.com.

[42] On the contentious patents, such as RiceTec's, that form the basis of "biopiracy", see *V.* Shiva, "Intellectual Property Protection in the North/South Divide", in Heath and Kamperman Sanders (eds.), *Intellectual Property in the Digital Age* (2001, The Hague – London – Boston, Kluwer Law International) 113.

[43] On the saga of Bud versus Bud, see W. Keegan and M. Green, *Global Marketing* (1999, Prentice Hall) at 202–3.

"export" a large number of domestic geographical indications. Many nations simply do not have the resources to monitor all new applications for registration of GIs. Conversely the relative costs that are presently exclusively put toward the protection of wines and spirits are high and benefit few. A broad extension of Art. 23 can lower these costs to the benefit of many.

Another issue of raised costs can be exemplified by the "Texmati" example. If producers of Texmati rice were obliged to remove the descriptive "Long Grain American Basmati Rice", or even change their mark to something not ending in "mati", search and transaction costs for consumers will be increased,[44] albeit probably only for a while. In the long run, consumers will be able to rely on the authenticity of the GI used in relation to a product.[45]

The Budweiser case raises yet another problem of cost, namely that of trade disruption. In the unlikely event that the Czech Republic would be allowed to reclaim the GI "Budweiser" for beer, if only in a number of jurisdictions, Anheuser-Bush would lose trade.

The argument of increased cost raised against the multilateral register, however, touches upon the European Union proposal of notification of GIs, possibly leading to automatic (extended) protection. Any WTO member would be able to notify the WTO of a GI for which protection is claimed. The proposal then envisages an 18-month period for examination or opposition by other WTO members. If the GI is challenged, the members will have to enter into bilateral negotiations, which may lead to a waiver of an obligation to protect the GI in that WTO member country. This approach leaves unaffected the fact that right holders remain responsible for enforcement, and the application of existing obligations in all member states. The system also enables potential right holders to obtain protection in all WTO member states at low cost. The system of "object or protect" is, however, burdensome for developing countries that may have to sift through large numbers of applications, an expense they cannot afford. The cost may thus be displaced from the potential beneficiary of GI protection to member states that have to set up a bureaucratic system dealing with objections to GI notifications. It would therefore make sense to exempt the least developed countries from the obligation to protect newly registered GIs for a certain period of time or to extend or defer the period for opposition for these WTO members. Also, limits on the number of GI applications may be imposed on all members so as to allow objections to be raised.

---

[44] WTO Document IP/C/W/289 at 7, available at WTO website http://docsonline.wto.org.

[45] WTO Document IP/C/W/308/Rev.1, para 14, available at WTO website http://docsonline.wto.org.

G. Conclusion

Concerns over the protection of GIs through a multilateral register are primarily concerns over costs and may be resolved. The debate over the Art. 23 extension to goods other than wines and spirits, however, will not be so easily resolved. The "Old World / New World" divide and the all-pervasive issue of "genericism" is in danger of overshadowing the benefits of GI protection and opportunities for economic and regional development, especially for economies that are oriented towards the production of agricultural products or handicraft items. Whereas the opposition procedure envisaged by the EU proposal for the establishment of a multilateral register, as well as the limitations contained in Arts. 23 and 24 may eliminate the opposition to the Old World / New World stand-off over genericism, they will not overcome the fundamental objections to the extension of Art. 23 protection to goods other than wines or spirits.

Annex – TRIPS Agreement, Arts. 22–24

GEOGRAPHICAL INDICATIONS
Article 22
Protection of Geographical Indications

1. Geographical indications are, for the purposes of this Agreement, indications which identify a good as originating in the territory of a Member, or a region or locality in that territory, where a given quality, reputation or other characteristic of the good is essentially attributable to its geographical origin.
2. In respect of geographical indications, Members shall provide the legal means for interested parties to prevent:

   (a) the use of any means in the designation or presentation of a good that indicates or suggests that the good in question originates in a geographical area other than the true place of origin in a manner which misleads the public as to the geographical origin of the good;
   (b) any use which constitutes an act of unfair competition within the meaning of Article 10bis of the Paris Convention (1967).

   3. A Member shall, ex officio if its legislation so permits or at the request of an interested party, refuse or invalidate the registration of a trademark which contains or consists of a geographical indication with respect to goods not originating in the territory indicated, if use of the indication in the trademark for such goods in that Member is of such a nature as to mislead the public as to the true place of origin.
   4. The protection under paragraphs 1, 2 and 3 shall be applicable against a geographical indication which, although literally true as to the territory, region or locality in which the goods originate, falsely represents to the public that the goods originate in another territory.

Article 23
Additional Protection for Geographical Indications for Wines and Spirits

1. Each Member shall provide the legal means for interested parties to prevent use of a geographical indication identifying wines for wines not originating in the place indicated by the geographical indication in question or identifying spirits for spirits not originating in the place indicated by the geographical indication in question, even where the true origin of the goods is indicated or the geographical indication is used in translation or accompanied by expressions such as "kind", "type", "style", "imitation" or the like.

2. The registration of a trademark for wines which contains or consists of a geographical indication identifying wines or for spirits which contains or consists of a geographical indication identifying spirits shall be refused or invalidated, ex officio if a Member's legislation so permits or at the request of an interested party, with respect to such wines or spirits not having this origin.

3. In the case of homonymous geographical indications for wines, protection shall be accorded to each indication, subject to the provisions of paragraph 4 of Article 22. Each Member shall determine the practical conditions under which the homonymous indications in question will be differentiated from each other, taking into account the need to ensure equitable treatment of the producers concerned and that consumers are not misled.

4. In order to facilitate the protection of geographical indications for wines, negotiations shall be undertaken in the Council for TRIPS concerning the establishment of a multilateral system of notification and registration of geographical indications for wines eligible for protection in those Members participating in the system.

Article 24
International Negotiations; Exceptions

1. Members agree to enter into negotiations aimed at increasing the protection of individual geographical indications under Article 23. The provisions of paragraphs 4 through 8 below shall not be used by a Member to refuse to conduct negotiations or to conclude bilateral or multilateral agreements. In the context of such negotiations, Members shall be willing to consider the continued applicability of these provisions to individual geographical indications whose use was the subject of such negotiations.

2. The Council for TRIPS shall keep under review the application of the provisions of this Section; the first such review shall take place within two years of the entry into force of the WTO Agreement. Any matter affecting the compliance with the obligations under these provisions may be drawn to the attention of the Council, which, at the request of a Member, shall consult with any Member or Members in respect of such matter in respect of which it has not been possible to find a satisfactory solution through bilateral or plurilateral consultations between the Members concerned. The Council shall take such action as may be agreed to facilitate the operation and further the objectives of this Section.

3. In implementing this Section, a Member shall not diminish the protection of geographical indications that existed in that Member immediately prior to the date of entry into force of the WTO Agreement.

4. Nothing in this Section shall require a Member to prevent continued and similar use of a particular geographical indication of another Member identifying wines or spirits in connection with goods or services by any of its nationals or domiciliaries who have used that geographical indication in a continuous manner with regard to the same or related goods or services in the territory of that Member either (a) for at least 10 years preceding 15 April 1994 or (b) in good faith preceding that date.

5. Where a trademark has been applied for or registered in good faith, or where rights to a trademark have been acquired through use in good faith either:

(a) before the date of application of these provisions in that Member as defined in Part VI; or

(b) before the geographical indication is protected in its country of origin;

measures adopted to implement this Section shall not prejudice eligibility for or the validity of the registration of a trademark, or the right to use a trademark, on the basis that such a trademark is identical with, or similar to, a geographical indication.

6. Nothing in this Section shall require a Member to apply its provisions in respect of a geographical indication of any other Member with respect to goods or services for which the relevant indication is identical with the term customary in common language as the common name for such goods or services in the territory of that Member. Nothing in this Section shall require a Member to apply its provisions in respect of a geographical indication of any other Member with respect to products of the vine for which the relevant indication is identical with the customary name of a grape variety existing in the territory of that Member as of the date of entry into force of the WTO Agreement.

7. A Member may provide that any request made under this Section in connection with the use or registration of a trademark must be presented within five years after the adverse use of the protected indication has become generally known in that Member or after the date of registration of the trademark in that Member provided that the trademark has been published by that date, if such date is earlier than the date on which the adverse use became generally known in that Member, provided that the geographical indication is not used or registered in bad faith.

8. The provisions of this Section shall in no way prejudice the right of any person to use, in the course of trade, that person's name or the name of that person's predecessor in business, except where such name is used in such a manner as to mislead the public.

9. There shall be no obligation under this Agreement to protect geographical indications which are not or cease to be protected in their country of origin, or which have fallen into disuse in that country.

7

The Conflict Between Trade Marks and Geographical Indications – The Budweiser Case in Portugal

ANTONIO CORTE-REAL

A. Introduction

Trade marks (TM) and geographical indications (GI) share the fact that they both serve to communicate certain information to consumers about the origin of the goods.

In general terms, a TM serves the purpose of distinguishing the goods or services of one undertaking from the goods or services of another, while a GI is a sign indicating a link of the goods with their place of origin.

TMs need to be distinctive to indicate a connection between the goods and an individual producer or an individual trader, while GIs are descriptive of certain characteristics of the goods and therefore in principle should not be the subject matter of a trade mark right. TMs are normally protected in terms of private property rights while GIs are protected in terms of public or common property and may be used by all traders in a particular geographic location for goods which emanate from that location.

But despite this basic conceptual differentiation, these two categories of intellectual property law frequently come into conflict with one another.

B. Trade Marks Containing a Geographical Indication.

I. In General

For the relationship between trade marks and geographical indications it is vital to analyse the problem of registration of TMs containing a GI. In Europe there are two basic principles to be considered.

First, a TM should not be registered if it exclusively consists of signs or indications which may serve, in trade, to designate the place of origin of the goods. This constitutes an absolute ground for refusal that should be applied by the Trade Mark Office.[1] For example, under this principle, the word PARIS was not accepted as a TM for perfumes. If the mark is complex (in the sense that it contains distinctive elements other than the geographical sign), registration is possible. However in such a case the exclusive right of

---

[1] *Ex officio* or at the request of any interested party.

the trade mark owner cannot extend to the geographical indication.[2] Where the mark contains a geographical indication or other generic element, the applicant or a third party may request the Office to include a disclaimer in its granting decision (this is possible at least in Portugal).

The rationale behind this principle is not only that the geographical element may be deemed descriptive of characteristics of the categories of the goods concerned but also that it is in the public interest that the geographical sign remains available for other competitors in the same place of origin to use. One of the reasons for protecting competitors is that associating the goods with a place may give rise to a favourable response from consumers.[3]

Second, misleading geographical signs are excluded from trade mark registration, e.g. when the mark contains a geographical sign indicating that the good in question originates in a geographical area other than the true place of origin *in a manner which misleads the public* as to the geographical origin of goods. It may not be easy to determine such misconception. What needs to be assessed is whether the geographical indication is liable to mislead consumers or may perform the normal function of a reference to the manufacturer.

In fact, there are signs that despite their literal geographical meaning are not likely to produce a misconception of the public. The public may recognise a geographical content in the mark, but for several reasons will not perceive it as being the true origin of the goods. For example, the words HOLLYWOOD (for coffee from a Spanish company)[4], TAHITI (for a deodorant from an American company)[5], ARC DE TRIOMPHE (for tobacco products from a German company)[6] or CHAMPS ELYSÉES (for tobacco products from a German company)[7] have been accepted as trade marks in Portugal. Also in this line of reasoning, the Portuguese Supreme Court allowed the registration of the mark BRISTOL for pharmaceuticals (Portuguese applicant)[8], or the mark SCOTCH-TRED (and other marks with the word SCOTCH) for coating products (US applicant)[9].

---

[2] Except where the geographical indication contained in the mark despite of being originally descriptive has acquired distinctive character through use in trade.

[3] As noted in joined Cases C–108/97 and C–109/97 *Windsurfing Chiemsee* [1999] ECR I–2779, paragraph 26.

[4] Civil Court of Lisbon, judgement of 22 February 1991, Industrial Property Bulletin 5–92, p. 2337.

[5] Civil Court of Lisbon, judgement of 27 April 1992, Industrial Property Bulletin 5–92, p. 2336.

[6] Civil Court of Lisbon, judgement of 20 January 1965, Industrial Property Bulletin 2–65, p. 170.

[7] Civil Court of Lisbon, judgement of 5 January 1963, Industrial Property Bulletin 1–63, p. 6.

[8] Supreme Court of Justice, judgement of 30 January 1985, Justice Ministry Bulletin 343, p. 347.

[9] Supreme Court of Justice, judgement of 20 February 1970, Industrial Property Bulletin 4–70, p. 563.

This approach has been a prevailing orientation in the Portuguese courts based on different justifying circumstances.[10] It may be that the geographical name is unknown to the public in general (this would probably be the case of BUDWEISER). It may be simply because the same word may have other meanings and the public is less aware of the geographical meaning or it may be that the geographical name is known to the public in general, but there is no specific connection of the goods to the place in question.

Nevertheless, it must be mentioned that the TRIPS Agreement established a stronger (absolute) protection for geographical indications of certain products: according to Art. 23 (1) and (2) of TRIPS, protection should be provided to GIs identifying wines or spirits regardless of any misconception on the side of the public and even where the true origin of the goods is indicated or the GI is used in translation or accompanied by expressions subs as "kind", "type", "style", "indication", or the like (see also Art. 7.1j Community Trade Mark Regulation).

Stronger protection is also provided for GIs where the GI was registered earlier than the TM and the normal rules of priority apply, at least with regard to trade marks for similar goods, regardless of a misconception on the side of the public. Further, the protection of GIs emerging from bilateral treaties is also not dependant on the risk of a misconception.

II. Collective Marks

The EC Trade Mark Directive allows Member States to provide that signs or indications which may serve in trade to designate the geographical origin of the goods or services may constitute collective, guarantee or certification marks. Although a registration for GIs already existed in Portugal, the possibility of registering GIs as collective marks is also foreseen under Portuguese law.

Collective marks are "association marks" or "certification marks". An association mark is a sign belonging to an association of natural or legal persons whose members use or have the intent to use the sign for products or services connected with the activity of the association. A certification mark is a sign belonging to a corporate body that controls the products or services or establishes the rules producers have to comply with and that apply to such products or services.

Collective trade mark owners are required to have an internal regulation governing the use of the mark. Such a regulation must be recorded in the Trade Mark Office and should specify the persons authorised to use the mark, the conditions of use of the mark, and the rights and obligations of the interested parties in the case of infringement.

The scope of protection of collective marks is basically the same as for individual marks. The proprietor will not be able to prohibit a third party

---

[10] In line with this is also the interpretation of the Directive in the above cited *Windsurfing Chiemsee* decision in paragraphs 31 and 33.

from using such signs or indications in the course of trade, provided he uses them in accordance with honest practices in industrial or commercial matters. Further, such a mark may not be invoked against a third party who is entitled to use the geographical name.

C. Conflicts Between Marks and Geographical Indications

I. Trade Marks and Geographical Indications

Controversial conflicts between TM and GI arise time and again. It appears that one source for such controversy has been the different approaches taken when solving conflicts between earlier TMs and GIs.

In trade mark law, conflicts among trade marks are solved according to the priority principle, that is to say, the supremacy of the prior right. The same solution can be found in conflicts amongst other industrial rights for distinctive signs such as company names or shop names and conflicts between such distinctive signs and trade marks. Furthermore, under Portuguese law it is also undisputed that an earlier GI, when registered, takes precedence over a later trade mark.

However, the same solution is not necessarily applicable in conflicts between earlier trade marks and GIs. Under the Lisbon Agreement, an appellation of origin that has been registered takes precedence over a prior trade mark use by third parties: according to Art. 5 (6), the competent national Trade Mark Office shall have the right to allow such third parties a period not exceeding two years to terminate such use. The EC regulations for wine products have taken a similar approach and, in the case of the TORRES trade mark, have been a cause for conflict in Portugal.

In Portugal, TORRES was a trade mark for wine and brandy products registered by a Spanish company.[11] The mark TORRES was registered in a significant number of countries and in Portugal at least since 1963. It was considered a well-known trade mark with an international reputation in the relevant sector of the public. In 1989, the EC Council passed a regulation concerning the designation and presentation of wines, in particular quality wines produced in specified regions (Quality Wines PSR).[12] The first version of this regulation provided that trade marks used in connection with wines were likely to be confused with the name of a specified region adopted for a quality wine PSR, and only limited and transitory exceptions were foreseen for trade marks registered until 31 December 1985. In 1989, Portugal adopted a law for the protection of the word "Torres" as a GI (for the wine-producing region near the town of Torres Vedras) to be used with

---

[11] Miguel Torres, S.A.
[12] Council Regulation (EEC) No. 2392/89 of 24 July 1989 laying down general rules for the description and presentation of wines and grape musts (OJ 1989 L 232, p. 13).

the Community designation quality wines PSR.[13] Consequently the prior
trade mark TORRES was meant to be cancelled as of 31 December 2002.

In light of this conflict the EC changed its rules:[14] The geographical name
designating a specified region should be sufficiently precise so that, taking
account of the existing situations, confusion could be avoided. Furthermore
a second exception was drafted for registered well-known trade marks.[15] As
a result of this change, Portugal also modified its national legislation and the
GI "TORRES" was replaced by the GI "TORRES VEDRAS".

A different approach was followed in the EC Regulation 2081/92 for
foodstuffs and agricultural products: according to Art. 14(3) a designation of
origin or geographical indication shall not be registered where, in the light of
a trade mark's reputation and the length of time it has been used, registration
is likely to mislead the consumer as to the true identity of the product.
Consequently, an earlier renown and reputed trade mark may block the
registration of a GI.

II. Generic Geographical Indications and Trade Marks

In other cases, a trade mark applicant may be interested in using and/or
acquiring rights over a GI which is considered generic.

Under the law of trade marks, the proprietor's right may be cancelled if
the mark, as a result of the activity or inactivity of the proprietor, becomes a
common designation in trade for the product or service for which it was
registered. The transformation of a GI into a generic indication is a similar
situation: in the mind of consumers, the GI turns into a name that describes
not its geographical origin but the type of product or a production method.
Several generic geographical names may be found in the current language
and practices of trade in Portugal (e.g. FLAMENGO for cheese,
FRANKFURT for sausages, CHINA for ink).

However, for a protected GI this consequence is practically excluded by
law. A GI protected under the EC Regulation 2081/92 may not become
generic (Art. 13(3)). Further, an appellation of origin protected under the
Lisbon Agreement cannot be deemed generic, as long it is protected as an
appellation of origin in the country of origin (Art. 6). Finally, Portuguese law
permits that a registered GI may be cancelled when the indication is deemed

---

[13] Decree Law No. 331/89, of 27 September 1989.

[14] Council Regulation (EEC) No. 3897/91 of 16 December 1991 (OJ 1991 L 368, p. 5).

[15] Conditions are that it was a well-known brand name for a wine or grape must which
contains wording that is identical to the name of a specified region or the name of a geographical unit smaller than a specified region where it corresponds to the identity of its
original holder or of the original provider of the name, provided that the brand name
was registered at least 25 years before the official recognition of the geographical name in
question by the producer Member State in accordance with the relevant Community
provisions as regards quality wines PSR and that the brand name has actually been used
without interruption.

generic. Excluded are geographical indications for wine, mineral waters and "other products which are protected and controlled in their country of origin" (Sec. 315, Industrial Property Code). As only a handful of industrial or handicraft products would normally not be subject to special legislation in the country of origin, the exception is limited.

III. Well-known Geographical Indications and Trade Marks

Another situation that has already been decided in the Portuguese courts is the use of a well-known GI in products other than the typical goods of the GI. For instance, the use of the word CHAMPAGNE for beers rather than sparkling wines.[16]

In the case at issue, a US company (Miller Brewing Company) had applied for the registration of the mark MILLER HIGH LIFE – THE CHAMPAGNE OF BEERS. The disputed goods were beers. This application was opposed by the French INAO (the competent French institute – Institut National des Appellations d'Origine des Vins et Eaux-de-Vie) based on the appellation of origin No. 231 registered under the Lisbon Agreement. The examiner rejected the opposition because in his opinion the words THE CHAMPAGNE OF BEERS could not cause the misconception amongst consumers that the beer originated from the French region of Champagne. The INAO appealed this decision and the court reversed the Office's decision. The court ruled that not only national law but also the Lisbon Agreement prohibited the use of a registered appellation on products originating in other places even for non-similar goods because it was necessary to protect the producers and local entities in the specific regions such as the Champagne region.[17]

The new Portuguese Industrial Property Code adopted in 2003 provides for the protection of geographical indications against use for non-similar goods in terms corresponding to those that may be found under trade mark law. According to Art. 312(4) IPC, the use of a protected GI for non-similar goods will be forbidden provided that the GI has a reputation in Portugal or in the EC, and use without due cause would take unfair advantage of, or be detrimental to, the distinctive character or the repute of the earlier GI.

---

[16] Civil Court of Lisbon, judgement of 3 December 1999, Industrial Property Bulletin 4–2000, p. 1762.

[17] The Portuguese INPI has now rejected several attempts to register trade or service marks using the word CHAMPAGNE for goods not related to wines (e.g. Application No. 255141 CHAMPAGNE KNIT for clothing, refused on 31 October 1994; Application No. 333709 CHAMPAGNE CLUB for services of education, providing of training, entertainment, sporting and cultural activities, refused on 29 June 2001).

D. The Budweiser Case in Portugal

I. Introduction and Facts

The name Budweiser is known as a trade mark for a beer produced in the United States by an American company (Anheuser-Busch, Inc. (AB)) but also as a GI referring to a city in the Bohemian[18] region of the Czech Republic. The current official name of the Czech city is Ceské Budejovice, but it was known in the past as Budweis.[19] Even now in the Czech Republic it is common to see traffic signs and advertising inscriptions indicating the name Budweis with or without its Czech translation Ceske Budejovice. The city of Budweis has an old tradition of beer-brewing that goes back to the XIII century and the beer from Budweis (mainly traded under the name Budweiser Budvar) achieved a good reputation due to its quality and flavour. The American brewery started using the Budweiser trade mark in the US at the end of the 19th century.

In Portugal the dispute started in 1982 with the American company filing two applications for the marks *Budweiser* and *Bud*, both in class 32 covering, *inter alia*, beer and non alcoholic beverages.[20]

The Czech brewery opposed these applications based on the registration of the appellations of origin *Budweiser Bier, Budweis Beer, Bière de Budweis, Budweiser Budvar*, and *Bud*, under the Lisbon Agreement.[21] The Czech brewery also provided evidence of previous though not systematic use

---

[18] Bohemia – historic country of central Europe that was a kingdom in the Holy Roman Empire and subsequently a province in the Habsburgs' Austrian Empire. Bohemia was bounded on the south by Austria, on the west by Bavaria, on the north by Saxony and Lusatia, on the northeast by Silesia, and on the east by Moravia. From 1918 to 1939 and from 1945 to 1992 it was part of Czechoslovakia. "Bohemia." Encyclopædia Britannica. 2004. Encyclopædia Britannica Premium Service <http://www.britannica.com/eb/article?eu=82555>.

[19] Budweis, city, capital of Jihocesky kraj (region), Czech Republic. It is a regional cultural and industrial centre lying amid lakes at the confluence of the Vltava (Moldau) and Malse rivers. Founded and fortified in 1265 by the Bohemian king Otakar II, the city is rich in medieval architecture. "Ceske Budejovice." Encyclopædia Britannica. 2004. Encyclopædia Britannica Premium Service <http://www.britannica.com/eb/article?eu=22514>.

[20] Application 211727 *Budweiser* and application 211728 *Bud* were both filed on 19 May 1981. Official publication for opposition purposes was made on 13 January 1982.

[21] Appellations of origin 49, 50, 51, 52 (registered on 22 November 1967) and 598 (registered on 10 March 1975). The Lisbon Agreement for the Protection of Appellations of Origin and their International Registration (1958), was revised at Stockholm (1967), and amended in 1979. On 15 January 2001, the Lisbon Agreement had 20 Member States: Algeria, Bulgaria, Burkina Faso, Congo, Costa Rica, Cuba, Czech Republic, France, Gabon, Haiti, Hungary, Israel, Italy, Mexico, Portugal, Republic of Moldova, Slovakia, Togo, Tunisia, and Yugoslavia.

through sales of *Budweiser Budvar* and *Budweiser Beer*, in Portugal, since 1956. In addition to these prior rights the opponent had obtained several international trade mark registrations containing the words Budweiser or Bud, but those registrations had meanwhile been cancelled for Portugal.[22]

In a 1989 action brought by the US brewery in the civil courts for cancellation of the appellations of origin registrations, the plaintiff claimed invalidity of the registrations for lack of the legal requirements provided in Art. 2 Lisbon Agreement. In a default judgment, the Lisbon First Instance Court decided to order cancellation of the appellations of origin.[23]

Based thereupon, the Portuguese IP Office dismissed the oppositions and granted both registrations to Anheuser-Busch.

The Czech brewery filed an appeal against the Portuguese IP Office decisions and the courts dismissed the appeal in respect of the mark Bud, while sustaining the Czech allegations based on a bilateral treaty on the reciprocal protection of geographical indications between the Czech Republic and Portugal, and consequently refused registration of the mark Budweiser. The decisive point in this decision is a bilateral treaty that Portugal had signed in 1987 with the Czechoslovakian Socialist Republic for the protection of certain geographical indications, including Ceské Budejovice. The Budweiser dispute did not involve contract law questions, although this was the case in other jurisdictions.

II. Questions of Trade Mark Law

The main question under trade mark law was the inherent registrability of the mark Budweiser. Was it possible to monopolise the word Budweiser as a trade mark for beers when a place known as Budweis with beer brewing tradition existed? Literally, the law seemed not to allow this situation but the interpretation of the courts based on public perception did not support this, because the mark was not considered geographical in Portugal, that is to say, it was unlikely that the public in Portugal would identify Budweiser as geographical (also because there was some degree of recognition of the American brand in Portugal).

III. Questions of the Law of Geographical Indications

1. *The Czech Appellations of Origin*

The Czech Republic had registered the appellations of origin *Budweiser Bier*, *Budweis Beer*, *Bière de Budweis*, *Budweiser Budvar*, and *Bud*, under the Lisbon Agreement. In 1989, AB filed a cancellation action claiming invalidity of the registrations for lack of the legal requirements established in Art. 2 Lisbon Agreement.

---

[22] For example, the International Registration R342158 *Budweiser Budvar* dated 26 January 1968.

[23] Civil Court of Lisbon (13 chamber, 3 section, case 7906), judgement of 8 March 1995, unpublished.

The court expunged the registrations of the appellations of origin in a default judgment and based on evidence by mere individual declarations (affidavits). The question of whether the national courts may declare a registration under the Lisbon Agreement invalid was not specifically addressed by the court. When examining the appellations of origin, the court declared the following:

> "Neither the beer manufactured by the defendant nor any other beer have characteristics or qualities that are exclusively or essentially connected to natural factors (soil, climate, etc.) or to human factors existing only in the locality where they are manufactured or any other specific locality. The characteristics and properties of any beer are determined by the raw materials used in the manufacture and in the manufacturing method itself. Neither the raw materials nor the manufacturing method are influenced by natural or human factors existing only in a determined place or are exclusively or essentially related with that place or area. Therefore it is perfectly possible to manufacture beer with the same qualities and characteristics in different geographical places or areas."

This is not well founded. As C. Heath points out, the ingredients of the Bohemian Budweiser beer are closely linked to soil and climate and one of the main reasons why beer from Austria, Germany and Czechoslovakia is not widely exported is the limited quantities of production due to the close connection to a specific place of origin.[24]

2. Bilateral treaty

Despite the fact that the Lisbon Agreement registrations were cancelled, the Czechs were able to reverse the decision of the Portuguese IP Office.

In 1986, Portugal had concluded a bilateral treaty with Czechoslovakia for the protection of indications of origin, appellations of origin, and other geographical designations and similar names.[25] The treaty came into force on 7 March 1987. In the Appendix A of the treaty under the heading "Beer", the names "Ceskobudejovické pivo" and "Ceskobudejovicky Budvar" are listed.

The treaty provides for an extensive protection of geographical names not only for beers but also for winery products, foodstuffs and agricultural products, handicrafts and some industrial products. Under Art. 5 of the Treaty, protection applies even when the names or designations are used in translation or transcription, even if the true origin of the products is mentioned, or if the words constituting the appellation or indication are accompanied by qualifiers such as "kind," "type," "form", "manner", "imitation" or "quality". The treaty is followed by a protocol where the parties agree that protection also applies to grammatical alterations of the names or designations and that Latin words are to be considered as translations of the

---

[24] C. Heath, Budweiser Blues, 36 IIC 2004 (forthcoming).
[25] Government Decree no. 7/87 adopted on 27 November 1986 and published on 4 February 1987.

protected designations. There are also specific provisions addressing the
problem of conflicts with previously registered trade marks but this was not
relevant for the *Budweiser* mark, as at that time there was no registration.
Protection of the GIs and indications of source covered by the treaty was
granted regardless of any registration system. In addition, protection was
absolute and not subject to any risk of misleading the public.

The court held that the trade mark *Budweiser* was contrary to the treaty
since it refers to Budweis, which is the German name for the Czech city of
Ceskebudejovice in the region of Bohemia. As to the *Bud* mark, the court
ruled that the treaty protection did not apply, not only because it was absent
from the Appendixes, but also for the reason that it is an English word and an
abbreviation of other German words.

The US brewery sustained also that the applicability of the treaty in
respect of translations of the protected geographical designations was limited
to the translation of Czech words into Portuguese and vice versa. It would
be pointless to protect the designations in third country languages that could
not be of any relevance to the average Portuguese consumer. Therefore a
translation into German should not be considered. Notwithstanding this
interpretation, it was clear that the treaty protected some Portuguese geographical designations such as *Port Wine* and *Madeira Wine* in several other
languages. Highlighting this and the principle of reciprocity on which the
treaty was based, the Supreme Court held that a translation into any other
language was relevant even if the translation was not known to the average
consumer.

An argument brought by the US brewery was that protection of geographical designations emerging from the bilateral treaty had been superseded by virtue of the registration system set up by the Regulation (EEC)
2081/92. The appellant submitted that the protection granted by the system
of the Regulation was of an exclusive nature and asked for a reference to the
European Court of Justice.[26]

The court rejected the argument based on Art. 12 that provides that the
Regulation may apply to an agricultural product or foodstuff from a third
country "without prejudice to international agreements". This question was
recently addressed by the judgment of the ECJ of 18 November 2003 (in case
C–216/01) concerning a similar bilateral treaty between Austria and The
Czech Republic regarding the designation BUD. The ECJ ruled that
Regulation No 2081/92 does not preclude the application of a provision of
a bilateral agreement between a Member State and a non-member country

---

[26] The question was the interpretation of Article 17 of the Regulation (EEC) No.
2081/92 of 14 July 1992 on the protection of geographical indications and designations of
origin for agricultural products and foodstuffs (OJ 1992 L 208, p. 1). Against the exclusivity of the protection system of Regulation (EEC) No. 2081/92, F.K. Beier / R. Knaak,
The Protection of Direct and Indirect Geographical Indications of Source in Germany
and the European Community, 25 IIC 1 (1994).

under which a simple and indirect indication of geographical origin from that non-member country is accorded protection in the importing Member State, whether or not there is any risk of consumers being misled, and the import of a product lawfully marketed in another Member State may be prevented.

The US brewery also objected that the Czech geographical name could not prevail over the trade mark Budweiser because the trade mark benefited from the exception foreseen in Art. 24.5 TRIPS Agreement. A measure to implement protection of a GI under TRIPS should not prejudice the registration or use of a trade mark where the trade mark has been applied for or registered in good faith or where rights to the trade mark have been acquired through use in good faith:

- before the date of application of Articles 22 to 24 in a Member State or
- before the geographical indication is protected in its country of origin.

It is not clear if Art. 24.5 TRIPS Agreement establishes a solution of co-existence between a prior TM and a later GI or a solution of exclusivity of the TM. In any case, as the court pointed out, the argument could not overcome the fact that good faith had not been substantiated. Moreover, subsection 5 concerns "measures adopted to implement this Section" while the decision of the Office (and the bilateral treaty provisions) were prior to the date of entry into force of TRIPS in Portugal (1 January 1996) and therefore could not be considered as such "measures".

8
Software and Computer-Related Inventions: Protection by Patent and Copyright

GIOVANNI F. CASUCCI

A. The Definition of "Software"

The meaning of the term "software" has varied according to the legal source defining it.

In particular, the WIPO[1] adopted a definition according to which software could be considered as a set of instructions that, once transferred to a computer readable support, could carry out a function or realise a task, or obtain a particular result by means of a machine that processed the transmitted information.

According to the American Copyright Act, software is defined as "a set of statements or instructions to be used directly or indirectly in a computer to bring about certain results".[2]

The Australian Copyright Act adopted the same definition as the U.S.,[3] specifying that a "computer program includes any literal work that is a) incorporated in, or associated with, a computer program; and b) essential to the effective operation of a function of that computer program".[4]

In other cases, due to the high speed of obsolescence of any definition in such a field, it was preferred to avoid any sort of definition, only providing the recognition of legal protection to the (undefined) subject matter "computer programs".[5] A clear sign of the effect of definition–obsolescence can be recognised in the fact that at present the key words used in the software field are "computer related inventions" or, according to the last document provided by the European Commission,[6] "computer-implemented inventions".

Nevertheless, a definition is required to determine the subject matter of protection and the specifics aims of the requested protection.

---

[1] WIPO, "Disposition types sur la protection du logiciel" (Provisions Type about the Software protection), (Geneva 1978).

[2] US Copyright Act, sec. 101.

[3] AUS Copyright Act, sec. 10.

[4] AUS Copyright Act, sec. 47AB. Previously definition was "a computer program is an expression, in any language code or notation, of a set of instructions intended to cause a device having digital information processing capabilities to perform a particular function".

[5] European Council Directive 91/250/EEC of 14 May 1991 on the legal protection of computer programs.

[6] See part 7 of this chapter.

The Courts have made a remarkable effort trying to explore all the technical issues related to computer programs.[7]

Finally, it is generally accepted that software could be considered as an intellectual creation expressed in a symbolic language, having the purpose of communicating instructions and /or to executing functions in an electronic device.

B. Technical Issues Involved

It is necessary to analyse preliminarily the steps that are usually involved in software creation. Following such approach it shall be easier to determine the subject-matter of a juridical relevance.

Programmer activities can be summarised in four steps:

(1) the identification of a principle finalised to a specific target;
(2) the choice among alternative ways to perform the final target;
(3) the writing of the specific list of selected steps (source code);
(4) the translation of the source code to object code (binary code).

Such activities involve a different kind of work and substantially different contributions. During activities (1) and (2), the programmer appears to perform work similar to the inventor, i.e., trying to find a solution to a specific problem, or to find the way to achieve a specific result. This work could have as its final outcome a new concept or a new solution idea. In particular, it could be said that the logical sequential steps made under the activity (2) could be defined as an algorithm. An algorithm has been defined as "a prescribed set of well-defined, unambiguous rules or processes for the solution of a problem in a finite number of steps".[8]

There is also a legal rule codified in the Japanese Copyright Act, according to which "algorithm means methods of combining, in a program, instructions given to a computer".[9] According to the Japanese Copyright Act, the algorithm could not be protected as copyright as in other jurisdictions, because such methods could have various expressions, and, in fact, they are methodological ideas of solutions.

The other two activities (3 and 4) are related to the final expression of the concept (or the solution idea), where the programmer codifies the specific list of instructions to be followed.

As said before, the codification consists of two steps:

a) the elaboration of the source code, entailing the codification of the instructions in a way that could be comprehensible to humans; and

---

[7] See in particular, Samuelson, Davis, Kapor & Reichmann, A Manifesto Concerning the Legal Protection of Computer Programs, 9 Col.L. Review 2308 [1994].

[8] See Samuelson, Davis et al. (above fn. 7), 2321 fn. 37.

[9] See Copyright Act of Japan, sec 10(3)(iii).

b) the drafting of the object code, entailing the translation of the algorithm into the binary code (i.e., the machine's language).

There is another consideration that should be made. In Directive 98/71 on the on the legal protection of designs[10] there is another express exclusion of "computer programs" from the subject matter of protection. Such an exclusion might appear a little bit strange: why exclude something that is in fact a methodological set of instructions for an electronic device? The previous analysis made is limited to the appreciation of software as an element that interacts only with an electronic device. Nevertheless software has another evident role: to communicate with the human user, giving him the tools needed to instruct the electronic device in doing determined functions (calculation, typing, etc.).

The specific command keys (constructed as command "texts" or as command "icons" or the predefined list of commands constructed in Menu and Sub Menu) represents the important role that the software plays as an interface between human beings and an electronic machine. It is self evident that some electronic devices are more reliable just because the software interface is more user friendly, or more intuitive (see, e.g., the cellular phone's commands menu, where the logic of the functions management could significantly determine the choice of an informed or professional user). This second function, that plays a "communicative" role, in relation to the choice of the internal logic of the software functioning is in principle capable of characterising the visual aspect of software as visible human interface. Directive 98/71 excluded it from design protection. No express motivation is made on the "recital" of the Directive. Yet it should be considered that the more evident "expressive" characteristics of software were considered protected only via copyright and not via a wider "scope of protection" right. In the famous Apple Computer *v.* Microsoft case,[11] the alleged infringement of the video displays by "Windows" was not considered a copyright infringement by the

---

[10] EC Directive 98/71 – Article 1 Definitions

"For the purpose of this Directive:

(a) 'design' means the appearance of the whole or a part of a product resulting from the features of, in particular, the lines, contours, colours, shape, texture and/or materials of the product itself and/or its ornamentation;

(b) 'product' means any industrial or handicraft item, including inter alia parts intended to be assembled into a complex product, packaging, get-up, graphic symbols and typographic typefaces, but excluding computer programs;

(c) 'complex product' means a product which is composed of multiple components which can be replaced permitting disassembly and reassembly of the product."

[11] Apple Computer, Inc. *v.* Microsoft Corp. [1988]. See, S. Menell, An analysis of the scope of Copyright Protection for Application Programs, [1989] Stanford Law Review 1049.

Court, because the same idea of "iconisation "of the commands was expressed in a different way by Microsoft.[12]

To summarise, various components are found in the programmer's activity:

(1) the solution of a technical problem, by a technical (procedural or methodological) teaching;
(2) the specific expression of the procedural steps chosen as instructions to be executed by an electronic device;
(3) the specific expression of the interface chosen to communicate to the end user the visual instructions to interact and to instruct the electronic device.

C. The Legal Perspective: Object and Scope of Protection of the Possible Exclusive Rights

From a judicial point of view, the various kinds of the above-mentioned activities and contributions could require different kinds of protection.

a) The technical concepts are usually protected under the patent system. The aim of the patent system is traditionally identified as a sort of agreement between the inventor and the State: the State's interest is that the inventor will share his knowledge with the public under a long term policy of incremental innovation development. The inventor's interest is to receive protection from the public authority over the intellectual property generated with the invention. Therefore the State, in exchange for full public disclosure of the invention, grants the inventor an exclusive right of exploitation for a limited period of time (20 years). The scope of protection of the exclusive right granted covers the reproduction of the claimed teaching, made either in an identical or an equivalent way. In practice, the patent covering the concept is disclosed independently from the way chosen to express such a teaching.

b) The formal expressions are usually protected under the copyright system. Copyright is not based on the "rewarding" approach that is usually found in the patent system. Copyright, moreover, does not protect ideas or concepts, but just the specific expression of an idea. The aim of copyright protection is to recognise the author's exclusive right to reproduce his creation. Consequently the scope of protection of copyright is very narrow and cannot prevent third parties from creating similar though non-identical works that might embody the same

---

[12] In such a case the Court also expressed its position asserting that certain elements of interfacing human being and electronic devices (such a commands expression/text/symbols) should constitute a publicly available technical standard.

idea.[13] In practice, copyright protection covers the expression of a work independently from the idea or the concept involved.

D. The Copyright Approach to Software Protection

The idea of applying the copyright system to software was adopted in the '80s in Europe, through the legislation and/or the jurisprudence of the various member States[14] as an alternative method of protection due to the expressed exclusion of the patent protection (see below).

In reality, the first mover in this direction was the United States who on 12 December 1980 adopted the "Computer Software Amendment Act". In 1991[15] the European Community adopted Directive 91/250 on the protection of computer programs. The Directive was adopted on the basis of the recognition of investments related to software and the significant risk of illicit copying made by third parties[16] and for the purpose of eliminating the differences among the member states on the juridical protection of computer programs.[17] The Directive expressly declared that the choice to use copyright for the legal protection of software should be considered merely a first step.[18] Accordingly, the Directive limits the protection conferred on computer programs (including preparatory materials) "per se", expressly excluding the ideas and the principles on the basis of the said computer programs.[19] Subsequently, the TRIPs Agreement of 1994 in Art. 10 stated that "Computer Programs, whether in source or in object code, shall be protected as literary works under the Berne Convention (1971)".

By following this approach we could easily come to the conclusion that computer programs "per se" are internationally protected by the copyright system. The practical enforcement of said discipline is relevant mainly in cases of piracy, that is cases of illicit duplication of software. Very few cases exist in which there was a real judicial discussion of the full or partial duplication of the source code of a program, independently of the duplication of all the software (possibly having a different users interface). In general, the very limited scope of protection of the copyright was affirmed.[20]

---

[13] In certain cases also identical (or quasi-identical) creations should be tolerated, in the case of ascertained independent creation from two different authors. This is the case of the "creative coincidences".

[14] Germany: Law of 24 June 1985; France: Law of 3 July 1985; United Kingdom: Law of 16 July 1985.

[15] Directive 91/250 of 14 May 1991.

[16] Recital (2) – EC Directive 91/250.

[17] Recital (5) – EC Directive 91/250.

[18] Recital (6) – EC Directive 91/250.

[19] Arts. 1,2 – EC Directive 91/250.

[20] Recently the Italian Supreme Court (13 December 1999, n° 13937 in Rivista di Diritto Industriale, II, 15 [2001]) held the new release of a previous software to be an illicit partial reproduction of software.. Previously, the Federal Court of Australia, in the case

E. The Patent Approach to Software Protection

Concerning patent protection, there is an express ban on the granting of patents for computer programs. The European Patent Convention, signed on 5 October 1973, expressly excluded computer programs from the subject matter list.[21] Such exclusion was introduced just before the approval of the Convention, and no mention was made at the Strasbourg Convention of 1963 either. Various reasons exist for this exclusion. In general, it was argued that computer programs are intellectual and abstract products. In particular, the objective difficulty in examining software claims was also raised. Nevertheless, the exclusion of computer programs is limited to the computer program "as such". The obvious consequence is that it could be, theoretically, patentable as an electronic device characterised by computer program. In fact the European Patent Office started to grant patents for products characterised by software.[22] There have been some relevant decisions in this area that can be summarised as follows:

"The non-patentability of computer programs as such does not preclude the patenting of computer-related inventions. However, the real technical contribution to the state of the art which the subject-matter claimed, considered as a whole, adds to the known art, should be ascertained (the subject-matter may also be defined by a mix of technical and non-technical features)."[23]

Decision T 208/8424 set out the principles governing the patentability of computer-related inventions. Even if the idea underlying an invention may be considered to reside in a mathematical method, a claim directed to a technical process in which the method is used does not

---

Data Access Corporation *v.* Powerflex Services, 9 February 1996, held that infringement of copyright had occurred despite there having been no literal copying of computer code. See K.Fong, Non-literal Copying Infringes Copyright in Software, [1997] EIPR 256; see also D. Hunter, Mind Your Language: Copyright in Computer Languages in Australia, [1998] EIPR 98.

  [21] Art. 52, EPC

    "(1) European patents shall be granted for any inventions which are susceptible of industrial application, which are new and which involve an inventive step.
    (2) The following in particular shall not be regarded as inventions within the meaning of paragraph 1:
    . . . C) programs for computers
    (3) the provisions of paragraph 2 shall exclude patentability of the subject-matter or activities referred to in that provision only to the extent to which a European patent application or European patent relates to such subject-matter or activities as such".

  [22] See G. Kolle, Patentability of Software Related Inventions in Europe, 22 IIC 660 [1991]. See also, from a different perspective, L. Van Raden, Technology Dematerialised: Another Approach to Information-related Inventions, [1997] EIPR 384.
  [23] See T 26/86 OJ 1988, 19 – Koch Sterzel; T 209/91 (norm) in Case Law of the Boards of Appeal of the European Patent Office, 3.

seek protection for the mathematical method as such. A claim directed to a technical process carried out under the control of a program (whether by means of hardware or software) cannot be regarded as relating to a computer program as such. A claim which can be considered as being directed to a computer set up to operate in accordance with a specified program (whether by means of hardware or software) for controlling or carrying out a technical process cannot be regarded as relating to a computer program as such.

The next leading case, decision T 26/86,[25] examined whether an X-ray apparatus incorporating a data processing unit operating in accordance with a routine was patentable. The board considered that the claim related neither to a computer program on its own and divorced from any technical application, nor to a computer program in the form of a recording on a data carrier, nor to a known, general purpose computer in combination with a computer program. It found instead that the routine in accordance with which the X-ray apparatus operated produced a technical effect, i.e. it controlled the X-ray tubes so that by establishing a certain parameter priority, optimum exposure was combined with adequate protection against overloading of the X-ray tubes.

The invention was therefore patentable irrespective of whether or not the X-ray apparatus without this computer program formed part of the state of the art. The board held that an invention must be assessed as a whole. If it made use of both technical and non-technical means, the use of non-technical means did not detract from the technical character of the overall teaching. The EPC does not prohibit the patenting of inventions consisting of a mix of technical and non-technical elements.

The board therefore regarded it as unnecessary to weigh up the technical and non-technical features in a claim in order to decide whether it related to a computer program as such. If the invention defined in the claim used technical means, its patentability was not ruled out by Art. 52(2)(c) and (3) and it could be protected if it met the requirements of Art. 52 to 57.

In decision T 6/83[26] the board found that an invention relating to the co-ordination and control of the internal communication between programs and data files held at different processors in a data processing system having a plurality of interconnected data processors in a telecommunications network, the features of which were not concerned with the nature of the data and the way in which a particular application program operated on them, was to be regarded as solving a problem which was essentially technical. The control program was therefore comparable to the conventional operating programs required for any computer to coordinate its internal basic functions and thereby permit the running of a number of programs for specific applications. Such an invention was to be regarded as solving a problem which was essentially technical and thus an invention within the meaning of Art. 52(1).

In decision T 158/88[27] the board stated that a method for the display of characters (e.g. Arabic characters) in a particular preset shape chosen from several possible character shapes did not in essence describe a technical method of operating a data processing system and its visual display unit, but an idea for a program. A computer program did not become part of a technical operating method if the teaching claimed was confined to changing data and did not trigger any effect over and above mere data processing. When examining whether the method in question

[24] OJ 1987, 14 – Vicom.
[25] See above 23.
[26] OJ 1990, 5.
[27] OJ 1991, 566.

served to solve a technical problem which could make the program defined in the claim patentable as part of a teaching on technical operations, the board came to the conclusion that where the data to be processed according to a claimed method represented neither operating parameters nor a device, nor had a physical or technical effect on the way the device worked, and no technical problem was solved by the claimed method, the invention defined in the claim did not make use of any technical means and in accordance with Art. 52(2)(c) and (3) could not be regarded as a patentable invention within the meaning of Art. 52(1).

In T 59/93[28] a method for entering a rotation angle value into an interactive draw graphic system was claimed. This method, implemented on a programme-controlled computer, its operator being the user, allowed the rotation of displayed graphic objects with increased accuracy. The board held that the method claim defined, by the steps the method comprised, the functional features of said system. These features were neither regarded as relating to mathematical methods as such (the calculating steps were considered to be only means used within the overall method), nor as claims to computer programs as such (the operation of the system, in its use under the control of such programs, brought about technical effects which solved a problem which was to be regarded as involving technical considerations), nor as relating to the presentation of information as such (the excluded subject-matter was not claimed as such, but was only a tool for implementing certain steps of the method claimed as a whole). The board held that methods comprising excluded features, but nevertheless solving a technical problem and bringing about technical effects, were to be considered as making a technical contribution to the art.

In T 953/94,[29] claim 1 of the main request related to a method of generating with a digital computer a data analysis of the cyclical behaviour of a curve represented by a plurality of plots relating two parameters to one another. The board held that such a method could not be regarded as a patentable invention, because an analysis of the cyclical behaviour of a curve was clearly a mathematical method excluded as such from patentability. The reference to a digital computer only had the effect of indicating that the claimed method was carried out with the aid of a computer, i.e. a programmable general-purpose computer, functioning under the control of a program excluded as such from patentability. The fact that the description disclosed examples in both non-technical and technical fields confirmed that the problem solved by the claimed mathematical method was independent of any field of application and could thus lie, in the case at issue, only in the mathematical and not in a technical field.

The fifth auxiliary request read as follows: 'A method of controlling a physical process based on analysing a functional relationship between two parameters of the physical process comprising the steps of: measuring the values of the two parameters, and generating with a digital computer a data analysis of the cyclical behaviour of a curve represented by a plurality of plots relating the two parameters to one another, . . .' The last feature was worded as follows: '(h) extending the range of said one parameter in accordance with the data generated for displaying on a visual display unit the prolongation of said curve for use in the control of said physical process.'

---

[28] T 59/93 (norm) in Case Law of the Boards of Appeal of the European Patent Office, 4.

[29] T 953/94 (norm) in Case Law of the Boards of Appeal of the European Patent Office, 4.

The board emphasised that claim 1 of the fifth auxiliary request was not excluded from patentability only because of the insertion of the expression 'for use in the control of said physical process'. Contrary to the decision of the opposition division the board decided that this wording limited the claim in a technical sense. Claim 1 no longer referred to the mere possibility of using the mathematical method in a technical or physical process. It was agreed that if the expression 'for use' were understood as merely indicating that the claimed extension of the range of a parameter for displaying the prolongation of the curve would be 'suitable' for use in the process control, such an interpretation might cast doubt on the effectiveness of the limitation of the claim. However, in conjunction with the expressly intended restriction of the claimed method to a 'method of controlling a physical process' the word 'for', in the board's view, could no longer be interpreted as merely meaning 'suitable' but as 'used to control a physical process'. The board concluded that the subject-matter of the fifth auxiliary request in its proper interpretation was not excluded from patentability."

Accordingly

"A computer program as such, i.e. if claimed by itself such a program listing, a record on a carrier or when loaded into a known computer, is not patentable subject matter, whereas a process for operating in a computer in accordance with a given program or a computer programmed to operate in a given way is, in general, patentable if a technical effect can be identified. Also, a program-controlled manufacturing or control process normally involves patentable subject-matter".[30]

Various member States followed the same EPO approach in their jurisdictions.[31] Nevertheless significantly conflicting approaches emerged, mainly due to rulings of the UK and German courts.

"As to the specific differences which exist between the case law of the U.K. courts and that of the EPO Board of Appeal, these concern the manner in which the law is interpreted in relation to excluded matter in general. Under U.K. jurisprudence (in contrast to that of the EPO), a computer program related invention that amounts to, for example, a method for doing business or a mental act, is considered non-patentable even if a technical contribution (in terms defined in this Directive) can be found. This is illustrated by Merrill Lynch, for business methods, and by Raytheon Co's Application, for mental acts.

On the other hand, it had been thought that German jurisprudence did not exclude the possibility that business methods having a technical aspect could be patentable even if the only contribution that the invention makes is non-technical. Such an interpretation would open the door to significant extension of patentability into this field. Relevant cases include the "Automatic Sales Control" case and Speech Analysis Apparatus. While the Bundesgerichthof recently clarified the position by affirming that the correct approach is the one adopted by the EPO Board of Appeals and this Directive, namely that an inventive technical contribution is an essential prerequisite for inventive step, this example clearly illustrates the potential for judicial

---

[30] G. Kolle, (above fn. 22), 675.

[31] See, for Germany, W. Tauchert, Patent Protection for Computer Programs – Current Status and New Developments, in 31 IIC 812 [2000]; see for the United Kingdom, A. Brimelow, Claims to Program for Computers, UK Patent Office, www.patent.gov.uk/patent/notices/practice/computer.htm [1999].

interpretation to develop the law in such a manner as to result in major changes to the scope of patentability at the national level."[32]

Recent decisions made by the Board of Appeal of the EPO clearly confirmed the new perspective, in particular

- T 769/92 of 31 May 1994[33];
- T 1173/97 of 1 July 1998[34];
- T 1194/97 of 15 March 2000[35];
- T 931/95 of 8 September 2000[36].

In such decisions "the Board of Appeal considered that a computer program product may possess a technical character because it has the potential to cause a predetermined further technical effect when the program runs on a computer".[37]

Accordingly, on 31 August 2001 the EPO decided to amend the EPO Guidelines for the Examination:

". . . while programs for computers are included among the items listed in art. 52(2), if the claimed subject-matter has a technical character, it is not excluded from patentability . . . if a computer program is capable of bringing about, when running on a computer, a further technical effect going beyond these normal physical effects, it is not excluded from patentability, irrespective of whether it is claimed by itself or as a record on a carrier. . . . As a consequence, a computer program claimed by itself or as a record on a carrier or in the form of a signal may be considered as an invention within the meaning of the Art. 52(1) if the program has the poten-

---

[32] COM (2002) 92 final, 2002/0047, Explanatory Memorandum, 10.

[33] In T 769/92 (OJ 1995, 525) the board held that an invention comprising functional features implemented by software (computer programs) was not excluded from patentability under Art. 52(2)(c) and (3) if technical considerations concerning particulars of the solution of the problem the invention solved were required in order to carry out that same invention. Such technical considerations lent a technical nature to the invention in that they implied a technical problem to be solved by (implicit) technical features. An invention of this kind was considered not to pertain to a computer program as such under Art. 52(3). The decision set out that non-exclusion from patentability could not be destroyed by an additional feature which as such would itself be excluded, as in the present case features referring to management systems and methods which might fall under the "methods for doing business" excluded from patentability under Art. 52(2)(c) and (3).

[34] See Gilian Davies, Computer Program Claims, [1998] EIPR 429.

[35] OJ 2000, 525.

[36] OJ 2001, 413.

[37] "Accordingly the supply of an infringing computer program on a carrier would be a direct infringement of the claims. In addition the Board of Appeal indicated that claims to a computer program product independent of any carrier or media are acceptable as long as the computer program has technical character or a further technical effect. This latter form of claim will have impact on the on-line distribution of computer programs using for example the Internet. It remains to be seen, however, how the Courts will interpret these claims." R. Hart, Holmes, J. Reid, The Economic Impact of Patentability of Computer Programs, 19 October 2000, 24, available at http://ftp.ipr-helpdesk.org/softstudy.pdf.

tial to bring about, when running on a computer, a further technical effect which goes beyond the normal physical interactions between the program and the computer."[38]

Such a position was considered by some[39] as a sort of juridical "coup", because the EPO anticipated the effects related to the discussed project to extend patent protection to computer programs via an EC Directive.

As far as a comparative approach is concerned, it should be mentioned that in 1989 a comparative study was prepared by the European Patent Office in connection with the Trilateral Cooperation between the EPO, JPO and USPTO.[40] In this study the first comparative approach was made to the basic criteria and tests for assessing patentability of computer related inventions.

The U.S.

The U.S. does not have statutory exclusions for inventions and it identifies four categories of patentable subject matter: process, machine, manufacture and composition of matter. The Supreme Court has identified three categories of subject matter that do not fall within the boundary of the statute "laws of nature, natural phenomena, and abstract ideas".

The U.S. Patent Office guidelines specifically identify that the utility of an invention must be within the technological arts. A computer related invention is within the technological arts. Claims to computer programs on a carrier are statutory on the grounds that they define an article of manufacture.

The State Street Bank case[41] has removed the mathematical algorithms and method of doing business "exceptions" and has defined that the focus for patentability in United States is "utility" which is defined as "the essential characteristics of the subject matter" and the key to patentability is the production of a "useful, concrete and tangible result".[42]

The USPTO Guidelines for examination of computer-related inventions offer a large panorama of examples of inventions with a complex claim analysis.[43]

Japan

The Japanese system has exceptions and requires that an invention be a highly advanced creation of technical ideas by which a law of nature is

---

[38] EPO Guidelines for Examination, Part C, chapter IV, 2.

[39] Eurolinux Alliance.

[40] Patentability of Computer-related Inventions, 21 IIC 817 [1990].

[41] State Street Bank & Trust *v.* Signature Financial Group Inc., US District Court of Massachusetts, 26 March 1996 in [1996] EIPR D-243; reversed by Court of Appeal for the Federal Circuit, decided on 23 July 1998, 149 F 3d. 1368, 47 U.S.P.Q. 2d.1596, No. 93 – 1327. Also available on www.webpatent.com/cases/statest.htm.

[42] R. Hart, Holmes, J. Reid, (above fn. 37), 23. See also, for a previous panorama D.R. Syrowik, R.J. Cole, The Challenge of Software-related Patents: A Primer on Software-related Patents and the Software Patent Institute, Software Patent Institute [1994].

[43] Available on www.uspto.gov/web/offices/pac/compexam/examcomp.htm.

utilised. The Japanese system does permit claims of a computer readable storage medium as a product with the programs functionally defined.[44]

In December 2000 the Japanese Patent Office revised the Examination Guidelines for Computer Software – related inventions. According to the new approach :

"(1) 'a computer program' which specifies the multiple functions performed by a computer can be defined as 'a product invention'.

(2) When information processing by software is concretely realised by using hardware resources, the said software is deemed to be 'a statutory invention' prescribed in the Patent Law."[45]

The Japanese approach therefore appears more open to the patentability of software inventions.

Finally it should be noted that

"The fundamental difference, however, between the United States and Europe turns on the requirement that the invention must provide a technical contribution in Europe, **whereas**, in the U.S. to be patentable computer program related inventions are of the technological arts and they need only provide a useful, concrete and tangible result which for example includes the computerised transformation of data representing dollar amounts into a final share price using a practical application of a mathematical formula or calculation. It is the requirement of technical contribution that will bar a large number of business method inventions that will be patentable in the U.S."[46]

F. The Recent Draft Directive on the Patentability of Computer-implemented Inventions

In March 1999 the European Commission announced its intention to update the European Patent Convention in relation to the patentability of the computer programs; in October 2000, it launched consultations on the patentability of computer-implemented inventions;[47] and in the same period, published a study on "The Economic Impact of Patentability of Computer Programs".[48]

Finally, on 2 February 2002 a draft Directive on the patentability of computer-implemented inventions was published.[49] The Explanatory Memorandum of the draft Directive indicates that despite the formal exclusion of the patentability for computer programs, "thousands of patents for computer implemented inventions have been granted by the European

[44] R. Hart, Holmes, J. Reid, (above fn. 37), 23.

[45] Available in www.jpo.go.jp/saikine/tt1301-008.htm .

[46] R. Hart, Holmes, J. Reid, (above fn. 37), 24.

[47] The consultation document could be found at the internet website: http://europa.eu.int/comm/internal_market/en/intprop/indprop/index.htm.

[48] R. Hart, Holmes, J. Reid, (above fn. 37).

[49] COM (2002) 92 final, 2002/0047.

Patent Office (EPO) and by national patent offices. The EPO alone accounts for more than 20,000 of them".[50] The draft Directive demonstrates the crucial relevance of computer programs in technological innovation, which is the reason for harmonisation capable of ensuring an optimum environment for developers and users of computer programs.[51] In any event, the draft Directive limits the protection to computer implemented inventions that make a "technical contribution" to the state of the art.[52]

Accordingly in

"a defined procedure or sequence of actions when performed in the context of an apparatus, such a computer may make a technical contribution to the state of the art and thereby constitute a patentable invention. However, an algorithm which is defined without reference to a physical environment is inherently non-technical and cannot therefore constitute a patentable invention."[53]

This express reference to the algorithm means that the algorithms are different from the source code and confirm the fact stated before under paragraph 1 of the present article: the activity related to the definition of the sequences related to the solving of a technical problem/solution could generate an inventive concept and therefore be patentable.[54]

Art. 2 of the proposal defines the meaning of computer-implemented invention as: "any invention the performance of which involves the use of a computer, computer network or other programmable apparatus and having one or more prima facie novel features which are realised wholly or partly by means of a computer program or computer programs".

Under Art. 4 the "technical contribution" is defined as a condition, part of the inventive step requirement.[55] Art. 5 provides the dual possibility to

---

[50] Ibid., 2.

[51] Ibid., recital (4), 17.

[52] Ibid., recital (11), 18; See at 11: "While the patent system has to be adapted where appropriate to meet the need for protection of inventions in new fields of technology, such developments should be based on the general principles of European patent law as they have evolved historically. These are expressed, in particular, in the rule that an invention, to be patentable, must make a technical contribution to the state of the art. Having reached this stage, the Commission believes it is right that the Community should, for the time being at least, refrain from extending the patent protection available for computer-implemented inventions, for example by dispensing with the technical contribution requirement. . . . By codifying the requirement for a technical contribution, the Directive should ensure that patents for 'pure' business methods or more generally social processes will not be granted because they do not meet the strict criteria, including the need for technical contribution."

[53] Ibid., recital (13), 19.

[54] "The term 'algorithm' may be understood in its broadest sense to mean any detailed sequence of actions intended to perform a specific task. In this context, it can clearly encompass both technical and non-technical processes." Ibid., 7.

[55] Art. 2 contains also a definition of the technical contribution as "a contribution to the state of the art in a technical field which is not obvious to a person skilled in the art".

claim a computer implemented invention as a product or as a process. Art. 6 provides that the patent protection does not affect in any way the special rules contained in Directive 91/250 on decompilation and interoperability.[56] Arts. 7 and 8 provide a system of monitoring and reporting the impact and the effects of the Directive.

In practice the proposal limits the effect of integrating the approach of the European Patent Office, allowing the patenting of computer implemented inventions (not software claimed "as such"), codifying the requirement of the "technical contribution" (to avoid the risk of business method patenting) and confirming the validity of the decompilation rule, set out in Directive 91/250.

G. The Competition Issues

Usually, the exclusive rights conferred by a patent or a copyright are considered as full and unlimited. There is only one specific rule, usually contained into the national patent Laws related to the compulsory licence. This institution represents a sort of compromise between the monopolistic effect of a patent and the public interest of other competitors in exploiting the patented invention. In fact, the real enforcement of such a rule was practically insignificant, due to the peculiarities of the legal conditions that have to be met in order to grant a compulsory licence.[57]

In certain fields of technology the existence and the exploitation of the exclusive rights has a particularly negative effect. In the field of software such a risk was evident from the beginning.

Previously, in the mid–1980s, the EC Commission initiated proceedings against the IBM[58] Corporation in relation to the disclosure of interface information. Nevertheless "that proceeding was suspended by an undertaking of IBM to provide certain information".[59] In fact

"when the manufacturer of a computer system elects not to disclose such interface information, or to make it available only on contractual condition that it cannot be used to create a competitive product but only to run the product acquired by user from the system manufacturer, questions have been raised under antitrust or competition law principles. . . . In terms of the Sherman Act, the question is whether it is an act of monopolisation, or is conduct that would support a claim of attempt to monopolise, to refuse to provide information that permits a competitor to offer a product that can substitute for one's own product. This question has been

---

[56] Such argument is analysed in the following paragraph.

[57] For instance in Italy, a compulsory licence could be granted only if a) the patent was not exploited after four years from the filing date; or b) in case of dependent inventions, the subsequent patent represents relevant technical progress and in any event evidence must be given about the fact that it was previously denied a licence under equitable conditions (Art. 54 Italian Patent Act).

[58] Commission Decision 84/233.

[59] C.B. Cohler and H. E. Pearson, Software Interfaces, Intellectual Property and Competition Policy, [1994] EIPR 434.

posed as one involving an 'essential facilities' doctrine, where the interface information is said to be essential to permit the opportunity for competition."[60]

That is why Directive 91/250 expressly created a rule based on a competition policy rule: the decompilation clause (Art. 6).[61]

The decompilation right for the purpose of interoperability does not mean that the requested information shall be made available by the copyright owner: the interested party should invest time and resources to study and to apply reverse engineering techniques. In fact the decompilation clause could not be considered a sort of compulsory licence because of lack of any publicly available content related to the interoperability information. Such evidence was, in particular, raised by the various associations that developed a completely different philosophy based on the "free software" or "open source" approach.[62]

---

[60] Ibid., 435

[61] Art. 6, EC Directive 91/250:

" Article 6 Decompilation
1. The authorisation of the right holder shall not be required where reproduction of the code and translation of its form within the meaning of Article 4 (a) and (b) are indispensable to obtain the information necessary to achieve the interoperability of an independently created computer program with other programs, provided that the following conditions are met:

(a) these acts are performed by the licensee or by another person having a right to use a copy of a program, or on their behalf by a person authorised to do so;
(b) the information necessary to achieve interoperability has not previously been readily available to the persons referred to in subparagraph (a); and (c) these acts are confined to the parts of the original program which are necessary to achieve interoperability.

2. The provisions of paragraph 1 shall not permit the information obtained through its application:

(a) to be used for goals other than to achieve the interoperability of the independently created computer program;
(b) to be given to others, except when necessary for the interoperability of the independently created computer program; or (c) to be used for the development, production or marketing of a computer program substantially similar in its expression, or for any other act which infringes copyright.

3. In accordance with the provisions of the Berne Convention for the protection of Literary and Artistic Works, the provisions of this Article may not be interpreted in such a way as to allow its application to be used in a manner which unreasonably prejudices the right holder's legitimate interests or conflicts with a normal exploitation of the computer program."

[62] "The term 'free software' is occasionally preferred, but the term 'open software' appears to be prevailing in the trade press. Open source software must be distinguished from the terms 'public domain software', 'free software' and 'shareware'. Shareware is a sales concept in which software is made available free of charge for a limited time or for a limited use, in order to give the user an opportunity to test it. The term 'public domain software' can only be understood against the background of US law. According to this

"The aim of the Free Software Foundation is to write and distribute 'free software' and also to secure the freedom of this software in legal terms. In this context, 'free' does not mean free of charge , nor is economic exploitation by commercial distribution intended to be entirely excluded. 'Free' on the contrary expresses that everyone should be allowed to copy, distribute, modify and in turn distribute modified versions of 'free software' or open source software."[63]

Such a disclosure is based, nevertheless, on a voluntary system.

For what expressly concerns EC competition rules, it should be noted that

"In early cases the European Court of Justice developed a distinction between the existence and exercise of an intellectual property right in applying both the free movement of goods and the competition law provisions of the Treaty or Rome. To apply that distinction, the concept of 'specific subject matter' of the right concerned was developed. The specific subject matter of copyright is the exclusive right to reproduce, which includes the right to refuse licenses. Normally, the exercise of the specific subject matter will not offend against either the free movement or the competition rules, but this is not absolute. If the right is exercised under special circumstances that it creates an unacceptable obstacle to either free trade or free competition, then it may overridden".[64]

---

position, copyright does not exist for such software. For this reason, the term cannot be applied similarly by continental – European legal circles. Nonetheless, the term has become established in the computer branch to designate software that the user can adapt according to whatever need he has. That does not mean, however, that the source code is disclosed. The use of the term 'freeware' is also vague. Some hold the view that freeware also allows the user to make changes. Nevertheless, public domain software and freeware differ in a significant point from the open source software. The definition of 'open software' entails not only distribution without license fees, but also the obligation to disclose the source code and to allow modifications". A. Metzeger and T. Jaeger, Open Source Software and German Copyright Law, 32 IIC 52 [2001]. See also, Software Patents Damage Society, available on http://bim.bsn.com/~jhs/txt/patents.html, where is expressly stated "Copyright is sufficient – Software Patents are excessive. I am Not against copyright pertaining to software. As a programmer myself, I & associates are often required to assign copyright, on hand over rights to custom software developed for specific requirements. I see no problem with copyright, except that, obviously where (to speed development & reduce costs) modules of pre-existing public code are used (mine or other peoples), pre-existing copyrights apply unchanged. I see a node to protect actual implemented code with copyright (except where the author makes it public domain etc), but I am against software patents that would bar programmers from even independently dreaming up the same nifty idea & re-implementing a similar solution". Moreover see the petition that Eurolinux directed to the European Parliament against the danger of the software patents: http://noepatents.org/index_html?LANG=en. See also Protecting Information Innovation Against the Abuse of the Patent System, in http://swpat.ffii.org.

[63] A. Metzger and T. Jaeger, (above fn. 62), 55–56.
[64] C.B. Cohler and H. E. Pearson, (above fn. 59), 438.

In the Magill case[65] the Court of Justice confirmed the fact that the exercise of an exclusive right (legitimately existing) could be considered abusive if the behaviour of the IP owner (consisting of the denial of licence or of access of the information) is only directed at preventing third parties from creating a new product or service not already offered by the owner.

H. The "Cumulation" of Rights

The complementary nature of patents and copyrights is expressly asserted by the Commission:

"legal protection may exist in a complementary manner in respect of the same program both by patent and by copyright law. The protection may be cumulative in the sense that an act involving exploitation of a particular program may infringe both the copyright in the code and a patent whose claims cover the underlying ideas and principles."[66]

---

[65] ECJ cases C–241/91 and C–242/91, of 6 April 1995:

"2. The conduct of an undertaking in a dominant position, consisting of the exercise of a right classified by national law as 'copyright', cannot, by virtue of that fact alone, be exempt from review in relation to Article 86 of the Treaty.

In the absence of Community standardisation or harmonisation of laws, determination of the conditions and procedures for granting protection of an intellectual property right is admittedly a matter for national rules and the exclusive right of reproduction forms part of the author's rights, with the result that refusal to grant a licence, even if it is the act of an undertaking holding a dominant position, cannot in itself constitute abuse of a dominant position.

However, the exercise of an exclusive right by a proprietor may, in exceptional circumstances, involve abusive conduct. Such will be the case when broadcasting companies rely on copyright conferred by national legislation to prevent another undertaking from publishing on a weekly basis information (channel, day, time and title of programmes) together with commentaries and pictures obtained independently of those companies, where, in the first place, that conduct prevents the appearance of a new product, a comprehensive weekly guide to television programmes, which the companies concerned do not offer and for which there is a potential consumer demand, conduct which constitutes an abuse under heading (b) of the second paragraph of Article 86 of the Treaty; where, second, there is no justification for that refusal either in the activity of television broadcasting or in that of publishing television magazines; and where, third, the companies concerned, by their conduct, reserve to themselves the secondary market of weekly television guides by excluding all competition from the market through denial of access to the basic information which is the raw material indispensable for the compilation of such a guide."

The Magill TV Guide case concerned the availability of information as to the time, channel and title of television broadcasts so as to permit publication of a weekly compilation of such information. None of the broadcasters of TV programmers agreed to provide information to Magill which wished to publish a weekly guide incorporating the listing of the broadcasters. C.B. Cohler and H. E. Pearson, (above fn. 59), 436.

[66] The patentability of computer implemented inventions, Consultation Paper by the Services of the Directorate General for the Internal Market, Brussels, 10 October 2000, 5.

Accordingly, the Explanatory Memorandum of draft Directive 2002/0047 recognises that:

"... legal protection may exist in a complementary manner in respect of the same program both by patent and by copyright law. The protection may be cumulative in the sense that an act involving exploitation of a particular program may infringe both the copyright in the code and a patent whose claims cover the underlying ideas and principles."[67]

From the practical point of view, the coexistence of the two kinds of protection will offer a double possibility to protect their innovations to the software developer and to the software companies, only in relation to software that offers a "technical contribution".

I. Conclusion

One may conclude that the dilemma about the choice of protection between copyright and patent protection does not exist.[68] Moreover the EC study finds "no evidence that European independent software developers have been unduly affected by the patent positions of large companies or indeed of other software developers."[69] Accordingly,

"the differences between the subject-matter of protection under patent and copyright law, and the nature of the permitted exceptions, the exercise of a patent covering a computer-implemented invention should not interfere with the freedoms granted under copyright law to software developers by the provisions of the Directive 91/250/EEC".[70]

"Moreover, as regards developing interoperable programs, the requirement for each patent to include an enabling disclosure should facilitate the task of a person seeking to adapt a program to another, pre-existing one incorporating patented features (the requirement of disclosure has no analogue under copyright law).

Finally, it should be said that in the event that patent rights are exercised in abusive way, compulsory licenses may be available as a remedy, as well as possible recourse to competition law."[71]

At present, therefore, the real problems will concern:

a) the broad or the strict interpretation that will be given by the EPO to the requirement of "technical contribution";[72]

---

[67] COM (2002) 92 final, 2002/0047, 8.

[68] D.C. Derrick, It Doesn't Fit: The Dilemma of Computer Softward and Patent /Copyright Law, E Law – Murdoch University Electronic Journal of Law, Vol. 3, No. 1 [1996], available at www.murdoch.edu.au/elaw/issues/v3n1/derrick.html.

[69] R. Hart, P. Holmes, J. Reid, (above fn. 37), 3, Conclusions 1.

[70] COM (2002) 92 final, 2002/0047, 9.

[71] COM (2002) 92 final, 2002/0047, 9.

[72] "To address the difference between the scope of protection in the U.S. and Europe it would be necessary to either amend the implementing regulations (rules 27 and 29) or to give a broader interpretation to technical contribution, such as that suggested by the United Nations where technology is defined as 'a combination of equipment and knowledge'." R. Hart, P. Holmes, J. Reid, (above fn. 37), 24.

b) the need to verify the enabling disclosure in patents to permit more advantageously the exercise of the decompilation clause;

c) the need to have a more relevant approach on the competitive issues, re-thinking the issues of the IP rights abuse and the compulsory licence system.

9
The Protection of Aesthetic Creations as Three-Dimensional Marks, Designs, Copyright or Under Unfair Competition

CHRISTOPHER HEATH

A. Introduction

With the enactment of the European Design Directive (October 1998) and the Design Regulation (January 2002), design protection in Europe has changed its face. While not all countries yet have implemented the Design Directive, the Design Regulation has been operative since 1 January 2003, when the European Trade Mark Office opened its doors to applicants for Community designs. This paper will thus begin with a brief introduction into European design protection (II). The Design Directive explicitly states that the protection of an aesthetic creation as a design must not preclude protection under copyright law where the protection requirements are otherwise met. Copyright protection would thus be the second tier of protection available under the laws of national member states and is explored under (III) for Europe, the US and Japan. Increasingly, attempts have been made to obtain protection for aesthetic creations also as indications of origin either by registration as three-dimensional marks or by claiming protection against so-called "slavish imitation". These issues are further explored under (IV) and (V). Also in these cases, a comparison is made between Europe, Japan and the US.

B. Design Protection

The most common way of protecting aesthetic creations is of course design protection. Despite a certain harmonisation of the minimum requirements of protection under the TRIPS Agreement (Arts. 25, 26), the protection systems in Europe, the US and Japan show a number of differences.

I. Design Protection in Europe

1. Registered designs

The protection of designs in Europe has been significantly harmonised by the Design Directive[1] and the Design Regulation.[2] While the Design

---

[1] Directive 98/71/EC of 13 October 1998, OJ L 289/28 of 28 October 1998.
[2] Council Regulation 6/2002 of 12 December 2001, OJ L 3/1 of 5 January 2002.

Directive has harmonised national design laws, the Design Regulation has created a European design right by either registration with the Alicante Trade Mark Office or by protection as an unregistered design. While the Design Regulation became operative in 2003, to date not all EU countries have implemented the Design Directive.[3]

The definitions of a design are contained in Art. 3 Design Regulation, according to which the term design "means the appearance of the whole or a part of a product resulting from the features of, in particular, the lines, contours, colours, shape, texture and/or materials of the product itself and/or its ornamentation." The definition of a product is fairly broad and also comprises graphic symbols and typographic typefaces, yet excludes computer programs.[4]

In order to obtain protection, a design must be new and have individual character. Where the design is applied to or incorporated in a complex product, novelty and individual character require the component part to remain visible during the normal course of use, and be new and individual in itself, Art. 4. The novelty test is measured against the previous publication of an "identical design". Novelty is thus assumed if there have been no designs on the market that are identical or that differ only in immaterial details from the design for which protection is sought. The date to determine novelty in the case of a registered design is the application date, in the case of an unregistered design, the day when the design is first made available to the public, Art. 5. The novelty standard is neither Community-wide nor worldwide novelty, but relies on a different test. Novelty is lost if the previous design could "reasonably have become known in the normal course of business to the circles specialised in the sector concerned, operating within the Community." Given the increasing ubiquity of the Internet, the standard may come close to worldwide novelty, though.

The "individual character" requires a distinction in the overall impression produced by the design on an informed user vis-à-vis previously existing designs. Individual character must also be measured against the degree of freedom the designer has in developing the design, Art. 6. Consequently, designs solely dictated by their technical function cannot be protected, Art. 8. However, designs that are only partly technical, in particular that allow the assembly within a modular system, are not per se considered functional.

The scope of protection corresponds to the test for determining individual character, and thus includes designs that do not produce a different overall impression on the informed user.

[3] C. Penteroulakis, Die Umsetzung der Richtlinie 98/71/EG über den rechtlichen Schutz von Mustern und Modellen in den EU-Mitgliedsstaaten, 2002 GRUR Int. 668.

[4] This is a welcome clarification insofar as in the UK two-dimensional colour arrangements were not deemed "configurations" under Sec. 51(3) Patents, Designs and Copyright Act 1988: Lambretta Clothing *v*. Teddy Smith, English High Court, 23 May 2003, [2003] R.P.C. 728, 737.

The protection period for an unregistered design (see below b) is three years from the date of first marketing, for a registered design, a maximum period of 25 years from the date of filing, comprising five terms of five years. The registered design lapses unless the renewal fees for the extension periods are paid.

The rights conferred by a Community design extend to basically all acts of use, yet do not confer a monopoly that would extend to independent creations by third parties, Art. 19(2) Design Directive. Excluded are further acts of private and non-commercial use, experimental use and the reproduction for the purpose of teaching. Exhaustion is recognised as a limitation, yet only on a Community-wide scale, Art. 21.

Community designs are enforced in certain designated national courts, and can be invalidated either by an invalidation action before the Trade Mark Office, or in the course of a counter-claim in infringement proceedings.

The Community Design has been well received by the business community: Until August 2003, that is, within the first eight months, exactly 6,400 design applications were received in Alicante. Of these, 19% came from Germany, 12% from the UK and Italy, each, and 11% from the US.

Month	Number of Applications	Request for single design	Request for multiple design
January	120	65	190
February	260	145	655
March	780	360	3500
April	1190	530	3750
May	1050	450	2870
June	890	340	2280
July	1160	70	360
August	950	3	35
Total	6400	2263	13640

2. Unregistered designs

A novelty in the European design approach is the unregistered design that has its roots in English law. The reason for protecting unregistered designs was the fact that under English law, designs were substantively examined, which led to gaps in protection, particularly for short-lived designs. These could neither be protected under copyright law (as explained below under III), nor was there an issue that protection could be obtained under unfair competition law (see below V). Unregistered designs, of course, can only be obtained where the protection requirements are met. Thus, for designs that lack novelty or individual character, design protection cannot be obtained.

However, one should be aware that the unregistered design as introduced in the United Kingdom was closer to copyright, while the one introduced on a Community level is a fully fledged exclusive right similar to registered designs. As to the prior UK design, the English Court of Appeal explained this in the following words:

"Although it has been suggested that the unregistered design right in Pt III of the 1988 Act is a conceptual cocktail of copyright and registered designs, it is plainly a right in the nature of copyright: the only exclusive right conferred is restricted to the copying of the design. Although Mr Watson occasionally lapsed in oral submissions, as well as in his skeleton argument, into calling it a 'statutory monopoly', it is not a monopoly right in the same sense as patents or registered designs, where innocence and coincidental similarity of result in independent creation are no defence to liability for infringement. The monopolies formally granted after official scrutiny under the Patents Act and the Registered Designs Act provide a radically different kind of protection than does copyright informally acquired by the very act of creation. The purpose of copyright and of design right is not to protect the 'novelty' of the work against all competition; it is to provide limited protection against unfair misappropriation of the time, skill and effort expended by the author of design on the cration of his work.

In some respect unregistered design right is different from artistic copyright: its duration is shorter (10 years from sale of the article instead of life of the author and 70 years from the death of the author of an artistic work); the protection from copying is more restricted (copyright protects an artistic work from being reproduced not only in its entirety but also in respect of any substantial part of it–design right is protected from reproduction which is substantially similar).

Those differences do not, however, make unregistered design right more like a registered design than like copyright. There are more significant differences between unregistered designs and registered designs. In particular, the latter, which are of longer duration (maximum 25 years), do not protect the shape or configuration of a design which is dictated solely by the function which it has to perform. Functional designs may be protected as unregistered designs, which are not limited to designs which appeal to the eye or have aesthetic qualities."[5]

In one of the first cases regarding an unregistered Community design, the US dollmaker Mattel was able to obtain a Europe-wide injunction against the sale of infringing dolls by Simba Toys Germany.[6]

3. Relationship between designs and copyright

It is important to note that Community design protection is not preemptive and still allows individual member states to apply domestic laws either where design protection fails, or for cumulative effects. Vis-à-vis copyright law, the Design Regulation and Directive expressly allow such cumulative effect. Considerations 31 and 32 of the Design Regulation read:

---

[5] Farmers Build Ltd *v*. Carier Bulb Materials Handling Ltd, Court of Appeal, [1999] R.P.C. 461, 481.

[6] Order made on 24 October 2003, Managing Intellectual Property, December 2003/January 2004, 6. The defendant admitted liability prior to the delivery of the decision.

"This Regulation does not preclude the application to designs protected by Community designs of the industrial property laws or other relevant laws of the Member States, such as those relating to design protection acquired by registration or those relating to unregistered designs, trade marks, patents and utility models, unfair competition or civil liability. "In the absence of the complete harmonisation of copyright law, it is important to establish the principle of cumulation of protection under the Community design and under copyright law, whilst leaving Member States free to establish the extent of copyright protection and the conditions under which such protection is conferred."

In other words, member states may not exclude copyright protection for aesthetic creations only because these can be protected under design law. However, where member states decide that aesthetic creations of industrial applicability, viz. applied art, do not meet the threshold of copyrightability, this is not contrary to the Design Directive or Regulation.

II. Design Protection in the US

Unlike the European design system, but in conformity with that of Japan, designs in the US are substantively examined. Protection is not afforded based on a tailor-made design act, but rather on the basis of "design patents" in §§ 171–173 of the US Patent Act (35 U.S.C.). Design patents can be obtained for "any new, original and ornamental design for an article of manufacture". Regarding application and enforcement procedures, design patents are treated no different from invention patents.

However, court law has modified the standard of non-obviousness. While under patent law, obviousness is determined by a person having ordinary skill in the art, in design law it should be "the designer of ordinary capability who designs article of the type presented in the application."[7] The courts understand ornamentality as the opposite of "functionality". Functionality is not examined for the article as such, but for the functionality of the particular design of such article.[8]

The scope of protection is determined based on the overall impression when comparing the two designs:

"If, in the eye of an ordinary observer, giving such attention as a purchaser usually gives, two designs are substantially the same, if the resemblance is such as to deceive such an observer, inducing him to purchase one supposing it to be the other, the first one patented is infringed by the other."[9]

In contrast to European design law, federal protection of designs in the US preempts further protection under state unfair competition laws or specific legislation to similar effects.[10]

---

[7] In re Nalbandian, United States Court of Customs and Patent Appeals 661 F.2d 1214 (1981).

[8] Avia Group International *v*. LA Gear California, CAFC, 853 F.2d 1557 (1988).

[9] Gorham *v*. White, 81 U.S. 511 (1871).

[10] E.g. for a California law prohibiting the use of the "direct molding process" to duplicate unpatented articles: Bonita Boats *v*. Thundercraft Boats, Supreme Court, 489 U.S. 141 (1989); for unfair competition protection of designs that lack novelty Sears, Roebuck

Functionality generally excludes protection for designs. For a further elaboration on this aspect, see the section on trade marks below at (IV).

III. Design Protection in Japan

The design system in Japan is characterised by substantive examination and a fairly elaborate set of rules for the application procedure.

Designs are protected only to the extent that they are embodied in an article, i.e. a movable three-dimensional object. Icon designs cannot be protected. In order to qualify for protection, the article where the design is embodied in must be visible (which would exclude, e.g. objects such as toner cartridges) and must be independently traded if part of a more complex article. Prior to the 1998 amendment of the Design Act, no portions of an article could be protected. If, e.g. a company wanted to protect the lens design of the well-known "Ixus" cameras, it needed to do so by supplying not only the lens design, but the complete camera shape. Since camera shapes were manifold, this required a high number of similar applications, which could be accommodated by the system of associated designs. Associated designs could be registered during the life span of the parent design and only required similarity to the latter. Interestingly enough, the filing date of the associated design was deemed the filing date of the parent design, ultimately leading to irreconcilable friction in cases where a third party design dissimilar to the parent design was filed later than the latter, yet before the filing of an associated design extending the scope of the parent design to reach a degree of similarity with the third party design.[11] The 1998 revision brought about two important changes. For one, the system of associated designs was practically abolished. Similar designs by the same owner can be filed on the same day and are treated as independent designs. They may not be filed later, however, as in such case, the previously filed design will be invoked by the Patent Office to protect the later application, even if by the same applicant. Even if filed on the same day by the same applicant, it has to be indicated that the design filed is an associated design. Even under the new system, no independent licences or transfers of the associated design can be made, although an associated design "survives" cancellation of the parent design. The second important amendment relates to the possibility of protection portions of an article, i.e. the lens design of a camera. A design filed for only part of an article would be treated differently from a design for the entire article, thus giving rise to questions of dependent designs if, e.g. a design is filed only for part of the camera, e.g. the lens and subsequently a third party files a design for the entire camera embodying the lens, the designs as such would be

---

v. Stiffel, Supreme Court, 376 U.S. 225 (1964); and Compco Corp. *v.* Day-Brite Lighting, Supreme Court, 376 U.S. 234 (1964).

[11] Supreme Court, 24 February 1995, 1997 GRUR Int. 265, holding that in such case, the associated design should indeed prevail over the third party design. This, in turn, led to the ultimate abolition of the associated design system.

treated different and registrable, yet the owner of the camera design may need permission from the owner of the previously filed lens design in order to use the lens design for his camera. Traditionally, the scope of similarity has been interpreted fairly narrowly and must relate to identity/similarity of both design and embodied article.[12]

Designs must be novel (standard of absolute novelty with a grace period of six months) and show a certain creativity or individual characteristics so that it could not have been easily created based on prior art.

To a certain extent, the scope of a design can be broadened by the registration as a design for a set of articles, Sec. 7. The maximum number of items permitted is 56.

In the application, it is necessary to indicate the article or part of the article to which the design is applied. The Japanese design classification (different from the Locarno international design classification) contains about 5,000 articles. A valid application requires six views of the design/article drawn with the orthogonal projection and having the same scale. Alternatively, it is permitted to submit drawings showing two-dimensional views by using the isometric projection method. The perspectives to be shown are top plan, bottom plan, front elevation, rear elevation, left side and right side view.

C. Copyright Protection

The protection of so-called applied art under copyright law does not follow a uniform pattern. As is further elaborated in the following, in principle the following approaches can be distinguished:

(1) The exclusion of copyright protection in favour of designs where the object of copyright protection (that is, the work) has been copied more than a number of times, thus confirming its industrial application;[13]

(2) Application of copyright law to any work that could be registered as a design: this position is only taken by France;

(3) Concurrent application of copyright and design laws, yet with a higher threshold of originality required for copyright protection: this is the position applied in Germany, Austria, Switzerland and Japan;

---

[12] Supreme Court, 19 March 1974, Supreme Court, 19 March 1974, 28–2 Minshû 308: the Supreme Court requires similarity of the object as considered by an ordinary consumer, similarity of the design and a degree of originality that puts the registered design beyond generally recognised shapes or forms.

[13] This would be the case for India where the Copyright Act 1957 makes copyright cease to exist in any design capable of being registered under the Design Act as soon as any article to which the design is applied is reproduced more than 50 times by an industrial process. Confirmed by the High Court of Dehli, Samsonite *v*. Vijay Sales, 20 May 1998, [2000] Fleet Street Reports 463.

(4) Copyright protection only for those designs that are incorporated into a work of art distinguishable from any utilitarian function: this appears to be the position of Italy, the UK and the US.

An interesting point of reference for comparison are the "Le Corbusier" furniture cases that were decided for the same objects in Germany, Austria, Switzerland and Italy. Works of applied art are usually those for which design protection could be requested.

I. France

French law is perhaps the most generous in providing protection for works of applied art. The principle of cumulative protection under copyright and design law has been enshrined in Art. L. 112–1 and 112–2, Art. L 511–1 Code de la Propriété Intellectuelle, but has been good law since time immemorial.[14] The author has the option between copyright and design protection, and is thus not obliged to register a design right in order to enjoy protection for his work.[15] This *cumul absolu* leads to the doctrine that what can be an object of design protection may equally be protected under copyright law. The author of a work may even rely on design protection in the first instance of a trial, and subsequently switch to copyright protection if he deems this more favourable to his claim, e.g. in view of moral rights protection.[16]

II. Germany

In Germany, works of applied art can find protection under Sec. 2(1)(iv) Copyright Act. It is immaterial to what extent concurrent protection under design law could have been obtained. "Independent of the purpose of use of the object in question it is decisive if such object shows a level of creativity [*Gestaltungshöhe*] that would justify categorising such work as one of the fine arts . . . Rather, what is decisive, independent of the use made of the work, is that the level of creativity is sufficient to classify the product in the category of the fine arts. . . . In this respect, one has to include the circumstances at the time the work was created and the interest that the work has found amongst specialists and the public in general. . . . Also the presentation . . . in museums and exhibitions may give clues to the relevant classification."[17]

---

[14] The leading case in this respect is Cour de Cassation Criminelle Jurisclasseur Privé 1961, II, 12242 – "Panier à Salade". An overview over the historical development is given by Zech, Der Schutz von Werken der angewandten Kunst im Urheberrechts Deutschlands und Frankreichs, Cologne 1999, 11–33.

[15] Although some remedies in the area of enforcement may depend on a registered right.

[16] Cour de Cassation Req., Annales 1931, 81.

[17] German Supreme Court, 10 December 1986, GRUR Int. 1987, 903, 904 – "Le Corbusier Möbel".

Copyright protection of the Le Corbusier chairs was thus affirmed in a number of German decisions.[18]

However, one should note that the decisions always concern individual objects of art and it is impossible to generalise in this respect. It should also be noted that even the Le Corbusier decisions were not unanimous in their approach, and that the lower courts in some cases denied protection of certain objects. While it is clear that purely functional elements cannot find copyright protection, the degree of originality necessary for protection is difficult to measure. It is not important that the objects are bought for practical purposes or that they can be industrially realised.

It is thus not easy to foresee protectability prior to raising a lawsuit.

III. Austria

Also in Austria, protection of a work as applied art requires a certain level of originality. When it comes to applied art, the case of course must be decided on the individual object in question, giving rise to some uncertainty. The leading case by the Austrian Supreme Court gives the following guidance:

"According to the literature and case law, a product of the human intellect is an individual intellectual creation (a 'work') within the meaning of Sec. 1 of the Copyright Act if it is the result of creative intellectual activity and if the uniqueness distinguishing it from other works is derived from the personality of its author. . . . In the field of works of art (Sec. 3, Copyright Act) this form must be conceptually linked with a certain degree of originality. Here a certain creativity in a work is necessary, an idea that has been given a form that bears the mark of the author's personal individuality, or at least is distinguishable by virtue of a personal touch from other products of a similar kind (1985 ÖBl. 24). Words belonging to an artistic style whose intention is to derive the aesthetic shapes of utility objects exclusively from their purpose, avoiding any decorative additions ('functional form'), could have an aesthetic effect, but are not necessarily protected as works of art as a result. If an artistic movement deliberately rejects all non-functionally determined elements of design, thus by its very nature having less scope for design at its disposal than other artistic styles, *i.e.* permitting less of the author's individuality to enter into the work, then the protection to which it is entitled is also correspondingly diminished (1985 ÖBl. 24, with further references). . . .

In the same decision, this Court also held that novel technical solutions are not entitled to copyright protection. In the case of a combination of technology and art in one work, examination must be made of the extent to which the design elements used are determined by technical factors and to what extent they have been selected for reasons of form, taste, beauty, or aesthetics. Nor is the choice of a geometrical shape alone sufficient to justify recognition as a work of art, since the geometrical shape of itself is in the public domain. Nor, likewise, can an artistic style be eligible for copyright protection in its own right. . . .

Despite its functional purpose, the chair designed by Le Corbusier and his assistants in 1928 contains an abundance of details that impose upon it the mark of uniqueness. Mention should

---

[18] E.g. Frankfurt Appeal Court, 19 June 1992, GRUR 1993, 116 – "Le Corbusier Möbel"; Frankfurt Appeal Court, 4 June 1987, GRUR 1988, 302 – "Le Corbusier Sessel".

be made here above all of the particular contrast between the broken line formed by the sitting and reclining surface and the arc-shaped supporting structure that serves both as contact element to the base and to enable infinite adjustment. It is not apparent that the chair only makes use of known features, or that its form is the necessary result of the technical function of the individual elements. In addition, the design of the head and foot of the chair also reveals traits of individuality; these latter shapes are neither determined by the purpose of the chair, nor made up of elements of a particular artistic style. All of these individual characteristics can be seen in the illustration of the prototype submitted in evidence;"[19]

From the above, one could thus distil the following principles:

(1) Copyright protection of works of applied art depends on a certain degree of originality and a corresponding status as a work. The border between copyright protection and design protection must not be set too low.

(2) Copyright protection only applies to the elements of shape that are selected for aesthetic reasons. Elements of shape imposed for technical reasons, geometrical shapes in the public domain or as certain style of art as such cannot enjoy protection.

IV. Switzerland

Switzerland takes the same approach as Germany and Austria in granting protection for works of applied art to the extent that they show a certain individuality or originality. "The utilitarian purpose is not as such sufficient to deny protection for an object that shows individual character. . . . This applies even to objects of utility for which design protection has been requested, yet that also meet the requirements of protection of the Copyright Act. It is only different where the form of the object is conditioned by its utilitarian function or the individual expression is so much limited by previously known forms that there really is no room for individual or original qualities."[20] The Supreme Court also attached importance to the fact that the defendant explicitly sold his chairs as "copies of Le Corbusier's works", thus indirectly referring to the individual and original character of the these chairs.

In Germany, Austria and Switzerland, Le Corbusier chairs could thus find protection under copyright law. Yet, one should be aware that the fame of Le Corbusier and the interest his works evoked amongst specialists certainly helped this result. In addition, one should be cautious in applying the above-mentioned principles to different fields of art. The decisions were rendered for furniture, and may be regarded differently for, e.g. jewellery or clothing. Finally, it has to be mentioned that certain fashion styles such as Bauhaus, Art Deco, etc., cannot be protected. Consequently, objects made in a certain

---

[19] Austrian Supreme Court, 5 November 1991, 25 IIC 128 – "Le Corbusier Chair".
[20] Swiss Supreme Court, 5 May 1987, GRUR Int. 1988, 263 – "Le Corbusier Möbel".

style will be judged only for those elements that are not determined by such specific style.

V. Italy

A radically different approach towards the protection of works of applied art is taken by the Appeal Court Florence with respect to the same Le Corbusier chairs.[21] According to the Florence Appeal Court, also works of applied art can be protected under Art. 2iv Italian Copyright Act. Yet, protection is limited to those works that are based upon a work of sculpture, painting or other expressive art. To the extent that such painting or sculpture is then used as a blueprint for a work of applied art, also the latter is protected. In other words, in order to determine protectability as a work of applied art, the artistic idea incorporated in such work has to be separated from the utilitarian purpose and it has to be determined to what extent the separated artistic contents represent a work of sculpture, painting, drawing, etc. In the case of the Le Corbusier furniture, this was not the case.

It is clear that this approach severely limits the protection of applied designs, and that some categories of applied art, e.g. embroidery, might be easier to protect under this definition than, e.g. furniture.

VI. The UK

A similar approach to Italy is taken in the United Kingdom, however, in this respect, Cornish writes as follows:

"In considering the impact of these broad notions, the key is to remember the governing consideration: what is the design *for*?[22] If a document is drawn for the purpose of making a sculpture, an etching or an engraving, then the exclusion of copyright from industrial infringement does not apply. In New Zealand, for instance, a Frisbee, made from plastic, was held to be an engraving, given the concentric ridges on its body.[23] Assuming this to be good law in the united Kingdom, a design for making the Frisbee would be one for an artistic work and so, under section 51, full copyright would survive.

If, however, the design is for something which is not itself an artistic work–such as, to take another New Zealand example, a kiwi-fruit box[24] – the mere fact that a three-dimensional

---

[21] Diritto d'Autore 1990, 444 – "Le Corbusier Furniture".

[22] Taylor and Dworkin [1990] E.I.P.R. 33.

[23] Wham-O *v.* Lincoln [1985] R.P.C. 127, C.a. (N.Z.). The forced logic of this decision depended in part on a definition of "engraving" which has not survived in the 1988 Act, so it may no longer be applicable (see equally in the UK, James Arnold *v.* Miafern [1980] R.P.C. 397; Breville *v.* Thorn EMI (1985) [1995] F.S.R. 77). There were signs of discomfort. In Wham-O the court could not bring itself to say that the Frisbees were sculptures, because (it seems) they did not express the intent of a sculptor. In Davis *v.* Wright [1988] R.P.C. 403, Whitford J. considered dental casts to be too temporary to be sculptures. Cf. also Greenfield *v.* Rover-Scott Bonnar (1990) 17 I.P.R. 417, where Pincus J. refused to regard moulds for plastic products as engravings.

[24] Plix Products *v.* Winstone [1986] F.S.R. 608.

model (itself counting as a sculpture) is made as a stepping stone towards final production will not exclude section 51. The intermediate version is not the end, only a means to it."[25]

The fact that design protection is not available, e.g. for two-dimensional designs (see above II), does not necessarily make copyright protection available.[26]

Thus, copyright protection in the United Kingdom appears to be as narrow as in Italy.

VII. Japan

Protection under the **Design Act** is possible for "shapes, patterns or colour, or a combination of these in an article which produces a visual aesthetic impression", Sec. 2(1) Design Act, and which must be capable of "industrial manufacture", Sec. 3(1) Design Act. Designs can only be registered on condition that they have not been made public elsewhere prior to the filing date. The same applies to **utility models** under the Utility Model Act ("an advanced technical innovation embodying a scientific process or processes"), and **patents** under the Patent Act ("highly advanced realisations of technical ideas in which a scientific principle is utilised"). Yet, even though protection under these laws is available, application procedures are cumbersome, especially for products with short life cycles. Since designs are still examined before being registered, application procedures may well take two years or more. Before registration, however, injunctive relief against infringement cannot be sought. The same applies to patents. Only in the case of utility models is no examination necessary. Yet an infringement suit can only be lodged after the registered (but at that time unexamined) utility model has been examined by the Patent Office. Thus, while registration can be effected without examination, such examination has to be undertaken before an infringement suit can be brought. As all these procedures involve the participation of the Patent Office, a certain delay is inevitable. Such delay can be fatal if the life cycle of a product is shorter than the examination procedure.

As distinct from industrial property laws, **copyright protection** does not require prior registration. Yet, a number of decisions have excluded protection under the Copyright Act for industrially made goods,[27] while others

---

[25] W.R. Cornish, Intellectual Property (3rd ed.), Sweet & Maxwell, London 1996, 496.

[26] English High Court, Lambretta Clothing *v.* Teddy Smith, 23 May 2003, [2003] R. P.C. 728, 742.

[27] Osaka High Court decision, 14 February, 1990, final appeal rejected by the Supreme Court decision, 28 March 1991 – "Neetier" (reported by Ushiki (1992)); Tokyo District Court decision, 24 January 1992 – "Decorative Window Bars"; Nikkei Design 61 [1992].

have upheld it.[28] In a decision of the Tokyo High Court of 17 December 1991, the court reasoned that

"according to Sec. 2(1) Copyright Act, a work of art is defined as the 'creative expression of ideas or feelings within the scope of literature, science, art or music'. In addition, Sec. 2(2) Copyright Act provides that 'works of art under the Copyright Act include works of craftsmanship'. Thus, the provision of Sec. 2(1) Copyright Act clearly establishes that works of 'applied art' which only use fine art techniques and which are merely utilitarian, can only be utilitarian goods themselves. The Copyright Act only protects craft works made in very small numbers.

As for works of applied art which fall outside the scope of craft works, the Copyright Act does not clearly define how far they can be protected under copyright law. It is certainly possible to protect works of applied art which serve as prototypes for mass-produced utilitarian goods, since it is the purpose of the Act to promote the creation of such prototypes and thereby the progress of industrial development (Design Act, Sec. 1). Also qualifying for protection are the forms, patterns and colouring of such products, including their associations as a subject of design rights (Design Act, Sec. 2). Apart from this, even if the product in question has only been produced as a prototype for mere utilitarian goods – if, for example, a famous artist has created a work of high artistic value (as a highly creative expression of ideas or feelings) and such work can be said to have the quality of art – it should be protected as a work of art under the Copyright Act."[29]

This decision aptly sums up the view inherent in later decisions that the Copyright Act can only protect craft works produced in small numbers. Although in some jurisdictions (e.g. Australia) the quantity of reproductions determines their fate, there is a different approach in countries that require a significantly high degree of originality.[30] In effect, excluding designs (which must be capable of industrial manufacture) from copyright protection because they are mass produced would only mean effectively depriving them of all copyright protection. But apparently, the Tokyo court would not go as far as this since it established in its decision that

"the *communis opinio* would not regard the designs as real works of art. The original drawing cannot be considered a work of art under copyright law accordingly".

It therefore seems more likely that despite some hiccups in terminology, Japanese courts determine copyrightability in terms of the degree of

---

28 Nagasaki District Court decision, 7 February 1973 – "Hakata Dolls", 5–1 Mutaishû 18 [1973]; Kobe District Court decision, 9 July 1979 – "Altar Statues", 11–2 Mutaishû 371 [1979]; Osaka District Court decision, 21 December 1970 – "California T-shirts", 2 Mutaishû 654 [1979].

29 Tokyo High Court, 17 December 1991, 25 IIC 805 [1994] – "Decorative Veneer".

30 N. Monya, Ishôhô to shuhinhô (The Design Act and related laws), 12 Nihon Kôgyô shoyûken hôgakukai nempô (Annual of the Association of Industrial Property Law) 118–133 [1989].

originality rather than the production method[31] and it is certainly true that in many cases industrially-made products lack the degree of originality necessary to qualify for copyright protection.

In fact, as Teramoto has conclusively proven, courts tend to grant copyright protection for applied art by subtracting the "degree to which expression in a work is restricted by its utilitarian function" from the work's creative value. The same approach that Teramoto has detected in judging works of applied art seems to be taken for judging logos and trade marks. Here, the courts also reject copyright protection unless a sufficient degree of originality can be established.[32]

VIII. The US

Also in the United States, the interface between copyright and design protection for works of applied art has received considerable judicial attention. The first case that came up before the Supreme Court was decided in 1954 and concerned male statuettes that were intended for use as bases for table lamps, with electric wiring circuits and lampshades attached. The Supreme Court basically affirmed that protection could be concurrently available under copyright and design law:

"Unlike a patent, a copyright gives no exclusive right to the art disclosed; protection is given only to the expression of the idea–not the idea itself. Thus, in Baker v. Selden, 101 U.S. 99, 25 L.Ed. 841, the Court held that a copyrighted book on a peculiar system of bookkeeping was not infringed by a similar book using a similar plan which achieved similar results where the alleged infringer made a different arrangement of the columns and used different headings. The distinction is illustrated in Fred Fisher, Inc. *v.* Dillingham, D.C., 298 F. 145, 151, when the court speaks of two men, each a perfectionist, independently making maps of the same territory. Though the maps are identical each may obtain the exclusive right to make copies of his own particular map, and yet neither will infringe the other's copyright. Likewise a copyrighted directory is not infringed by a similar directory which is the product of independent work. The copyright protects originality rather than novelty or invention–conferring only 'the sole right of multiplying copies.' Absent copying there can be no infringement of copyright. Thus, respondents may not exclude others from using statuettes of human figures in table lamps; they may only prevent use of copies of their statuettes as such or as incorporated in some other article. Regulation § 202.8 makes clear that artistic articles are protected in 'form but not their mechanical or utilitarian aspects.' The dichotomy of protection for the aesthetic is not beauty and

---

[31] S. Teramoto, Copyrightability and scope of protection for a work of utilitarian character under the copyright law of Japan, 28 International Review of Industrial Property and Copyright Law (IIC) 51 [1997].

[32] In one case, the plaintiff Asahi had tried to stop a third party using the trade mark "Asax" and based the claim on trade mark law and unfair competition law. When this was rejected (Tokyo District Court decision, 28 March 1994, 1994/10 Patent 96), the plaintiff tried to enjoin the continued use of the "Asax" logo by the defendant under copyright law. However, the Tokyo High Court (26 January 1996, 249 Hanketsu Sokuhô 3 [1996]), denied protection because of lack of originality.

utility but art for the copyright and the invention or original and ornamental design for design patents. We find nothing in the copyright statute to support the argument that the intended use or use in industry of an article eligible for copyright bars or invalidates its registration. We do not read such a limitation into the copyright law.

Nor do we think the subsequent registration of a work of art published as an element in a manufactured article is a misuse of the copyright. This is not different from the registration of a statuette and its later embodiment in an industrial article"[33]

The issue has subsequently been treated less favourably for designers, however. Human torsos that functioned to display clothing were denied copyright protection. The court held, *inter alia*:

"The legislative history thus confirms that, while copyright protection has increasingly been extended to cover articles having a utilitarian dimension, Congress has explicitly refused copyright protection for works of applied art or industrial design which have aesthetic or artistic features that cannot be identified separately from the useful article. Such works are not copyrightable regardless of the fact that they may be 'aesthetically satisfying and valuable.' H.R.Rep. No. 1476, supra, at 55, 1976 U.S.Code Cong. & Ad.News at 5668."[34]

A number of efforts have been made to clarify these perhaps contradictory decisions. One decision relied on the physical separability of a work of art (a simulated antique telephone) and the utilitarian object contained therein (a pencil sharpener).[35] Another court tried the approach of conceptual separability holding that,

"If design elements reflect a merger of aesthetic and functional considerations, the artistic aspects of a work cannot be said to be conceptually separable from the utilitarian elements. Conversely, where design elements can be identified as reflecting the designer's artistic judgment exercised independently of functional influences, conceptual separability exists."[36]

Sec. 101 US Copyright Act excludes "useful articles" from copyright protection. These are defined as articles "having an intrinsic utilitarian function that is not merely to portray the appearance of the article or to convey information. An article that is normally a part of a useful article is considered a 'useful article'." Articles are utilitarian if that is their primary purpose.[37] It is not relevant for protection under copyright law if the article has already been registered as a design.

On the academic side, Goldstein gives the following definition of when three-dimensional objects can be protected under copyright law:

---

[33] Mazer *v.* Stein, US Supreme Court, 1954, 347 U.S. 201, 74 S.Ct. 460, 98 L.Ed. 630, 100 U.S.P.Q. 325.

[34] Carol Barnhart Inc. *v.* Economy Cover Corp., US Court of Appeals, Second Circuit, 1985, 773 F.2d 411, 228 U.S.P.Q. 385.

[35] Ted Arnold *v.* Silvercraft, 259 F.Supp. 733 (Southern District of New York 1966).

[36] Brandir International *v.* Cascade Pacific Lumber, 834 F.2d 1142, 1145 (2d Cir. 1987).

[37] Gay Toys *v.* Buddy Corp., 703 F.2d 970, 973 (6th Circuit 1983).

"[a] pictoral, graphic or sculptural feature incorporated in the design of a useful article is conceptually separable if it can stand on its own as a work of art traditionally conceived, and if the useful article in which it is embodied would be equally useful without it."[38]

IX. Problems of Reciprocity

It should also be noted that with a narrow approach on copyright protection such as the one in Italy and the UK, Italian and English artists face difficulties in obtaining copyright protection abroad: Art. 5(1) Berne Convention establishes the principle of national treatment. That means that nationals of member states enjoy protection of their works abroad in accordance with such foreign copyright laws and no different than nationals of these respective countries. In some cases, however, the Berne Convention deviates from the principle of national treatment and follows the principle of reciprocity. This is particularly the case for works of applied art according to Art. 2(7) Berne Convention. In such case, works of foreign nationals are only protected if the country where the work originates also provides protection for the same category of works. According to the Frankfurt Appeal Court, the above-mentioned decision of the Appeal Court Florence clearly indicates that Italy does not provide for copyright protection for works of applied art with the consequence that Italian works of applied art are not protectable in other countries as well.[39] This consequence applies to countries outside the EU, however, thanks to the ECJ's *Phil Collins* decision that prohibits a discriminatory treatment of EC citizens also in respect of the exercise of intellectual property rights.[40]

D Three-dimensional Marks

I. General Issues

It is the field of trade marks that has been the most interesting in recent years when it comes to the protection of three-dimensional shapes. This is unsurprising given the fact that trade marks can be maintained for an unlimited period of time and grant a comparatively broad monopoly. The issues relate both to registered and unregistered trade marks. In Europe, most cases concerned the registrability of marks under the Community Trade Mark Regulation; in the US, issues both of registrability as such, and of protection of an unregistered mark as a trade dress. In both cases, the same issues are at stake: To what extent would a three-dimensional get-up be capable of indicating an origin. This can only be the case where the mark is distinctive and

---

[38] Goldstein, Copyright § 2.5.3.1 (Vol. 1), 1996.

[39] Frankfurt Appeal Court, 19 June 1992, GRUR 1993, 116 – "Le Corbusier Furniture".

[40] European Court of Justice, 20 October 1993, GRUR Int. 1994, 53 – "Phil Collins".

not functional. Accordingly, these two issues are at the centre stage of litigation. In the European context, the Community Trade Mark Regulation and the Trade Mark Directive both have specific grounds for excluding protection for three-dimensional marks that go beyond the mere issue of functionality.

Three-dimensional objects may be registered as trade marks in certain limited circumstances. In this respect, the European Court of Justice has rendered two leading decisions under the European Trade Mark Directive/Regulation, and a couple of other decisions have been rendered by national courts. Registration as such may be effected as a two-dimensional drawing that is then applied for a three-dimensional mark object. Protection, however, also extends to the two-dimensional registration.[41]

Even those shapes that are not novel can be registered. This was clarified by the Milan Ferragamo decision.[42] The trade mark in that case consisted of an ornamental design of a woman's shoe produced by the Italian company Ferragamo. Registration was contested on the grounds that Ferragamo had already registered this ornament as a design and should not be able to register yet another industrial property right over the same subject matter. The court correctly held that anticipation by a previous design registration had no impact on registration of a trade mark. On the other hand, novelty as such is insufficient to show distinctiveness. This was so held by the OHIM Board of Appeal with respect to the head of a toothbrush.[43]

Rather, registrability has to be determined according to distinctiveness and functionality.

II. Distinctiveness

It is distinctiveness rather than functionality that is most often argued about in trade mark cases.[44]

1. *The Maglite cases*

In a decision on 7 February 2002, the European Court of Justice denied the distinctive character of three-dimensional trade mark applications for torches. Basis of the rejection was Art. 7(1)(b) EC Trade Mark Regulation.[45] The case concerned the rejection of the three-dimensional trade mark

---

[41] English High Court, Philips *v.* Remington, [1998] R.P.C. 283.

[42] Milan District Court, 30 December 1999, Revista di Diritto Industriale 2001, 265 – "Ferragamo".

[43] OHIM Board of Appeal, 28 March 2001, Case R406/2000–3 – "In re Gillette".

[44] Folliard-Monguiral and Rogers, The Protection of Shapes by the Community Trade Mark, [2003] E.I.P.R. 169–179; Firth, Gredlex and Maniatis, Shapes and Trade Marks: Public Policy, Functional Considerations and Consumer Perception, [2001] E.I.P.R. 86–99.

[45] Case T88/00 Mag Instrument *v.* Community Trade Mark Office.

application both before the European Trade Mark Office and the German Federal Patent Court.[46] Both institutions held the trade mark not distinctive. The Federal Patent Court held the following in this respect:

"The shape was that of a typical cylindrical flashlight which, despite a certain elegance, remained within the limits usual on the market. In this product sector, the consumers would not regard the shape of the goods as being an indication of their origin from a particular enterprise. In the light of the minor differences to the rival products, even the attentive customer would hardly be capable of identifying one particular manufacturer from memory. Nor could distinctive character be established by comparison with those word trade marks in which it was only a graphic effect that established a capacity for trade mark protection. The distinctive character of the shape of goods was subject to stricter criteria than conventional trade mark forms such word and picture marks."[47]

The case gave the European Court of Justice an opportunity to interpret Art. 3(1)(b) European Trade Mark Directive (equals Art. 7(1)(b) European Trade Mark Regulation) that denies registrability to "trade marks which are devoid of any distinctive character".

The court first of all made an important clarification regarding three-dimensional marks. While the German Federal Supreme Court[48] found that "distinctiveness" should be interpreted stricter for three-dimensional marks than for others, the ECJ rejected this approach. It would be inappropriate to apply more stringent requirements to three-dimensional marks than to ordinary marks. The legislature offered no basis for such distinction.[49]

However, already the European Court of First Instance noted that although the standard of distinctiveness might be the same, consumer perception in this respect is different, thus indirectly confirming the opinion held by the German Federal Supreme Court. The CFI held as follows:

"Account must be taken of the fact that the perception of the relevant section of the public is not necessarily the same in relation to a three-dimensional mark consisting of the shape and the colours of the product itself as it is in relation to a word mark, a figurative mark or a three-dimensional mark not consisting of the shape of the product. Whilst the public is used to recognising the latter marks instantly as signs identifying the product, this is not necessarily so where the sign is indistinguishable from the appearance itself."[50]

In the Maglite case, the court examined the five shapes for torches and found that the cylindrical shapes were rather common for such products.

---

[46] The case was then submitted by the German Federal Supreme Court, 23 November 2000, 33 IIC 886 [2002] – "Flashlights".

[47] As above, 33 IIC 886, 887.

[48] German Federal Supreme Court, 14 December 2000, 33 IIC 892 [2002] – "Swatch".

[49] In fact, the German Federal Supreme Court did not base this distinction on legislation, but rather on consumer perception, as consumers would be less used to connecting a certain shape with an origin than they would be in the case of word or picture marks.

[50] Court of First Instance, 19 September 2001, Case T–129/00 – "Tabs".

Even the specific features of the five shapes could not alter this point of view, as consumers were used to similar shapes in a wide variety of designs for torches.

Thus, the court clarified two issues.

(1) examination criteria for distinctiveness regarding three-dimensional marks were the same as those for other marks, neither more nor less stringent, and

(2) even unusual variance of a common shape is unlikely to pass the threshold of distinctiveness.

2. Secondary meaning

There is no doubt that a non-distinctive shape as such can be overcome by secondary meaning. This was so held in the case of the Ferragamo mark.[51] What is strange, however, is that the court did not indicate by what level of use such secondary meaning was indeed obtained. This was much different in the cases decided by OHIM's Board of Appeal. In the case of the form for certain little chocolates, the board found the mark as such non-distinctive and then went on to consider secondary meaning:

"Neither can the applicant rely on secondary meaning of its mark within the Community, as the furnished documents did not give sufficient evidence in this respect. To some extent, they only referred to the German market, while the other figures indicated that neither use within the whole Community nor even a substantial part of the relevant markets could be assumed. This leads to the conclusion that no sufficiently large part of the circles of purchasers within the economic area of the European Union would regard this form of chocolates as a mark."[52]

A new decision by the New Zealand Patent Act seems to indicate that a non-distinctive three-dimensional mark can under no circumstances overcome this obstacle by secondary meaning.[53] The decision is not final, however.

A recent South African decision made the following three-step test:

"The first was whether the mark, at the date of its application for registration, was inherently capable of distinguishing the goods of the first appellant and, if the answer was in the negative, the next inquiry was whether it was presently so capable of distinguishing by reason of its use to date . . . The fact that other manufacturers had used the same or similar shapes and that such shapes appeared in pharmaceutical reference works established conclusively that the particular shape in issue was not inherently capable of distinguishing in the trade mark sense."[54]

---

[51] Tribunale di Milano, 30 December 1999, 30 December 1999, Revista di Diritto Industriale 2001, 265 – "Ferragamo".

[52] OHIM Board of Appeal, 8 March 2001, Case R203/2000–3 – "Schogette".

[53] In New Zealand, the shape of Nestle's Kit Kat chocolate bar was deemed unregistrable as a trade mark on the understanding that the shape was not a "sign". The decision is reported by the Simpson and Grierson Newsletter of December 2002. A date was not given.

[54] Triomed *v.* Beecham Group, Supreme Court of South Africa, 19 September 2002, [2003] F.S.R. 475, 476.

Although millions of such tablets had been dispensed annually, distinctiveness was denied, as "no pharmacist would regard the shape alone as a guarantee that the tablet came from the first appellant."

3. Related decisions in other countries

Distinctiveness of three-dimensional marks has been subject to a number of decisions both in Europe and outside. It would be fair to say that most courts show a certain reluctance in accepting the registration of three-dimensional marks.

In a recent Australian decision on three-dimensional marks, the court held that whether a mark is inherently adapted to distinguish must

> ". . . be tested by reference to the likelihood that other persons, trading in goods of the relevant kind and being actuated only by proper motives – in the exercise, is to say, of the common heritage, for the sake of the signification which they ordinarily posses – will think of the [shape] and want to use it in connection with similar goods in any manner would infringe a registered trade mark granted in respect of it. . . . Children relate spontaneously and strongly to animals and animal-like creatures. Moreover, confectionary is highly malleable . . . To allow registration of the shape of a real or readily-made imagined animal would be to commence a process of 'fencing in the common' which would speedily impose serious restrictions upon other traders."[55]

Or, regarded from the consumer's point of view:

> As with all other trade mark forms, the sole decisive factor for three-dimensional shape trade marks representing the product itself is that the public addressed – for whatever reason – regards the filed mark as an indication of origin."[56]

III. Functionality and Other Obstacles

European law makes a clear distinction between the refusal of protection for lack of distinctiveness and other specific obstacles against the registration of three-dimensional marks. The relevant Art. 3 Trade Mark Directive is quoted verbatim in order to appreciate this difference:

> "(1) The following shall not be registered or if registered shall be liable to be declared invalid:
> (a) signs which cannot constitute a trade mark;
> (b) trade marks which are devoid of any distinctive character;
> (c) trade marks which consist exclusively of signs or indications which may serve, in trade, to designate the kind, quality, quantity, intended purpose, value, geographical indication, or the time of production of the goods or of rendering of the service, or other characteristics of the goods or service;
> (d) trade marks which consist exclusively of signs or indications which have become customary in the current language or in the bona fide and established practice of the trade;
> (e) signs which consist exclusively of:
> – the shape which results from the nature of the goods themselves, or

---

[55] Kenman Kandy *v*. Registrar of Trade Marks, Federal Court of Australia, 3 August 2001, [2001] 52IPR 137.

[56] Federal Supreme Court, 14 December 2000, 33 IIC 892 [2002] – "Swatch".

- the shape of goods which is necessary to obtain a technical result, or
- the shape which gives substantial value to the goods."

The difference is important for the following reason: under European law, obstacles to registration under (b) may be overcome by secondary meaning, obstacles under (e) not.

While other jurisdictions have also debated the issue of functionality, the other two exclusions under European trade mark law (nature of the goods in themselves, shapes which give substantial value) have not been argued in other jurisdictions.

1. *Functionality in Europe: The Philips Shaver decision*

The second important European decision related to three-dimensional marks concerned the well-known Philips shaver that Philips developed in 1966. In 1985, Philips filed an application to register a trade mark consisting of a graphic representation of the shape and configuration of the head of such a shaver, comprising three circular heads with rotating blades in the shape of an equilateral triangle. The trade mark was registered. In 1995, Remington, a competitor, began to manufacture and sell a competing product in the United Kingdom which also consisted of a shaver with three rotating heads forming a equilateral triangle. Philips sued Remington for infringement. Two questions arose in this respect. First, if secondary meaning could also be obtained due to the fact that the trade mark owner, thanks to a prior registration of the shape as a design, held a monopolistic position. And, second, if the "shape necessary to obtain a technical result" as a barrier to registration could be overcome by establishing that there were other shapes which allowed the same technical result to be obtained.

The Advocate General in the Philips decision interpreted Art. 3(1)(e) of the Directive as follows:

"The legislature acknowledged the basic similarity of those three grounds [listed in Art. 3(1)(b)–(d)] of exclusion in providing, in Article 3(3), that they do not apply if, before the date of application for registration and following the use which has been made of it, it has 'acquired a distinctive character'. Subparagraph (e), however, is not of the same legal nature. It applies to three-dimensional signs which arise solely from the nature of the goods themselves, seek to obtain a technical result or give substantial value to the goods. This exclusion is based not on the lack of distinctiveness of certain natural, functional or ornamental shapes – in which case it would only serve to define the scope of subparagraph (b) – but reflects the legitimate concern to prevent individuals from resorting to trade marks in order to extend exclusive rights over technical developments. Consistent with that logic, the legislature did not include subparagraph (e) among the grounds for refusal which may be overcome by virtue of Article 3(3). Natural, functional or ornamental shapes are incapable, by express intention of the legislature, of acquiring a distinctive character. It is altogether otiose – as well as contrary to the scheme of the Directive – to consider whether or not such shapes have acquired distinctiveness."[57]

---

[57] Opinion of Advocate General Ruiz-Jarabo Colomer, delivered 23 January 2001 for Case C–299/99.

In other words, subsection (e) is a public policy exclusion that resembles the old German doctrine of a public interest in keeping signs free for general use.[58]

   This being so, the court strictly speaking was in no need of answering the question to what extent secondary meaning could also count when obtained under monopolistic conditions. Rather, that question would belong to what was discussed under 1 above, that is, in connection with Art. 3(1)(b) Trade Mark Directive. Nonetheless, the court's opinion in this respect is helpful for clarifying future cases where three-dimensional shapes applied for as trade marks have been previously registered as designs. The positions of both parties of the suit were the following:

> "According to Philips, the criterion in Art. 3(3) of the Directive is satisfied where, because of the extensive use of a particular shape, the relevant trade and public believe that goods of that shape come from a particular undertaking. Moreover, Philips submits that a longstanding *de facto* monopoly on products with the relevant shape is important evidence which supports the acquisition of distinctiveness. If a trader wishes to base an application for registration upon distinctiveness acquired through use, a *de facto* monopoly is almost a prerequisite for such registration. Remington submits that in the case of a shape which is made up of functional features only, strong evidence is required that the shape itself has been used also as an indication of origin so as to confer on that shape a sufficient secondary meaning to justify registration. Where there has been a monopoly supplier of goods, particular care needs to be taken to ensure that the factual analysis is focused on the relevant matters."

The court – correctly in this author's opinion – did not attach importance to the fact that others could be excluded from using the same shape, but to the actual use made in order to obtain secondary meaning.

> "As is clear from paragraph 51 of the judgment in *Windsurfing Chiemsee*, in assessing the distinctive character of a mark in respect of which registration has been applied for, the following may, *inter alia*, also be taken into account: the market share held by the mark; how intensive, geographically widespread and longstanding use of the mark has been; the amount invested by the undertaking in promoting the mark; the proportion of the relevant class of persons who, because of the mark, identify goods as originating from a particular undertaking; and statements from chambers of commerce and industry or other trade and professional associations . . . In the light of those considerations, the answer to the third question must be that, where a trader has been the only supplier of particular goods to the market, extensive use of a sign which consists of the shape of those goods may be sufficient to give the sign a distinctive character for the purposes of Art. 3(3) of the Directive in circumstances where, as a result of that use, a substantial proportion of the relevant class of persons associates that shape with that trader and no other undertaking or believes that goods of that shape come from that trader. However, it is for the

---

[58] On this issue, see, e.g. Fox, Does the Trade Mark Harmonisation Directive Recognise a Public Interest in Keeping Non-distinctive Signs Free for Use? [2000] E.I.P.R. 1; more specifically for three-dimensional marks: Firth/Gredley/Maniatis, Shapes as Trade Marks: Public Policy, Functional Considerations and Consumer Perception, [2001] E.I.P.R. 86.

national court to verify that the circumstances in which the requirement under that provision is satisfied are shown to exist on the basis of specific and reliable data, that the presumed expectations of an average consumer of the category of goods or services in question, who is reasonably well informed and reasonably observant and circumspect, are taken into account and that the identification, by the relevant class of persons, of the product as originating from a given undertaking is as a result of the use of the mark as a trade mark."[59]

These considerations are important for those cases where secondary meaning can overcome the obstacle of non-distinctiveness. They are, as was observed by the Advocate General, of no use where the obstacle to registration stems from public policy considerations. The court interpreted Art. 3(1)(e) Trade Mark Directive as follows:

"The rationale of the grounds for refusal of registration laid down in Art. 3(1)(e) of the Directive is to prevent trade mark protection from granting its proprietor a monopoly on technical solutions or functional characteristics of a product which a user is likely to seek in the products of competitors. Art. 3(1)(e) is thus intended to prevent the protection conferred by the trade mark right from being extended, beyond signs which serve to distinguish a product or service from those offered by competitors, so as to form an obstacle preventing competitors from freely offering for sale products incorporating such technical solutions or function or characteristics in competition with the proprietor of the trade mark.

As regards, in particular, signs consisting exclusively of the shape of the product necessary to obtain a technical result, listed in Art. 3(1)(e), second indent, of the Directive, that provision is intended to preclude the registration of shapes whose essential characteristics perform a technical function, with the result that the exclusivity inherent in the trade mark right would limit the possibility of competitors supplying a product incorporating such a function or at least limit their freedom of choice in regard to the technical solution they wish to adopt in order to incorporate such a function in their product.

As Art. 3(1)(e) of the Directive pursues an aim which is in the public interest, namely that a shape whose essential characteristics perform a technical function and were chosen to fulfil that function may be freely used by all, that provision prevents such signs and indications from being reserved to one undertaking alone because they have been registered as trade marks (see, to that effect, *Windsurfing Chiemsee*, paragraph 25).

As to the question whether the establishment that there are other shapes which could achieve the same technical result can overcome the ground for refusal or invalidity contained in Art. 3(1)(e), second indent, there is nothing in the wording of that provision to allow such a conclusion . . . [T]he ground for refusal or invalidity of registration imposed by that provision cannot be overcome by establishing that there are other shapes which allow the same technical result to be obtained."

In other words, it is up to the registering authorities or opponent to show that a given shape was necessary to obtain a technical result. Once this is proven, it does not help the applicant to show that this public policy objection can be helped by competitors using different shapes that might obtain the same result.

---

[59] ECJ, Philips Electronics *v.* Remington Consumer Products, quoted from [2003] R.P.C. 25–27. The case is also reprinted in 33 IIC 849 [2002] – "Philips *v.* Remington".

One wonders already at that point how a design could have been registered for the Philips in the first place. After all, also designs whose features are functional cannot be registered.[60]

2. *Comparable cases in other jurisdictions*

(1) Germany

Prior to the ECJ decision, the view that the defence of other possible shapes was precluded was not shared by all national courts in Europe. The German courts held that the application of Art. 3(1)(e) was restricted to cases where only one shape was possible for technical reasons, leaving no viable alternative for competitors.[61]

(2) The US

The situation in the US seems to be more ambiguous, as demonstrated by one case regarding an accessory to a wheelchair. Here, the trade mark owner argued in an infringement procedure that alternative designs were available to reach the same result. The court rejected this, but not specifically because the defence as such was not available, but rather because it was not convinced that other designs could achieve the same functions:

> "This evidence certainly supports [the plaintiff's] contention that adequate alternative designs exist which 'admirably' do the job, but to [the plaintiff's] detriment, it goes further. Because the product review not only demonstrates that a design such as the Ortho [a design developed by an unrelated third party] may be 'highly functional and useful', it also indisputably shows that the Ortho does not 'offer exactly the same features as [the plaintiff's design]', in particular the secured-grip handle, and thus fails as matter of law to support [the plaintiff's] interest in precluding competition by means of trade mark protection . . . In *Leatherman* we held that a product's manufacturer 'does not have rights under trade dress law to compel its competitors to resort to alternative designs which have a different set of advantages and disadvantages. Such is the realm of patent law' . . . Here [the plaintiff] does not dispute that some customers may prefer a specific functional aspect of the SAFECUT [the plaintiff's design], namely its closed-grip handle, even though other functional designs may ultimately get the job done just as well. As *Leatherman* reminds us, though, a customer's preference for a particular functional aspect of a product is wholly distinct from a customer's desire to be assured 'that a particular entity made, sponsored or endorsed a product'."[62]

Other cases have held differently, though. According to a fundamental Supreme Court decision of 2001, a trade mark, registered or not, is functional "when it is essential to the use or purpose of the device or when it

---

[60] E.g. Art. 7 European Design Directive: Directive 98/71/EC of 13 October 1998, OJ L289/28 of 28 October 1998. Art. 7 reads. "A design right shall not subsist in features of appearance of a product which are solely dictated by its technical function."

[61] German Federal Supreme Court, GRUR 1998, 1018 – "Honigglas".

[62] Tietech *v.* Kinedyne, 9 Circuit, 11 July 2002, reprinted in BNA 64 No. 1582, 299, 300.

affects the cost or quality of the device."[63] More recent case law has thus held that once functionality of a product feature is established, there is no need to engage in speculation about other design possibilities, and the existence of alternative designs therefore cannot negate the functionality of trade dress. However, the existence of alternative designs may indicate whether the trade dress itself embodies functional or merely ornamental aspects of a product.[64] Thus, also under US law, the existence of alternative designs does not make certain design non-functional, although in order to determine functionality of a design, the existence of alternatives might suggest non-functionality.

3. Issues of legal doctrine

While of course it has to be acknowledged that European trade mark law does not allow overcoming the obstacle of functionality by showing secondary meaning, it is questionable if, even without such explicit wording, the result should be different. To start with, it should be reiterated that a functional design should not receive protection under design law in the first place. Both design and trade mark law require shapes to be arbitrary rather than functional. The reasons for this are different, however. Design law gives protection to aesthetic features, and what is functional cannot be aesthetic, as aesthetic features require a certain degree of originality that is *per se* absent where the design is meant to achieve a certain technical result. In the case of trade marks, functionality makes it difficult for a mark to fulfil its function as an indication of origin, not because it *cannot* serve as such indication, but as it *may not*. This has also been recognised under unfair competition prevention law where functional getups do not get protection either as indications of origin[65] or as achievements to be protected against slavish imitation.[66]

Excluding technical shapes from trade mark protection thus oscillates between trade mark function and public policy: a technical function at least initially cannot confer an origin. Therefore, registration should be excluded due to lack of distinctiveness. That a technical shape can never obtain secondary meaning is not *prima facie* true, however. That it *should not* is an issue of public policy.

---

[63] TrafFix Devices *v.* Mktg Displays, 532 U.S. 23, 33 (2001),

[64] Talking Rain Beverage *v.* South Beach Beverage, US Court of Appeals 9th Circuit, 4 November 2003, 68 USPQ 2d 1764: functionality affirmed for a water bottle to be carried on bicycles; Antioch *v.* Western Trimming, US Court of Appeals 6th Circuit, 20 October 2003, 68 USPQ 2d 1673: functionality affirmed for a scrapbook album to be use for inserting photographs.

[65] See, e.g. the Japanese decision of the Tokyo District Court, 21 September 1994, 26–3 Chizaishû 1095 [1994] – "Foldable Containers".

[66] E.g. Italian Supreme Court, 9 March 1998, 32 IIC 349 [2001] – "LEGO Bricks III" (see below).

4. *Shapes which result from the nature of the goods*

European law also excludes shapes which result from the nature of the goods from protection as a three-dimensional mark regardless of secondary meaning. As yet, no final decision of the European Court of Justice has ruled on what "the goods" actually means. There are a number of interpretations. The Court of First Instance construes the exception very narrowly and finds it sufficient that "there are other shapes of soap bar in the trade without those features",[67] thus finding a soap bar registered for soap not a shape which results from the nature of the goods. Advocate General Colomer in the Philips case thought that the exception should be limited to naturally occurring shapes rather than artificially created ones.[68] The English Court of Appeal in the Philips case referred to a comparison between the shape at issue and the specification of goods for which the shape was registered:

> "In my judgment the words 'the goods' refer to the goods in respect of which the trade mark is registered. Those are the goods which it must be capable of distinguishing and in respect of which the proprietor obtains, on registration, the exclusive right to use the trade mark. The words I used to refer to any of the goods falling within the class for which the trade mark is registered. For example, registration of a picture of a banana in respect of 'fruit' would be just as objectionable as registration of that word would be in respect of 'bananas'. The purpose of this subsection is to prevent traders monopolising shapes of particular goods and that cannot be defeated by the skill of the applicant when selecting the class of goods for which registration is sought."[69]

In a case that is currently before the ECJ, the English High Court slightly differed in that the court compared the registered shape with the kind of article regarded as an article of commerce.[70]

5. *Shapes that give substantial value to the goods*

Another exclusion from registrability that cannot be overcome by secondary meaning concerns "signs which consist exclusively of the shape which gives substantial value to the goods". Also here, no ECJ decision is available at the moment to interpret this provision. The judge in an English High Court case referred to the ECJ, thought that the appearance of "Viennetta" ice cream bars were "obviously intended to attract customers as compared with other designs. It is clearly arguable, probably strongly arguable, that the appearance adds value to the product and may serve only that purpose being essentially an aesthetic creation. Unilever indeed registered the shape as a design."[71]

---

[67] European Court of First Instance, 16 February 2000, 32 IIC 214 [2001] – "Procter & Gamble *v.* OHIM".

[68] Opinion of the Advocate General in Philips *v.* Remington, [2001] R.P.C. 745, 751.

[69] English Court of Appeal, Philips *v.* Remington, [1999] R.P.C. 809, 820.

[70] English High Court, Unilever PLC's Trade Mark Application, 18 December 2002, [2003] R.P.C. 651, 656. The three-dimensional mark at issue was registered for ice cream products and was shaped as an ice cream bar with certain decorations.

[71] English High Court, Unilever PLC's Trade Mark Application, 18 December 2002, [2003] R.P.C. 651, 656.

6. *The interest in limiting monopolistic rights*

Even where none of the absolute exclusions regarding three-dimensional marks apply, and where distinctiveness has been obtained through monopolistic use thanks to a previous design registration, some courts have denied protection. This was the case in the so-called LEGO disputes in the United Kingdom. Here, registration of the "patent of 4/6/8 raised knobs or stubs applied to the upper surface of a toy brick" was rejected. The registrar held:

"I do not place any reliance whatsoever on the terms of the 1994 Trade Mark Act. I merely refer to it in the context that the 1994 Act appears to envisage a much more liberal attitude to the registration of trade marks as compared to the 1938 Act and yet it also bars the registration of certain marks on the basis that shapes as trade marks should not perpetuate indefinitely temporary monopolies granted through other forms of intellectual property law."[72]

On appeal it was held that

"The decision whether to register a trade mark can, at least in some cases, involve a balancing exercise, particularly in light of the very substantial benefit accorded to a proprietor if he succeeds in registering his mark and the public interest against monopolies in products (as opposed to marks) . . . The fact that an applicant has, or has had, the benefit of the protection of a registered patent in respect of the very thing which (or part of which) he seeks to register as a trade mark as a factor, which, at least in some cases, ought to be taken into account."[73]

E. Slavish Imitation

At present, protection against slavish imitation is one of the most disputed areas in the field of unfair competition law. There is a degree of distinction between civil law countries which tend to grant such protection, and common law countries which are more reluctant to do so. In detail:

I. General Outline and International Developments

a) The idea that achievements benefiting the public should receive protection as absolute rights has gained ground only in the last century and led to the introduction of protection for innovations in technical and aesthetic fields, for trade marks and for creative works.[74] Protection was not provided for financial investments, but for achievements in the field of science and art. Recently, however, it has been questioned whether this system of protection through patents, utility models, designs, trade marks and copyrights may not be too narrow. While the development of type faces, computer programs,

---

[72] Controller of Patents, in re. Interlego AG's application, [1998] R.P.C. 69.
[73] English High Court, in re. Interlego AG's application, [1998] R.P.C. 69.
[74] For a historical overview, see: G. Tarde, Les lois de l'imitation, (Paris 1921) 335–348; Ladas, The International Protection of Industrial Property (1930) 691–720, esp. 717–719.

semiconductor chips and databases has involved huge financial commit-
ments, the results have been found to be incapable of protection in most cases
because they were not thought to meet the high level of creativity required
under copyright law. However, in the case of record producers and artists,
additional protection has been deemed just and necessary (so-called
neighbouring rights). In most cases, legislation has responded to demands for
additional protection, but only belatedly.

Providing additional protection for otherwise unprotected achievements
may sometimes be desirable, but also runs counter to the principle of "freedom of imitation". All intellectual property rights are based on the principle
that creative achievements can only be protected under certain, sometimes
very narrowly-defined circumstances. Circumventing the requirements of
protection under intellectual property laws by providing for a very broad
"protection against imitation" would certainly not be compatible with the
system.

Insofar as imitation implied confusion, protection could be sought as
an extension of trade mark protection. However, without the element of
confusion, the theoretical foundations of protection against imitations are
much more difficult to define and in fact represent one of the most disputed
areas of unfair competition today. So far, in fact, common law countries have
refused to grant protection beyond the scope covered by passing-off actions.
However, since additional protection against imitation is in large measure
only necessary where intellectual property laws fail, the need for protection
is not as urgent where, e.g. very broad concepts of copyright protection,
such as in common law countries, can cover investments on a much broader
basis ("sweat-of-the-brow" doctrine).[75]

b) At present, protection against slavish imitation is one of the most disputed
areas in the field of unfair competition protection. There is a degree of distinction between civil law countries which tend to grant such protection,
and common law countries which are more reluctant to do so.

While there is no explicit provision against slavish imitation in the
WIPO's model Unfair Competition Prevention Act, a lively discussion has
been going on at the **AIPPI** level.[76] In its resolution, it was recommended
that slavish or quasi-slavish imitations should be unlawful under the following circumstances:

". . . 2.6 Slavish or quasi-slavish imitation of goods or services should be considered acts of
unfair competition not only if there is a danger of confusion, but also when there is exploitation
of the original product or service or if distinction between the original and the imitation is
seriously impeded,

---

[75] Limited for copyright law in the US Supreme Court decision Feist Publications Inc.
v. Rural Telephone Service Company, Inc., 27 March 1991, 18 USPQ 2nd 1275.

[76] Question 115, discussions of the XXXVI AIPPI congress in Montreal, 25–30 June,
1995.

... 2.8 Slavish or quasi-slavish imitation of goods or services should not be considered acts of unfair competition insofar as they may be necessary to achieve a particular technical function with regard to the products or services."[77]

Generally speaking, slavish imitation can be acknowledged in cases where there is a certain confusion as to the identity of goods, even in common law countries (so-called passing-off).[78]

II. Individual countries

1. Germany

While in Germany, imitation which does not give rise to confusion is deemed legal in principle *(Nachahmungsfreiheit)*, additional elements may make it unlawful.[79] In fact, most of the cases which are dealt with under the heading "slavish imitation" *(sklavische Nachahmung)* require confusion as to origin in one way or another.

In the absence of confusion, direct adoption is not unlawful per se,[80] but only in certain cases because of the "special features" of the product,[81] if imitation is very easy (especially by electronic means,[82] and also for databases[83]), when otherwise incentives for development would be stifled[84] or when imitation was undertaken systematically and for a whole range of goods.[85] But the clearest example of protection being provided beyond the (purposely limited) protection possible under intellectual property laws is the (undisputed) protection of fashion designs for one season[86] or more, if fair and equitable.[87] Again, the courts judge on the basis of a balance of interests. Since the law denies fashion designs specific protection (either because the fashion has been around once before, or because design law is too cumbersome) and designers have to make their profits quickly, protection is necessary and justified.

---

[77] Reprinted in GRUR Int. 1996, 1043.

[78] For Germany: German Supreme Court, 3 May 1986, GRUR 1968, 591 – "Pulver Behälter".

[79] Baumbach/Hefermehl, UWG Kommentar, 22nd ed. 2000, marginal note 438 et seq., Reimer, 190 et seq.; Emmerich, 158 et seq.; Walch, Ergänzender Leistungsschutz nach § 1 UWG, 1991.

[80] German Supreme Court, 21 November 1991, NJW 1992, 1316 – "Leitsätze".

[81] German Supreme Court, 19 June 1974, WRP 1976, 370 – "Ovalpuderdose".

[82] German Supreme Court, 30 October 1968, GRUR 1969, 186 – "Reprint".

[83] German Supreme Court, 10 December 1987, GRUR 1988, 310 – "Informationsdienst": the plaintiff's business was threatened by the continuous use of data by a competitor.

[84] German Supreme Court, 4 June 1986, GRUR 1986, 895 – "OCM".

[85] German Supreme Court, 10 December 1986, GRUR 1987, 905 – "Le Corbusier Möbel".

[86] German Supreme Court, 19 January 1973, GRUR 1973, 480 – "Modeneuheit".

[87] German Supreme Court, 10 November 1983, GRUR 1984, 453 – "Hemdblusenkleid": the skirt was a sort of "all year round" wear.

Also in another specific case, the German Supreme Court found slavish imitation in the absence of confusion unlawful: where a competitor manufactured products which are interchangeable with a product series manufactured by the original creator and where the original series per se was meant to be expanded, completed or complemented.[88]

2. Italy

Also in Italy, the LEGO dispute gave rise to an interesting discussion about the protection of aesthetic creations in the absence of confusion. The court held as follows:

"In our legal system, substitution without differentiation is only permitted if it is found that it is impossible to apply distinctive features without impairing the function, and does not follow automatically, as the Court of Appeals seems to assume, from the reproducibility of the function. It is permitted to copy the functional idea of another, but it is not permitted also to copy those shapes where reproduction simply leads to the product's no longer being distinguishable on the market, thus alone the party making the copy not only to use the idea, as is his right, but also to use the goodwill of another. It is precisely this distinction that justifies the theory acknowledged in case law of non-functional harmless deviation: Even if the law must prevent an exploitation monopoly continuing in perpetuity beyond the duration of the property right, it cannot as a matter of principle permit what is ultimately a transfer of the revenue from another's investments. Such a solution would itself result in a restriction of competition, since it would eliminate a condition for competition on the market, namely the possibility of acquiring customers in accordance with the rules of commercial honesty . . . By failing to determined whether it is possible to differentiate the product in a way that is harmless to function but at the same time capable of avoiding a complete reproduction, the Court of Appeals in effect generally and hence arbitrarily excluded the possibility that the tort of slavish imitation can be admitted with respect to utility designs that reproduce functional shapes."[89]

3. Japan

Japan in 1994[90] introduced a new provision in its Unfair Competition Prevention Act that prohibited:

"the act of transferring or dealing in (including the display for such purpose), exporting or importing goods that imitate the form of another party's goods (excluding such forms that are

---

[88] German Supreme Court, 6 November 1963, GRUR 1964, 621 – "Klemmbausteine"; German Supreme Court, 7 May 1992, GRUR 1992, 619 – "Klemmbausteine II". The cases concerned the LEGO system, and the court tried hard to find convincing arguments as to why in the absence of any intellectual property protection, the manufacturer of parts interchangeable with the LEGO series was objectionable. That the approach is not entirely convincing may have dawned on the court itself that tried to limit the application of such rule in Supreme Court, 8 December 1999, GRUR 2000, 521 – "Modulgerüst".

[89] Italian Supreme Court, 9 March 1998, 32 IIC 349 [2001] – "Building Bricks III". A strong protection against slavish imitation is also advocated by P. Frassi, Protection of Modular Products Under Italian Law, 32 IIC 267 [2001].

[90] Law No. 47/1993, in force since 1 May 1994.

commonly used for such or similar goods or that have an identical or similar function or effect), provided that not more than three years from the date of first commercial circulation have elapsed;"

This provision also goes beyond the scope specified in the Paris Convention and codifies recent Japanese jurisdiction.[91] The prohibition does not extend to configurations commonly used for a certain purpose, and limits protection to three years from the marketing date. This provision, influenced by moves in Europe to introduce a system of unregistered designs, should be interpreted within the context of unfair competition law. E.g. the protected configuration does not have to show novelty, as it would if protected under industrial property laws. Since the provision is clearly new in the Japanese context, its interpretation poses a number of interesting problems.[92]

4. Common law countries

As has been explained above, the **common law countries** have based protection against unfair competition on the tort of *passing-off* with some examples of extended interpretation in order to protect famous or well-known trade marks. In addition, the threshold for protection under copyright has traditionally been very low.[93]

In the United States, particular attention has been given to acts of slavish imitation in the newspaper industry, while apparently other fields of law have not followed suit. In a US Supreme Court case of 1918, it was found unlawful for a competitor in the newspaper industry to misappropriate the process of gathering information by using information assembled from another newspaper in his own:

"Stripped of all disguises, the [defendant's] process amounts to an unauthorised interference with the normal operation of the complainant's legitimate business precisely at the point where the profit is to be reaped in order to divert the material portion of the profit from those who have earned it to those who have not. The transaction speaks for itself, and the court of equity ought not to hesitate long in characterising it as unfair competition in business."[94]

---

[91] See the "Decorative Veneer" decision of the Tokyo High Court, 17 December 1991, cited above.

[92] For details, see C. Heath, The System of Unfair Competition Prevention in Japan, London 2001, 128–140.

[93] In the Scottish case Leslie *v.* Young that went to the House of Lords, it was held that there was copyright in a railway timetable (House of Lords, [1894] A.C. 329); similar decisions were rendered for TV programme guides: BBC *v.* Wireless League Gazette Publishing Co, English High Court, [1926] Ch 433 and Independent Television Publications Limited *v.* Time Out, English High Court, 9 May 1983, [1984] FSR 64. This approach has made restrictions necessary by a control of possible anti-competitive behaviour by the British Monopolies and Mergers Commission, and not least by the European Commission as well: Radio Telefis Airann *v.* Independent TV Publications, European Court of Justice 6 April 1995, 27 IIC 78 [1996].

[94] International News Service *v.* Associated Press, 248 U.S. 215 (239–240) [1918].

But just as the German courts seem to have created a special law for the designer industry, the US courts were not persuaded to extend prohibition of slavish imitation from newspapers to other fields of industry.[95] One reason may be that in the US, there is no federal statute on unfair competition.

F. Conclusion

Finding the appropriate manner of protection for works of applied art has been difficult throughout. The most uncontroversial form of protection has been the design. Particularly in countries with a substantive examination system, such protection is often insufficient, however, due to the relatively lengthy examination procedure and the short-lived cycle of fashion.

The international protection of applied art under copyright law was introduced into the Berne Convention at the Berlin Revision Conference in 1908. The approach was fraught with difficulties, however, as no common denominator could be found under which circumstances and to what extent works of applied art that would also merit design protection could and should be protected under copyright law. In this respect, Ladas states the following:

> "It is safe to assume that . . . a subject-matter in which the artistic element is not predominant but is rather an aesthetic feature of an industrial product, such as the configuration of a motor car body, a shoe pattern, the shape of a drinking glass, will not be protected by the copyright law. On the other hand, artistic works, such as statuettes, figurines, etc., although used for utilitarian purposes, for instance, as containers, and the like, will be generally protected by such law. In between these two classes there is a large field of creations on which uncertainty prevails under the existing laws in the various countries."[96]

Indeed, even today there is no harmonised approach towards protection. The only issue that has been clarified in Europe is that double protection may not be excluded per se. On an international level, the difficulties in obtaining copyright protection are heightened by the somewhat untypical requirement of reciprocity that the Berne Convention stipulates in Art. 2(7).

Both designs and copyright protect certain aesthetic achievements. The issue is less clear for unfair competition prevention law that in some countries would be extended to the protection of aesthetic creations even without any danger of confusion (Japan, Germany), while in others would only protect aesthetic features to the extent that their copying creates confusion in the market (common law protection of passing-off). While the latter is an established principle of protection, the former is not internationally recognised as an act of unfair competition.

---

[95] See particularly, R. Callmann, 55 Harvard Law Review 595 [1942].
[96] Ladas, The International Protection of Literary and Artistic Works, New York 1938, 260.

Finally, also trade mark protection is meant to prevent confusion in trade and thus requires the aesthetic creation to be distinctive and non-functional in order to serve as an indication of origin. Most three-dimensional creations fail to meet this standard. In order to prevent aesthetic forms to be mono-polised in perpetuity, the registration of three-dimensional marks should only be granted where secondary meaning has been established.

10
Copyright, Contract and the Legal Protection of Technological Measures: Providing a Rationale to the 'Copyright Exceptions Interface'

THOMAS HEIDE

A. Introduction

The relationship between copyright, contract and the legal protection extended to technological measures is important and one due to increase in prominence as copyright owners increasingly rely on contracts and technology in the delivery of copyrighted material.

The interrelationship between copyright on the one hand and contract and legal protection extended to technological measures used by rights-holders, on the other, is herein referred to as the 'copyright exceptions interface'.[1] This term is used to refer to how legislators envisage that users of copyright material can benefit from copyright exceptions despite attempts to restrain or prevent certain uses either through contract or technology. The copyright interface is thus of key relevance to both users and rights-holders. For users, the interface indicates what contractual restrictions they can consider to be null and void and in what instances they can circumvent rights-holders' technological measures. For rights-holders, the interface indicates what type of obligations they may be under in enabling users to benefit from exceptions under copyright law.

One would have thought that the WIPO Copyright Treaty (WCT) – the international treaty drafted specifically to address copyright in the digital environment – would have addressed the copyright exceptions interface. However, it only extends legal protection to technological measures, and does not set out an interface for such measures. This is because the WCT does not indicate how acts 'permitted by law' are to apply where technological measures applied by rights-holders restrict such acts.[2]

---

[1] The 'copyright exceptions interface' is composed of the interface with contract ('the contract interface') and the interface with technological measures ('the technological measures interface').

[2] Article 11 of the WIPO Copyright Treaty (WCT) only sets out the obligation concerning legal protection of technological measures:

'Contracting Parties shall provide adequate legal protection and effective legal remedies against the circumvention of effective technological measures that are used by authors in connection with the exercise of their rights under this Treaty or the Berne

Despite this, both the US and EU have introduced a copyright exceptions interface. This article reviews the respective US and EU interfaces and argues that they are insufficient because they do not provide an interface for the core aspect of copyright: the aspect which encourages innovation by enabling the re-use or productive use of works. It is submitted that this core aspect of copyright is important especially because of its economic effects, in particular its effects on competition between copyrighted works and its effects on rights-holders' use of contractual restrictions and technological measures.

This article first elaborates why the copyright exceptions interface is necessary and then goes on to offer economic analysis to underscore why any copyright exception enabling productive use must be included within an exceptions interface. After examining and critiquing the US and EU approaches to the copyright interface, the article discusses the EC Software Directive. It is submitted that, despite the Software Directive only addressing copyright law relative to computer software, it can be looked to as a model precedent because it is the only piece of legislation which provides a complete copyright exceptions interface – that is, both for contract and technological measures – for copyright exceptions which enable productive use.

B. Why a Copyright Exceptions Interface Is Necessary

It is widely recognised that digital technology and the Internet present serious challenges to copyright owners and the law. Despite recent legislative efforts to bolster copyright law, rights-holders concerned about losing control over their material increasingly rely on contractual restrictions and technological measures to minimize the risks of unauthorised use and distribution.[3] For users of copyright materials the resort to contract and technological measures is of significant concern because such means can easily frustrate the ability to benefit from exceptions specifying lawful acts under copyright law. Indeed, the concern is that 'digital lock-up' will result.[4]

Convention and that restrict acts, in respect of their works, which are not authorized by the authors concerned or permitted by law.'

Acts 'permitted by law' refers to the exceptions under copyright law.

[3] Indeed, the recent report on 'Copyright and Contract' of the Australian Copyright Law Review Committee observed this to be taking place. *See* Australian Copyright Law Review Committee's Report on Copyright and Contract (October 2002), available at http://www.law.gov.au/www/clrHome.nsf

[4] 'Digital lock-up' occurs where exceptions specifying lawful uses under copyright law are without practical effect either due to contractual restrictions which require any user to agree to terms restricting the lawful use or uses before copyright material can be used or because a rights-holder's technological measures frustrate or make it impossible to use copyright material in a way permitted by copyright law.

Notwithstanding the nature and extent of both copyright owner and user concerns, there is little question that copyright law remains the body of law best suited to regulating productive use of materials. At the most fundamental level, the idea expression dichotomy, now part of the international copyright treaties, indicates that the ideas underlying copyright works can be re-used.[5] Certain national exceptions also permit productive use of otherwise protected expression. This is the case under the US fair use doctrine,[6] the UK fair dealing exceptions,[7] and for any copyright or author's right exception permitting quotation, parody, or for that matter, the inclusion of a part of a work in another.[8] It is also the case for the reverse engineering or decompilation exceptions found under US and EC law.[9]

It should not be controversial that these aspects of the law cannot have effect unless the exceptions enabling productive use can be applied.[10] Similarly, if the law allows copyright owners to deposit only one or a few

---

[5] WCT Article 2.

[6] 17 U.S.C. 107 (2000).

[7] *See*, in particular, Copyright, Designs and Patents Act (CDPA) (1988), §§29–30.

[8] Thus what is in issue here is described by Professor Landes and Judge Posner as a 'productive use' and such use results whenever the number of copyrighted *works* is increased. The 'productive use' should be contrasted with the 'reproductive use' which merely increases the number of *copies*. *See* W. Landes and R. Posner, 'An Economic Analysis of Copyright Law', 18 Journal of Legal Studies 325, 360 (1989). The label 'transformative' use is synonymous with 'productive use' and was adopted by the US Supreme Court in Campbell *v*. Acuff-Rose Music, Inc., 114 U.S. 1164 (1994). A use is 'transformative' where it alters 'the original with new expression, meaning, or message.' Ibid, 1164. As the Court points out, 'transformative' use was discussed by Judge Leval where he states:

> 'Transformative uses may include criticizing the quoted work, exposing the character of the original author, proving a fact, or summarizing an idea argued in the original in order to defend or rebut it. They also may include parody, symbolism, aesthetic declarations, and innumerable other uses.'

See P. Leval, 'Toward a Fair Use Standard', 103 Harvard Law Review 1105, 1111 (1990).

[9] *See* 17 U.S.C. 1201(f) (2000) and Council Directive 91/250/EEC of 14 May 1991 on the legal protection of computer programs ('Software Directive'), (O.J. L122, 17.5.1991, p. 42). *See* also, e.g., the US decision in Atari Games Corp. *v*. Nintendo, 975 F.2d 832 (Fed. Cir. 1992) which held that reverse engineering of computer programs can constitute fair use under US copyright law.

[10] The EC Copyright Directive practically encourages the contractual override of copyright exceptions. Although the Directive sets out a technological measures interface it does not even apply where copyright works are made available to the public on agreed contractual terms. At least in the online environment, any use can be contractually restricted or technologically blocked. *See* Recitals 45 and 53 and Article 6(4), fourth subparagraph, discussed below in Sections III(A) and (C). Directive 2001/29/EC of the European Parliament and of the Council of 22 May 2001 on the harmonisation of certain aspects of copyright and related rights in the information society ('Copyright Directive'), (O.J. L167, 22.6.2001, p.10).

hard-copies of their copyright material free from technological measures in order to side-step the obligation to allow users in EU Member States to benefit from certain copyright exceptions despite the application of technological measures, not many users intent upon productive use are realistically likely to be able to benefit from those exceptions.[11] Productive use may also become only academically possible if users have to resort to 'the old-fashioned way' to make re-use of copyright materials.[12]

The copyright exceptions interface provides the mechanism through which it may be possible to apply copyright exceptions despite attempts to restrain or prevent certain uses either through contract or technology.[13] The interface is necessary because the presumption about copyright works being available in a way that allows users to apply exceptions cannot be said to hold in the environment predominated by click-on licences and technological measures.[14] Without a copyright interface, rights-holders will be able to use contractual restrictions and technological measures to target exceptions, including those enabling productive use.[15] However, whilst the need for an

---

[11] Indeed, the obligation to provide a technological measures interface for the private copying exception, Article 5(2)(b) of the Copyright Directive, does not arise if 'reproduction for private use has already been made possible by rightholders to the extent necessary to benefit from' this exception. Moreover, rights-holders are free to adopt 'adequate measures regarding the number of reproductions.' *See* Article 6(4), second subparagraph, of the Copyright Directive.

[12] *See* e.g. Universal City Studios *v.* Corley, 273 F.3d 429, 459 (2nd Cir. 2001) ('We know of no authority for the proposition that fair use, as protected by the Copyright Act, much less the Constitution, guarantees copying by the optimum method or in the identical format of the original. . . .Fair use has never been held to be a guarantee of access to copyrighted material in order to copy it by the fair user's preferred technique or in the format of the original.') *See* also United States *v.* Elcom Ltd., 62 USPQ 1736, 1749 (ND Cal. 2002) ('. . . nothing in the DMCA prevents anyone from quoting from a work or comparing texts for the purpose of study or criticism. It may be that from a technological perspective, the fair user my find it more difficult to do so – quoting may have to occur the old fashioned way, by hand or by re-typing, rather than by "cutting and pasting" from existing digital media').

[13] The interface is necessary because most copyright exceptions are not of mandatory effect and can be overridden through contract. Moreover, copyright exceptions are exceptions only to the rights under copyright, not to other rights. They do not, for instance, apply to the rights structure established by extending legal protection to technological measures. It is therefore apparent why Article 11 of the WCT (above fn. 2) does not provide an interface: it introduces legal protection for technological measures but does not specify that copyright exceptions apply to it.

[14] The presumption in the hard-copy or analogue world seems to be that exceptions can be applied only to copyrighted material once it has been published. For example, the Berne Convention in Article 10(1) states that '[i]t shall be permissible to make quotations from a work which has already been lawfully made available to the public, . . .'.

[15] *See*, e.g., the recent decision in Bowers *v.* Baystate Technologies, Inc. 64 USPQ 2d 1065 (Fed. Cir. 2002). In this decision, the Court of Appeal for the Federal Circuit upheld the copyright owner's shrink-wrap licence which prohibited reverse engineering of its computer program.

interface should be plain, the difficulty remains in deciding which exceptions to specify an interface for – those enabling productive use or all copyright exceptions.[16]

C. Copyright's Promotion of Innovation-Driven Competition: A Rationale for the 'Copyright Exceptions Interface'

Innovation is a key part of today's policy landscape and copyright has an important role in promoting it.[17] Whilst it is commonly recognised that copyright promotes innovation through the rights it extends to creators, it is submitted that copyright also promotes innovation through its encouragement of productive use.

This section highlights the economic effects of copyright's encouragement of productive use. It is shown that the promotion of productive use has an important effect on competition, herein referred to as innovation-driven competition. This type of competition is shown to be capable of acting as a check and balance not only on the price charged by rights-holders but also on contractual restrictions and technological measures used along with a work.[18] For these reasons, the copyright exceptions which promote

---

[16] We could recommend the mandatory application of all copyright exceptions, an approach taken by the Belgian legislature. Similarly, the Australian Copyright Law Review Committee recently recommended that the Australian Copyright Act be amended so that agreements or provisions which exclude or modify the Act's copyright exceptions have no legal effect. However, we submit that making such a broad declaration may have several adverse effects. For one, it may require that aspects of copyright law (e.g. time-shifting) are applicable even to new ways of distributing works where they may not fit. Secondly, if copyright law is made too broadly applicable, it may not provide the degree of flexibility needed to efficiently address challenges posed by technology or the marketplace. For the Belgian law, *see* Article 23 Loi Coordonnee du 30 Juin 1994 relative au droit d'auteur et aux droits voisins, as amended by the law of 31 August 1998. The recommendation of the Australian Copyright Law Review Committee can be found in the report cited above in fn. 3. It should also be pointed out that the decision to address potential contractual overrides does not address the challenge of technology to the copyright exceptions and the need for a technological measures interface. As is discussed in section III, these issues have to be addressed together.

[17] *See* e.g. Recital 4 of the Copyright Directive. *See* also, e.g., the recent WIPO publication, Kamil Idriss, 'Intellectual Property – A Power Tool for Economic Growth' (2003).

[18] Moreover, we submit that because the ability of any copyright owner to impose unfair terms or technologically restrict access to a work is limited by innovation-driven competition, it follows that there is less of a chance that an abuse of a dominant market position or a clash with fundamental interests such as freedom of expression will take place. Innovation-driven competition therefore has the potential to minimise the need to resort to other bodies of law, including antitrust or competition law, to regulate the content of contractual restrictions or the use of technological measures.

innovation-driven competition (i.e. the exceptions enabling productive use) cannot be ignored and must form the basis of any copyright exceptions interface.

I. Copyright and 'Innovation-Driven Competition'

Innovation-driven competition is defined as the type of competition which results from the appearance of innovative products as encouraged by law.[19] This type of competition is best understood when compared to a market in which it does not take place. Considering the market for information products, including the market for entertainment and knowledge based information products, it is uncontroversial that the available attention of the consumer is subject to constraints on both time and energy. Accordingly, all works in such a market compete for the limited attention of the consumer and a degree of substitutability and resulting competition between works can be said to exist. Moreover, because competitive forces are present in this market, changes in price or features of an information product occur over time.

Where innovation-driven competition is applicable, productive use of works is permitted which results in an increased number of works available for consumption. If the constraints on the available attention of the consumer are considered to remain constant, an increased number of works translates into an increased degree of competition between those works. In addition, because competing works share ideas or protected expression, a higher degree of substitutability than would be the case without productive use is present. Thus, the competition any one work experiences is intensified compared to where a lesser degree of substitutability is present. As a result, changes in price or features of a work occur at a faster pace than would be the case without productive use. In sum, innovation-driven competition is notable because it is characterised by an increased level of competition more intensive and occurring at a faster pace than normally applicable competitive forces.[20]

---

[19] In short, as revealed in this section, productive use permitted under copyright law brings about substitution between works and the resulting substitution enhances competition between those works.

[20] Innovation-driven competition as introduced by copyright law can be said to fit Schumpeter's description of dynamic competition propelled by the introduction of new products and new processes. Joseph Schumpeter stressed that potential competition from new products and processes is the most powerful form of competition, stating

> 'in capitalist reality, as distinguished from its textbook picture, it is not that kind of [price] competition that counts but the competition that comes from the new commodity, the new technology, the new source of supply. . . . This kind of competition is much more effective than the other as bombardment is in comparison with forcing a door, and so much more important that it becomes a matter of comparative indifference whether competition in the ordinary sense functions more or less promptly.'

J. Schumpeter, Capitalism, Socialism and Democracy, 84–85 (1942). Indeed, innovation-driven competition as introduced by copyright can be said to reflect a particular striking

This view of the economic effect of intellectual property rights has recently been explicitly embraced by the European Commission. In its Evaluation Report on the Technology Transfer Regulation, the Commission states that:

'. . . innovation in new products and new technologies are the ultimate source of substantial and major competition over time.'[21]

It is important to distinguish innovation-driven competition as promoted by copyright law. Because copyright law targets infringing uses of works, in particular the use of the entirety of a work, it prevents complete or near complete free-riding from taking place. Accordingly, copyright excludes the type of competition where competition arises from initial creators and free-riders offering the *same* information product to consumers.[22] Innovation-driven competition therefore revolves around the type of competition based on partial or incomplete free-riding as permitted by law.

II.   The Effects of Innovation-driven Competition

It is submitted that innovation-driven competition is indiscriminate and results in competitive pressures being imposed on rights-holders both in terms of price and the use of contractual restrictions and technological measures. These competitive pressures mean that there is a constant need for rights-holders of pre-existing works and new creators alike to be able to benefit not only from copyright exceptions enabling productive use but also from any copyright interface for such exceptions.[23]

1.   *The Effect on the Price of Copyright Works*

Fundamental economic principles indicate that where supply expands due to an increase in the number of works available for consumption, price will decrease where demand remains constant. Moreover, due to the substitutability introduced to the market by the encouragement of productive use, the ability of a copyright owner to charge supra-competitive prices for his information product is lessened as any increase in price will lead consumers

---

case of what Schumpeter had in mind because it can be said to speed up the process of competition by encouraging substitutes.

[21] *See* Commission Evaluation Report on the Technology Transfer Block Exemption regulation 240/96, paragraph 190, (2002), available at http://europa.eu.int/comm/competition/antitrust/technology_transfer/

[22] This type of competition is discussed by Professor Lehmann and is distinguishable from the innovation-driven competition in issue here. In short, it involves a 'reproductive use' as opposed to a 'productive use'. *See* M. Lehmann, 'The Theory of Property Rights and the Protection of Intellectual and Industrial Property', 16 IIC 525 (1985) and M. Lehmann, 'Property and Intellectual Property – Property Rights as Restrictions on Competition in Furtherance of Competition', 20 IIC 1 (1989).

[23] Professor Landes and Judge Posner make a similar point but indicate that copyright owners might find it in their self-interest to limit copyright protection because stronger or more extensive copyright protection raises the cost of expression to both 'earlier' and 'later' authors. *See* Landes and Posner, (above fn. 8), 333.

to substitute other cheaper information products in place of his information product. The overall effect of innovation–driven competition is therefore lower prices and the maintenance of lower prices when compared to a market where productive use is unduly restricted through contractual provisions and technological measures.

2. The Effect on the Use of Contractual Restrictions and Technological Measures

As indicated above, innovation-driven competition intensifies the competitive pressures brought to bear on any given work due to copyright law's encouragement of increased substitutability. Such competitive pressures may force a copyright owner to evaluate the entire market presentation of his work and compete not only on price but also on features, including any contractual restrictions and technological measures regulating permissible use.[24]

Where every aspect of the market presentation of a work becomes a competitive parameter, the copyright owner is less able to control permissible uses through technological measures or restrictive contractual terms. Any attempt to impose restrictive contractual terms and technological measures which frustrate certain uses will cause consumers to shift their consumption to available substitutes. The overall effect of innovation-driven competition forces consideration of the features of a work made publicly available, including its contractual restrictions and any technological measures used in its delivery.[25] It may lead to less onerous contractual restrictions and technological measures when compared to a market where productive use is unduly restricted through the use of contractual restrictions and technological measures.

III. The Economic Case for the Copyright Exceptions Interface

As is plain, innovation-driven competition as promoted by copyright law only applies where the copyright exceptions enabling productive use are available and can be applied by users. However, in the environment where copyright owners increasingly rely on contracts and technological measures in the delivery of copyrighted material, it must be asked whether these copyright exceptions can be applied. In its recent report on Copyright and Contract, the Australian Copyright Law Review Committee found that this was not the case. The report observed that electronic trade in copyright

---

[24] This 'features based' competition was recognised by Judge Easterbrook when he indicated that '[t]erms of use are no less a part of "the product" than are the size of the database and the speed with which the software compiles listings.' *See* ProCD, Inc. *v.* Zeidenberg, 86 F.3d 1447, 1453 (7 Cir. 1996). In this decision, the 7 Circuit Court of Appeals upheld a contractual term in a shrink–wrap licence agreement limiting the user of ProCD CD-ROM telephone directories to consumer uses.

[25] Ibid. Judge Easterbrook also indicated that '[c]ompetition among vendors, not judicial revision of a package's contents, is how consumers are protected in a market economy.' However, as is discussed just below, we submit that the forces of competition will only properly work where they are unfettered. They are not unfettered where innovation-driven competition as promoted by copyright law is curtailed.

materials is commonly subject to contracts which purport to exclude or modify copyright exceptions.[26] It also observed that technological measures are being used to curtail the applicability of copyright exceptions. It is submitted that 'digital lock-up' is taking place particularly with respect to the copyright exceptions enabling productive use.[27] The effect in terms of innovation-driven competition is not difficult to appreciate: Where the copyright exceptions enabling productive use do not apply they do not result in the substitution effect which enhances competition between information products. As a consequence, the price and features-based competition promoted by copyright law is altogether eliminated or significantly curtailed. The latter results where a rights-holder is able to pick and choose the applicable copyright exceptions whilst targeting others through contractual restrictions and/or technological measures, thereby manipulating both the degree and timing of any competition that the information product will face.[28] For example, a rights-holder can influence the degree of applicable competition by deciding to permit only the most benign productive uses of his work – such as quotation – and restricting uses viewed as involving a greater competitive threat.[29] Likewise, the timing of any applicable innovation-driven competition can be affected where the rights-holder targets exceptions enabling productive use and restricts users applying these exceptions. This is because the lead-time the copyright owner enjoys before the effect of innovation-driven competition 'bites' may be increased when compared to the hard-copy world where copyright exceptions commonly apply once a work has been made publicly available.[30]

---

[26] *See* paragraph 4.106 of the Australian Copyright Law Review Committee's report (above fn. 3). In relation to Australia, the report observed that 'this phenomenon prima facie alters the copyright balance established by the Copyright Act, which partly defines the rights of copyright owners in terms of the limits placed upon those rights by the exceptions.'

[27] The definition of 'digital lock-up' is set out above in fn. 4.

[28] It is notable that the recent report on the DMCA observed that:

'. . . the movement at the state level toward resolving questions as to the enforceability of non-negotiated contracts coupled with legally-protected technological measures that give right holders the technological capability of imposing contractual provisions unilaterally, increases the possibility that right holders, rather than Congress, will determine the landscape of consumer privileges in the future.'

See Study Examining 17 U.S.C. Sections 109 and 117 Pursuant to Section 104 of the Digital Millennium Copyright Act, xxxi–ii, (2001), available at http://www.copyright.gov/reports/studies/dmca/dmca_study.html

[29] For instance, 'shrink-wrap' and 'click-wrap' licences generally contain restrictions on reverse engineering or decompilation. This was also observed in the Australian Copyright Law Review Committee's report (above fn. 3).

[30] *See* above fn. 14. As copyright law generally leaves only the basic building blocks necessarily requiring the investment of time and effort to bring works to the marketplace, the law privileges the rights-holder with lead-time, a time period during which he is able to exploit his work without a next generation of works appearing on the market. *See* section I for a discussion of provisions enabling productive use.

A copyright exceptions interface is thus necessary in order to avoid innovation-driven competition either being eliminated or significantly curtailed. It is further submitted that, given the effects of innovation-driven competition as promoted by copyright law, it is not sufficient to leave the copyright exceptions enabling productive use to be applied, as the Elcom case put it, 'the old fashioned way'.[31] Only by specifying an interface for these exceptions can the user public and new creators alike enjoy the benefits of innovation-driven competition in the environment already predominated by contractual restrictions and technological measures.

D. Legislative attempts on the 'Copyright Interface"

This section examines and evaluates the 'copyright exceptions interface' in the DMCA and the EC Copyright Directive.[32] With regard to the contract interface, we examine whether there is any indication that contractual ordering is permissible or not, in which case the provision in point can be said to be of mandatory effect or incapable of contractual derogation.[33] With regard to the technological measures interface, as technological measures may not enable a user to benefit from copyright exceptions, we examine whether it is permissible to circumvent the rights-holder's technological measures in order to apply copyright exceptions. In addition, as circumvention devices may be necessary to enable a user to circumvent, we look to whether either the US or EU legislation indicates that it is permissible to develop devices which enable circumvention.[34]

It is submitted that the contract and technological measures interfaces need to be treated together. Otherwise, it will be easy to undo through

---

[31] *See* above fn. 12.

[32] §§1201(d)–(j) of the Digital Millennium Copyright Act of 1998, Pub. L. No. 105–304 ('DMCA'); Article 6(4) of the Copyright Directive. This legislation can be found in Appendixes 1 and 2, respectively.

[33] Otherwise, the assumption is that provisions can be contractually overridden.

[34] In considering the US and EU copyright exceptions interfaces, it is important to keep DMCA §1201(c)(1) in mind. §1201(c)(1) states:

'Nothing in this section shall affect rights, remedies, limitations, or defenses applicable to copyright infringement, including fair use, under this title.'

A similar provision is included in Recital 51 of the Copyright Directive, which states that '[t]he legal protection of technological measures applies without prejudice to public policy, as reflected in Article 5, or public security.' However, these provisions do not by themselves indicate whether contractual ordering of exceptions is acceptable or whether it is permissible for users to circumvent technological measures. Indeed, this interpretation was confirmed in respect of §1201(c)(1) in Universal City Studios *v.* Corley, 273 F.3d 429, 443, 459 (2d Cir. 2001), which rejected the contention that §1201(c)(1) should be read to allow the circumvention of encryption technology.

contract whatever interface is set out for technological measures.[35] However, neither the DMCA nor the Copyright Directive sets out a contract interface.[36] But, as indicated below, the Copyright Directive does indicate its approach to the interrelationship between copyright exceptions and contract.[37]

In terms of introducing legal protection for technological measures, the DMCA introduced §1201, which includes provisions dealing both with access control-technology (§1201(a)) and copy-protection (§1201(b)). As detailed below, the DMCA only really introduces an interface for one copyright provision enabling productive use, the provision enabling reverse engineering. In the EU, the Member States are currently in the process of implementing the Copyright Directive.[38] Article 6 sets out the obligations concerning technological measures. It sets out an intricate interface which is ultimately likely to be of little, if any, effect, especially for copyright exceptions enabling productive use.

I. The DMCA and Copyright Directive: The Contract Interface

The DMCA does not address the issue of contracting around exceptions and therefore leaves the ability to benefit from exceptions, including benefiting from any exceptions where a technological measures interface has been specified subject to contractual ordering (see Section III(B) below). Any challenge would fall, if at all, under the preemption doctrine.[39]

Under the Copyright Directive, it is made clear that all of the exceptions are deemed capable of contractual ordering. Indeed as the following recital spells out, it is practically encouraged:

---

[35] Indeed, as we argue in section III(B), it seems possible to contractually seek to prevent a user from benefiting from the technological measures interface specified in the DMCA.

[36] This is because they do not address contract law issues. However, this would not prevent them from specifying a contract interface. Indeed, as section IV elaborates, this has been done under the EC Software Directive.

[37] For example, the Uniform Computer Information Transactions Act (UCITA), the contract code adopted by the NCCUSL in the US, indicates in its comments that contracts are unlikely to be able to override a user's ability to engage in reverse engineering. *See* the Official Comment to Section 105, available at http://www.ucitaonline.com/. UCITA has been adopted by two states, Maryland and Virginia. The District of Columbia, Illinois, Maine, New Hampshire, New Jersey, Oregon, and Texas are presently considering whether to adopt UCITA.

[38] The implementation deadline was 22 December 2002. At the time of writing only Denmark and Greece have met this deadline.

[39] 17 U.S.C. 301 (2000). The decision in Bowers (above fn. 15) is illustrative as to the potential applicability of the 'statutory' preemption doctrine. The Bowers court considered 'statutory' preemption and found it inapplicable to the facts before it because the contract claim in issue was considered 'qualitatively different from copyright infringement.' The Court of Appeal in Bowers effectively adopted the reasoning of the 7 Circuit in ProCD *v.* Zeidenberg (above fn. 24).

'The exceptions and limitations referred to in Article 5(2), (3) and (4) should not, however, prevent the definition of contractual relations designed to ensure fair compensation for the rightholders insofar as permitted by national law.'[40]

This is arguably also the case for the mandatory provision concerning certain types of temporary copying.[41] Although it is mandatory for the EU Member States to implement this exception – as opposed to the exceptions found in Article 5(2) and 5(3) which are optional, there is no indication that Article 5(1) cannot be overridden through contract. It is submitted that with no treatment similar to that afforded the mandatory provisions under the Software and Database Directives,[42] this provision can also be overridden through contract.

II. The DMCA Technological Measures Interface

The DMCA introduces seven exceptions to the anti-circumvention and anti-manufacturing provisions introduced in §§ 1201(a)(1) and (2).[43] Only one of these exceptions is also introduced as an exception to the anti-manufacturing and trafficking provisions in §1201(b).[44] In all, these exceptions are far from being co-extensive with the exceptions under copyright law.[45]

---

[40] Recital 45 of the Copyright Directive.

[41] Article 5(1) of the Copyright Directive.

[42] *See* Directive 96/9/EC of the European Parliament and of the Council of 11 March 1996 on the legal protection of databases (O.J. L77, 27.3.1996, p. 20) ('Database Directive').

[43] They include exceptions for reverse engineering of computer programs, law enforcement, intelligence and other government activities, security testing and encryption research. There is also an exception for non-profit libraries and educational institutions to determine if they wish to acquire a work (the so-called shopping exception), an exception to permit discovering and disabling an undisclosed feature that collects personally-identifying information, and an exception to prevent access by minors to inappropriate material on the Internet.

[44] This is the reverse engineering exception, §1201(f). The DMCA does not include a prohibition on the act of circumvention for technological measures that protect the rights of copyright owners. However, there is still a ban on manufacturing and trafficking in such devices, which is found in §1201(b).

[45] The DMCA contains an administrative rule-making procedure (§1201(a)(1)(C)) which allows the Librarian of Congress to examine whether users of a copyrighted work are, or are likely to be, in the succeeding three-year period, adversely affected in their ability to make non-infringing uses of a particular class of copyrighted works because of the anti-circumvention prohibition contained in §1201(a). If this is found to be the case, the Librarian of Congress can exempt certain classes of works from the prohibition against circumventing access controls in §1201(a)(1). In the initial rulemaking proceeding, the prohibition against circumvention of access controls was lifted with respect to two categories of works until 28 October 2003: (1) compilations consisting of lists of web-sites blocked by filtering software applications, and (2) literary works, including computer programs and databases, protected by access control mechanisms that fail to permit access because of a malfunction, damage or obsolescence. Although the rule-making only applies to the

The exception for reverse engineering is the only exception that can be said to primarily address copyright issues.[46] This exception permits circumvention by a person who has lawfully obtained a right to use a copy of a computer program for the sole purpose of identifying and analysing elements of the program necessary to achieve interoperability with other programs, to the extent that such acts are permitted under copyright law.[47] This provision also permits the development of technological means for the act of circumvention.[48]

However, as there is no indication in the US Copyright Act or the case law interpreting it that any of these exceptions are of mandatory effect, the ability to benefit from any of these exceptions and even the exceptions interface would seem to be subject to contractual ordering.[49]

III. The Copyright Directive Technological Measures Interface

The Copyright Directive sets out the possibility that eight copyright exceptions can be benefited from despite the application of technological measures by a copyright owner. These exceptions include: reprography, private copying, certain permitted acts by libraries, educational institutions, museums and archives, the making of certain ephemeral recordings and archival copies by broadcasters, the reproduction of broadcasts by certain 'social institutions", certain uses for scientific or research purposes, certain uses by the disabled, and certain uses for public security or administrative, parliamentary or judicial proceedings.[50]

Unlike the US reverse engineering exception, the Copyright Directive does not provide authorisation for circumvention or the development of devices to assist in such circumvention. Instead, the arrangement is intricate.

Under the Directive, users must in the first instance rely on 'voluntary measures' undertaken by rights-holders to enable them to benefit from the

---

anti-circumvention provision it is possible that it can apply to a broad class of works (e.g. all literary works) as was decided in the first rulemaking proceeding. For purposes of this article, this is an important development because a broadly applicable exception to §1201(a) would be necessary for any amendment affecting copyright exceptions enabling productive use. A second rule-making is currently taking place and is expected to be completed during 2003.

[46] 17 U.S.C. 1201(f) (2000).

[47] 17 U.S.C. 1201(f)(1) (2000).

[48] 17 U.S.C. 1201(f)(2) (2000). This section applies notwithstanding the anti-manufacturing provisions found in §§1201(a)(2) and (b). For interpretation of this provision, *see* Universal City Studios, Inc. *v.* Reimerdes, 111 F. Supp.2d 294 (SDNY 2000) and Universal City Studios Inc. *v.* Reimerdes, 82 F. Supp.2d 211 (SDNY 2000).

[49] For instance, whilst a number of US cases support the ability to reverse engineer under the fair use provision, other case law has found it permissible to contractually prohibit reverse engineering. Compare the decisions of the US Court of Appeal for the Federal Circuit in Atari *v.* Nintendo (above fn. 9) with its recent decision in Bowers (above fn. 15).

[50] These are respectively Article 5(2)(a), 2(c), 2(d), 2(e), 3(a), 3(b), 3(e). The private copying exception is found in Article 5(2)(b) of the Copyright Directive.

specified exceptions.[51] Only where such 'voluntary measures' do not exist are the EU Member States obligated to 'take appropriate measures to ensure that rightholders make available to the beneficiary of an exception or limitation [specified in Article 6(4), first and second subparagraphs] . . . the means of benefiting from that exception or limitation. . . .'[52]

However, it is possible for rights-holders to completely side-step the interface – including any 'voluntary measures' and possible Member State obligations – if their copyright work is delivered online with contractual restrictions attached.[53] Whilst this also applies to the private copying exception, the further possibility exists to side-step this exception even where it is potentially available. The obligation to provide an interface for this exception is not imposed where the rights-holder has already made reproduction for private use possible by alternative means.[54]

IV. The US and EU Copyright Exception Interfaces: Critique & Evaluation

It is plain that both the US and the EU do not address the issue of the contractual overriding of copyright exceptions, leaving them open to contractual ordering.[55] What is most striking about the interface that is provided in their respective legislation is that both the US and EU technological measures interfaces are not really available to users of copyright works. This is because the DMCA does not provide a technological measures interface for works other than computer programs. Whilst the Copyright Directive does set out a broader interface for technological measures, it only potentially applies in the off-line world, thus significantly limiting its effectiveness.[56] It

---

[51] What constitutes 'voluntary measures' is not indicated, but they include 'agreements between rightholders and other parties concerned.'

[52] Article 6(4), first and second subparagraphs, of the Copyright Directive.

[53] Recital 53 and Article 6(4), fourth subparagraph, states that the interface 'shall not apply to works or other subject matter made available to the public on agreed contractual terms in such a way that members of the public may access them from a place and at a time individually chosen by them.' Thus, copyright owners need not even try to contractually restrict the ability of users to benefit from the interface.

[54] See Article 6(4), third subparagraph, of the Copyright Directive. Similar to the DMCA, Article 12 of the Copyright Directive requires the European Commission to make an assessment to determine, amongst other issues, whether the protection provided for technological measures in Article 6 is sufficient. Importantly, the assessment must also examine whether 'acts which are permitted by law are being adversely affected by the use of effective technological measures'. The first report is due on 22 December 2004. Subsequent reports must be submitted every three years thereafter.

[55] As indicated in Section III(B), it would also be possible in the US to seek to contractually override a user's ability to benefit from the technological measures interface specified for the reverse engineering exception.

[56] However, Recital 53 of the Copyright Directive states that '[n]on-interactive forms of online use *should* remain subject to' the interface. (emphasis added). This language is hardly confidence inspiring.

must additionally be remembered that even this interface is only available where the exceptions specified in the interface have been implemented by the individual EU Member States. As each of these exceptions is optional to implement, so is the interface accompanying it.

Where the exceptions are implemented under the Copyright Directive, the interface arrangement is complicated. Users, who must be lawful users, have to rely on rights-holders agreeing 'voluntary measures' in the first instance.[57] Only where the so-called 'voluntary measures' do not materialise are the EU Member States obligated to provide users with the opportunity of benefiting from the specified exceptions. Whilst the European legislator is plainly giving rights-holders the first opportunity to provide users the possibility of benefiting from the specified exceptions, it must be asked whether this 'voluntary measures'regime is really workable. After all, are rights-holders willing to agree 'voluntary measures'for any but the most benign use of their works? If the Member States have to step in to fulfil their obligations – which does not arise for the private copying exception if a rights-holder has somehow made reproduction for private use possible[58] – will it be possible to benefit from the exceptions using any means other than paper and pencil or other 'low tech'utensils?[59]

Despite the obvious shortcomings of both the US and EU interfaces, each addresses productive use in its own way. This is most clearly the case for the DMCA reverse engineering exception. Indeed, it is particularly notable that the US legislators drafting the exception recognised the importance of this exception: the legislative history cogently indicates that '[t]he purpose of this section is to foster competition and innovation in the computer and software industry.'[60] Whilst this statement is directly in line with the argument advanced in this article – that copyright promotes innovation and competition through its exceptions – it must be asked why competition and innovation should only be fostered for the software industry and not for copyright industries in general. The argument can be made that if the reverse

---

[57] Presumably this is why the interface only addresses circumvention – even though such circumvention is not undertaken by the user – and not the manufacture of circumvention devices to assist in circumvention.

[58] This requirement would seem to be satisfied, for instance, where a rights-holder deposits one or a couple of copies of his copyright material in just one library in each of the Member States. This arrangement is similar to the Software Directive which makes it possible to prevent a user decompiling a computer program if the information necessary to achieve interoperability is 'readily available'. *See* below fn. 65. However, whilst the Software Directive requires that the information be 'readily available', it would seem possible, for instance, for a copyright owner to deposit one or a few hard copies of a work in a remote library in the north of Sweden in order to prevent the private copying interface from applying in Sweden.

[59] Or, to use the phraseology of the Elcom case (above fn. 12), will it only be possible to engage in such uses in 'the old fashioned way'?

[60] S. Rep. 105–190 p. 32 (1998).

engineering exception is important enough to merit a technological measures interface, other exceptions also recognised as enabling productive use
merit a similar interface.

With regard to the Copyright Directive interface, several of the eight
exceptions specified in the interface could result in productive use by
individual users. This would seem most clearly to be the case for the three
exceptions addressing certain uses for scientific or research purposes, certain
uses by the disabled, and certain uses for public security or administrative,
parliamentary or judicial proceedings.[61] The remaining five interface exceptions would seem to enable 'reproductive' use, and not productive use.[62]
However, as these five exceptions are exceptions to the reproduction right,
the possibility exists that once a reproduction is made in accordance with
those exceptions, other exceptions enabling productive use could be applied
and result in such uses.[63]

E. The EC Software Directive: A Model Precedent

From the previous sections, it has become plain that: (1) copyright law,
through its exceptions, has an important role to play through its effects on
price and the use of contractual restrictions and technological measures; and
(2) the DMCA and the EU Copyright Directive do not provide a sufficient
copyright interface for exceptions enabling productive use.

The question arises whether there is an existing precedent which both
addresses copyright exceptions which enable productive use and provides an
appropriate copyright interface, including interfaces for contract and technological measures. As can be seen below, the EC Software Directive meets
both of these requirements.[64]

I. Contract Interface

In Article 9(1) the Software Directive addresses any attempts at contractual
overriding of certain of the exceptions addressed by the Directive:

---

[61] These exceptions are specified in Articles 5(3)(a), (3)(b), and (3)(e) of the Copyright
Directive. Because Article 6(4), fourth subparagraph, indicates that the Copyright
Directive interface also applies to the Database and the Rental Rights Directives, it
notably means that the exception for scientific or research purposes found under these
Directives will also be available where technological measures have been applied to pro-
tect the rights under those Directives. *See* Article 6(2)(b) of the Database Directive and
Article 10(1)(d) of the Rental Rights Directive. Council Directive 92/100/EEC of 19
November 1992 on rental right and lending right and on certain rights related to copyright
in the field of intellectual property (O.J. L346, 27.11.1992, p. 61).

[62] *See* above fn. 8 for the distinction between 'reproductive use' and 'productive use'.

[63] This possibility presupposes that contractual terms or technological measures do not
restrict such further uses.

[64] Relevant provisions of the Software Directive can be found in Appendix 3.

'The provisions of this Directive shall be without prejudice to any other legal provisions such as those concerning patent rights, trade-marks, unfair competition, trade secrets, protection of semi-conductor products or the law of contract. Any contractual provisions contrary to Article 6 or to the exceptions provided for in Article 5 (2) and (3) shall be null and void.'

As indicated, this contract interface addresses three exceptions under the Directive: the making of backup copies, the privilege to observe, study or test the functioning of the program in order to determine the ideas and principles which underlie any element of the program, and decompilation.[65] The only other exception under the Directive, covering certain acts as referred to in Article 4 where they are necessary for the use of the computer program by the lawful acquirer in accordance with its intended purpose, including for error correction, remains subject to contractual ordering.[66] It is important to note that two of these exceptions concern productive use, namely Articles 5(3) and 6.

In terms of specifying the contract interface, the 'such as' language of the first sentence indicates that the list of legal provisions is not exhaustive. As such, the sentence indicates that the rights structure under the Directive (i.e. copyright as applicable to software) should be deemed capable of co-existing with a potentially unlimited number of other rights structures. By indicating that 'any' contractual provision is caught, the Directive indicates that the exceptions specified in the second sentence cannot be made inapplicable through contract.[67]

Where a different rights structure to copyright is applicable, the overall effect of Article 9(1) is that users can still benefit from Articles 5 and 6. These exceptions would be available, for instance, where a software patent also applied to the computer software.[68] This is not because the Software Directive's exceptions become applicable to the rights under another rights structure by virtue of Article 9(1). Instead, as long as a computer program

---

[65] These are, respectively, Articles 5(2), 5(3) and 6 of the Software Directive. For Article 6 (decompilation) to apply, the interoperability information must not otherwise be 'readily available' and invoking the provision must be 'indispensable'. *See* Article 6(1) of the Software Directive.

[66] Article 5(1) of the Software Directive.

[67] As is evident from the second sentence of Article 9(1), beyond declaring any contractual derogation 'null and void', the Software Directive does not otherwise sanction a rights-holder's or user's conduct. Accordingly, a rights-holder is under no legally imposed duty not to seek terms restricting decompilation, for instance. Similarly, a user is under no duty not to engage in such contractual derogation. Nevertheless, this sanction makes the Directive's exceptions mandatory.

[68] This same point has also been made in relation to a rights structure supported by the EC Conditional Access Directive. Directive 98/84/EC of the European Parliament and of the Council of 20 November 1998 on the legal protection of services based on, or consisting of, conditional access (O.J. L320, 28.11.1998, p. 54). *See* T. Heide, 'Access Control and Innovation under the E.U. Electronic Commerce Framework', 15(3) Berkeley Technology Law Journal 993 (2000).

satisfies the requirements for copyright protection, the Software Directive's provisions apply and this means that its exceptions will be available and, crucially, that the policy underlying those exceptions – i.e. the copyright policy of productive use – applies. As the copyright exceptions cannot be made inapplicable through contract, they continue to be available to users.

This interpretation is confirmed by the recent proposed EC Software Patents Directive. Article 6 of the proposed Directive is very careful in seeking to ensure that the result achieved through the earlier Software Directive is not undermined through the extension of patent protection to software. It states that:

> 'Acts permitted under Directive 91/250/EEC on the legal protection of computer programs by copyright, in particular provisions thereof relating to decompilation and interoperability, or the provisions concerning semiconductor topographies or trade marks, shall not be affected through the protection granted by patents for inventions within the scope of this Directive. (emphasis added).'[69]

This point is further underscored by the Commission's Explanatory Memorandum which states that 'Article 6 [of the proposed Software Patents Directive] expressly preserves the application of the provisions on decompilation and interoperability in Directive 91/250/EEC.'[70]

II. Technological Measures Interface

Article 7 establishes the legal protection extended to technological measures. As indicated in Article 7(1)(c) it seeks to restrict:

> '. . . any act of putting into circulation, or the possession for commercial purposes of, any means the sole intended purpose of which is to facilitate the unauthorized removal or circumvention of any technical device which may have been applied to protect a computer program.'

The interface with this provision is also set out in Article 7 because that Article is explicitly declared to be 'without prejudice to' both the rights and exceptions found under the Directive.[71] To phrase it differently, the legal protection in Article 7(1)(c) shall leave intact and in no way affect the rights and exceptions under the Directive. With regard to the exceptions, the 'without prejudice to' means that all of copyright law which applies to computer programs can be made applicable despite the existence of technological measures which may interfere with such exceptions.

---

[69] Recital 18 of the Directive contains the identical language.

[70] *See* Proposal for a Directive of the European Parliament and of the Council on the patentability of computer-implemented inventions (COM(2002)92), 15. The proposed Directive is currently being considered by the European Parliament (Committee for Legal Affairs), and can be found at http://www.europa.eu.int/comm/internal_market/en/indprop/comp/com02-92en.pdf

[71] Article 7(1) Software Directive states that it is '[w]ithout prejudice to the provisions of Articles 4, 5 and 6'.

It becomes apparent from reading the first paragraph of Article 7 in conjunction with the language of sub-section (c) that it is permissible both to engage in circumvention in order to apply any of the exceptions and to develop any device necessary to engage in the circumvention.[72]

The first proposition is apparent because the legal protection extended to technological measures is to be deemed 'without prejudice to' the exceptions in Article 5. As such, the Directive indicates that the extension of protection must not interfere with the ability to benefit from the exceptions under the Directive. Presumably, if the technical devices imposed by the rights-holder somehow interfered with the ability to benefit from the exceptions, it would be possible to take the necessary steps to benefit from the exceptions. It is submitted that only in that way could the legal protection remain 'without prejudice to' the exceptions.[73]

The second proposition – that it is permissible to manufacture any device necessary to engage in authorised removal or circumvention – is evident from the face of sub-section (c). This provision targets only those means 'the sole intended purpose of which is to facilitate the unauthorized removal or circumvention' of the rights-holder's technical device.[74] In the case of a device required to enable a user to benefit from the exceptions under the Directive, it could not be targeted by this provision as its 'sole intended purpose' is not to 'facilitate the unauthorised removal or circumvention' of a technical device. It is submitted that even if its sole intended purpose was the removal or circumvention of a technical device it could not be targeted under the Directive because, where the circumvention device is used to enable a user to benefit from an exception, in line with the analysis above, the underlying act would not be 'unauthorised'.

This interpretation is confirmed by the Copyright Directive, but only in regard to Articles 5(3) and 6. Recital 50 indicates that the legal protection for technological measures in the Copyright Directive 'should neither inhibit nor prevent the development or use of any means of circumventing a technological measure that is necessary to enable acts to be undertaken in accordance with the terms of Article 5(3) or Article 6 of Directive

---

[72] In contrast, other commentators indicate that Article 7 only condones circumvention where necessary to facilitate lawful reverse engineering. *See*, e.g., T. Vinje, Copyright Imperiled? [1999] EIPR 192–207.

[73] Sub-section (c) only addresses the 'unauthorised removal or circumvention of any technical device . . .'. As the protection is to be deemed 'without prejudice to' the exceptions in Article 5, any removal or circumvention in order to benefit from the exceptions cannot be 'unauthorised'. In other words, where necessary, there is legal authority to remove or circumvent any technical device in other to benefit from the exceptions.

[74] We use 'technical device' merely to conform to the language of the Software Directive. It is to be considered synonymous with the more recent and frequently used term, 'technological measure'.

91/250/EEC."[75] In short, as stated above, the use and development of technological means necessary to benefit from these two exceptions should be
considered permissible.

It is also important to note that any attempt to contractually override the
technological measures interface which accompanies the exceptions under
the Directive would also be caught by Article 9(1) of the Software Directive.
This is because it broadly states that 'any contractual provisions contrary' to
the Directive's exceptions are affected. As such, rights-holders seeking to
prevent users benefiting from the technological measures interface through
the use of contractual provisions would not be able to do so.

III. A Model Interface

The most crucial aspect to note about the Software Directive is that it
provides a complete copyright exceptions interface – an interface both for
contract and for technological measures.[76] The Directive importantly provides this interface for copyright exceptions which enable productive use
and thereby promote innovation-driven competition.

Similar to the DMCA interface for reverse engineering, the Software
Directive's interface offers the most direct route for the application of certain
exceptions enabling productive use. Like the DMCA provision, only a lawful user is permitted to circumvent in order to benefit from the exceptions
under the Directive.[77] In addition, it is possible to manufacture devices necessary for the circumvention because such devices are not targeted by the
Directive.[78] There is no need, as is the case under the Copyright Directive,

---

[75] Although the Copyright Directive's recital comports with the analysis advanced
herein, recitals in and of themselves do not enjoy legal effect under EC law. Accordingly,
this recital and the interpretation it advances cannot take precedence over the wording of
the Software Directive which indicates that the interface applies to all four exceptions
under the Directive.

[76] An examination whether this interface has actually been implemented in all of the
EU Member States is outside of the scope of this article. However, it has not been implemented in either Germany or the UK. See §69f of the German Copyright Act and CDPA
§296, respectively.

[77] It is important to note that the Directive limits the ability to benefit from the exceptions under the Directive to the lawful acquirer of a copy of the computer program
(Article 5(1)), to the person having a right to use a copy of a program (Articles 5(2); 5(3);
6), or to the licensee (Article 6). Thus, not any person can benefit from the exceptions and
the interface. This should minimise the concern of rights-holders that only persons having
lawful access to the program can benefit from the interface.

[78] It is notable that the DMCA reverse engineering exception §1201(f) sets out the
necessary permissible steps, thereby increasing legal certainty for both users and rights-
holders. The exception explicitly permits circumvention of a technological measure that
'effectively controls access to a particular portion' of a computer program. It also enables
the person seeking interoperability to 'develop and employ technological means to
circumvent a technological measure, or to circumvent protection afforded by a technological measure'. In contrast, similar steps have to be implied under the Software
Directive. *See* section IV(B).

to rely on 'voluntary measures' or, absent the existence of such measures, steps being undertaken by the EU Member States to allow users to benefit from certain copyright exceptions.[79]

It is submitted that making exceptions directly applicable is likely to be the most appropriate for exceptions which enable productive use. This is because rights-holders in existing works are not likely to welcome competition with their works – especially not innovation-driven competition given its effects.[80] They can hardly be expected to make it easy for users to benefit from exceptions – whether through 'voluntary measures' or other means. As such, legislative steps have to be taken to allow users to benefit from the exceptions enabling productive use.[81]

The Software Directive also goes further than the DMCA provision in two main ways. First, it also includes a contract interface and this interface addresses the same exceptions as are addressed under the technological measures interface.[82] This allows the Software Directive's productive use exceptions and the policy underlying them to be applicable whatever attempts are made to contractually override them. It also short-circuits any attempts to contractually override the technological measures interface. Secondly, although the Software Directive only addresses copyright as applied to computer software, it provides a broader interface for such works than the DMCA does. This is because it provides an interface for the idea expression dichotomy as applied to computer programs.[83]

---

[79] In addition, we submit that the Copyright Directive's approach is inadequate because it presumes that those copyright exceptions not included in the specified interface can be applied by users without more or 'the old fashioned way'. It remains to be seen whether in the environment predominated by technological measures and contractual restrictions this will be true. In this regard it is notable that only 8 of the 20 'optional' exceptions in Article 5 of the Copyright Directive are included in the Article 6(4) interface.

[80] Section II above discusses the effects of innovation-driven competition.

[81] *See* section II(C) for this argument.

[82] As indicated in section III(A), the Copyright Directive also does not specify a contract interface.

[83] Compare Article 5(3) and 6 of the Software Directive with 17 U.S.C. 1201(f). Under §1201(f) – similar to Article 6 of the Software Directive – reverse engineering is only permissible for the 'sole purpose of identifying and analyzing those elements of the [computer] program that are necessary to achieve interoperability of an independently created computer program . . .' In contrast, Article 5(3) of the Software Directive permits a user 'to observe, study or test the functioning of the [computer] program in order to determine the ideas and principles which underlie any element of the program . . .'. It is curious why the application of the idea/expression dichotomy should be treated differently under the Software and the Copyright Directives since the Copyright Directive is implementing the WCT which explicitly sets out the dichotomy in Article 2. Perhaps the underlying assumption is that the dichotomy can be applied without more or 'the old fashioned way'.

F. Conclusion

In light of recent US and EU legislative treatment of the copyright exceptions interface, this article urges re-consideration of the type of exception where such an interface is appropriate. As copyright law remains the body of law best suited to regulating productive use of materials, there is a strong case to be made why any copyright exceptions interface must include exceptions enabling productive use.

This article has bolstered the case for including exceptions enabling productive use in any copyright exceptions interface. It has offered economic analysis to show how such exceptions promote innovation-driven competition and result in important economic benefits not only for the user public but also for new creators seeking to make productive use of existing copyright material. It has identified the EC Software Directive as a model precedent which establishes a complete exceptions interface addressing both contract and technological measures. It is submitted that this Directive, with minor adjustment, could provide the basis of a broader interface applicable to all types of copyright works for those exceptions enabling productive use.

Appendix 1:

Section 1201 of the U.S. Copyright Act, introduced with the Digital Millennium Copyright Act of 1998

§ 1201. Circumvention of copyright protection systems

(a) VIOLATIONS REGARDING CIRCUMVENTION OF TECHNOLOGICAL MEASURES. – (1)(A) No person shall circumvent a technological measure that effectively controls access to a work protected under this title. The prohibition contained in the preceding sentence shall take effect at the end of the 2-year period beginning on the date of the enactment of this chapter.

(B)   The prohibition contained in subparagraph (A) shall not apply to persons who are users of a copyrighted work which is in a particular class of works, if such persons are, or are likely to be in the succeeding 3-year period, adversely affected by virtue of such prohibition in their ability to make noninfringing uses of that particular class of works under this title, as determined under subparagraph (C).

(C)   During the 2-year period described in subparagraph (A), and during each succeeding 3-year period, the Librarian of Congress, upon the recommendation of the Register of Copyrights, who shall consult with the Assistant Secretary for Communications and Information of the Department of Commerce and report and comment on his or her views in making such recommendation, shall make the determination in a rulemaking proceeding on the record for purposes of subparagraph (B) of whether persons who are users of a copyrighted work are, or are likely to be in the succeeding 3-year period, adversely affected by the prohibition under subparagraph (A) in their ability to make noninfringing uses under this title of a particular class of copyrighted works. In conducting such rule-making, the Librarian shall examine –
(i)   the availability for use of copyrighted works;
(ii) the availability for use of works for nonprofit archival, preservation, and educational purposes;
(iii) the impact that the prohibition on the circumvention of technological measures applied to copyrighted works has on criticism, comment, news reporting, teaching, scholarship, or research;

(iv) the effect of circumvention of technological measures on the market for or value of copyrighted works; and

(v) such other factors as the Librarian considers appropriate.

(D) The Librarian shall publish any class of copyrighted works for which the Librarian has determined, pursuant to the rulemaking conducted under subparagraph (C), that non-infringing uses by persons who are users of a copyrighted work are, or are likely to be, adversely affected, and the prohibition contained in subparagraph (A) shall not apply to such users with respect to such class of works for the ensuing 3-year period. (E) Neither the exception under subparagraph (B) from the applicability of the prohibition contained in subparagraph (A), nor any determination made in a rulemaking conducted under subparagraph (C), may be used as a defense in any action to enforce any provision of this title other than this paragraph.

(2) No person shall manufacture, import, offer to the public, provide, or otherwise traffic in any technology, product, service, device, component, or part thereof, that – (A) is primarily designed or produced for the purpose of circumventing a technological measure that effectively controls access to a work protected under this title; (B) has only limited commercially significant purpose or use other than to circumvent a technological measure that effectively controls access to a work protected under this title; or (C) is marketed by that person or another acting in concert with that person with that person's knowledge for use in circumventing a technological measure that effectively controls access to a work protected under this title.

(3) As used in this subsection –

(A) to circumvent a technological measure means to descramble a scrambled work, to decrypt an encrypted work, or otherwise to avoid, bypass, remove, deactivate, or impair a technological measure, without the authority of the copyright owner; and (B) a technological measure effectively controls access to a work if the measure, in the ordinary course of its operation, requires the application of information, or a process or a treatment, with the authority of the copyright owner, to gain access to the work. (b) ADDITIONAL VIOLATIONS. – (1) No person shall manufacture, import, offer to the public, provide, or otherwise traffic in any technology, product, service, device, component, or part thereof, that –

(A) is primarily designed or produced for the purpose of circumventing protection afforded by a technological measure that effectively protects a right of a copyright owner under this title in a work or a portion thereof;

(B) has only limited commercially significant purpose or use other than to circumvent protection afforded by a technological measure that effectively protects a right of a copyright owner under this title in a work or a portion thereof; or

(C) is marketed by that person or another acting in concert with that person with that person's knowledge for use in circumventing protection afforded by a technological measure that effectively protects a right of a copyright owner under this title in a work or a portion thereof.

(2) As used in this subsection –

(A) to circumvent protection afforded by a technological measure means avoiding, bypassing, removing, deactivating, or otherwise impairing a technological measure; and (B) a technological measure effectively protects a right of a copyright owner under this title if the measure, in the ordinary course of its operation, prevents, restricts, or otherwise limits the exercise of a right of a copyright owner under this title.

(c) OTHER RIGHTS, ETC., NOT AFFECTED. – (1) Nothing in this section shall affect rights, remedies, limitations, or defenses to copyright infringement, including fair use, under this title.

(2) Nothing in this section shall enlarge or diminish vicarious or contributory liability for copyright infringement in connection with any technology, product, service, device, component, or part thereof.

(3) Nothing in this section shall require that the design of, or design and selection of parts and components for, a consumer electronics, telecommunications, or computing product provide for a response to any particular technological measure, so long as such part or component, or the product in which such part or component is integrated, does not otherwise fall within the prohibitions of subsection (a)(2) or (b)(1).

(4) Nothing in this section shall enlarge or diminish any rights of free speech or the press for activities using consumer electronics, telecommunications, or computing products. (d) EXEMPTION FOR NONPROFIT LIBRARIES, ARCHIVES, AND EDUCATIONAL INSTITUTIONS. – (1) A nonprofit library, archives, or educational institution which gains

access to a commercially exploited copyrighted work solely in order to make a good faith determination of whether to acquire a copy of that work for the sole purpose of engaging in conduct permitted under this title shall not be in violation of subsection (a)(1)(A). A copy of a work to which access has been gained under this paragraph –
(A) may not be retained longer than necessary to make such good faith determination; and
(B) may not be used for any other purpose.
(2) The exemption made available under paragraph (1) shall only apply with respect to a work when an identical copy of that work is not reasonably available in another form. (3) A nonprofit library, archives, or educational institution that wilfully for the purpose of commercial advantage or financial gain violates paragraph (1) –
(A) shall, for the first offense, be subject to the civil remedies under section 1203; and (B) shall, for repeated or subsequent offenses, in addition to the civil remedies under section 1203, forfeit the exemption provided under paragraph (1).
(4) This subsection may not be used as a defense to a claim under subsection (a)(2) or (b), nor may this subsection permit a nonprofit library, archives, or educational institution to manufacture, import, offer to the public, provide, or otherwise traffic in any technology, product, service, component, or part thereof, which circumvents a technological measure. (5) In order for a library or archives to qualify for the exemption under this subsection, the collections of that library or archives shall be –
(A) open to the public; or
(B) available not only to researchers affiliated with the library or archives or with the institution of which it is a part, but also to other persons doing research in a specialized field. (e) LAW ENFORCEMENT, INTELLIGENCE, AND OTHER GOVERNMENT ACTIVITIES. – This section does not prohibit any lawfully authorized investigative, protective, information security, or intelligence activity of an officer, agent, or employee of the United States, a State, or a political subdivision of a State, or a person acting pursuant to a contract with the United States, a State, or a political subdivision of a State. For purposes of this subsection, the term information security means activities carried out in order to identify and address the vulnerabilities of a government computer, computer system, or computer network. (f) REVERSE ENGINEERING. – (1) Notwithstanding the provisions of subsection (a)(1)(A), a person who has lawfully obtained the right to use a copy of a computer program may circumvent a technological measure that effectively controls access to a particular portion of that program for the sole purpose of identifying and analyzing those elements of the program that are necessary to achieve interoperability of an independently created computer program with other programs, and that have not previously been readily available to the person engaging in the circumvention, to the extent any such acts of identification and analysis do not constitute infringement under this title.
(2) Notwithstanding the provisions of subsections (a)(2) and (b), a person may develop and employ technological means to circumvent a technological measure, or to circumvent protection afforded by a technological measure, in order to enable the identification and analysis under paragraph (1), or for the purpose of enabling interoperability of an independently created computer program with other programs, if such means are necessary to achieve such interoperability, to the extent that doing so does not constitute infringement under this title.
(3) The information acquired through the acts permitted under paragraph (1), and the means permitted under paragraph (2), may be made available to others if the person referred to in paragraph (1) or (2), as the case may be, provides such information or means solely for the purpose of enabling interoperability of an independently created computer program with other programs, and to the extent that doing so does not constitute infringement under this title or violate applicable law other than this section.
(4) For purposes of this subsection, the term 'interoperability' means the ability of computer programs to exchange information, and of such programs mutually to use the information which has been exchanged.
(g) ENCRYPTION RESEARCH. –
(1) DEFINITIONS. – For purposes of this subsection –
(A) the term encryption research means activities necessary to identify and analyze flaws and vulnerabilities of encryption technologies applied to copyrighted works, if these activities are conducted to advance the state of knowledge in the field of encryption technology or to assist in the development of encryption products; and

(B) the term encryption technology means the scram-bling and descrambling of information using mathematical formulas or algorithms.

(2) PERMISSIBLE ACTS OF ENCRYPTION RESEARCH. – Notwithstanding the provisions of subsection (a)(1)(A), it is not a violation of that subsection for a person to circumvent a technological measure as applied to a copy, phonorecord, performance, or display of a published work in the course of an act of good faith encryption research if – (A) the person lawfully obtained the encrypted copy, phonorecord, performance, or display of the published work; (B) such act is necessary to conduct such encryption research; (C) the person made a good faith effort to obtain authorization before the circumvention; and (D) such act does not constitute infringement under this title or a violation of applicable law other than this section, including section 1030 of title 18 and those provisions of title 18 amended by the Computer Fraud and Abuse Act of 1986.

(3) FACTORS IN DETERMINING EXEMPTION. – In determining whether a person qualifies for the exemption under paragraph (2), the factors to be considered shall include – (A) whether the information derived from the encryption research was disseminated, and if so, whether it was disseminated in a manner reasonably calculated to advance the state of knowledge or development of encryption technology, versus whether it was disseminated in a manner that facilitates infringement under this title or a violation of applicable law other than this section, including a violation of privacy or breach of security; (B) whether the person is engaged in a legitimate course of study, is employed, or is appropriately trained or experienced, in the field of encryption technology; and (C) whether the person provides the copyright owner of the work to which the technological measure is applied with notice of the findings and documentation of the research, and the time when such notice is provided.

(4) USE OF TECHNOLOGICAL MEANS FOR RESEARCH ACTIVITIES. – Notwithstanding the provisions of subsection (a)(2), it is not a violation of that subsection for a person to – (A) develop and employ technological means to circumvent a technological measure for the sole purpose of that person performing the acts of good faith encryption research described in paragraph (2); and (B) provide the technological means to another person with whom he or she is working collaboratively for the purpose of conducting the acts of good faith encryption research described in paragraph (2) or for the purpose of having that other person verify his or her acts of good faith encryption research described in paragraph (2).

(5) REPORT TO CONGRESS. – Not later than 1 year after the date of the enactment of this chapter, the Register of Copyrights and the Assistant Secretary of Communications and Information of the Department of Commerce shall jointly report to the Congress on the effect this subsection has had on – (A) encryption research and the development of encryption technology; (B) the adequacy and effectiveness of technological measures designed to protect copyrighted works; and (C) protection of copyright owners against the unauthorized access to their encrypted copyrighted works. The report shall include legislative recommendations, if any.

(h) EXCEPTIONS REGARDING MINORS. – In applying subsection (a) to a component or part, the court may consider the necessity for its intended and actual incorporation in a technology, product, service, or device, which – (1) does not itself violate the provisions of this title; and (2) has the sole purpose to prevent the access of minors to material on the Internet.

(i) PROTECTION OF PERSONALLY IDENTIFYING INFORMATION. – (1) CIRCUMVENTION PERMITTED. – Notwithstanding the provisions of subsection (a)(1)(A), it is not a violation of that subsection for a person to circumvent a technological measure that effectively controls access to a work protected under this title, if – (A) the technological measure, or the work it protects, contains the capability of collecting or disseminating personally identifying information reflecting the online activities of a natural person who seeks to gain access to the work protected; (B) in the normal course of its operation, the technological measure, or the work it protects, collects or disseminates personally identifying information about the person who seeks to gain access to the work protected, without providing conspicuous notice of such collection or

dissemination to such person, and without providing such person with the capability to prevent
or restrict such collection or dissemination;
(C) the act of circumvention has the sole effect of identifying and disabling the capability
described in subparagraph (A), and has no other effect on the ability of any person to gain access
to any work; and
(D) the act of circumvention is carried out solely for the purpose of preventing the collection or
dissemination of personally identifying information about a natural person who seeks to gain
access to the work protected, and is not in violation of any other law.
(2) INAPPLICABILITY TO CERTAIN TECHNOLOGICAL MEASURES. – This subsec-
tion does not apply to a technological measure, or a work it protects, that does not collect or
disseminate personally identifying information and that is disclosed to a user as not having or
using such capability.
(j) SECURITY TESTING. –
(1) DEFINITION. – For purposes of this subsection, the term security testing means accessing
a computer, computer system, or computer network, solely for the purpose of good faith
testing, investigating, or correcting, a security flaw or vulnerability, with the authorization of
the owner or operator of such computer, computer system, or computer network. (2)
PERMISSIBLE ACTS OF SECURITY TESTING. – Notwithstanding the provisions of
subsection (a)(1)(A), it is not a violation of that subsection for a person to engage in an act of
security testing, if such act does not constitute infringement under this title or a violation
of applicable law other than this section, including section 1030 of title 18 and those provisions
of title 18 amended by the Computer Fraud and Abuse Act of 1986. (3) FACTORS IN
DETERMINING EXEMPTION. – In determining whether a person qualifies for the exemption under paragraph (2), the factors to be considered shall include – (A) whether the information derived from the security testing was used solely to promote the security of the owner or
operator of such computer, computer system or computer network, or shared directly with the
developer of such computer, computer system, or computer network; and (B) whether the
information derived from the security testing was used or maintained in a manner that does not
facilitate infringement under this title or a violation of applicable law other than this section,
including a violation of privacy or breach of security. (4) USE OF TECHNOLOGICAL
MEANS FOR SECURITY TESTING. – Notwithstanding the provisions of subsection (a)(2),
it is not a violation of that subsection for a person to develop, produce, distribute or employ
technological means for the sole purpose of performing the acts of security testing described in
subsection (2), provided such technological means does not otherwise violate section (a)(2).

Appendix 2:

Directive 2001/29/EC of the European Parliament and of the Council of 22 May 2001 on
the harmonisation of certain aspects of copyright and related rights in the information society
Official Journal L 167 , 22/06/2001 P. 0010–0019
. . .

Article 5
Exceptions and limitations

1. Temporary acts of reproduction referred to in Article 2, which are transient or incidental
[and] an integral and essential part of a technological process and whose sole purpose is to enable:
(a) a transmission in a network between third parties by an intermediary, or (b) a lawful use of a
work or other subject-matter to be made, and which have no independent economic
significance, shall be exempted from the reproduction right provided for in Article 2. 2.
Member States may provide for exceptions or limitations to the reproduction right provided for
in Article 2 in the following cases: (a) in respect of reproductions on paper or any similar
medium, effected by the use of any kind of photographic technique or by some other process
having similar effects, with the exception of sheet music, provided that the rightholders receive
fair compensation; (b) in respect of reproductions on any medium made by a natural person for
private use and for ends that are neither directly nor indirectly commercial, on condition that
the rightholders receive fair compensation which takes account of the application or non-
application of technological measures referred to in Article 6 to the work or subject-matter

concerned; (c) in respect of specific acts of reproduction made by publicly accessible libraries, educational establishments or museums, or by archives, which are not for direct or indirect economic or commercial advantage; (d) in respect of ephemeral recordings of works made by broadcasting organisations by means of their own facilities and for their own broadcasts; the preservation of these recordings in official archives may, on the grounds of their exceptional documentary character, be permitted; (e) in respect of reproductions of broadcasts made by social institutions pursuing non-commercial purposes, such as hospitals or prisons, on condition that the rightholders receive fair compensation. 3. Member States may provide for exceptions or limitations to the rights provided for in Articles 2 and 3 in the following cases: (a) use for the sole purpose of illustration for teaching or scientific research, as long as the source, including the author's name, is indicated, unless this turns out to be impossible and to the extent justified by the non-commercial purpose to be achieved; (b) uses, for the benefit of people with a disability, which are directly related to the disability and of a non-commercial nature, to the extent required by the specific disability; (c) reproduction by the press, communication to the public or making available of published articles on current economic, political or religious topics or of broadcast works or other subject-matter of the same character, in cases where such use is not expressly reserved, and as long as the source, including the author's name, is indicated, or use of works or other subject-matter in connection with the reporting of current events, to the extent justified by the informatory purpose and as long as the source, including the author's name, is indicated, unless this turns out to be impossible; (d) quotations for purposes such as criticism or review, provided that they relate to a work or other subject-matter which has already been lawfully made available to the public, that, unless this turns out to be impossible, the source, including the author's name, is indicated, and that their use is in accordance with fair practice, and to the extent required by the specific purpose; (e) use for the purposes of public security or to ensure the proper performance or reporting of administrative, parliamentary or judicial proceedings; (f) use of political speeches as well as extracts of public lectures or similar works or subject-matter to the extent justified by the informatory purpose and provided that the source, including the author's name, is indicated, except where this turns out to be impossible; (g) use during religious celebrations or official celebrations organised by a public authority; (h) use of works, such as works of architecture or sculpture, made to be located permanently in public places; (i) incidental inclusion of a work or other subject-matter in other material; (j) use for the purpose of advertising the public exhibition or sale of artistic works, to the extent necessary to promote the event, excluding any other commercial use; (k) use for the purpose of caricature, parody or pastiche; (l) use in connection with the demonstration or repair of equipment; (m) use of an artistic work in the form of a building or a drawing or plan of a building for the purposes of reconstructing the building; (n) use by communication or making available, for the purpose of research or private study, to individual members of the public by dedicated terminals on the premises of establishments referred to in paragraph 2(c) of works and other subject-matter not subject to purchase or licensing terms which are contained in their collections; (o) use in certain other cases of minor importance where exceptions or limitations already exist under national law, provided that they only concern analogue uses and do not affect the free circulation of goods and services within the Community, without prejudice to the other exceptions and limitations contained in this Article. 4. Where the Member States may provide for an exception or limitation to the right of reproduction pursuant to paragraphs 2 and 3, they may provide similarly for an exception or limitation to the right of distribution as referred to in Article 4 to the extent justified by the purpose of the authorised act of reproduction. 5. The exceptions and limitations provided for in paragraphs 1, 2, 3 and 4 shall only be applied in certain special cases which do not conflict with a normal exploitation of the work or other subject-matter and do not unreasonably prejudice the legitimate interests of the rightholder.

CHAPTER III PROTECTION OF TECHNOLOGICAL MEASURES AND RIGHTS-MANAGEMENT INFORMATION

Article 6
Obligations as to technological measures

1. Member States shall provide adequate legal protection against the circumvention of any effective technological measures, which the person concerned carries out in the knowledge, or with

reasonable grounds to know, that he or she is pursuing that objective. 2. Member States shall provide adequate legal protection against the manufacture, import, distribution, sale, rental, advertisement for sale or rental, or possession for commercial purposes of devices, products or components or the provision of services which: (a) are promoted, advertised or marketed for the purpose of circumvention of, or (b) have only a limited commercially significant purpose or use other than to circumvent, or (c) are primarily designed, produced, adapted or performed for the purpose of enabling or facilitating the circumvention of, any effective technological measures. 3. For the purposes of this Directive, the expression "technological measures" means any technology, device or component that, in the normal course of its operation, is designed to prevent or restrict acts, in respect of works or other subject-matter, which are not authorised by the rightholder of any copyright or any right related to copyright as provided for by law or the sui generis right provided for in Chapter III of Directive 96/9/EC. Technological measures shall be deemed "effective" where the use of a protected work or other subject-matter is controlled by the rightholders through application of an access control or protection process, such as encryption, scrambling or other transformation of the work or other subject-matter or a copy control mechanism, which achieves the protection objective. 4. Notwithstanding the legal protection provided for in paragraph 1, in the absence of voluntary measures taken by rightholders, including agreements between rightholders and other parties concerned, Member States shall take appropriate measures to ensure that rightholders make available to the beneficiary of an exception or limitation provided for in national law in accordance with Article 5(2)(a), (2)(c), (2)(d), (2)(e), (3)(a), (3)(b) or (3)(e) the means of benefiting from that exception or limitation, to the extent necessary to benefit from that exception or limitation and where that beneficiary has legal access to the protected work or subject-matter concerned. A Member State may also take such measures in respect of a beneficiary of an exception or limitation provided for in accordance with Article 5(2)(b), unless reproduction for private use has already been made possible by rightholders to the extent necessary to benefit from the exception or limitation concerned and in accordance with the provisions of Article 5(2)(b) and (5), without preventing rightholders from adopting adequate measures regarding the number of reproductions in accordance with these provisions. The technological measures applied voluntarily by rightholders, including those applied in implementation of voluntary agreements, and technological measures applied in implementation of the measures taken by Member States, shall enjoy the legal protection provided for in paragraph 1. The provisions of the first and second subparagraphs shall not apply to works or other subject-matter made available to the public on agreed contractual terms in such a way that members of the public may access them from a place and at a time individually chosen by them. When this Article is applied in the context of Directives 92/100/EEC and 96/9/EC, this paragraph shall apply mutatis mutandis. . . .

Appendix 3

Council Directive 91/250/EEC of 14 May 1991 on the legal protection of computer programs *Official Journal L 122 , 17/05/1991 P. 0042 – 0046*

. . . Article 5 Exceptions to the restricted acts

1. In the absence of specific contractual provisions, the acts referred to in Article 4 (a) and (b) shall not require authorization by the rightholder where they are necessary for the use of the computer program by the lawful acquirer in accordance with its intended purpose, including for error correction. 2. The making of a back-up copy by a person having a right to use the computer program may not be prevented by contract insofar as it is necessary for that use. 3. The person having a right to use a copy of a computer program shall be entitled, without the authorization of the rightholder, to observe, study or test the functioning of the program in order to determine the ideas and principles which underlie any element of the program if he does so while performing any of the acts of loading, displaying, running, transmitting or storing the program which he is entitled to do.

Article 6 Decompilation

1. The authorization of the rightholder shall not be required where reproduction of the code and translation of its form within the meaning of Article 4 (a) and (b) are indispensable to obtain the information necessary to achieve the interoperability of an independently created computer

program with other programs, provided that the following conditions are met: (a) these acts are performed by the licensee or by another person having a right to use a copy of a program, or on their behalf by a person authorized to do so; (b) the information necessary to achieve interoperability has not previously been readily available to the persons referred to in subparagraph (a); and (c) these acts are confined to the parts of the original program which are necessary to achieve interoperability. 2. The provisions of paragraph 1 shall not permit the information obtained through its application: (a) to be used for goals other than to achieve the interoperability of the independently created computer program; (b) to be given to others, except when necessary for the interoperability of the independently created computer program; or (c) to be used for the development, production or marketing of a computer program substantially similar in its expression, or for any other act which infringes copyright. 3. In accordance with the provisions of the Berne Convention for the protection of Literary and Artistic Works, the provisions of this Article may not be interpreted in such a way as to allow its application to be used in a manner which unreasonably prejudices the right holder's legitimate interests or conflicts with a normal exploitation of the computer program.

Article 7 Special measures of protection

1. Without prejudice to the provisions of Articles 4, 5 and 6, Member States shall provide, in accordance with their national legislation, appropriate remedies against a person committing any of the acts listed in subparagraphs (a), (b) and (c) below: (a) any act of putting into circulation a copy of a computer program knowing, or having reason to believe, that it is an infringing copy; (b) the possession, for commercial purposes, of a copy of a computer program knowing, or having reason to believe, that it is an infringing copy; (c) any act of putting into circulation, or the possession for commercial purposes of, any means the sole intended purpose of which is to facilitate the unauthorized removal or circumvention of any technical device which may have been applied to protect a computer program. 2. Any infringing copy of a computer program shall be liable to seizure in accordance with the legislation of the Member State concerned. 3. Member States may provide for the seizure of any means referred to in paragraph 1 (c).

11
Essential Facilities and Appropriate Remuneration of Achievements

ANSELM KAMPERMAN SANDERS

A. Commodification of Information and the Depletion of the Commons

The "commons" are under threat, or at least that is what many commentators would like us to believe.[1] It is said that the traditional balance underpinning the Intellectual Property Law system is disturbed by encroachments on the public domain and traditional liberties are reduced to window-dressing to obscure the unbridled expansion of property rights benefiting only big industry. This is a nice mantra, but some critical observations are in order. Whereas the level of IP protection has undoubtedly increased on a worldwide level, so has piracy. So where exactly does this purported disturbance of the IP balance[2] take place? Intellectual property monopolies are limited in time and upon expiry of the copyright and patent term discrete items of private property are returned to the commons. Most intellectual property rights are never relied upon, let alone enforced. Limitations and exceptions enable citizens, researchers and even competitors to access and use information, industrial products and processes. Furthermore the

---

[1] N. Elkin-Koren/N. Weinstock Netanel (eds.), *The Commodification of Information* (2002, The Hague, Kluwer Law International). Sherman B., "Digital Property and Digital Commons", in C. Heath/A. Kamperman Sanders (eds.), *Intellectual Property in the Digital Age* (2001, The Hague, Kluwer Law International) at 95; Y. Benkler, *Free As the Air To Common Use: First Amendment Constraints on Enclosure of the Public Domain*, 74 N.Y.U. L. Rev. 354 (1999); See also http://www.law.duke.edu/pd/papers.html, which provides access to the papers of the Duke Law School conference on the public domain, and most notably P. Samuelson, "Digital Information, Digital Networks, and The Public Domain", who provides a map of the public domain.

[2] E. Kaufer, *The Economics of the Patent System* (1989, Chur, Harwood Academic Publishers GmbH); W. Landes/R. Posner, "An Economic Analysis of Copyright Law", 18 *Journal of Economic Studies* 325 (1989) 347; F. Warren-Boulton/K. Baseman/ G. Woroch, "The Economics of Intellectual Property Protection for Software: The Proper Role for Copyright", Paper prepared for the American Council on Interoperable Systems, June 1994, Washington D.C.; W. Cornish/J. Phillips, "The Economic Function of Trademarks: An Analysis With Special Reference to Developing Countries", (1982) 13 *IIC* 41; N. Economides, "The Economics of Trademarks", 78 *TMR* 523 (1988); W. Landes/R. Posner, "Trademark Law: and Economic Perspective", *IPLR* 229 (1989).

extended reach of intellectual property rights merely serves as a guarantee for return on the investments necessary to produce new technology, drugs and information products. This stimulus to innovation and creation will at a later stage enlarge the commons. Genome,[3] aerospace, seabed, and nanotechnology research are at the forefront of industrial activity and require vast investments and collective efforts to advance knowledge in these areas. Intellectual property rights therefore not only serve as guarantees for return on investment, but they also act as a conduit for collaborative research, development and marketing efforts by providing the framework for licensing agreements.[4] Even the open source software movement is IPR intensive in that it relies on intellectual property rights to enforce licences that maintain a common status of certain software kernels and interfaces.[5] Robust rights over innovation and creativity in software therefore enable creation of semi-commons, where there was exclusive property.

More worrying is the accumulation and stacking of various intellectual property rights, the introduction of technical protection mechanisms, database protection, as well as contractual and tortious principles[6] which enable rightholders to layer their intangible industrial and creative assets with digital barbwire and ancient restrictions previously used to prevent access to land. Competition law is mooted as a counterbalance to the unbridled exercise of intellectual property rights. Yet, the interface between intellectual property law and competition law is under-explored and underdeveloped. Left as a stopgap solution to prevent abuse of a dominant position, competition law is a last resort. Courts are furthermore struggling to come up with an acceptable balance between the existence and exercise of intellectual property rights. This contribution offers an overview of the expansion and bolstering of intellectual property rights and provides an analysis of a number of cases dealing with the interface between intellectual property rights and competition law.

---

[3]   See the EC Workshop Report on Managing IPR in a Knowledge-based Economy – Bioinformatics and the Influence of Public Policy (2001, EC Commission DG Research, EUR 20066).

[4]   See in this respect Workshop Reports on IPR (Intellectual Property Rights) Aspects of Internet Collaborations (2001, EC Commission DG Research, EUR 19456) and on the Role and Strategic Use of Intellectual Property Rights in International Research Collaborations (2002, EC Commission DG Research, EUR 20230).

[5]   See http://www.opensource.org/ for licensing examples and statements of principle.

[6]   See *Thrifty-Tel v. Bezenek* 54 Cal Rptr 2d 468 (1996); *eBay v. Bidder's Edge* 100 F Supp 2d 1058 (N D California, 24 May 2000). See T. Hardy, "The Ancient Doctrine of Trespass to Web Sites", 1996 *J. Online L.* 7.; and also J. Adams, [2002] *Intellectual Property Quarterly* 1, who argues that the correct form of action should have been trespass on the case.

B. The EC Database Directive

The EC Database Directive[7] is still pretty much work in progress. The EU Commission enlisted the Amsterdam-based legal firm of Nauta Dutilh to conduct an independent evaluation of the directive by the end of 2002,[8] but still has to present its own report to the European Parliament. Protection under the Database Directive comprises copyright protection of databases which ". . . by reason of the selection or arrangement of their contents, constitute the author's own intellectual creation . . ."[9] This produces an equivalent effect to the decision of US Supreme Court in *Feist v. Rural Telephone Services*[10] in most European jurisdictions subject to the Directive. A clear line is drawn for protection under copyright between original and non-original works.[11]

In order to fill the resulting gap comprising of works that are non-original, but require investment to accumulate and verify, the Directive requires member states to introduce a new *sui generis* protection. Article 7 defines the object of protection as follows:

"1. Member States shall provide for a right for the maker of a database which shows that there has been qualitatively and/or quantitatively a substantial investment in either the obtaining, verification or presentation of the contents to prevent extraction and/or re-utilization of the whole or of a substantial part, evaluated qualitatively and/or quantitatively, of the contents of that database.

2. For the purposes of this Chapter:(a) 'extraction' shall mean the permanent or temporary transfer of all or a substantial part of the contents of a database to another medium by any means or in any form;(b) 're-utilization' shall mean any form of making available to the public all or a substantial part of the contents of a database by the distribution of copies, by renting, by on-line or other forms of transmission. The first sale of a copy of a database within the Community by the rightholder or with his consent shall exhaust the right to control resale of that copy within the Community; Public lending is not an act of extraction or re-utilization."

For both databases that do not pass the threshold for copyright protection, and for databases that do, *sui generis* protection is available. This right is much stronger than copyright, as it is primarily designed to provide the producer of a database with control over the access and use of a database. Copyright is

---

[7] Directive 96/9/EC of the European Parliament and of the Council of 11 March 1996 on the Legal Protection of Databases, 1996 O.J. L77/20.

[8] *The Implementation and Application of Directive 96/9/EC on the Legal Protection of Databases* Study – Contract ETD/2001/B5-3001/E/72, available by request on the DG Internal Market website at http://www.europa.eu.int.

[9] Article 3.1.

[10] *Feist Publications Inc. v. Rural Telephone Service Company Inc,* 111 S Ct. 1282; 113 L Ed 2d 358; 20 IPR 129 (US Supreme Court, 1991).

[11] See in this respect also the *Van Dale v. Romme*, Dutch Supreme Court, 4 January 1991, NJ 1991, 608, in which protection was denied to a list of words in a dictionary.

infringed by reproduction of a material part of a work, which is judged quantitatively and qualitatively, so that the occasional entry into a database and the extraction of a small part of it, may well not infringe copyright in that database. Infringement of the *sui generis* right is defined as "extraction and/or re-utilization of the whole or of a substantial part, evaluated qualitatively and/or quantitatively, of the contents of that database". At first sight, this might not appear much stronger than copyright, but, Article 3.5 provides:

> "The repeated and systematic extraction and/or re-utilisation of insubstantial parts of the contents of the database implying acts which conflict with normal exploitation of that database or which unreasonably prejudice the legitimate interests of the maker of the database shall not be permitted."

Although the initial term of database right is only 15 years from the first of January following completion of the database, substantial changes, evaluated quantitatively and qualitatively to the database including changes resulting from successive additions, deletions or alterations, which would result in the database being considered as having undergone substantial new investment, evaluated quantitatively and qualitatively, result in a renewal of the term of protection. The effect of this is that up-to-date and time-sensitive databases will enjoy perpetual database right.

In terms of the efficacy of the Directive in terms of its objective to stimulate database industries in the EU, the picture is not at all clear. Upon introduction of the Directive there was a sharp increase in the number of companies entering the database market in France, Germany and the UK.[12] Whereas this provides credence to the idea that IP protection fosters investment, this increase has since petered out. Protection under the Directive has primarily been sought by companies generating so-called "synthetic data", which is not collected, but made-up. Unlike genuine information, for example, in the area of genomics or nuclear physics, synthetic data is not available through independent research. Telephone directories, horse-racing[13] and other sporting events information, broadcast schedules, cannot

---

[12] S. Maurer/P. Hugenholtz/H. Onsrud, "Europe's Database Experiment", *Science* vol. 294, 26 October 2001, 789, available at http://www.ivir.nl/publications/hugenholtz/maurer.pdf (as visited 19-07-2004).

[13] In *British Horseracing v. William Hill Ltd.* [2001] All ER (D) 111, the Horseracing Board, the governing body for horse racing in Great Britain maintained a computerised database containing information relating to horse races to be run in the country. The Board licenses the use of such information for use in Licensed Betting Offices run by firms of bookmakers. William Hill is one of the leading off-track bookmaking firms in the United Kingdom. It had started to provide betting services over the Internet. The Horseracing Board sued on the basis that such use was on unlicensed use of its data and an infringement of its database rights. The judge concluded that for a "database right to exist, there must be investment in its creation and, in particular, that investment must be directed at obtaining, verifying or presenting the contents". He concluded: "William Hill's actions of taking information from [an intermediary] and loading it onto its own computers for the purpose of making it available on its website is an unlicensed act of

be duplicated through independent invention or creation. It is in this area where anti-trust considerations over abuse of dominant positions in primary markets to control downstream markets are most prevalent. The Dutch courts have been most active in addressing this concern and designed a way around this problem by refusing to extend protection to databases based on investments that the producer has made as a result of other, non-database-related, activities.[14]

Scientific or genuine information databases suffer the problem that resources are hard to acquire and may sometimes be funded once only. The mixing of public and private funds and resources may furthermore add insult to injury when it comes to monopolistic concerns when private parties claim their rights.[15] Yet, concerns apart, the impact of the database directive appears minimal in this area based on the number of cases brought, although possible negative effects on licensing practice and emerging monopolies over standards may not yet be visible.

---

extracting a substantial part of the [Board's] Database and the subsequent transmission of that data onto its website for access by members of the public is a re-utilization. The defendant infringes [the Board's] rights in both ways." On appeal, the Court of Appeal indicated that it was inclined to follow the judge's views but that some questions should be referred to the European Court of Justice for a preliminary opinion (see the opinions of AG Stix-Hackl of 8 June 2004 in ECJ Case C–203/02 and the Fixtures marketing cases C–444/02, C–46/02 and C–338/02).

[14] See *KPN Telecom B.V. v. Xbase Software Ontwikkeling B.V.*, Pres. Distr. Ct. The Hague, 14 January 2000, KG 99/1429, (2000) *Mediaforum* 64, AMI 2000, 71 which involved a software program running on the world wide web that allowed users to extract information from the KPN database containing telephone numbers, bypassing the advertising banners. This was held to be a clear infringement of the Database right; conversely see *Vermande B.V. v. Bojkovski*, Pres. Distr. Ct. The Hague, 20 March 1998, [1998] IER 111; *Denda v. KPN,* Court of Appeal Arnhem 15 April 1997 and 5 August 1997, (1997) Mediaforum B72, AMI 1997, 214. In the telco cases the point was also advanced that the investments made were not primarily geared towards the creation of databases of phone numbers. The argument that spin-off databases should not be protected for lack of substantial investment was not accepted. See, however, *NOS v. De Telegraaf,* Court of Appeals of The Hague 30 January 2001, (2001) Mediaforum 90; and Dutch Supreme Court, 6 June 2003, AMI 2003, 141. And *De Telegraaf/NOS and HMG,* Netherlands Competition Authority/NMa 10 September 1998, AMI 1999, 12; NMa 16 February 2000, *Mediaforum* 2000, nr. 22; Pres. District Ct. Rotterdam, 22 June 2000, LJN-no. AA6280; NMa 3 October 2001; District Ct. Rotterdam, 11 December 2002, LJN-no. AF1811; College van Beroep voor het Bedrijfsleven (the highest court in competition matters in the Netherlands), 9 April 2003, LJN-nummer AF7441 (De *Telegraaf/NOS HMG*) and 15 July 2004, LJN-no. AQ1727 (NOS/De Telegraaf), all involving a refusal to license broadcasting information, which was ultimately held not to amount to an abuse of a valid intellectual property right. See also P. Hugenholtz, "The New Database Right: Early Case Law from Europe", (2001) available at http://www.ivir.nl/publications/hugenholtz/fordham2001.pdf (as visited 11-04-2002), listing cases involving web pages and classified ads in a newspaper.

[15] See the EC Commission Working Paper, *Managing IPR in a Knowledge-Based Economy – Bioinformatics and the Influence of Public Policy* (2001, Brussels, EUR 20066).

C. Torts of Lore

In the US case of *eBay v. Bidder's Edge,*[16] Bidder's Edge, an auction aggre-
gation site, utilised software robots to access eBay 100,000 times per day,
burdening their system capacity. eBay moved for preliminary injunctive
relief to prevent Bidder's Edge from accessing eBay based on nine causes of
action, including copyright infringement. The court, however, moved in a
totally different direction when it found for eBay based on a trespass to
chattels claim. The preliminary injunction issued prevented Bidder's Edge
from accessing eBay altogether without written authorisation. In effect this
type of protection is even stronger than the *sui generis* right under the EC
Directive, since trespass is committed merely by access, and, subject to
proof of special damage, does not require any extraction at all. It is therefore clear to see that this type of action has a clear impact on the commons
in the sense that it is not even possible to find out what commons and what
exclusive property is. Simple access to the information is prevented from
the outset.

D. Contract Law

Another possibility lies in the application of contract law. The use of
information products may be limited or by express contractual agreement
setting the terms for delivery of the information service, but also through use
of *shrink-wrap* licences connected to the information product.[17] In the US
case of *ProCD v. Zeidenberg*[18] defendants Matthew Zeidenberg and Silken
Mountain Web Services, Inc., purchased copies of plaintiff's Select Phone
TM CD-ROM software program, downloaded telephone listings stored on
the CD-ROM discs to Zeidenberg's computer. Zeidenberg made these
listings available to Internet users by placing the data onto an Internet host
computer. In support of their copyright infringement claims, breach of the
express terms of the parties' software licensing agreement was part of the
claim. Zeidenberg argued that the data they downloaded from plaintiff's
program were not protected by copyright, and that they were not bound by
the software licensing agreement. The Court accepted that, in principle,

---

[16] See the EC Commission Working Paper, *Managing IPR in a Knowledge-Based
Economy – Bioinformatics and the Influence of Public Policy* (2001, Brussels, EUR 20066).

[17] See P. Samuelson/K. Opsahl, "The Tensions between Intellectual Property &
Contracts in the Information Age: An American Perspective" in: F. Grosheide/K. Boele-
Woelki, *Molengrafica 1998* (1998, Lelystad, Vermande) at 163–93 on Article 2B proposal
of the Uniform Commercial Code.

[18] *ProCD, Inc. v. Matthew Zeidenberg, and Silken Mountain Web Services* 86 F 3d 1447
(7th Cir. 1996).

end-user licences are enforceable when the user breaks the plastic film wrapped around a software package, but held that Zeidenberg had not been offered reasonable opportunity to take cognisance of the licence terms, because they were inside the box. The Zeidenberg judgment prompted the American Law Institute, drafters of proposed new US Uniform Commercial Code (UCC), to suggest a provision following the ProCD judgment, that would make standard form licences enforceable if:

"prior to or within a reasonable time after beginning to use the intangible pursuant to an agreement, the party
  1. signs or otherwise by its behavior manifests assent to a standard form license; and
  2. had an opportunity to review the terms of the license before manifesting assent, whether or not it actually reviewed the terms".

The UCC revision has sparked controversy over the question whether contract law can and should override copyright law.[19] The controversy continues, but the principle that contract law can enhance the rights of authors as well as producers of databases remains an important principle that has been carried forward to the US Uniform Computer Information Transactions Act (UCITA).[20]

E. Technical Protection Mechanisms

The WIPO copyright treaties[21] have introduced obligations concerning technological measures that are embedded in information products to prevent piracy. Although important for the safe marketing of digital products prone to easy copying and dissemination, this digital barbwire may operate irrespective of the idea/expression dichotomy and irrespective of limitations and exceptions provided by law. This has been recognised by the European Commission, which in its implementation Directive 2001/29/EC of the European Parliament and of the Council of 22 May 2001 on the harmonisation of certain aspects of copyright and related rights in the information society[22] obliges its member states to ensure that access to materials, where

---

[19] See M. Lemley, "Beyond Preemption: The Law and Policy of Intellectual Property Licensing", 87 *Calif. LR* (1999) 111; and D. McGowan, "Free Contracting, Fair Competition, and Article 2B: Some Reflections on Federal Competition Policy, Information Transactions, and "Aggressive Neutrality", 13 *Berkeley Techn. L.J.* (1998) 1173.

[20] Uniform Computer Information Transactions Act, http://www.law.upenn.edu:80/library/ulc/ucita/cita10st.htm.

[21] Article 11 WCT.

[22] Official Journal L 167/10.

and when appropriate, is provided.[23] How this is to be effectuated is not at all clear. Although Member States are free in their implementation of this obligation, the present author thinks that it would be appropriate for national libraries to act as depositories for works that are free from technological constraints. National libraries would then be in a position to provide and preserve access to the materials for present and future generations. The irony of this situation for counties that have consistently resisted to follow the US

---

[23] Article 6 EC Directive 2001/29/EC Obligations as to technological measures 1. Member States shall provide adequate legal protection against the circumvention of any effective technological measures, which the person concerned carries out in the knowledge, or with reasonable grounds to know, that he or she is pursuing that objective. 2. Member States shall provide adequate legal protection against the manufacture, import, distribution, sale, rental, advertisement for sale or rental, or possession for commercial purposes of devices, products or components or the provision of services which: (a) are promoted, advertised or marketed for the purpose of circumvention of, or (b) have only a limited commercially significant purpose or use other than to circumvent, or (c) are primarily designed, produced, adapted or performed for the purpose of enabling or facilitating the circumvention of, any effective technological measures. 3. For the purposes of this Directive, the expression "technological measures" means any technology, device or component that, in the normal course of its operation, is designed to prevent or restrict acts, in respect of works or other subject-matter, which are not authorised by the rightholder of any copyright or any right related to copyright as provided for by law or the sui generis right provided for in Chapter III of Directive 96/9/EC. Technological measures shall be deemed "effective" where the use of a protected work or other subject-matter is controlled by the rightholders through application of an access control or protection process, such as encryption, scrambling or other transformation of the work or other subject-matter or a copy control mechanism, which achieves the protection objective. 4. Notwithstanding the legal protection provided for in paragraph 1, in the absence of voluntary measures taken by rightholders, including agreements between rightholders and other parties concerned, Member States shall take appropriate measures to ensure that rightholders make available to the beneficiary of an exception or limitation provided for in national law in accordance with Article 5(2)(a), (2)(c), (2)(d), (2)(e), (3)(a), (3)(b) or (3)(e) the means of benefiting from that exception or limitation, to the extent necessary to benefit from that exception or limitation and where that beneficiary has legal access to the protected work or subject-matter concerned. A Member State may also take such measures in respect of a beneficiary of an exception or limitation provided for in accordance with Article 5(2)(b), unless reproduction for private use has already been made possible by rightholders to the extent necessary to benefit from the exception or limitation concerned and in accordance with the provisions of Article 5(2)(b) and (5), without preventing rightholders from adopting adequate measures regarding the number of reproductions in accordance with these provisions. The technological measures applied voluntarily by rightholders, including those applied in implementation of voluntary agreements, and technological measures applied in implementation of the measures taken by Member States, shall enjoy the legal protection provided for in paragraph 1. The provisions of the first and second subparagraphs shall not apply to works or other subject-matter made available to the public on agreed contractual terms in such a way that members of the public may access them from a place and at a time individually chosen by them. When this Article is applied in the context of Directives 92/100/EEC and 96/9/EC, this paragraph shall apply mutatis mutandis.

in its assertion that the US registration requirements for copyright works does not violate the Berne Convention is not lost on the author.

F. Is the Law is Stacked Against Commons?

The picture that emerges is one of relaxation over the status of the commons when IPR enhancements are viewed individually. Practice, however, is that various IPRs are converging into layers of rights attaching to various aspects of intellectual and industrial creativity. Portfolio management of these rights is aimed at obtaining the most advantageous bargaining position for cross-licensing purposes and market share. Digital barbwire, contractual gloss and access rights cement these layers to formidable dams that stop any leakage of IPR to commons. User rights should provide some relief to the individual citizen or researcher, but for the larger economic interest of consumer and competitor alike, the immune exercise of intellectual property rights should sometimes be questioned in order to prevent monopolies to run unchecked.

G. The IPR Anti-trust Dichotomy

Whereas monopoly pricing is left to anti-trust authorities, reliance on intellectual property rights to safeguard assets and associated pricing is generally left unaffected.[24] Intellectual property policy and anti-trust policy are still perceived as separate domains. Where enhancements to the IPR system are argued based on investment and return analysis and market failure assessment, it is submitted that because of the roots in competition law, database protection, contractual enhancements and other additional layers to intellectual property rights should follow the contours of market reality. This means that they be, contrary to intellectual property rights proper, subject to a higher level of scrutiny when it comes to anti-trust policy. In their work *Information Rules*,[25] Carl Shapiro and Hal Varian succinctly describe the characteristics of the network economy, pointing to the fact that there are many more factors, such as network effects, tying, bundling, lock-in and switching costs, versioning,[26] and encryption technologies[27] that may also

---

[24] The rightholder is therefore permitted to maximise income. Only on cases of price discrimination between classes of purchasers are authorities prepared to act. For an overview of the plethora of means a marketer has at his disposal and the way in which US courts have reacted: see M. Katz/C. Shapiro, *Antitrust in Software Markets*, Paper presented at the Progress and Freedom Foundation conference, *Competition, Convergence and the Microsoft Monopoly*, 5 February 1998.

[25] H. Varian/C. Shapiro, *Information Rules – A Strategic Guide to the Network Economy* (1999, Boston, Harvard Business School Press).

[26] H. Varian, "Versioning Information Goods" 1997, http://www.sims.berkeley. edu/~hal/people/hal/papers.html (visited 25-05-2004).

[27] These techniques may be applied to the underlying software, but also to the data itself.

serve as barriers to access to and free flow of information goods. Some argue[28] that in the new economic reality old economic axioms do not apply, as new information products possess different characteristics, which means regulators should stay well away from this emerging market. Others[29] argue that normal scenarios still apply. The Microsoft browser and media player cases in the US[30] and Europe,[31] however, shows that the latter position is still prevalent.[32] Whereas there may be a certain reluctance to impose a duty on intellectual property rightholders to provide essential facilities,[33] the creation of a horizontal right to information may be construed under the essential facilities doctrine when there is only reliable source available. Still, practical limitations on the exercise of intellectual property rights on account of competition concerns are often illusionary, as lengthy legal procedures are necessary to prove abusive exercise of intellectual property rights.

H. Abuse of a Dominant Position

Just as there are compelling arguments for the protection of a trader's market through property- or liability-rule systems, there is also a compelling argument for the curbing of abuse of monopoly power resulting from either system. Whereas any monopoly leads to a situation in which market entry for new entrants is restricted, the abuse of monopoly power does so without heeding the justifiable reasons for restricting market entry for new incumbents, which can be found in the incentive- and reward-based paradigms. Instead the undertaking uses its monopoly right to seek excessive rents in an abusive manner through its position of dominance. Article 86 of the Treaty of Rome has the effect that in those circumstances in which an undertaking

---

[28] See the contributions of G. Reback/K. Kelly to *Wired*, August 1997; see also K. Kelly, *New Rules for the New Economy* (1998, New York, Viking Press).

[29] Note above.

[30] *United States of America v. Microsoft Corporation*, US District Court for the District of Columbia, 12 November 2002; *Sun Microsystems v. Microsoft Corporation* US District Court for the District of Maryland, 26 June 2003; and http://www.microsoft.com/presspass/legal/settlement.asp for further documentation. Furthermore a decision of the US District Court in the Northern District of Illinois, Eastern Division of 11 August 2003 in *Eolas v. Microsoft Corporation* ironically saw Microsoft held liable for patent infringement of webbrowser technology that forms the basis of Microsoft Internet Explorer.

[31] Decision of the EG Commission of 24 March 2004, Case COMP/37.792 – MICROSOFT/ W2000, (C(2004)900 final) calling for the making available by Microsoft of server software interface codes, as well as imposing a fine of 497,196,304. Microsoft has appealed.

[32] R. Posner, "Antitrust in the New Economy", *Tech Law Journal* 14 September 2000.

[33] M. Katz/C. Shapiro, *Antitrust in Software Markets*, Paper presented at the Progress and Freedom Foundation conference, *Competition, Convergence and the Microsoft Monopoly*, 5 February 1998, at 39 when discussing interfaces in software markets.

abuses its dominant position in the market, that undertaking may be forced not to exercise its monopoly power.[34] In *United Brands Co. and United Brands Continental BV v. EC Commission*[35] a dominant position was described as: "a position of economic strength enjoyed by an undertaking which enables it to prevent effective competition being maintained on the relevant market by giving it the power to behave to an appreciable extent independently of its competitors, customers and ultimately of its consumers". It is appropriate to point out at this point that intellectual property rights may contribute to a large extent to the dominant market position an undertaking can achieve and lead to a situation where: an undertaking's market share, either in itself or when combined with its know-how, access to raw materials, capital or other major advantage such as trademark ownership, enables it to determine the prices or to control the production or distribution of a significant part of the relevant goods. It is not necessary for the undertaking to have total dominance such as would deprive all other market participants of their commercial freedom, as long as it is strong enough in general terms to devise its own strategy as it wishes, even if there are differences in the extent to which it dominates individual sub-markets.

It is equally appropriate to point out that the mere existence and exercise of an intellectual property right as such does not constitute an abuse, since it is a legally recognised exclusive right to reproduction that is a restriction on competition which is devised to create a market for an intangible in the first place. This point can be found in many abuse cases.[36] It is therefore important to distinguish between the existence of intellectual property rights conferred by national legislation of a Member State, which is not affected by the Treaty of Rome, the exercise of the "specific subject matter", which is a justifiable restriction on the freedom of trade but may come within the prohibitions of the Treaty,[37] and the use of market power, which may also come within the prohibitions of the Treaty.[38] Over a number of years the European Court of Justice (ECJ) developed the doctrine of the "immune exercise", meaning that an exercise of a right corresponding with the core of

---

[34] For a description see *V*. Korah, *An Introductory Guide to EC Competition Law and Practice* (5th ed. 1994, London, Sweet & Maxwell).

[35] (Case 27/76) [1973] ECR 215.

[36] *Etablissements Consten SA & Grundig-Verkaufs-GmbH v. EC Commission* (Case 56/64) [1966] ECR 299, [1966] CMLR 418; *Deutsche Grammophon Gesellschaft GmbH v. Metro-SB-Großmärkte GmbH & Co. KG* (Case 78/70) [1971] ECR 487, [1971] 1 CMLR 631.

[37] Ibid. See also Article 30–36 of the Treaty of Rome. For a description see N. Green, "Intellectual Property and the Abuse of a Dominant Position under European Union Law: Existence, Exercise and the Evaporation of Rights", [1993] *Brooklyn Journal of International Law* 141; G. Tritton, *Intellectual Property in Europe* (1996, London, Sweet & Maxwell), ch. 7.

[38] *Radio Telefis Eireann and Independent Television Publications v. EC Commission* (Cases C241 and 242/91) [1995] ECR I–743.

an intellectual property right cannot in itself constitute an abuse.[39] "Specific circumstances" are needed in order to make the exercise abusive. These additional "specific circumstances" may be abuses of market power that are clearly separate from the existence/exercise of an intellectual property right,[40] or certain exercises of rights related to intellectual property rights, such as licensing and demanding royalties, which fall within the subject matter of the right. With this latter category the boundaries of what is part of the existence, the exercise, and the specific subject matter is not evident.[41] It is not at all clear to what extent such exercises are subject to Art. 82 of the Treaty. As a consequence the question whether a refusal to license on the basis of an intellectual property right constitutes an abuse is not self-evident, for it presupposes that the aims of Community competition law are included in the essential function of an intellectual property right. The position of the ECJ on this matter has been described by a leading academic as having evolved from a hostile attitude towards IPRs, as evidenced in the *Magill* case, towards recognition of the importance of IPR as a means to stimulate investment in innovation.[42] The reasons for the early hostility are said to have been brought about by the influence of the ordo-liberal thinking of the school of economics in Freiburg. As backlash to the Nazi ideas, the pursuit of liberty was to be effectuated by the dispersion of political and economic power. Patent monopolies were not only seen as an economic power that ought not be exercised, they were also evaluated *ex post* in terms of their efficacy to ensure incentives to invest, leading to a situation where: "By the time an intellectual right holder exercises its rights, the investment that led to the right is water under the bridge".[43] Limitations to intellectual property rights were thus not perceived as reductions to the incentive to make the investment leading up to the existence of these rights.

---

[39] *Parke Davis & Co. v. Probel* (Case 24/67) [1968] ECR 55, [1968] CMLR 54.; *Hoffman-La Roche & Co. AG v. Centrafarm Vertriebsgesellschaft Pharmazeutischer Erzeugnisse GmbH* (Case 102/77) [1978] ECR 1139, [1978] CMLR 217; *Consorzio Italiano della Componentistica di Ricambio per Autoveilici (CIRCA) and Maxicar v. Régie Nationale des Usines Renault* (Case 53/87) [1988] ECR 6039, [1990] 4 CMLR 265; *Volvo AB v. Erik Veng (UK) Ltd* (Case 237/87) [1988] ECR 6211, [1989] 4 CMLR 122.

[40] One can think of practices such as tying, discriminatory policies, refusal to supply customers who might resell, refusals to honour guarantees, and operating secretly and unilaterally a policy of differential discounts. This was the case in *Hilti AG v. EC Commission* (Case C–53/92P) [1992] 4 CMLR 16, an appeal from Commission Decision 22 December 1987, *Eurofix-Bauco v. Hilti AG* (Cases 30/787 and 31/488) [1989] 4 CMLR 677, where eight distinct abuses were put forward, all of which were exercises of market power, not of patent rights, although one of the abuses consisted of the frustration or delay of legitimately available licences under Hilti's patent, by demanding exorbitantly high royalties.

[41] As was pointed out by C. Miller, "Magill: Time to Abandon the 'Specific Subject-matter' Concept", [1994] *EIPR* 415.

[42] V. Korah, "The Interface between Intellectual Property and Antitrust: The European Experience", [2001] *Antitrust Law Journal* 801–39.

[43] Ibid. at 803.

I. Refusal to License or Supply

In *Commercial Solvents*,[44] the case revolved around a refusal by Commercial Solvents to supply Zoja with the raw materials to make ethambutol, a drug used for the treatment of tuberculosis. Commercial Solvents was the only commercial player in this market possessing the knowledge to make the raw material and had been supplying Zoja in the past. When Commercial Solvents obtained half an interest in Istituto Chemioterapico, the only other producer of ethambutol, it changed its policy on supplying Zoja. The ECJ held that this refusal amounted to an abuse of a dominant position, and that its condemnation of the refusal was prompted by a desire to protect a small firm rather than free competition for the benefit of consumers.

In *Volvo AB v. Erik Veng (UK) Ltd*,[45] rights within the specific subject matter of design rights[46] were exercised in "special circumstances".[47] Because he was refused a licence, the defendant imported spare parts (front wings) for the Volvo 200 series from Italy and Taiwan via Denmark into the United Kingdom, where these parts were protected under the Registered Designs Act 1949. In considering the exercise by Volvo of its intellectual property right, the ECJ stated that to oblige "the holder of a protected design to grant third parties a licence to supply products incorporating the design, even in return for reasonable fees, would result in depriving the holder of the substance of its exclusive right", but that nevertheless Volvo's refusal amounted to an abuse of its dominant position. This was because Volvo itself was no longer producing the parts in question and thus created market conditions that obliged the consumer to buy a new car, where the old model was still in circulation. Whereas in *Volvo* the "specific circumstances" elevate the exercise of a design right to an abusive exercise,[48] the distinction between

---

[44] *Istituto Chemioterapico Italiano SpA v. Commission*, Cases 6 & 7/73, [1974] ECR 223, [1974] 1 CMLR 309, CMR 8209.

[45] *Volvo AB v. Erik Veng (UK) Ltd* (Case 237/87) [1988] ECR 6211, [1989] 4 CMLR 122.

[46] For the definition of specific subject mater of patents as the reward for inventive effort, see *Centrafarm BV and De Peijper v. Sterling Drug Inc.* (Case 15/74) [1974] ECR 1147, [1974] 2 CMLR 480; For trade marks see *Hoffman-La Roche & Co. AG v. Centrafarm Vertriebsgesellschaft Pharmazeutischer Erzeugnisse GmbH*, note 35 above, defining as the essential function of a trade mark the guarantee of the origin of the product. See *Ciné Vog Films v. CODITEL (Compagnie Générale pour la Diffusion de la Télévision)* (Case 62/79) [1980] ECR 881, [1981] 2 CMLR 362, where the right to demand a royalty for the public performance of a work was held to be an essential function of copyright, a position rejected by the AG in Magill. The difference between "specific subject-matter" and the "essential function" of intellectual property rights is not always clear, nor is the relevance for making it. See in this respect on Gulmann AG's Opinion in *Magill*, S. Haines, "Copyright Takes the Dominant Position" [1994] 9 *EIPR* 401, 402.

[47] See the definition in *Hoffman-La Roche & Co. AG v. Centrafarm Vertriebsgesellschaft Pharmazeutischer Erzeugnisse GmbH* (Case 102/77) [1978] ECR 1139, [1978] CMLR 217.

[48] See in this respect also *IBM/370 Settlement*, Commission 14th Report on Competition Policy (1984), paras. 94–95.

existence and exercise is not so clear in the *Magill* case.[49] The case concerned the exercise of copyright in broadcast listings in the United Kingdom and Ireland, which the television broadcasters RTE, BBC and ITV provided on a daily basis free to newspapers. Weekly listings were provided by each broadcaster in separate television guides. When an Irish publisher, Magill, launched its comprehensive weekly guide, it was faced with an injunction by the Irish courts on the basis of the broadcasters' respective copyrights. When the ECJ finally upheld the decisions of the Commission and the Court of First Instance, both holding that the broadcasters had indeed abused their dominant position in holding that the reliance on copyright amounted to the monopolisation of a derivative market, much thought was given by commentators to the question whether the ECJ's judgment presented an overly broad incursion into the "immune exercise" of the broadcaster's copyright.[50] It is important to note at this point that the protection of moral rights and the ensuring of a reward for creative effort were judged to be within the "essential function" of copyright, but that the approach taken in *Coditel*,[51] where the right to demand a royalty for the public performance of a copyright work was held to be an "essential function", was not adopted.[52] This factor notwithstanding, *Magill* prompts the question of what the "special circumstances" were that made the otherwise legitimate exercise by the broadcasters of their copyright in their refusal to grant a licence an exercise of a dominant position that is abusive. Commentators have looked at *Magill* on the basis of parallels with *Volvo*,[53] stating the refusal to license in that case amounted to an obstruction of the reproduction of products; *Magill* involved the monopolisation of a derivative market. By the exercise of its copyright, Magill would not only retain its primary product; it would also prevent the production of comprehensive television guides based on raw data, and thus impair the genesis of a new market.[54] This is why *Magill* is not so much a

---

[49] *Radio Telefís Eireann and Independent Television Publications v. EC Commission* (Cases C241 and 242/91) [1995] ECR I–743.

[50] See C. Miller, note above; M. van Kerckhove, "Magill: A Refusal to License or a Refusal to Supply?", [1995] 51 June/July *Copyright World* 26; H. Calvet/T. Desurmont, "The Magill Ruling (1): An Isolated Decision?", 167 [1996] *RIDA* 2.

[51] *Ciné Vog Films v. CODITEL (Compagnie Générale pour la Diffusion de la Télévision)* note above; and *CODITEL (Compagnie Générale pour la Diffusion de la Télévision) v. Ciné Vog Films (No 2)* (Case 262/81) [1982] ECR 3381, [1983] 1 CMLR 49.

[52] See on this point note above, 418, where Miller attributes much of the controversy surrounding the Magill case to the incorrect application, as he sees it, of this distinction by the ECJ. It can be suggested that the ECJ's assessment of the abusive adverse effects on competition, which according to the Court lay in the monopolisation of a market in weekly television guides by exercise of copyright in raw data, was in fact a covert attempt by the ECJ to interfere with the immune exercise of UK copyright, which happens to grant protection, where other Member States do not. See also the Broadcasting Act 1990, s. 176.

[53] Note above; S. Haines, note above.

[54] Treaty of Rome Article 86(b) defines it as dealing with abuse consisting in "limiting production, markets or technical development to the prejudice of consumers".

refusal to license case, as a refusal to supply case,[55] comparable to *Commercial Solvents Corp. and Istituto Chemioterapico Italiano SpA v. EC Commission.*[56] This distinction is important to the Court's finding of "exceptional circumstances",[57] which rendered the broadcasters' behaviour abusive. The fact that raw data are susceptible to copyright in the United Kingdom, if incorporated in an original literary work,[58] stems from a nationally recognised right, the exercise of which is within the essential function of copyright. This could not be seen to be the basis for the ECJ's decision. The Court is indeed silent on the matter, but one cannot help thinking that at the back of the Court's mind were the provisions on decompilation in the Council Directive on the Legal Protection of Computer Programs,[59] and the compulsory licensing provisions that were part of the Database Directive as proposed at the time.[60] Exercise of a dominant position supported by intellectual property rights, resulting in the creation of extremely high barriers to entry for new market entrants, can thus be mediated by Art. 86 of the Treaty of Rome. It is, however, important to realise that the modifying effects of the essential facilities doctrine can only be relied upon if a refusal to license or supply results in an exclusion of competition in a secondary market.

In *Oscar Bronner v. Mediaprint*[61] the ECJ accepted that a supply service consisting of a home-delivery scheme for daily newspaper media constitutes a separate market. The Advocate General's opinion insisted that supply of facilities be essential to enter downstream markets, but spelled out that compulsory licences to provide access to assets should be rare,[62] particularly in

---

[55] M. van Kerckhove, note above.

[56] (Cases 6 7/72) [1974] ECR 224, [1974] 1 CMLR 309, a case in which the applicants produced the raw materials nitropropane and aminobutanol, needed for the production of ethambutanol, which was subsequently used in the production of a tuberculosis drug. The applicant refused to sell aminobutanol to a competitor because they wanted to enter the derivatives market themselves. This refusal to sell essential raw materials to a competitor was held to be an abuse of a dominant position.

[57] It is interesting to note that the ECJ speaks of "exceptional circumstances" and not of "special circumstances". This displays the extraordinary position Magill takes in the Art. 86 case law and supports the position taken by H. Calvet/T. Desurmont, note above.

[58] N. Mallet-Poujol, "The Information Market: Copyright Unjustly Tormented . . .", [1996] 167 RIDA 92, 138: "[T]he Magill case reveals plainly the impasses to which an incorrect application of copyright leads, through a lax assessment of the originality of programme listings and doubtless a poor understanding of the implementation of the reproduction right".

[59] Council Dir. 91/250/EEC of 14 May 1991, [1991] OJ L122/42.

[60] See T. Cook, "The Final Version of the EC Database Directive – A Model for the Rest of the World?" [1996] 61 Copyright World 24, 27, on the removal of the provisions relating to compulsory licensing of commercially exploited databases that form the sole source of data from the final Dir. in the light of the Magill decision.

[61] Oscar Bronner GmbH Co, KG v. Mediaprint Zeitungs/und Zeitschriftenverlag GmbH Co. KG Case C–7/97 [1998] ECR I–7817, [1999] 4 CMLR 112, [1999] CEC 53.

[62] See in this respect the EC Commission's rejection in Info-Lab v. Ricoh of compulsory licences sought for the use of design rights in ink-cartridges on the ground that it

view of the maintenance of incentives for investment.[63] He furthermore enunciated that the objective of competition law is to protect consumers, rather than particular competitors, limiting the rationale for compulsory licensing. The Advocate General's opinion seems to have been persuasive. On the question of whether a refusal by Mediaprint, owner of the only nationwide Austrian home-delivery scheme, to allow rival publisher Oscar Bronner access to the service against payment of reasonable remuneration constitutes an abuse of a dominant position, the Court answered negatively. The Court construed *Magill* narrowly and said it was an exceptional case,[64] holding that even if it applied to other property rights than intellectual property rights, to find an abuse Oscar Bronner would have to establish:

(1) that the refusal would be likely to eliminate all competition in the daily newspaper market;

(2) that the refusal could not be objectively justified; and

(3) that the service be indispensable to carrying on Oscar Bronner's business, in that there was no potential substitute.

Mediaprint's refusal was held not to eliminate all competition in the daily newspaper market, and would also not create technical, legal or economic obstacles, making it impossible to establish a competing home-delivery scheme. Access to the home-delivery scheme was, in this sense, not an essential facility.[65]

The EC Commission brought essential facilities to the fore once more in the case of *IMS Health,*[66] when it required that a licence be given on a method of structuring a database that a German court had held to be the subject of copyright protection. The structure consisted of the compilation of information on sales and prescriptions of pharmaceutical products according to a "brick" structure, whereby the German territory was divided into 1860 zones, the scope of each determined by the weighing of utilitarian and data protection considerations. This means that a minimum of three pharmacies need to be included in each zone to prevent tracing of individual data,

---

could not be proven that the rightholder has a dominant position in a downstream market, Competition Report 1999, 169, Bulletin EU 1-2-1999 Competition (7/55).

[63] Note 61, para. 64.

[64] Note 61 paras. 39–41.

[65] See ECJ CFI Case T–504/93, [1997] ECR II 923, [1997] 5 CMLR 309 (Tiercé Ladbroke *v.* EC Commission), which did not consider television broadcasts, for which the French association of horse racing did not want to supply a licence, to be essential facilities gambling services. In view of the emerging US practice of patenting business methods, however, it is easily conceivable that even delivery schemes may become essential facilities. See Amazon.com *v.* Barnesandnoble.com 73 F. Supp.2d 1228, 53 USPQ2d 1115 (W.D. Wash. 1 December 1999) and State Street Bank and Trust Co. *v.* Signature Financial Group, Inc. 927 F.Supp.502, 38 USPQ2d 1530 (D. Mass. 1996).

[66] NDC Health / IMS Health: Interim Measures, Case COMP D/338.044 (3 July 2001), [2002] 4 CMLR 111.

whereas a maximum of four or five are required to keep the database structure stable and useful. IMS received help and information from pharmaceutical companies in establishing the brick structure, but subsequently invested in the system by fine-tuning the zones and adding new ones after German reunification. Until 1999 IMS was the sole provider of regional data. In 1999 competitor Pharma Intranet Information (PII) entered the market with a similar database. Initially PII used its own zone-description, resulting in different data output from IMS's system. PII soon found out that its information system was not picked up by the market, because of the territorial divisions already in use by pharmaceutical companies. In other words, the customers were not able or willing to make the switching costs. Faced with market realities PII started using the IMS brick system in 2000 and were promptly enjoined by the Landesgericht Frankfurt am Main because of copyright infringement. This decision also applied to NDC when it acquired PII and found that the Oberlandesgericht Frankfurt am Main confirmed the decision of the lower court on 12 July 2001 on the basis that the 1860-brickstructure could indeed be considered a copyright work.

A week earlier, however, the EC Commission, had required IMS to grant a licence in the geographical arrangement that was the basis of the brick system.[67] It did so by arguing that IMS's refusal to license amounts to an abuse of a dominant position, since the use of the brick system is essential as it has become an industry standard without substitute. What is remarkable is that the brick structure is licensed to be used in competing products to that of the licensor. The 1860 structure in itself is not a product that can be marketed separately. The Commission's interim measure controversially[68] extended Magill to encompass directly competing as opposed to separate downstream markets.[69] The

---

[67] Decision 2002/165/EC of 3 July 2001, Case COMP D/338.044 (NDC Health/IMS Health: Interim Measures).

[68] A. Narciso, "IMS Health or the Question Whether Intellectual Property Still Deserves a Specific Approach in a Free Market Economy", [2003] 4 Intellectual Property Quarterly 455; B. LeBrun, "Towards a Test for Mandatory Licensing?", [2004] 2 EIPR 84; D. Aitman and A. Jones, "Competition Law and Copyright: Has the Copyright Owner Lost the Ability to Control his Copyright?", [2004] 3 EIPR 137.

[69] In this respect it is interesting to note that an Austrian Supreme Court decision to grant a compulsory licence on a database containing "synthetic" public sector information follows the Commission's reasoning that a producer of a database abuses his dominant position if he refuses to licence single source information that constitutes an essential facility for the prospective licensee's business. Austrian Supreme Court decision of 9 April 2002, Geschäftszahl 4Ob17/02g ADV-Firmenbuch I, concluding: "[Es muss] als Missbrauch einer marktbeherrschenden Stellung (§ 35 Abs 1 KartG) angesehen werden, wenn dem Hersteller einer Datenbank, der diese nur unter der Bedingung wirtschaftlich sinnvoll betreiben kann, dass ihm zur Aktualisierung notwendige Veränderungsdaten zur Verfügung gestellt werden, vom monopolistischen Hersteller jener Datenbank, aus der allein die Veränderungsdaten bezogen werden können, ein Zugriff auf die Veränderungsdaten grundlos verweigert oder von der Zahlung eines unangemessenen Entgelts abhängig gemacht würde."

Commission did not specify the criteria for settling the licence fees, but ordered the parties to agree upon the terms of a licence fee within two weeks.

Upon appeal to the Court of First Instance of the European Court of Justice (CFI), IMS argued that the refusal to license did not amount to the abuse of a dominant position, that the central findings of fact contradicted those of the German courts, that the measures were not conservatory, and that its right to a fair hearing had been infringed. The Commission's interim measure was suspended,[70] resulting in a revocation of the interim order by the Commission.[71] This revocation was also prompted by the fact that the Landgericht Frankfurt am Main had put the following three prejudicial questions to the ECJ:

"(1) Is Article 82 EC to be interpreted as meaning that there is abusive conduct by an undertaking with a dominant position on the market where it refuses to grant a licence agreement for the use of a data bank protected by copyright to an undertaking which seeks access to the same geographical and actual market if the participants on the other side of the market, that is to say potential clients, reject any product which does not make use of the data bank protected by copyright because their set-up relies on products manufactured on the basis of that data bank?

(2) Is the extent to which an undertaking with a dominant position on the market has involved persons from the other side of the market in the development of the data bank protected by copyright relevant to the question of abusive conduct by that undertaking?

(3) Is the material outlay (in particular with regard to costs) in which clients who have hitherto been supplied with the product of the undertaking having a dominant market position would be involved if they were in future to go over to purchasing the product of a competing undertaking which does not make use of the data bank protected by copyright relevant to the question of abusive conduct by an undertaking with a dominant position on the market?"

In its decision of 29 April 2004,[72] the ECJ considers, with reference to *Bronner*,[73] that the refusal to license an industry standard in the absence of a reasonable alternative may constitute an abuse of a dominant position. In answering the question whether there is abusive behaviour, a national judge will have to take into account the fact that the pharmaceutical industry itself participated in setting and improving the standard it has become dependent on. This may result in significant switching costs that will make it difficult for a new market entrant to offer a viable alternative.

Whether a refusal to license an intellectual property right constitutes an abuse of a dominant position should, according to the ECJ, be answered

---

[70] IMS Health Inc. *v.* Commission, Order of the President of the CFI, Cases T–180/01 R, 10 August 2001, [2002] 4 CMLR 46 and Case T–184/01 RII, 26 October 2001, [2002] 4 CMLR 58.

[71] Decision 2003/742/EC of 13 August 2003, Case COMP D3/38.044 (NDC Health/IMS Health: Interim measures) OJ 2003 L 268.

[72] Case C–418/01 IMS Health/NDC Health.

[73] Note above.

according to the three cumulative criteria of its *Magill* decision, namely that refusal: 1) prevented the emergence of a new product for which there was a potential consumer demand; 2) was not justified by objective considerations; and 3) was likely to exclude all competition in the secondary market.

Although *Magill* still spoke of two separate markets, the ECJ now considers that it is not necessary to identify two distinct markets. It is enough that there is a potential, or even hypothetical market, where it is possible to discern two distinct, but interrelated stages of production.[74] As noted before, it is hard to see a separate market for the copyright work consisting of 1860-zones that has a separate economic significance without the database of which it is the defining structure. By introducing the notion of stages of production it is, however, still possible to speak of a primary market for the building block and a secondary market for the finished commercial product. The end result is that IMS has to compete on the market where it is economically active, that of the finished product.

The ECJ has therefore provided guidance on the interpretation of the first requirement set out in *Magill*. It makes clear that a:

"refusal by an undertaking in a dominant position to allow access to a product protected by copyright, where that product is indispensable for operating on a secondary market, may be regarded as abusive only where the undertaking which requested the licence does not intend to limit itself essentially to duplicating the goods or services already offered on the secondary market by the owner of the copyright, but intends to produce new goods or services not offered by the owner of the right and for which there is a potential consumer demand."[75]

The ECJ thus recognises that the primary function of the limiting effects of competition law on intellectual property rights lies in guaranteeing that innovative products are available to the consumer. What exactly constitutes a new product will no doubt be the topic of future litigation.[76] The present author submits that consumer perception, as well as a global appreciation of what is innovative, even if the product in question is composed of standardised elements, should play an important role in determining whether someone seeking a licence is not merely duplicating a service or product already provided.

So what should happen in terms of royalty calculation and mitigation of monopoly loss in case of a compulsory licence? Although cross licensing is

---

[74] Note above, paras 44–45.

[75] Note above, para 49.

[76] See note above, and Austrian Supreme Court, 28 May 2002, Geschäftszahl 4Ob30/02g ADV-Firmenbuch II, where it held that the innovative nature of defendant's product meant that plaintiff's action for database infringement could not be successful, and that a licence should not be refused. Conversely, see note above on College van Beroep voor het Bedrijfsleven of 15 July 2004, LJN-no. AQ1727 (NOS/De Telegraaf), where the lack of innovation in the supply of TV listings in newspaper supplement was used to reject a claim for a compulsory licence of such information.

customary practice when it concerns patents for dependent innovation,[77] it is not so common in copyright. A compulsory licence entitles the rightholder of the main patent to a cross-licence in the derivative creation. The reason for doing so is to make sure that the first rightholder is not left with an invention that has been rendered commercially redundant by the subsequent innovation.[78] In the area of copyright this is not always self-evident. A cross-licence is, for example, not necessary in case of derivative works, such as translations. There is scope for others to innovate without copying. This is different in those cases where copyright encompasses functional or technical elements. When copyright protection of computer programs is concerned, the EC Computer Programs Directive recognises the need for decompilation, which may result in a form of statutory licensing for which the consent of the rightholder is not required.[79] The idea behind decompilation is that compatible and derivative products that interoperate with the original computer program can be created unhindered. The proviso is, however, that the rightholder has not made interface code available and that the information obtained by decompilation is not used to develop a computer program that is substantially similar in expression to the original. As such Article 6 of the Computer Programs Directive aims to balance the interests of rightholders with that of competitors and the interest of society.

In cases such as *IMS Health* a strong case for cross licensing can also be made, as opposed to a payment of a licence fee only, to mitigate the fact that the licensor will have to tolerate competition in the (secondary) market for the finished product or service. If there is a close proximity between the original product or service and the innovation, the stronger the argument for duopolistic competition is likely to be. In this way the licensee is able to enter the market, and the licensor has access to the commercial advantage that the innovation brings.

---

[77] Council Regulation No. 17/62 of 6 February 1962 – First Regulation implementing Articles 85 and 86 of the Treaty; Commission Regulation (EEC) No. 418/85 of 19 December 1984 on the application of Article 85(3) of the Treaty to categories of research and development agreements; Commission Regulation (EEC) No. 4087/88 of 30 November 1988 on the application of Article 85(3) of the Treaty to categories of franchise agreements; Commission Regulation (EC) No. 240/96 of 31 January 1996 on the application of Article 85(3) of the Treaty on certain categories of technology transfer agreements.

[78] This may be exemplified by the situation in which a new invention which eliminates the adverse effects of a patented drug depends on obtaining a licence from the original patent holder. The original patent holder should be granted access to the innovation to in order to retain the market value in the patented drug. The resulting duopoly benefits both patent owners, but also society by introducing innovation and competition in the market.

[79] Council Directive of 14 May 1991 on the Legal Protection of Computer Programs, OJ L 122, p. 42, Art. 6.

J. In Conclusion

Cross-licensing practices have not yet developed in the copyright and database domain to the same extent as in the patent area.[80] The *Magill* and *IMS* decisions reinforce the argument for the application of framework antitrust law. In the past the EC Commission has contributed to the development of licensing practice in the patent area by the creation of block exemption regulations pertaining to certain types of potentially restrictive licensing agreements. The making available of essential facilities and an underlying licensing practice demonstrate that the scope and nature of intellectual property rights and their exercise are not necessarily unconditional. Consumer interest may prompt the courts to curtail the abusive exercise of intellectual property rights that frustrate the marketing of innovative products or services. Duopolistic competition through cross-licensing may lead to a balance of interest between licensors and licensees, especially where a compulsory licence leads to competition in the secondary market. Similarly, a balance of interests should be made visible in database and other intellectual property legislation, so that it is clear what the public domain is comprised of. This means that there is a further need for clarification of the interrelation between intellectual property and competition law.

---

[80] K. Dam, "Intellectual Property and the Academic Enterprise", John M. Olin Law & Economics Working Paper No. 68 (2d Series) (1998, The Law School, The University of Chicago).

12

Terminator Genes as "Technical" Protection Measures for Patents?*

Stephen Hubicki and Brad Sherman

A. Introduction

The last few decades have seen a number of changes in the way plant genetic resources are regulated and controlled. Many changes, such as the extension of plant breeders' rights to new varieties and patent protection for botanical innovation, have been incremental. Others, such as those initiated by the *Convention on Biological Diversity* and the *International Treaty on Plant Genetic Resources*, have the potential to be more broad-ranging. There have also been slow and, for the most part, unsuccessful attempts to protect the use made of indigenous biological knowledge. In this paper, we wish to explore yet another potential change in the way biological resources are regulated and used. *Genetic use restriction technologies*, or *GURTs*, is the name that has been given to a range of biotechnologies that have a variety of forms and functions. In general terms, these biotechnologies enable seed producers and plant breeders to control the expression of a gene associated with a particular trait, such as drought tolerance, for instance, or to control the expression of a gene or genes that have a vital role in plant reproduction. The former method of control has been termed "trait-specific" genetic use restriction technology, or T-GURTs, whilst the latter form of control has been dubbed "variety-level" genetic use restriction technology, or V-GURTs, because the technology affects the expression of all traits in the genetically modified plant. As the names imply, the aim of these technologies is to restrict the use of germplasm, or genes associated with value-added traits that have been integrated into the genome of a chosen plant. While the research to date has focused on broad-acre crops, there are plans to extend the application of GURTs to include aquaculture, trees, and livestock.

Although more than 50 patents have been granted worldwide covering various genetic use restriction technologies,[1] in this paper we wish to focus on one particular form of the technology that was jointly developed by scientists at the United States Department of Agriculture and the Delta (USDA) and Pine Land Company. This technology, officially known as the

* Thanks to Jay Sanderson.

[1] C. N. Pendleton, "The Peculiar Case of 'Terminator' Technology: Agricultural Biotechnology and Intellectual Property Protection at the Crossroads of the Third Green Revolution", (2004) *23 Biotechnology Law Report*, 1 at 6.

"Technology Protection System", is a type of V-GURT that has become the archetype of all genetic use restriction technologies, primarily as a result of the controversy which ensued upon the grant of a United States patent for the technology in 1998.[2] The technology soon became known in the international media under the moniker "Terminator Technology" because the technology entails a method of genetically modifying plants so that they produce sterile seed in the second generation.[3] Farmers who purchase seed from suppliers who utilise this technology will initially be able to generate a viable crop, but will not be able to use seed produced from that crop to generate further crops. Instead, he or she will have to return to the supplier each year to purchase new seed. Thus, genetic use restriction technologies are at once the ultimate embodiment of the Baconian fantasy of mind over matter and the fulfilment of intellectual property owners' long held desire to exert complete control over reproduction.

One of the defining characteristics of biological materials such as plants is that they carry with them the innate ability to replicate and reproduce themselves. In the same way that the dynamic nature of biological inventions creates problems for the application of traditional rules of patent infringement, in particular the notion of strict liability,[4] biological subject matter also engenders different problems for the patent owner in relation to detecting or ascertaining when and where an infringement has occurred. This problem is by no means novel or peculiar to biological inventions: detection of infringement of patents for chemical processes and new use patents, for example, is a long-standing problem. What sets those types of inventions and biological inventions apart, however, is that whilst the problems associated with ascertaining whether chemical inventions had been infringed were assuaged by legal means, for instance by reversing the onus of proof for patent infringement, the development of genetic use restriction technologies portends a biological solution to this problem. Before we explore the potential impact that this technology might have on the creation, circulation and use of plant genetic resources, it may be helpful to provide a brief overview of United States Department of Agriculture and the Delta and Pine Land Company's patent for the Technology Protection System. After looking at the context in which the technology developed, we will then look in more detail at the key features of the invention. We will then examine some of the claims made for and against genetic use restriction technologies, focusing on the specific issue of the relationship between this new technology and intellectual property law.

---

[2] M. J. Oliver, et al., "Control of Plant Gene Expression", United States Patent No. 5,723,765, 3 March 1998.

[3] The term "terminator technology" was first coined by Hope Shand of the Canadian NGO, Rural Advancement Foundation International (now known as the Action Group on Erosion, Technology and Concentration, or ETC).

[4] B. Sherman, "Biological Inventions and the Problem of Passive Infringement", (2002) *13 Australian Intellectual Property Journal*, 146.

B. Developing the Technology Protection System

The Technology Protection System arose out of informal discussions that took place in 1993 between Delta and Pine Land Company, the largest supplier of cotton seed in the United States, and scientists at the United States Department of Agriculture (USDA). According to Mel Oliver, the principal inventor of the Technology Protection System, the USDA approached Delta and Pine to see whether they were interested in developing hybrid cotton. Delta and Pine told the USDA that it was not interested in the proposal because, in their opinion, cotton hybrids do not provide enough of a yield advantage to make them commercially viable.[5] Despite this, Delta and Pine expressed an interest in investigating the possibility of developing a genetically-modified plant that would produce sterile seed.[6] By mid-1995, the two groups had successfully transformed tobacco plants to produce sterile seed, and on 7 June 1995 the USDA and Delta and Pine applied for a United States patent entitled "Control of Plant Gene Expression". The patent was granted on 3 March 1998.[7]

According to Oliver, the motivation for developing the technology was "[t]o come up with a system that allowed you to self-police your technology, other than trying to put on laws and legal barriers to farmers saving seed, and to try and stop foreign interests from stealing the technology".[8] The patent also foreshadowed that the invention might be useful for preventing gene flow from genetically modified crops.[9] But, if the official title given to the technology is any indication, the development of a technique that would prevent farmers from using saved seed from patented plants was foremost in the inventors' minds.[10] The practice of using saved seed to regenerate crops

---

[5] Interview with Dr. Mel Oliver, Agjournal.com (http://www.agjournal.com/agprofile.cfm?person_id= 27).

[6] Interview with Dr. Mel Oliver, Agjournal.com (http://www.agjournal.com/agprofile.cfm?person_id= 27).

[7] M. J. Oliver, et al., (above note 2). The patent contains a number of broad claims, including (in general terms): a method for making a genetically modified plant, a method for producing seed that is incapable of germination, and a method of producing non-viable seed. The patent also claims a number of products obtained by the use of these methods, including (again, in general terms): a transgenic plant stably transformed with three specific DNA sequences; plant seed that has been stably transformed with exogenous DNA; plant tissue that has been stably transformed with three specific exogenous DNA sequences; and a plant cell that has been stably transformed with exogenous DNA.

[8] L. Broydo, "A Seedy Business", *Mother Jones*, 7 April 1998 (http://www.motherjones.com). See also R. Edwards, "End of the Germ Line", *New Scientist* 2127 (1998): 22: "Our system is a way of self-policing the unauthorised use of American technology . . . It's similar to copyright protection".

[9] M. J. Oliver, et al., (above note 2), 5.

[10] We use the term "plants" broadly to include plants containing patented genetic material.

is almost universally condemned by agricultural biotechnology companies as an act of piracy which undermines investment in crop research.

Before the development of genetic use restriction technologies, the primary mode of regulating the use of saved seed was through the inclusion of restrictive covenants in patent licence "agreements", often attached to the bag in which the seed is sold. For example, a notification is printed on the bags of Monsanto's "Roundup Ready" soybean seeds that the seeds may be protected under one or more United States patents. It then provides:

> "The purchase of these seeds conveys no licence under said patents to use these seeds or perform any of the methods covered by these patents. A licence must first be obtained before these seeds can be used in any way. See your seed dealer to sign a Monsanto Technology/Stewardship Agreement. Progeny of these seeds cannot be saved and used for planting or transferred to others for planting".[11]

Monsanto advocates the use of these restrictions as part of a program of "seed stewardship".[12] A farmer is a "good steward" if he or she signs the Technology/Stewardship Agreement, complies with all agronomic and marketing guidelines, and agrees to plant purchased seed only for a single commercial crop.[13] A "good steward" also notifies Monsanto of individuals who do not comply with these standards. According to Monsanto, good stewardship "insures investment in research and development so that new technologies can be brought to market that provide growers and consumers benefits".[14]

Despite the inclusion of terms in patent licences that restrict the use of saved seed, there remains the problem, by no means peculiar to biological inventions, of identifying "bad stewards" who fail to comply with these terms and prosecuting them. Additionally, if the person alleged to have

---

[11] Monsanto's "Technology/Stewardship Agreement", which must be signed by a prospective purchaser before the seed can be purchased, contains a number of other restrictions on the use of saved seed. For example, Monsanto's 2004 United States Technology/Stewardship Agreement provides the purchaser with a limited licence to purchase and plant seed containing Monsanto technologies. In particular, this seed may only be used for planting a single commercial crop. In addition, the purchaser covenants not to: supply any of this seed to any other person or entity; save any crop produced from this seed for planting or supply seed to anyone for planting; use or allow others to use seed for crop breeding, research, generation of herbicide registration data, or seed production (unless the grower has entered into a valid, written production agreement with a licensed seed company). The full text of this agreement can be found at: http://www.monsanto.com/monsanto/us_ag/content/stewardship/tug/tug 2004.pdf.

[12] "Most growers understand property protection and know how to be good stewards of the land. In the same manner, Monsanto patents seed traits to protect the value of its property. When growers purchase patented seed, they agree to respect the property rights held by the seed and trait providers": Monsanto, (2003) "Seed Piracy Update" (http://www.monsanto.com/monsanto/us_ag/content/stewardship/training/course/SeedPiracyUpdate.pdf).

[13] Monsanto, (2004) "2004 Technology Use Guide" (http://www.monsanto.com/monsanto/us_ag/ content/stewardship/tug/tug2004.pdf).

[14] Monsanto, (2004) "2004 Technology Use Guide", 23.

infringed the patent acquired the seed from someone other than an author-ised licensee (i.e. "brown-bagging") and, as is likely, that person was unaware of these restrictions, then the patentee will be unable to sustain a claim for patent infringement against that person. This uncertainty, so the argument goes, made companies cautious of investing in research to develop improved non-hybrid, self-pollinating varieties, even with the promise of patent protection.[15] In part, the Technology Protection System was devel-oped as a solution to this problem.[16]

A key aim of the Technology Protection System was to develop a mechanism to protect genetic resources and innovations without having to conform to the existing intellectual property frameworks. That is, the USDA and Delta and Pine wanted to develop a technical means that would allow them to prevent the unauthorised propagation of cotton plants, without having to go to the cost and expense of obtaining intellectual property pro-tection.[17] To prevent reproduction, the inventors proposed to genetically modify plants so that they could be rendered sterile. However, given that the valuable oils and fibres of cotton plants do not develop until the plant reaches maturity, the inventors also needed to ensure that modified cotton plants were able to reach maturity: otherwise the plants would have been of no value to farmers. As such, they needed to develop a mechanism that could render seeds sterile, but did not inhibit the "normal" growth cycle of the transformed plant. At the same time, the inventors also needed to ensure that they were able to propagate successive generations of plants in order to gen-erate seed to supply to farmers. The Technology Protection System is an attempt to respond to these apparently conflicting demands.

According to Oliver, the solution to these conflicting problems came to him in a proverbial flash of genius "at an odd hour of the night".[18] In general terms, that solution entailed genetically modifying a chosen plant by inte-grating three recombinant genes into the genome of the plant.[19] One of

---

[15] Curiously, this marks one of the first occasions where it has been suggested that the incentive patents provide to invest in research is insufficient.

[16] As noted by the Nuffield Council on Bioethics, genetic use restriction technologies are "only the latest in a long line of more or less efficient ways of compelling farmers to buy seeds from the companies that have developed them . . .": Nuffield Council on Bioethics, *Genetically Modified Crops: The Ethical and Social Issues*, London: Nuffield Council on Bioethics, 1999, 77.

[17] Ironically, this is not the case with the genetic use restriction technology itself, which is patented in a number of countries.

[18] Interview with Dr. Mel Oliver, Agjournal.com (http://www.agjournal.com/agprofile.cfm?person_id= 27).

[19] The patent does not claim any of these genes as such. Taken by themselves, none of these genes are novel, nor are the mechanisms used to switch these genes on and off. On the contrary, several of them are patented and most of the techniques used to transfer them to the plant chromosomes and to switch them on and off are routine and widely used. What is novel about the technology is the way in which the inventors combine these materials and techniques to create a transgenic plant that produces non-viable seed.

these genes produces a protein that sterilises the plant seed, whilst the other two genes prevent this from occurring *unless* and until the seed is exposed to a specific chemical.[20] In the absence of this chemical, these genes are engineered to interact in a manner that prevents the protein that causes sterility from being made. However, when the seeds are exposed to this chemical, it triggers a sequence of events that ultimately lead to the sterility of the subsequent generation.[21] In this way, the technology enables seed producers to control reproduction.

The simplicity of this concept belies the complexity of the overall process. Before we examine this process in more detail, it may be helpful for those unfamiliar with molecular biology to briefly outline how a cell uses its genes to make the proteins necessary for its structure and function (a process known as "gene expression").

C. Technical Details of the Technology Protection System

Every cell of a multicellular organism, such as a plant, contains the same set of genes. As many of these genes produce proteins that are basic to the structure and function of every cell, they are used by every living cell. Other genes are only used by specific types of cells. For example, even though every cell carries the genes for haemoglobin, those genes are only used by red blood cells. In other cell types, these genes are "switched off". In fact, most genes are not being used by the cell all the time, but are "switched on" and "off" when needed. However, genes do not do this by themselves: they do so with the help of other genes which produce proteins called "transcription factors". A transcription factor works by attaching itself to a region of DNA called a promoter.[22] Each gene has its own promoter. In higher organisms,

[20] Strictly speaking, genes do not "produce" proteins, as such: cells do. Genes carry only the instructions, or recipe, for a protein. The process by which those instructions are used to make protein is called "gene expression". The chemical language contained in a gene is expressed just as human language, and just like human language, the message contained in a gene may be lost in the translation. The process of gene expression is therefore somewhat akin to a cellular game of Chinese whispers: Whilst the message is in most cases expressed in its intended form, these messages may be copied or translated incorrectly, for example. This is why this process is referred to as gene expression.

[21] The "creation" of genetically modified plants that produce sterile seed is only one application of the Technology Protection System. The patent broadly claims a number of methods which enable the control of plant gene expression. According to the patent, these methods can be used to control the expression of other genes, such as genes providing resistance to insecticides, drought, fungicides, or genes that alter secondary metabolism.

[22] To many biologists, a "promoter" is the site on DNA where RNA polymerase binds to initiate transcription after being recruited by transcription factors. Here, we prefer to use the term in its wider sense to mean the entire gene control region, which includes the site where RNA polymerase binds, as well as the regulatory sequences to which transcription factors bind: see M. Ridley, *Nature via Nurture*, London: Fourth Estate, 2003. G. A. Wray,

such as plants, promoters may consist of dozens of separate segments of DNA, most of which are located near the associated gene (although some of these segments can be located a large distance away from the gene). Each of these segments attracts a different transcription factor, which either activates (switches on) or represses (switches off) the associated gene.[23] For this reason, promoters are often likened to "gene switches" because the associated gene is either switched on or off depending on the type and number of transcription factors attached to the promoter. The function of many genes is therefore to help switch other genes on or off.[24] The Technology Protection System exploits this phenomenon of gene expression to control if and when a genetically modified plant produces a protein that sterilises second generation seed.

As noted above, the Technology Protection System is made up of three components: a gene that produces a protein that sterilises plant seed, and two other genes that are engineered to prevent this from occurring unless and until the seed is exposed to a specific chemical. We shall examine each of these in turn.

The *first* component of the Technology Protection System is a gene that is found in the seed of the *Saponaria officinalis* plant (commonly known as "Soapwort" or "Bouncing Bet"). This gene is referred to in the patent as a "lethal gene" because it produces a protein, called "saporin-6", that kills the cells in which it is produced. It is perhaps more accurately described as a "sterility gene" because it is only produced in the plant seed and does not otherwise affect the health of the plant. These cells die because saporin-6 causes irreparable damage to molecules called ribosomes,[25] which are an integral component of the cellular machinery involved in the manufacture of proteins. Without properly functioning ribosomes, the cell is unable to make proteins, and because proteins are necessary for many essential cellular functions, the cell will quickly die without them. For this reason, saporin-6 is felicitously known as a "ribosomal inactivating protein", or "RIP".[26]

Promoter Logic (20 March 1998) 279: 5358 *Science* 1871: An excellent lay account of the role of promoters is provided by Ridley at 31–37. What follows is an adaptation of that section.

[23] Transcription factors that switch on genes are called "gene activator proteins", whilst transcription factors that switch off genes are called "gene repressor proteins".

[24] These genes are referred to as "regulatory genes". For example, about 5–10% of the approximately 30,000 genes in the human genome produce transcription factors: Alberts, et al., *Molecular Biology of the Cell* (4th Edition), New York: Garland Science, 2002, 401.

[25] Specifically, by damaging the large ribosomal subunit, which disrupts the binding of elongation factors to ribosomes: L. Barbieri/M. G. Battelli/F. Stirpe, "Ribosome-inactivating Proteins from Plants", (1993) *Biochimica et Biophysica Acta* 1154 (3/4), 237–282.

[26] There are at least 9 other saporin proteins found in various tissues in Soapwort, including leaves, roots and seeds, however saporin-6 is the most widely used because it is easily obtainable and very stable. It is also the most toxic of the saporin proteins: L. Barbieri/M. G. Battelli/F. Stirpe, (above note 25), 240, 248.

The *second* component of the Technology Protection System is a gene switch (or promoter) that controls when and where the saporin-6 is produced. The ideal promoter for the sterility gene is one that is only active in seeds, and only after the plant has fully matured. One such promoter is a "late embryo-genesis abundant" or "LEA" promoter that is found in the seed of a particular variety of cotton. As its name suggests, this promoter does not switch on its associated gene until late in seed development (during embryogenesis), after most other fruit and seed structures have formed.[27] At this stage the seed is fully grown, has accumulated most of its storage oil and protein, and is drying down in preparation for the dormant period between leaving the parent plant and germination.[28] When the LEA promoter is fused to the sterility gene, it switches on production of the saporin-6 sterility gene in the seed during embryogenesis, halting embryo development. The rest of the seed is unaffected and is otherwise normal, except that it will be unable to germinate.

The most difficult problem facing the inventors of the Technology Protection System was that they needed to develop a mechanism that would enable them to switch the LEA promoter off. The reason for this was that they needed to be in a position whereby they could generate seed to sell to farmers. At the same time, however, they also needed to be able to switch the promoter back on prior to the point of sale. To solve this problem, the inventors developed a complex, multi-step solution. First, a segment of DNA is placed between the LEA promoter and the sterility gene. Whilst this blocking sequence remains in place, the sterility gene is unable to be switched on.[29] To remove the blocking sequence, the inventors integrated a second gene into the genome of the plant that produces a bacterial protein called "cyclization recombination recombinase", or "Cre". Cre, which is like a pair of genetic scissors, attaches itself to specific segments of DNA called "*lox*" sites. Once attached, the Cre severs the DNA at the *lox* sites and removes the hapless DNA that is located between them. To complete the process, Cre then splices the severed ends back together.[30] By placing *lox*

---

[27] M. J. Oliver, et al., (above note 2), 6. Late embryogenesis proteins are believed to function by protecting the seed against desiccation, which the seed is naturally exposed to in the period between leaving the parent plant and germination: See A. Garay-Arroyo/ J. M. Colmenero-Flores/A. Garciarrubio/A. A. Covarrubias, "Highly Hydrophilic Proteins in Prokaryoates and Eukaryotes Are Common During Conditions of Water Deficit", (2000) *Journal of Biological Chemistry* 275(8), 5668–5674.

[28] M. L. Crouch, "How the Terminator Terminates", An Occasional Paper of the Edmunds Institute, 1998 (http://www.edmonds-institute.org/crouch.html).

[29] This "blocking sequence" functions by disrupting the reading frame of RNA polymerase, the enzyme which initiates the process of using the information in the sterility gene to make saporin-6.

[30] This is a much simplified account of the Cre-*lox* system. For a comprehensive account of its mechanism of action, see: D. N. Gopaul/G. D. Van Duyne, "Structure and Mechanism in Site-specific Recombination", (1999) *Current Opinion in Structural Biology* 9: 14–20; A. Nagy, "Cre Recombinase: The Universal Reagent for Genome Tailoring", (2000) *Genesis* 26, 99–109.

sites at either end of the blocking sequence, the inventors ensured that the blocking sequence was able to be removed. The Cre then splices the LEA promoter and the sterility gene back together and the sterility gene is able to be activated.

The *third* component of the Technology Protection System is a mechanism for switching the Cre gene on and off. Once again, the solution comes from bacteria. Many bacteria produce a protein from a gene called "*tetA*" that protects them from the antibiotic tetracycline. However, these bacteria only produce this protein when exposed to tetracycline. In the absence of tetracycline, these bacteria produce a transcription factor that switches off the *tetA* gene by attaching itself to short segments of DNA within its promoter called "operators". When tetracycline enters the cell, it entices the transcription factor away from the operators and *tetA* is switched on again.[31] The inventors of the Technology Protection System adapted this process to switch the Cre gene on and off in the following way. First, the inventors modified a promoter that is ordinarily switched on all of the time by inserting a number of operator sequences in specific positions. The promoter is then fused with the Cre gene. Second, a third gene that produces the transcription factor that attaches to these operators is integrated into the genome of the plant. This is then fused to a promoter that is always switched on. The transcription factor is therefore constantly being produced, which means that the Cre gene is always switched off.

However, if the seeds are treated with tetracycline before they are sold, the transcription factor is drawn away from the operators by tetracycline and the Cre gene is switched on.[32] Tetracycline therefore acts as a catalyst that triggers a chain reaction that leads to all three genes being expressed: the Cre gene is switched on, which leads to the production of Cre. After binding to the *lox* sites flanking the blocking sequence, the Cre deletes the blocking sequence. As a result, the LEA promoter and the sterility gene are joined

---

[31] Again, this is a gross oversimplification. For a thoroughgoing analysis, see: C. Gatz, "Use of the Tn*10*-encoded Tetracycline Repressor to Control Gene Expression", in H. S. Reynolds (ed.), *Inducible Gene Expression in Plants*, Wallingford: CABI Publishing, 1999, 11–22; W. Hillen/C. Berens, "Mechanisms Underlying Expression of Tn*10* Encoded Tetracycline Resistance", (1994) *Annual Review of Microbiology* 48, 345–369.

[32] The tetracycline-inducible gene switch is just one of many possibilities available to regulate the production of proteins from transgenes, although it remains the most widely used. Other options include the steroids dexamethasone and estradiol, herbicide safeners, copper, ethanol, the inducer of pathogen-related proteins, benzothiadiazol, and the insecticide methoxyfenozide: W. Tang/R. J. Newton, "Regulated gene expression by glucocorticoids in cultured Virginia pine (*Pinus virginiana* Mill.) cells", (2004) *Journal of Experimental Botany* 55, 1499 at 1500. For a general review, see: C. Gatz/I. Lenk, "Promoters that respond to chemical inducers", (1998) *Trends in Plant Science* 3:3, 352; I. Jepson/A. Martinez/J. P. Sweetman, "Chemical-Inducible Gene Expression Systems for Plants – A Review", (1998) *Pesticide Science* 54, 360–367; R. Wang/X. Zhou/ X. Wang, "Chemically Regulated Expression Systems and their Applications in Transgenic Plants", (2003) *Transgenic Research* 12, 529–540.

together. When this occurs, the LEA promoter is switched on late in the development of the seed embryo and saporin-6 is made, halting the final stages of development of the seed embryo. The ultimate result is sterility of the subsequent generation of seed. But, prior to the application of the tetracycline the transformed plant has only a latent potential for sterility.

D. Implications of the Technology Protection System

One of the curious features of genetic use restriction technologies is that the policy debate has thus far preceded the science. As a consequence, one point that is frequently overlooked in those debates is that genetic use restriction technologies such as the Technology Protection System, taken by themself, are of little value.[33] To be commercially viable, the technology first needs to be coupled with some feature or features that improve the economic value of the target crop, for example genes conferring drought or frost tolerance, enhanced photosynthesis, more efficient use of nitrogen, or increased yield. In relation to hybrid crops, the point is often made that farmers are prepared to purchase new hybrid seed each year because the cost of purchasing new seed is offset by the economic benefits arising from the improved yield associated with hybrid crops. The situation is much the same with genetic use restriction technologies. Thus far, however, the search for value-added traits has, with a few exceptions, met with mixed results.[34] In many respects, the inventors of the Technology Protection System do not see it as an end in itself, but as a means to an end: by preventing the use of saved seed, the Technology Protection provides "an incentive to conduct breeding research in crop species and geographies which have received little or no research attention in the past, because there was no economic incentive to conduct costly research with no prospect of economic return. Increased breeding research and the subsequent production of new, improved varieties is obviously an advantage to the farmers to which these varieties become available".[35] In other words,

---

[33] Shoemaker, et al., *Economic Issues in Agricultural Biotechnology*, United States Department of Agriculture, Economic Research Service Agriculture Information Bulletin No. 762, Washington DC: United States Department of Agriculture, 2001, 42.

[34] The exceptions to this are the introduction of agronomic traits such as herbicide and insect resistance in crops such as corn, cotton, rapeseed, rice and soybean, and the introduction of value-enhanced traits such as altered flower colour in carnations and increased oil content in rapeseed and soybean. For a summary of current and future developments in this field, see: Shoemaker, et al., (above note 33), 16–22.

[35] H. B. Collins/R. W. Kruger, "Potential Impact of GURTs on Smallholder Farmers, Indigenous and Local Communities and Farmers Rights", paper presented to the Convention on Biological Diversity Ad Hoc Technical Expert Group on the Impact of Genetic Use Restriction Technologies on Smallholder Farmers, Indigenous People, and Local Communities, 19–21 February 2003, 1. This paper represents the official position of the International Seed Federation. This paper is available from: http://www.etcgroup.org/documents/collins_kreugerISF.pdf.

with the aid of the Technology Protection System those who invest in plant innovation can do so safe in the knowledge that their investment will not be diluted by nature's tendency to proliferate or by the "bad stewards" who save and reuse this seed.

Whilst the Technology Protection System and similar genetic use restriction technologies may provide an added incentive to conduct research into improving plant varieties, it is unclear whether this will lead to the production of new, improved varieties. For one thing, the Technology Protection System and similar transgenic technologies must first overcome a number of technical hurdles before they can be commercialised. Prime amongst these is the fact that the stable transformation of plants remains elusive, particularly where a number of genes are introduced into the target plant.[36] In particular, it is not possible to predict or control where the introduced genes will be located in the recipient genome or how many complete or partial copies will be inserted.[37] The mesmerising complexity of gene expression in eukaryotes further undermines attempts to stably transform plants: there are no guarantees as to the degree of expression of any gene introduced into a new genomic context, particularly where this involves the transfer of bacterial genes to eukaryotic genomes, as is the case with the Technology Protection System.[38] For example, in the Technology Protection System incompletely expressed genes could result in sterility of plant seed in the first generation, leaving the seed producer without any viable commercial seed. On the other hand, poor expression of the Cre gene may prevent expression of sterility gene, which would defeat the purpose of the Technology Protection System.[39]

In recent times, a number of concerns have also been raised about some of the genetic materials that may be used in the Technology Protection System. In particular, a number of scientists have raised concerns about the potential for the cauliflower mosaic virus promoter CaMV 35S, which is used in most

---

[36] Shoemaker et al., (above note 33), 42.

[37] D. R. Murray, *Seeds of Concern: The Genetic Manipulation of Plants*, Sydney: University of New South Wales Press, 2003, 33.

[38] Ibid. As Jefferson et al. note, "the robustness, reliability and accuracy of transgene expression seems to be affected by issues that are still somewhat obscure, including the quantity of gene expression, its timing and spatial integration, and the correlation of these features with the site of integration into the genome of the plant . . . Anticipating the effects of these phenomena . . . is not trivial. With current transgenic technology, securing sufficiently reliable control of introduced gene expression to meet the quality control needs of the seed industry is a daunting task": R. A. Jefferson, et al., "Genetic Use Restriction Technologies: Technical Assessment of the Set of New Technologies which Sterilise or Reduce the Agronomic Value of Second Generation Seed as Exemplified by U.S. Patent No. 5,723,765 and WO 94/03619", Annex to Convention on Biological Diversity Subsidiary Body on Scientific, Technical and Technological Advice, *Consequences of the Use of the New Technology for the Control of Plant Gene Expression for the Conservation and Sustainable Use of Biological Diversity*, UNEP/CBD/SBSTTA/4/9/Rev.1, 17 May 1999, at 29.

[39] Shoemaker, et al., (above note 33), 42.

transgenic plants and is suggested in the Technology Protection System patent to be a suitable promoter for both the Cre gene and tetracycline transcription factor gene, to recombine with other DNA in the host genome. Accordingly, it has been suggested that this makes the host genome susceptible to instability, and creates the potential for new viruses or other invasive genetic elements. However, this continues to be hotly debated.[40]

A number of other technical problems have also been identified with genetic use restriction technologies, such as the instability of tetracycline and its possible toxicity to plants grown in conditions of limited drainage.[41] A pioneer in the use of tetracycline gene switches in transgenic plants has also observed that tetracycline reduces root growth.[42] In addition, whilst the tetracycline gene switch and the Cre-*lox* systems are valuable laboratory tools, their utility in the field remains uncertain.[43] Notwithstanding these technical impediments, it remains to be seen where the increased in investment in crop research that is foreshadowed by the introduction of the Technology Protection System will be directed, and whether new, improved varieties will result from this investment. In time, these technical difficulties might be overcome. However, it is necessary to keep them in mind when considering the impact that the technology, which is yet to be finalised, may ultimately have.

E. Cost Benefit Analysis

A number of claims have been made about the possible benefits of genetic use restriction technologies if, and when, they are released commercially.

---

[40] See M. W. Ho/A. Ryan/J. Cummins, "Cauliflower Mosaic Viral Promoter — A Recipe for Disaster?" , (1999) *Microbial Ecology in Health and Disease* 11, 194–197; R. Hull/S. N. Covey/P. Dale, "Genetically modified plants and the 35S promoter: assessing the risks and promoting the debate", (2000) *Microbial Ecology in Health and Disease* 12, 1–5; M. W. Ho/A. Ryan/J. Cummins, "Hazards of transgenic plants containing the cauliflower mosaic viral promoter", (2000) *Microbial Ecology in Health and Disease* 12, 6–11; M. W. Ho/A. Ryan/J. Cummins, "CaMV 35S promoter fragmentation hotspot confirmed, and it is active in animals", (2000) *Microbial Ecology in Health and Disease* 12, 189; J. Hodgson, "Scientists Avert New GMO Crisis", (2000) *Nature Biotechnology* 18, 13; J. Cummins/M. W. Ho/A. Ryan, "Hazardous CaMV Promoter?", (2000) *Nature Biotechnology* 18, 363; J. Hodgson, "Reply to 'Hazardous CaMV Promoter?'", (2000) *Nature Biotechnology* 18, 363; M. A. Matzke/M. F. Matte/W. Aufsatz/J. Jakowitsch/ A. J. M. Matzke, "Integrated Pararetroviral Sequences", (2000) *Nature Biotechnology* 18, 579.

[41] I. Jepson/A. Martinez/J. P. Sweetman, (above note 32), 363.

[42] C. Gatz, (above note 32), 17.

[43] R. A. Jefferson, et al., "Genetic Use Restriction Technologies", Annex to Convention on Biological Diversity Subsidiary Body on Scientific, Technical and Technological Advice, *Consequences of the Use of the New Technology for the Control of Plant Gene Expression for the Conservation and Sustainable Use of Biological Diversity*, UNEP/CBD/SBSTTA/4/9/Rev.1, 17 May 1999, 31.

One of these claims is that they will advance agricultural productivity. This is particularly the case with crops that are planted yearly from seed. As such, genetic use restriction technologies will be important for fibre crops such as cotton and flax, soybean, sunflower and peanut; annual ornamental flowers; grain crops such as maize, wheat and sorghum; leaf crops such as tobacco; vegetable crops such as lettuce, carrot, broccoli, cabbage and cauliflower; and fruit crops such as tomato, zucchini, watermelon, cantaloupes and pumpkin.[44] To date, most of the agricultural benefits that are said to flow from genetic use restriction technologies have been confined to trait-specific modifications (T-GURTs). For example, it has been suggested that trait-specific genetic use restriction technologies have the potential to modify plants to make them resistant to drought, insects, and pathogen attack. As the USDA-Delta and Pine patent claims, genetic use restriction technologies can bring about "different growth habit, altered flower or fruit color or quality, premature or late flowering, increased or decreased yield . . . altered production of secondary metabolites, or an altered crop quality such as taste or appearance".[45]

While most of the agricultural advantages offered by genetic use restriction technologies will arise through the modification of genetic traits, the ability to restrict biological reproduction – as promised by the genetic use restriction technologies that operate to render plants sterile – is also said to offer a number of potential agricultural benefits. For example, it has been suggested that such genetic use restriction technologies could be used to prevent pre-harvest sprouting of wheat, thus making crops less susceptible to disease.[46] When applied to crops that reproduce vegetatively, genetic use restriction technologies are said to prevent growth during storage. This has the advantage of extending the shelf and storage life of roots, tubers and many ornamentals. In addition, the non-viable seed produced on genetically modified plants will prevent the possibility of volunteer plants, a major pest problem where rotation is not practised.[47] The ability to control the life-cycle of plants also means that crops can be standardised. This is particularly important for large scale mechanised farming, which requires uniform plants that fit with machines.[48]

One of the most controversial claims made for genetic use restriction technologies is that they offer a potential solution to the problem of genetic

---

[44] M. J. Oliver, et al., (above note 2), 8.

[45] M. J. Oliver, et al., (above note 2), 4.

[46] H. Collins, "Protecting Technology and Encouraging Development", (2001) *21 Seed Info: Official Newsletter of the WANA Seed Network*, 1 (available from: http://www.icarda.org/ News/Seed%20Info/21/SeedInfo21.htm).

[47] Ibid.

[48] One of the reasons why industrial farmers are said to be happy to buy hybrid corn seed each year is because it provides them with uniform and stable crops. Another potential use of V-GURTs is in relation to golf-courses where it is desirable to maintain turf grasses for a long time without seed production.

pollution. In particular, it has been suggested that as genetic use restriction technologies are able to bring about second generation sterility, if pollen from activated plants pollinate flowers of a wild related species, the resulting seed will be rendered non-viable. That is, genetic use restriction technologies will prevent the spread of transgenic plants because the subsequent generation will be unable to germinate.[49] Unsurprisingly, the supposed environmental benefits of genetic use restriction technologies have met with considerable scepticism.[50] For example, it has been said that "the promotion of terminator seeds as a "green" solution to pollution by genetically modified (GM) crops is the Trojan Horse of biotechnology. If terminator wins market acceptance under the guise of biosafety, it will be used as a monopoly tool to prevent farmers from saving and reusing seed".[51] Commentators have also raised concerns that if the sterility trait spreads beyond the confines of a field where the genetic use restriction technologies are planted, it could produce a "suicide-plant pandemic" that wipes out an entire species.[52] In response to arguments of this nature, it has been suggested that "sterility is one trait that does not spread in a population. By its very nature, it is only present for one

---

[49] Report of the Panel of Eminent Experts on Ethics in Food and Agriculture, FAO, Rome, 2001. Cited in FAO, "Potential Impacts of Genetic Use Restriction Technologies (GURTs) on Agricultural Biodiversity and Agricultural Production Systems" 14–18 Oct. 2002, CGRFA-9/02/17, 1.

[50] A number of other concerns have been raised about the impact of GURTs. See, for example, H. Shand, NGO Statement on Terminator Technologies, presented to UNEP/CBD/COP6, (10 April 2002).

[51] H. Shand, "Terminator No Solution to Gene Flow", (2002) *Nature Biotechnology* 20, 775. Debate continues to wage about whether the Technology Protection System and other genetic use restriction technologies are useful as an environmental control mechanism for genetically modified crops. See S. Tally, "Purdue Biotech Experts Say Genetic Plant Sterilisation Technology – Scorned by Environmentalists – Is Needed", (2002) *Ascribe Newswire* (available from: http://www.biotech-info.net/sterilization.html); ETC Group, "ETC Responds to Purdue University's Recent Efforts to Promote Seed Sterilization – or Terminator – as an Environmental Protection Technology", (2002) *Genotype*, 1 May 2002 (available from http://www.etcgroup.org/documents/geno2002 May1Perdue.pdf); S. Smyth/G. C. Khachatourians/P. W. B. Phillips, "Liabilities and Economics of Transgenic Crops", (2002) *Nature Biotechnology* 20, 537; H. Daniell, "Molecular Strategies for Gene Containment in Transgenic Crops", (2002) *Nature Biotechnology* 20, 581.

[52] J. Mander, "Machine Logic: Industrialising Nature and Agriculture", in A. Kimbrell (ed.), *The Fatal Harvest Reader: The Tragedy of Industrial Agriculture*, Washington: Island Press, 2002, 87 at 90. There are also fears that a farmer growing a non-GURTs crop next to a field of GURTs plants of the same species would not be able to save the non-GURTS seed because pollen flow from the GURTs crop would be rendered sterile. Arguments of this nature have been rejected by proponents of the technology because "the TPS target crops – soybean, wheat and rice – are highly self pollinated. Therefore plants of these crops will have produced seed fertilized by their own pollen prior to accepting pollen from the adjacent TPS crop. The frequency of outcrossing would be extremely low and therefore the amount if sterile seed produced on the non-TPS crop would be negligible and indiscernible": H. B. Collins, (above note 46), 2.

generation and because sterile seeds do not produce plants, these nonexistent plants cannot produce pollen with which to propagate more sterile plants".[53]

For our purposes, the most important claim made for genetic use restriction technologies is that they offer a way of controlling the way plant genetic resources are generated, used, and consumed. It is this issue that we wish to focus on here. In so far as genetic use restriction technologies prevent farmers, breeders and other users from reproducing protected plants, it provides genetic "in-built protection against unauthorised reproduction of the seed or the added-value trait".[54] As a result, it offers those who invest time and money in biological innovation a technological mechanism to protect genetic resources and innovations without the need of having to comply with the requirements of intellectual property law. The fact that genetic use restriction technologies operate as a copy-protection system is said to have a number of positive benefits. In particular, it has been suggested that it will make it more attractive for private organisations (as well as those public sector agencies who have adopted a more commercial approach to research) to invest in agricultural research and development.[55] The reason for this is that genetic use restriction technologies offer those who invest time and money in breeding a possible solution to the problem of leakage which occurs where third parties use but do not pay for biological resources. This will occur, for example, where farmers save seed or competitors rely upon the breeder's exemption to develop new varieties. The ability of genetic use restriction technologies to act as a copy-protection system will be particularly important where hybrid technologies or other natural control mechanisms are not well developed.[56] It will also be important where companies that invest in breeding are unhappy either with the level or nature of intellectual property protection.[57] To the extent that genetic use restriction technologies encourage additional funding for agricultural research, proponents of the technology claim that it will stimulate breeding, increase innovation in plant breeding, and ultimately lead to the development of improved varieties. It has also been suggested that as genetic use restriction technologies will encourage investment in smaller currently neglected areas of research, that it will promote genetic diversity and provide farmers with greater choice. As a representative of Delta Pine and Land said, "if a technology does not bring benefits and increased prosperity to our customers, the farmers, they will not purchase the technology. It is in everyone's interest

---

[53] Ibid.

[54] R. A. Jefferson, et al., (above note 43), 13.

[55] T. Goeschi/T. Swanson, "The Development Impact of Genetic Use Restriction Technologies: A Forecast Based on the Hybrid Crop Experience", (2003) 8 *Environment and Development Economics*, 149 at 151.

[56] See the International Seed Federation, "Position Paper of the International Seed Federation on Genetic Use Restriction Technologies", adopted at Bangalore, India in June 2003 (available from: http://www.worldseed.org/Position_papers/Pos_GURTs.htm).

[57] H. B. Collins, (above note 46), 2.

that more choices be available to all of the world's farmers, and the TPS is a means of achieving this goal".[58]

While the proponents of genetic use restriction technologies believe that its ability to protect botanical innovation will bring about a number of long-term benefits, critics have been more sceptical arguing that the technology will have a negative impact on the way that plant genetic resources are created, used, and consumed. In particular, critics have said that if genetic use restrictions technologies become available they would make the existing repertoire of intellectual property rights "largely redundant as property would be embedded in the material itself".[59] The concern here is that biologically based protection systems would effectively remove the policy control that governments have exercised when designing intellectual property law. More specifically, the concern is that the protection offered by genetic use restriction technologies will be broader (entire genome, any seed), more effective (100% control), and last much longer than is currently the case under intellectual property protection (in perpetuity rather than of limited duration).[60] Another problem that has been raised is that genetic use restriction technologies have the potential to undermine the defences and exceptions that currently exist in intellectual property law, notably the farmer's rights to save seed,[61] the exemptions in plant breeders rights that ensure that varieties are available for further breeding,[62] and the research exemption in patent law (where it exists in any meaningful form). To the extent that intellectual property is replaced by genetic use restriction technologies, a complex sensitive set of issues would be determined by technical fiat rather than by institutional negotiation.[63] To the extent that genetic use restriction technologies undermine the practice whereby farmers save grain from one year's crop to sow in subsequent years, the seasonal purchase of seed would effectively become obligatory.[64] If this occurs, farmers would become dependent upon seed manufacturers for the supply of seed and thus their livelihood. This would also be the case with breeders and researchers working on plant related materials.[65]

---

[58] H. B. Collins, (above note 46), 3.

[59] R. A. Jefferson, et al., (above note 43), 37.

[60] Convention on Biological Diversity, Subsidiary Body on Scientific, Technical and Technological Advice, "Note by the Executive Secretary", *Consequences of the Use of the New Technology for the Control of Plant Gene Expression for the Conservation and Sustainable Use of Biological Diversity*, UNEP/CBD/SBSTTA/4/9/Rev.1 17 May 1999, 9.

[61] *Act of 1991 of the International Convention for the Protection of New Varieties of Plants*, Chapter 5; Directive 98/44/EC of the European Parliament and of the Council of 6 July 1998 on the Legal Protection of Biotechnological Inventions, Article 11.

[62] With hybrids, elite parents are typically not available to breeders.

[63] A. Pottage, Untitled (manuscript on file with authors), 1.

[64] R. A. Jefferson, et al., (above note 43), 18.

[65] FAO, (above note 49), Annex, para. 15, 13.

F. Historical Parallels – Hybridisation

Many of these arguments will be familiar to intellectual property lawyers. For example, the idea that private sector organisations will only invest in agricultural research if they have some means of controlling reproduction is similar to the arguments used to justify the grant of patents, designs, copyright and plant breeders' rights. In turn, the fears raised about the replacement of intellectual property protection by biological protection systems has parallels with the growing use of (digital) technological protection systems to control access to works protected by copyright. The claims by the proponents of genetic use restriction technologies that the criticisms made of the technology are not supported by any factual or empirical evidence,[66] are similar to those used to counter ethical arguments against the patenting of living inventions. In so far as genetic use restriction technologies provide a system of genetic copy protection, there are obvious and useful parallels to the technological protection systems used in relation to digital technologies. There are also parallels with earlier biological technological protection systems that were used to control reproduction in plants and animals. These include the intentional infestation of sheep with liver fluke to render them infertile,[67] and the practice of inducing triploidy (three chromosomes instead of two) in fish breeding. Perhaps the most well known biological protection system, and the most obvious starting point when thinking about the potential impact that genetic use restriction technologies might have on the circulation and use of plant genetic resources, is provided by hybrid seed.

The process of hybridisation, which has been available for commercial seed since the 1920s, occurs when two highly inbred types are genetically crossed. While the hybrid system is not viable in all crops, over time hybridisation has been used in many cross-pollinated crops including maize, sorghum, sunflower and canola. One of the most important consequences of hybridisation is that it leads to "heterosis" or "hybrid vigour". That is, it leads to increased yield and to more standardised crops. Another notable feature of hybridisation is that while it increases yield in first generation crops, the quality and quantity of subsequent crops deteriorates, and continues to deteriorate, with each replanting.[68] While farmers are able to use seed to replant subsequent crops, the benefits in yield are not realised in subsequent generations. One of the consequences of this is that hybridisation operates as a de facto technological protection system and thus as a way of controlling the

---

[66] "Proposal of the United States of America Regarding Procedural and Substantive Issues on the GURTS Memorandum Submitted by the Office of the Union to the Convention on Biological Diversity", UPOV CAJ/47/7 (31 March 2003) Annex II, 5.

[67] H. Ritvo, "Possessing Mother Nature: Genetic Capital in Eighteenth-Century Britain", in J. Brewer/S. Staves (eds.) *Early Modern Conceptions of Property*, London: Routledge, 1995, 413.

[68] R. A. Jefferson, et al., (above note 43), 21; FAO, (above note 49), Annex, para. 3, 1.

way that plant genetic resources are used.[69] While farmers are technically able to use hybrid seed to re-sow new crops, hybrid seed is seldom saved for replanting due to "differences from the parent seed in the produced generation and resulting reduction in performance".[70] So long as the inbred parent lines that were used to develop the hybrid crop are not disclosed to the public, farmers need to purchase seed on an annual basis.

A number of claims have been made about hybridisation and the impact that it had, and continues to have, on the circulation and use of plant genetic resources. For example, it has been suggested that the protection offered by hybridisation has encouraged private firms to invest in research and development. Indeed, it has been argued that a primary motivation for the creation of hybrid cultivars was that it enhanced the scope for appropriating rents from research and development.[71] Whether or not this is the case, it is clear that private companies have been more willing to invest in crop innovations where they are able to control how the resulting varieties are used. Conversely, it has been suggested that private companies have been reluctant to invest in self-pollinated species that have proved difficult to hybridise, such as soybeans, wheat, rice and cotton.[72] The private investment in research facilitated by hybridisation is said to have a number of long-term benefits. For example, it is often suggested that the willingness of farmers to buy hybrid seed each year, rather than saving and replanting seeds from their previous crop, "insures quality while funding continued research that leads to new and improved varieties".[73]

As many commentators have noted, hybrid crops share a number of features in common with genetic use restriction technologies. In particular, both act as a form of use restriction and in so doing have the potential to shape the way plant genetic resources are modified and used. For example, it has been suggested on the basis of experience in relation to hybrid-based agriculture that genetic use restriction technologies will lead to a higher rate of investment by private industry in crop improvement "motivated by enhanced scope for rent capture".[74] It has also been argued on the basis of studies looking at the impact of hybrid maize that "there is good reason to be concerned that the rate of diffusion will be slow with genetic use restriction technologies, as the flow of plant materials and the level of public funding is restricted".[75]

---

[69] H. B. Collins, (above note 46), 1.
[70] Ibid.
[71] T. Swanson/T. Goeschi, "Genetic Use Restriction Technologies (GURTs): Impacts on Developing Countries"; (2000) 2 *International Journal of Biotechnology*, 56 at 74; R. A. Steinbrecher/P. Mooney, "Terminator Technology: The Threat to World Food Security", (1998) 28 *Ecologist*, 276.
[72] H. B. Collins, (above note 46), 1.
[73] Ibid.
[74] T. Goeschi/T. Swanson, (above note 55), 162.
[75] T. Swanson/T. Goeschi, (above note 71), 67–68.

While there are obvious parallels between hybridisation and genetic use restriction technologies, we must be careful about the conclusions we draw from this. In part, this is because genetic use restriction technologies will potentially provide a much more effective and more widespread system of use restriction.[76] In particular, while hybridisation has only been successfully used in a limited number of crops (it is not used in barley, cotton, millet, rice, soybeans and wheat), it is theoretically possible for genetic use restriction technologies to be applied to all seed-bearing crops.[77] Another difference is that while farmers are able to gain some benefit from the replanting of farm-saved hybrid seed, the replanting of seed protected by genetic use restriction technologies is expected to result in a 100% yield loss. Another reason why we should be careful about the conclusions we draw from the experience in relation to hybridisation is because the legal, political and economic environment that genetic use restriction technologies operate in today is markedly different from that which existed when hybridisation was first utilised in the 1920s. While it is important that we keep the lessons of history in mind when thinking about the impact that genetic use restriction technologies may have upon the creation use and consumption of plant genetic resources, it is also important that we situate genetic use restriction technologies within the environment in which they are likely to operate.

G. Technology Protection Systems and Intellectual Property

So long as the technical uncertainties surrounding genetic use restriction technologies are overcome, there is a real possibility that they will have a negative impact upon the creation, use and circulation of plant genetic resources. Ultimately, however, the impact that genetic use restriction technologies may have upon plant genetic resources will vary depending on a number of variables including whether the practical difficulties with the technology are overcome, whether the technology is commercially viable, the nature of the existing farming systems (such as the type of crop, the availability of hybrids, and reliance on local landraces), the level of mechanisation, the geographic region in question, and the extent to which farmers habitually save seed to re-sow annual crops. While these are all important considerations, we wish to focus on another equally important factor that has attracted less attention. This is that the last twenty or so years have seen the beginning of the juridification of plant genetic resources. That is, we have witnessed the growing impact of law on the creation, circulation, and use of

---

[76] GURTs are said to be "radically different in mechanism, scope and implications": R. A. Jefferson, et al., (above note 43), 17.

[77] GURTs are likely to have greater impact in those crops "for which hybridisation has not been carried out on a significant scale, such as wheat and rice": T. Goeschi/ T. Swanson, (above note 55), 152.

plant genetic resources. In particular, we have moved from a situation where intellectual property protection played, at best, a minimal role in the protection of botanical innovation, to a situation where it now plays a much more prominent role in the creation, circulation, and use of genetic resources. For example, ten years ago all of the wheat varieties grown in Victoria (Australia) were freely available to growers. By the end of 2005, however, it is expected that all of the major varieties of wheat grown in Victoria will be protected by plant variety rights. A similar situation exists in other States in Australia, and in many other developed countries around the world. While patents on biological innovations have not had much of an impact on agricultural practices in many countries to date, the US being the notable exception, this is likely to change in the immediate future. Indeed, recent figures show that agricultural patents are the fastest growing area of patent activity in the United States.[78]

Another notable development that has extended the reach of the law in this area has been the growing use of endpoint royalties as a way of collecting revenue for varieties protected by plant breeders' rights. Where endpoint royalties are included in seed contracts, farmers pay a percentage of the income on the crop grown rather than a royalty on the seed purchased. As well as sharing the risk of crop failure between farmers and breeders (in much the same way as authors and publishers share risk of the success of a book), endpoint royalties, at least on one reading, mark a shift in the scope of protection offered by plant breeders' rights away from merely being a right over propagating material to being a more general right. That is, the property provided by plant breeders' rights is changing to look more like that provided by patents. If this does occur, it may extend the reach of intellectual property rights beyond breeders and growers to also include bulk handlers, processors and possibly even manufacturers. Even if this does not transpire, the almost inevitable growth in the number of patents granted over plant genetic resources that seems likely to occur in the future will bring about similar changes. The ongoing juridification of plant genetic resources has been exacerbated by the increased use of grower agreements that attempt to control the way farmers deal with plant materials, particularly in relation to the saving of seed, and the increased use of material transfer agreements to regulate the transfer of germplasm. It has also been reinforced by the growing interest in the commercialisation of agricultural research that has occurred recently.

A number of changes have also taken place at the international level that reinforce the growing reach that the law has over biological materials. For example, the 1993 *Convention on Biological Diversity*, which introduced the

---

[78] J. King/P. Heisey, "Ag Biotech Patents: Who is Doing What?", (2003) *Amber Waves: The Economics of Food, Farming, Natural Resources, and Rural America*, November 2003 (available from: http://www.ers.usda.gov/AmberWaves/November03/pdf/agbiotech.pdf).

idea of national sovereignty over genetic resources into international law, set in play a number of changes that have altered the way plant genetic resources are used. Anecdotal evidence suggests that the *Convention on Biological Diversity* has slowed down and, in some cases, stopped the exchange of germplasm between countries who are still deciding how the Convention should be implemented domestically. While few countries have implemented the *Convention on Biological Diversity*, the introduction of benefit-sharing arrangements and the need to obtain prior informed consent are likely to influence the way that plant genetic resources are used. They are also likely to add to the costs of biological related inventions. The *International Treaty on Plant Genetic Resources*, which came into force on 29 June 2004, also has the potential to add to the juridification of plant genetic resources. To some extent the impact that the Treaty has will depend on the details of the Material Transfer Agreements developed under the Treaty, and the extent to which they allow recipients to take out intellectual property protection over inventions that are derived from plant genetic resources covered by the Treaty.

The process of juridification which has taken place over the last twenty or so years is likely to have a number of important consequences for the creation, circulation, and consumption of plant genetic resources. It will also play an important role in mediating the impact that genetic use restriction technologies have when and if they are released commercially. One of the most important consequences of the juridification of plant genetic resources is that it is highly unlikely that genetic use restriction technologies will replace intellectual property protection. In part, this is because the existing laws and practices are not only interwoven, they also often act as substitutes for each other. This is reinforced by the fact that genetic use restriction technologies only provide a means of controlling reproduction: they do not deal with the important follow-up issue of the manner and mode of exploitation and remuneration, nor with the issue of free-riding by imitators.[79] As such, breeders still need to develop mechanisms to deal with the way their biological innovations are exploited. In doing so, breeders who utilise genetic use restriction technologies to protect their biological innovations will inevitably rely upon structures, networks and institutions which are themselves either created by, or increasingly subject to, the law.

While it is unlikely that genetic use restriction technologies will replace intellectual property law, this does not mean that they will not play an important role in shaping the way intellectual property law develops in the

---

[79] As Jefferson et al. note, the use of genetic use restriction technologies does not protect "by itself the imitation of a certain product by other companies or entities that may possess the technical capabilities to reverse-engineer or otherwise duplicate the "technically protected" seed. Hence, patents, PBRs and trade secrets protection would continue to be important tools to secure control over certain materials in the relationship between the innovator and eventual imitators": R. A. Jefferson, et al., (above note 43), 37.

future. In particular, it is likely that breeders and those who invest in the breeding process will use genetic use restriction technologies as a strategic bargaining device to help them influence the shape and direction of intellectual property law. For example, in developing countries, particularly those countries who have to implement Article 27(3)(b) of TRIPS, genetic use restriction technologies may be used to place pressure on policy makers to ensure that new legislation does not contain exemptions for farmers or breeders.[80] In developed countries genetic use restriction technologies may be used as a way of pressuring policy makers to alter or sideline existing defences. This is in effect what the Seed Association of Australia has been doing in its campaign to have the innovation patent (which has fewer defences than plant breeders rights) extended to include plant and animal subject matter. There is also a possibility that genetic use restriction technologies will be used to shape the manner and level of remuneration payable where copy-protected genetic material is used. It is also likely that genetic use restriction technologies will act as a catalyst for the further juridification of plant genetic resources. This has already happened, to some extent, as we start to witness the first wave of responses to genetic use restriction technologies. For example, a Bill recently introduced in the US Congress proposes to impose a prohibition of non-fertile plant seeds. In particular, it provides that "a person may not manufacture, distribute, sell, plant, or otherwise use any seed that is genetically engineered to produce a plant whose seeds are not fertile or are rendered infertile by the application of an external chemical inducer".[81] In India, laws have been enacted that attempt to limit the scope and operation of genetic use restriction technologies.[82] The juridification of germplasm has been reinforced by the decision of the International Agricultural Research Centres that it will "not incorporate into their breeding materials any genetic systems designed to prevent seed germination".[83] In so far as the exclusion of genetic use restriction technologies needs to be monitored by legal means, it will entrench the role that the law plays in regulating the creation and circulation of plant genetic resources.

[80] International Seed Federation, "Position Paper of the International Seed Federation on Genetic Use Restriction Technologies", adopted at Bangalore, India in June 2003, 1.

[81] *Genetically Engineered Crop and Animal Farmer Protection Act of 2003*, H.R. 2918 (25 July 2003), section 9. The Bill has been referred to the Committee on Agriculture, Subcommittee on Conservation, Credit, Rural Development and Research.

[82] *Protection of Plant Variety and Farmers' Rights Act* (2001).

[83] Consultative Group on International Agricultural Research, (1998) *CGIAR News*, December 1998, 3 (available from: http://www.worldbank.org/html/cgiar/newsletter/dec98/dec98.pdf).

H. Conclusion

As Derrida reminds us, "an invention always pre-supposes some illegality, the breaking of an implicit contract; it inserts a disorder into the peaceful ordering of things, it disregards, the proprieties".[84] Genetic use restriction technologies follow this logic, but potentially do so in a much more violent way than to which we are accustomed. They turn Dawkins' conception of organisms as passive "survival machines" for their genes on its head: instead, genetic use restriction technologies enable the transformation of plants into "suicide machines".

Whilst genetic use restriction technologies disrupt the natural order of things, it remains to be seen what impact they will have upon existing legal and agricultural practices. And while these technologies are yet to be successfully transplanted from the laboratory to the field, they, and the debates that have crystallised around them, have raised a number of important issues. In terms of intellectual property law, they reinforce the fact that biological subject matter is very different from the subject matter of mechanical and chemical inventions, not only in terms of the grant of property rights but also, and perhaps more importantly, in terms of the use and exploitation of these rights. As such, they remind us of the folly of the notion of technological neutrality. They also remind us that many of the concepts, ideas and techniques used in intellectual property law were developed to deal with mechanical (and to a lesser extent chemical) inventions. Thinking through the possible impact that genetic use restrictions may have for plant genetic resources also highlights the fact that very little work that has been done on the relationship between intellectual property and agriculture. Before we are in a position to understand the impact that genetic use restriction technologies might have upon plant genetic resources, we first need to understand a lot more about the role that intellectual property plays in the creation, distribution and use of plant genetic resources. Given the increasingly important role that intellectual property plays in the regulation of plant genetic resources and the potentially important role that genetic use restriction technologies might play in changing the way that plant genetic resources are used and consumed, this is an urgent and pressing task.

---

[84] J. Derrida, "Psyche: Inventions of the Other" (trans. C. Porter), in L. Waters/ W. Godzich (eds.), *Reading de Man Reading*, Minnesota: University of Minnesota Press, 1989, 25–65 at 25.

13
Enforcing Industrial Property Rights: Patent Protection From a Comparative Viewpoint

DIETER STAUDER

A. Enforcement – A Key Current Issue

I. The Need for Effective Protection of Rights

The value of intellectual property rights in practice depends on whether the holder can take effective measures to prevent others from infringing them.[1] Apart from taking the infringer to court, the right-holder can issue a warning to refrain from the acts in question. The main object of this may be to arrive at a settlement with the infringing competitor, in which case the right-holder will merely send a letter to the other party, informing it of the position with regard to IP rights and offering to negotiate.

Before embarking on litigation, a warning letter is the most effective preventive instrument available, though it carries an element of risk which calls for the involvement of a qualified legal practitioner. However, any lawyer knows that warnings are useless unless the claim against the other party can be enforced effectively through the courts. Instituting civil proceedings to prevent further infringement is one indispensable weapon in the right-holder's armoury; applying for a preliminary injunction is another particularly effective means of stopping an infringer in his tracks.

Enforcement before the courts is therefore a major test of effectiveness for the rights conferred by the intellectual property system.[2] A key requirement is that effective protection against infringement be available at reasonable cost to the right-holder in terms of money, time and effort. However, the

---

[1] TRIPS, Part III "Enforcement of Intellectual Property Rights", Art. 41–61; on these provisions see Dreier, in From GATT to TRIPs, IIC-Studies Vol. 18, VCH 1996, Beier and Schricker (eds.), 248–277; for further info see: www.wto.org, under TRIPS; see, e.g. Report on implementation of TRIPS enforcement provisions, Commission on Intellectual and Industrial Property of 16 June 1997; Prof. W. R. Cornish's well-known book on "Intellectual Property", 5th ed. 2002 starts Chapter 2 "The Enforcement of Rights".

[2] See Stauder, Patent- und Gebrauchsmusterverletzungsverfahren in der Bundesrepublik Deutschland, Grossbritannien, Frankreich und Italien. Eine rechtstatsächliche Untersuchung, Cologne 1989; Bastian/Götting/Knaak/Stauder, Der Markenverletzungspozess in ausgewählten Ländern der Europäischen Wirtschaftsgemeinschaft. Eine rechtstatsächliche und rechtsvergleichende Untersuchung, Cologne 1993.

very existence of effective judicial procedures[3] is already a means of ensuring that IP rights are not violated.[4] The threat of court action has to be a genuine deterrent.

II. Prohibition: The Most Important Sanction

The legal protection[5] of intellectual property is chiefly based on the right to prevent others from doing certain things.[6] A right-holder can apply for an injunction to restrain[7] an infringer, who is usually also a major competitor, from making or distributing the infringing product, or from using it or performing certain other acts. This emphasis on the right to prohibit distinguishes intellectual property protection from the protection offered in other civil law matters involving the infringement of an owner's rights. The usual sanction[8] in the civil courts is the award of compensation to the plaintiff for infringements of his rights which have already occurred, generally in connection with personal injury or property damage, an example being the many road accidents whose consequences are resolved in this way. Monetary compensation also plays a central role in the commercial sphere, where it is the main remedy for breaches of contract. Prohibitory injunctions, on the other hand, are something which the public rarely becomes aware of, except in disputes over press complaints or infringements of the right to privacy.

In the field of intellectual property, the purpose of prohibitory injunctions is to protect the exclusive market position which the right-holder has established for a product or service. An award of damages is generally insufficient to compensate the right-holder for the injury incurred, since the cost to the infringer often barely exceeds that of licensing the invention, and the necessary funds can easily be found in his company budget.[9] The deterrent effect of compensation claims seems to be confined to the US.[10]

---

[3] The quality of courts and of judges, patent attorneys and attorneys-at-law is required to guarantee the necessary protection of IP holders. One condition is a effective competition among these persons and also between the courts of first instance. The appeal court, however, should have central jurisdiction like the CAFC in the US. Forum shopping is one important means to stimulate courts and other legal personnel involved.

[4] The term: "infringed" may be the correct legal term, however " violation" is sometimes used in European Continental law, which is based on the Roman legal tradition.

[5] In legal English: "remedy".

[6] Claims for injunction in German procedures: 90.4% in patents; 90.7% in trade marks; in most cases the preliminary measures are directed to an injunction; see fn. 2.

[7] Or: to refrain from doing certain acts.

[8] "Sanction" is the legal term now used in IP instead of "remedy"; this is for the same reason as stated in fn. 3.

[9] A never ending discussion: The measure of damages is mostly based on the licensing fees; for decades there has been pressure to increase the amount of damages awarded to the IP owner.

[10] See Art 41 (1) 1st sentence of TRIPS: ". . . including expeditious remedies to prevent infringement and remedies which constitute a deterrent to further infringements". See now: Proposal for a Directive of the European Parliament and of the Council on

Prohibition is necessary because allowing an infringing product to remain on the market will hurt the right-holder's sales and lead to a risk of market confusion. Trade mark infringement is a clear case in point: The appearance on the market of a product closely resembling a trademarked item has the effect of confusing potential customers, who are unsure of the product's origin. In time, the market may settle down again once consumers have learned to distinguish between the confusingly marked goods or services, but the right-holder still loses out by the weakening of the dominant position conferred by the trade mark. The same applies in patent law: If the market gets used to the idea that several technically equivalent products are available simultaneously, there is a risk that the customer will stop doing business with the proprietor of the patent and go to the competition instead.

Unlike the award of compensation, the prevention of infringing acts involves a time factor. The length of a court case leading to an award of compensation is not a matter of indifference; indeed, it may be very important, e.g. to a plaintiff claiming damages for personal injury or assault, to receive compensation as soon as possible. However, the time aspect is not crucial where there is an obligation to pay interest on any damages and where the injured party is more interested in maximising the amount of the award than in expediting the proceedings.

With prohibition, on the other hand, time is of the essence. A long court case can have a highly negative impact on the right-holder's market position. Demanding cessation of infringement only makes sense if a court order can be issued quickly. For this reason, preliminary injunctions, preventing further infringement until the court has decided on the merits of the case, play a major part in IP litigation.[11]

The demand for a quick procedure, leading to a very tough sanction, involves various additional requirements. Only judges fully versed in intellectual property matters will be prepared to make speedy use of this prohibitory instrument. It is also necessary to ensure the participation of well-trained legal practitioners and patent attorneys with the ability to prepare the brief.

A further aspect in Europe is that in cases of cross-border infringement, protection for single national markets is not enough. The Europeanisation of intellectual property is proof of the need for Europe-wide regulation in this field, accompanied by corresponding judicial arrangements. I shall explore this topic later.

Measures and Procedures to ensure the Enforcement of Intellectual Property Rights, Commission of the European Communities, COM (2003) 46 final, Brussels, 30.1.2003 with the intention to improve the situation of the IP owners, Art. 17 with explanatory memorandum.

[11] Provisional measures are of paramount importance, Explanatory memorandum of the EU proposal to Art. 10, see fn. 9 above; see also Art. 15. Preliminary injunctions in trade marks, Germany: 50.3% of the infringing actions; UK 86.4%; see fn. 2.

III. The European Movement in Intellectual Property

With the Community trade mark and the Community design,[12] the European Union has created two important Community instruments backed by a system of enforcement, involving the national courts and the European Court of Justice. A similar arrangement remains to be devised for copyright and patent law.

This is particularly surprising with regard to patents, in view of the central patent grant procedure established on the basis of the European Patent Convention (EPC) and the considerable degree of legal harmonisation accompanying centralisation. At the post-grant stage, however, the European patent continues to be a bundle of national rights, subject to national jurisdiction. The efforts of the EU to create a Community patent with its own judicial system have yet to bear fruit.

Within the framework of the European Patent Convention, moves have begun to conclude a special agreement setting up a new judicial system, with its own rules of procedure, for European patents. The EU Commission has similar plans for the Community patent.[13]

Before the launching of these initiatives, the existing situation in European patent law led to a form of competition among national courts. The basis for this was the 1968 Brussels Convention on Jurisdiction and the Enforcement of Judgments in Civil and Commercial Matters, which was recently replaced by a similarly worded Council Regulation.[14] This Community law, governing the competence of civil and commercial courts throughout the EU member states, extends the principle that jurisdiction rests with the member state in which the defendant is domiciled, by establishing that judgments of a court in one member state are automatically recognised and enforceable in others. Since infringement disputes in the field of intellectual property are civil matters, they too are covered by the Regulation.

The European domicile system would already have generated a large body of European case law, had it not been for two obstacles. The first of these consists in the fact that decisions on revocation or cancellation of a registered industrial property right may only be taken by the courts of the country for which the right has been granted.[15] Since the defendants in patent infringement proceedings – and to some extent in proceedings concerning other

---

[12] Competent Authority: The Office for Harmonisation in the Internal Market (OHIM), established by Council Regulation (EC) No. 40/94 of 20 December 1993, OJ EC 11/1994 L, p. 1 et seq.; homepage: europa eu.int.

[13] European Union: Community Patent – Common political approach of 3 March 2003, OJ EPO 2003, 218; Proposal for a Council Regulation of 16.4.2003.

[14] Council Regulation (EC) No. 44/2001 of 22 December 2000 on jurisdiction and the recognition and enforcement of judgments in civil and commercial matters, OJ EC 12/2001 L, p.1 et seq. – Brussels Regulation.

[15] Art. 22 No. 4 Brussels Regulation.

types of industrial property rights – usually file a counterclaim for invalidity, the potential for internationalising the domicile principle is limited. The rise of the cross-border injunction has led to divergences in the case law of the various EU member states. A second obstacle to liberalising the domicile principle arises from the fact that cross-border competence is normally limited to the courts of the country where the defendant is resident or has his principal place of business, and does not extend to the country where the infringing act occurred,[16] which, however, is of particular importance to the plaintiff.

As long as the divergence of approaches persists in Europe,[17] the effectiveness of industrial property protection, especially in the field of patent law, will continue to depend on the quality of the national courts. This is the topic to which I now turn.

B. Infringement Proceedings – The Most Common Form of Legal Action in Industrial Property

I. Types of Action in Intellectual Property

In industrial property, and probably in copyright too, the majority of legal disputes concern infringement, followed by issues of rights ownership[18] and licensing matters. The various types of procedure in this field include actions for performance and for obtaining positive and negative declaratory judgments. Compulsory licensing actions are rare.[19]

Licensing agreements often contain arbitration clauses, enabling disputes in this area to be settled by a tribunal. In infringement cases, arranging for arbitration – which can only be done after the event – is very rare. In certain areas, for example in disputes over domain names, arbitration and mediation have come to play a particularly prominent part.[20]

This trend is likely to continue with designations, since symbols tend to be short-lived, and in certain areas of the law relating to fashion. In the "classic"

---

[16] Art. 5 No. 3 Brussels Regulation: forum or court of the place of tort.

[17] Answer may come now from the ECJ : Reference of the OLG Düsseldorf of 5. December 2002 to the European Court of Justice for preliminary ruling, C – 4/03, relates to the interpretation of Art.16 No. 4 Brussels Convention whose text is identical with Art. 22 No. 4 Brussels Regulation.

[18] Action for entitlement to the patent or patent application; *action en revendication*.

[19] See, however, the discussion about Doha, 4th WTO Ministerial Conference, Qatar, 9.–14. 11. 2001; e.g. Nolff, Compulsory Patent Licensing in View of the WTO Ministerial Conference Declaration on the TRIPS Agreement and Public Health, JPOS 2002, 133 with the Declaration in the Annex; Report of the Commission on Intellectual Property Rights: Integrating Property Rights and Development Policy, Executive Summary, London, September 2002.

[20] Plant, Resolving International Intellectual Property Disputes, International Chamber of Commerce, 1999; see the activities of the WIPO Arbitration and Mediation Center, WIPO, Geneva.

fields of patent and trade mark law, there is little evidence as yet of a shift towards alternative dispute resolution (ADR).

II. Infringement Disputes – Towards a Definition

The defining feature of infringement proceedings in the IP field is that the plaintiff is the owner (or licensee) of a right which the defendant has allegedly breached. This, as we have seen, typically leads to applications for injunctive relief and damages, often accompanied by requests for information and the production of invoices. In some cases the plaintiff also demands the destruction or confiscation of the infringing goods, and the publication of the judgment. A further typical aspect of infringement disputes is the fact that the court begins by determining whether or not an infringement has occurred, before going on to hear an expert assessment of the injury caused and taking a further decision fixing damages.

C. Characteristics of Patent Infringement Proceedings

I. Frequency

Determining the frequency of patent infringement proceedings in Europe is difficult, because not all the courts keep detailed records. A survey (based on the years 1998–2000) carried out by the EU Commission in 2001 points to an annual maximum of 1,200 patent infringement cases being heard at first instance in the EU member states. However, no figures were available for Italy, a country where infringement actions could well be frequent. The statistical picture is also blurred by the fact that other kinds of action are bracketed with infringement proceedings in France and the UK, which are both major IP countries.

My own view is that the quoted figures need to be treated with caution. Infringement proceedings in Germany are a case in point. My research[21] showed that in the early 1970s the annual number of cases coming before the regional courts with jurisdiction for infringement totalled around 125. A study based on the year 1990 showed that the German courts had dealt with 286 disputes relating to patents, utility models and employee inventions. These figures also included an element of guesswork.[22] The annual average number of patent infringement actions in 1998–2000 is said to be 611 – a very steep rise.

This number of patent infringement actions may at first seem high, but the figure is in fact low in relation to the number of patents granted. The earlier

---

[21] See fn. 2.
[22] Hase, Mitteilungen der Deutschen Patentanwälte 1992, 23, and Mitt. 1993, 289.

results indicated that 0.1%[23] of the annual total of granted patents were involved each year in infringement proceedings. With an average patent life of around ten years, this means that only 1% of all patents ever become the subject of infringement litigation.

Moreover, at a rough estimate, only about one-third of patent infringement cases go as far as a first-instance decision. This figure varies from country to country, depending on national procedure: In Germany and France, for example, the proportions seem to be quite similar, but the picture is probably different in Italy, and certainly so in the UK. There, only about 5% of all legal actions – including those for patent infringement – lead to a first-instance decision. Of course, the statistical frequency of decisions says nothing at all about the quality and effect of proceedings before the courts. Here, too, the principle applies that a good out of court settlement is often better than a judgment.

II. Typical Issues in Infringement Proceedings

Patent infringement proceedings have certain recurrent features which provide an element of standardisation. Obviously, each case is individual, and the core issues of infringement can also open up a wide range of further civil law issues. However, most disputes revolve around two topics: validity/revocation and the extent of protection conferred by the patent. In the latter case, the key question is whether the allegedly infringing product or process actually infringes the patent by encroaching on the protected subject-matter.

From the procedural angle, discussion has been continuing for some years on the appropriate means of giving patent proprietors access to evidence held by the alleged infringer, especially with a view to proving that infringement has occurred.

1. Validity or revocation of the patent

The usual response to an infringement action is to file a counterclaim for revocation or, less commonly, an objection of nullity. The alleged infringer's legal representative has to resort to these counter-measures in order to safeguard his client's rights *lege artis*. With the system of separate first-instance proceedings for infringement and validity, the defendant will generally apply for revocation before the court with jurisdiction for such matters (in Germany, this is the Federal Patents Court). Under the "one-stop", consolidated procedure, defendants are more likely to counterclaim for revocation

---

[23] See Stauder, fn. 2, 21 (the 1% is a printing error); France 1%, see Véron, Les contentieux des brevets d'invention en Franc. Etude statistique, FNDE – ASPI, novembre 2001, 5 ; different figures in US, see Lanjouw and Schankerman, An Empirical Analysis of the Enforcement of Patent Rights in the United States, Paper prepared for the Conference on New Research on the Operation of the Patent System, October 2001, p. 2: 1.9%.

than under the "split proceedings" system, where filing separately for revocation involves considerable extra work.[24] With the latter system, a revocation action can be avoided if the parties reach a settlement after the initial infringement claim is filed. Experience has shown that claims and counterclaims for revocation are the most powerful weapons in the defendant's armoury.

In infringement proceedings, the issue of invalidity is nearly always decided before infringement *per se*, since the existence of a protective right is a logical precondition for assessing whether it has been infringed. Only in rare cases will the court refrain from examining this issue, where it is clear that no infringing act has taken place. The reason why this seldom happens is that a second-instance court may take a different view, which is problematic if the crucial initial question of the patent's validity was not examined at first instance.

Assessment for revocation and validity also requires the services of technical experts, who may be appointed by the parties or the court.

2. Extent of protection

Infringement proceedings regularly involve determining the extent of protection conferred by the patent and assessing whether the infringing subject-matter encroaches on it. Piracy, with infringement by identical goods, is a special case.

Following assessment as to validity, determining the extent of protection by interpreting the claims, with the help of the description and any drawings, is a central issue at the European level, too, where Article 69 EPC and the Protocol on Interpretation have had a harmonising effect.[25]

Expert witnesses are regularly called to give opinions on the facts. Without experts, it would scarcely be possible to explain the state of the art, determine what the ordinary skilled person would have known at the date of priority of the disputed patent,[26] and assess equivalent infringement. Here too, the experts can be appointed by parties or by the court, depending on national rules of procedure. In "one-stop" proceedings, taking infringement and revocation together, the same experts are likely to be consulted on both issues.

3. Infringing act actually committed

As a rule, the question whether the defendant has actually committed an infringing act and thereby breached the patent-holder's right to prohibit

---

[24] 44% of the German actions for infringement have been answered by a separate action for nullity; France: 81.0% in a united system; UK 92.8%; Italy 56.9%; see fn. 2.

[25] Cf. Singer/Stauder (Stauder) European Patent Convention. A commentary, 3rd ed. 2003, Carl Heymanns and Sweet & Maxwell, Art. 69 with comments, esp. note 39 et seq.

[26] The expert is giving his expert opinion on the state of the art which did exist at a date of the past! He has to be an expert in the history of the relevant technology.

others from doing certain things, is seldom asked.[27] Culpability, as a condition of liability for damages, is raised as an issue in some cases.[28]

4. Access to and preservation of evidence

In recent years, a good deal of attention has also been devoted to the question of how and to what extent the patent proprietor should be granted access to evidence held by the defendant, making it difficult or impossible for the right-holder to prove infringement. The key concept in this discussion is *saisie,* as applied in France. Practice in Europe as a whole seems to be moving towards the French model, albeit in a less rigorous form.

The English courts have come up with the "Anton Piller" or search order, a measure typical of English practice, which reconciles the patent proprietor's need to obtain evidence with the alleged infringer's right to protection from the consequences of what may be wrongful accusations. The overall situation has also improved in Germany, where the courts used to take a very restrictive line on applications for access to evidence. A recent judgment of the Federal Supreme Court,[29] accompanied by improvements in the Code of Civil Procedure, has aligned German practice with general European standards.

The toughest measure in the law of any European country is undoubtedly *saisie contrefaçon,*[30] which enables the right-holder to enter the alleged infringer's premises and seek evidence of infringement before instituting proceedings. The evidence is gathered by experts – generally patent attorneys – under the supervision of a bailiff. Orders for *saisie contrefaçon* are issued by the president of the first-instance court, without hearing the other party, and generally require no more than compliance with certain rules of procedure. The measure is too harsh and one-sided to be adopted as a general European model; however, as well as facilitating the taking and preservation of evidence, it also serves a further purpose, mentioned below, in the interests of the right-holder.

5. Further issues in the proceedings

Inevitably, a number of further legal issues also crop up in patent infringement proceedings. These include, in order of frequency: place of jurisdiction; ownership of the patent; legal responsibility (e.g. of managers) on the defendant's side; the question whether the allegedly infringing act was condoned by the grant of licences and other permissions, or allowed on the basis of exceptions such as experimental use in chemistry; and the exhaustion of rights.

---

[27] 13.7% of the German procedures; France: 6.6%.

[28] 6.4% Germany; 7.1% France.

[29] BGH of 2.5.2002, GRUR 2002, 1046 – Faxkarte –; Comment bei Tillman and Schreibauer, GRUR 2002, 1015.

[30] Véron, Saisie-contrefaçon, 1999; Treichel, Die französische Saisie-contrefaçon im europäischen Patentverletzungsprozess, GRUR Int. 2001, 690; Tornato, Beweissicherung bei Schutzrechtsverletzungen in Italien, VPP-Rundbrief 2003, 50.

These issues involve legal problems which require less specialised or strictly technical knowledge than the points outlined earlier, and can usually be decided by an ordinary court applying general principles of civil law.

III. "Europeanised" Questions

The issues relating to validity and revocation and the extent of protection, as determined by interpretation, have been unified, both in the EPC and at national level in the contracting states. The two main areas of dispute in patent infringement proceedings are therefore covered by European or at least harmonised law. One consequence of such Europeanisation is that the task of the courts has become easier, as the law they have to apply is unified, no matter whether it is European or the national law of either the country where the court has its seat or of another country, so that judges only need to familiarise themselves with one law for the whole of Europe.[31] The issues of jurisdiction and of what constitutes permissible non-infringing use have also been largely Europeanised.

In the national laws of the contracting states the definition of the exclusive rights conferred by the patent is also unified, together with a number of associated questions. In the area of sanctions, the prohibitory injunction also poses few problems, as it is granted without any need to show culpability; only the sanction of *astreinte* is different. Considerable variations are also found in levels of damages and the national procedures for fixing them.

Therefore, the biggest differences now lie in procedural law and the associated issues, such as those arising from *saisie*.

IV. Main Factors in Practice

Two aspects of patent infringement proceedings are of key practical importance. The first concerns the time factor, in view of the seriousness of the sanctions involved, which require that decisions be taken as quickly as possible. This brings us to the question of the preliminary injunction, as the toughest form of preventive action. Here, there is a conflict between urgency and technical complexity. Highly intricate content – especially in chemistry and similar fields – makes injunctive relief impossible and precludes quick proceedings.

In this area, it is often said that dealing with complex technical content requires judges with appropriate training and experience. Since the infringement courts are mainly staffed by lawyers, assisted in only some countries by technical judges, the call for experienced judges has a rather different meaning. Obviously, a judge in patent infringement proceedings must be prepared to address difficult technical matters, but he must also take a balanced, critical attitude to written or oral evidence given by experts, so as not to be dependent on their opinion or allow himself to be manipulated by them.

---

[31] Singer/Stauder (Stauder), Art. 1 and 2 EPC with comments.

The key virtue of the patent judge consists in applying his judicial abilities to the assessment of reports and experts, in order to Make the right decision.

Finally, costs are an issue of major practical importance. With the complexity of the subject-matter, retaining the services of experts, and of specialised legal practitioners in addition to patent attorneys, imposes a heavy financial burden on the parties. Measures such as taking evidence and carrying out tests and investigations on the infringing goods also involve further costs. Patent infringement proceedings therefore have to be evaluated from this angle, too, so as not to disadvantage the financially weaker party. The costs of the proceedings need to be rationalised.

D. Requirements for an Efficient Procedure

An efficient procedure requires a specialised court which can hear technically complex cases without losing sight of the time factor. The quality of the court rests on its experience in the field, i.e. on the professional knowledge of the judge. He in turn can only acquire such knowledge by dealing with sufficiently large numbers of patent cases over a considerable period. This means that patent cases, like other IP disputes, should be concentrated in a few courts; in smaller countries, only one or two courts should be given jurisdiction. Concentration makes it possible to establish a fund of expert knowledge at particular courts. It is also necessary for judges to stay at the same court for an extended period, instead of moving elsewhere after a short time. It would be make sense for the judiciary to create some form of specialised career structure, so that judges could stay within their chosen area and not have to move away for career reasons.

It is difficult to say how many cases a court would have to hear in an average year to meet the requirements for establishing a fund of specialist knowledge. This depends, *inter alia*, on the legal system of the country concerned. The smaller number of IP court cases in the UK, for example, might lead to the conclusion that a few cases is enough, but this would be mistaken: There, the judges are former barristers who are eminent practitioners in the field and already have the requisite degree of specialisation.

The soundest basis for an efficient court system consists in the familiarity of the judge with the subject-matter and the particular requirements of infringement proceedings.

The efficiency of patent infringement proceedings is further enhanced by conducting them in a manner adapted to their particular requirements. Two European examples may serve to indicate the lines along which some experts are thinking. The above-mentioned practice of *saisie* under French law – which also exists in a similar form in Belgium, Italy and Spain – is not only a means of uncovering and preserving evidence; it also has a deterrent effect on potential infringers. The speed and simplicity of the measure, and the directness of access to evidence, make it clear to the infringer that he is on dangerous ground. The measure also makes it difficult to play for time; initially, the right-holder has the upper hand. The second example comes from the Netherlands, where the summary proceedings known as *kort geding* have been developed as a quick and efficient solution which has proved popular – as evidenced by its use in obtaining cross-border injunctions – and also cheap. The court concentrates on the main issues – validity and extent of protection – and takes a quick decision.

IP infringement cases require a procedural approach which rules out the usual practice in civil litigation of playing for time and protects the interests of the right-holder by focusing attention on the main issues. Here, it would be useful to follow the lesson of English law, by ordering successful applicants for preliminary injunctions to post a substantial bond. This, as with *saisie,* makes it clear that resorting to such measures involves an element of risk.

This would also raise the question of the extent to which the parties are prepared, in view of the facts and the legal position, to accept an arbitration procedure leading to a reasonable compromise. But without the threat posed by an efficient court system, such reflections are of little value.

14
Criminal Enforcement of Intellectual Property Rights: Interaction Between Public Authorities and Private Interests

GREGOR URBAS[*]

A. Introduction

Intellectual property protection has emerged as a priority issue in the Asia–Pacific region over recent years, both in terms of international trading arrangements (e.g. China's membership of the World Trade Organisation) and as a significant area of concern for law enforcement agencies (e.g. Hong Kong's and other jurisdictions' legislative reforms directed against copyright and trade mark piracy). However, the division of labour between public and private enforcement of intellectual property not only varies considerably between countries, but is also often not clearly defined. Significant public / private sector interaction is often required at the investigation stage for the identification of pirated or counterfeit goods, and similarly for the collection and presentation of appropriate evidence in any subsequent criminal prosecution. Public law enforcement agencies may be reluctant to deal with intellectual property referrals because these are viewed as commercial disputes rather than criminal matters, and the general experience is that such investigations and prosecutions can be very expensive and often unsuccessful. A further complication is the presence or absence of restrictions against parallel importing, so that offences of infringement by unauthorised importation may turn on complex commercial market arrangements. However, where police action is undertaken, significant investigative resources including search warrants, powers of arrest, covert surveillance and even controlled deliveries may be deployed. This paper considers these issues in the light of recent experience in Australia and other countries in the region.

* This is a revised paper which was first presented at the Intellectual Property: Enforcement and Accumulation Seminar held at the Institute of European Studies (IEEM) in Macao on 27 June 2002. The author wishes to thank the seminar organisers and the IEEM.

B. Definitions and Framework

I. Intellectual Property Rights

Intellectual property rights are normally taken to encompass the following, with some divergence across countries depending on the historical origins of their legal systems:

(i)   Copyright, including "neighbouring rights" and moral rights;
(ii)   Trade marks;
(iii)   Patents / Utility models;
(iv)   Industrial designs;
(v)   Integrated circuit layouts;
(vi)   Plant breeders' rights;
(vii)   Confidential information / Trade secrets; and
(viii) Protection from unfair competition, misleading business conduct etc.

These rights may be defined and protected through legislation or under general principles developed through case law. Most countries in the Asia–Pacific region have specific legislation dealing with copyright, trade marks and patents and designs (including utility models in China, Japan and South Korea). Some have more specialised legislation dealing with topics such as integrated circuit layouts, and a few have legislative protection also for industrial or trade secrets.[1]

II. Protection of Intellectual Property Rights

Intellectual property rights are normally protected through civil and criminal infringement provisions in specific intellectual property legislation, as opposed to property offences under the general criminal law such as theft or larceny, fraud, and obtaining by deception. However, not all countries have criminal offence provisions in relation to all categories of intellectual property. In Australia, for example, such offences occur only in relation to copyright and trade mark infringement.[2] By contrast, in many Asian jurisdictions, substantial criminal penalties can also apply to patent, design and utility model infringement.[3]

---

[1] For an overview of computer crime and intellectual property offence provisions and penalties in the Asia–Pacific region: see Urbas 2001.

[2] Sections 132, 135AS, 248P, 248Q and 248QA of the *Copyright Act 1968* (Cth) provide penalties up to 5 years' imprisonment for copyright infringement, while sections 145–149 of the *Trade Marks Act 1995* (Cth) provide penalties up to to 2 years' imprisonment for false use of trade marks (see further Urbas 2000a).

[3] For example, maximum penalties of 5 years apply to patent infringement, and 3 years for design and utility model infringement: see Urbas 2001.

III. Public Enforcement

Intellectual property enforcement may involve a number of different public agencies:

(i) Customs / Border controls;
(ii) Police / Specialist public investigators;
(iii) Public prosecutors;
(iv) Courts with criminal jurisdiction and penalties (fines, imprisonment, forfeiture).

It is important, however, not to overlook the active role of many industry bodies in providing intelligence and operational support in such public enforcement activities. Operations may indeed be conducted jointly with investigators from such bodies as the Motion Picture Association (MPA),[4] the International Federation of Phonographic Industries (IFPI),[5] the Business Software Alliance (BSA)[6] or their local representative enforcement agencies. In Australia, for example, music copyright enforcement is conducted through the Music Industry Piracy Investigations (MIPI) unit of the Australian Recording Industry Association (ARIA) affiliated with IFPI.[7]

1. Arguments For Public Enforcement

In general, industry groups support a strong role for public agencies in the enforcement of intellectual property rights, based on factors including:

(i) The necessity of maintaining public order or ensuring regulation;
(ii) Protection of economic activity;
(iii) Protection of creative / cultural activity;
(iv) Increasing piracy levels;
(v) Prohibitive costs of enforcement for individual owners; and
(vi) Involvement of organised criminal groups.

The last of these has increasingly been raised in order to convince police and public prosecutors of the seriousness of the criminality associated with copyright piracy. For example, IFPI has described numerous enforcement operations in many countries which have uncovered evidence of organised, large-scale music piracy and distribution operations, sometimes linked to illegal arms or drug dealings, or conducted in tandem with smuggling of other illegal commodities across national borders. With the increasing

---

[4] See MPA anti-piracy website: http://www.mpaa.org/anti-piracy/ (accessed 20 May 2004).
[5] See IFPI website: http://www.ifpi.org/ (accessed 20 May 2004).
[6] See BSA website: http://www.bsa.org/ (accessed 20 May 2004).
[7] See ARIA website: http://www.aria.com.au/news.htm (accessed 20 May 2004). The operations of MIPI are further described in Williams 2002.

attention directed towards terrorism and its sources of funding, IFPI has also recently highlighted links between music piracy and terrorist financing.[8]

2. *Arguments Against Public Enforcement*

Public authorities are often reluctant to undertake intellectual property enforcement referrals, even when there is clear legislative foundation for them to do so. The reasons may vary from inexperience with these types of cases, to policy assessments that intellectual property matters are of low priority for police attention. The latter attitude may in turn rest upon further factors associated with intellectual property infringement:

(i)   Intellectual property infringement may be regarded as essentially commercial disputation rather than criminal activity;

(ii)   Investigations into intellectual property infringement are often complex and lengthy;

(iii) Prosecutions often have a low success rate;

(iv)   Penalties imposed upon conviction can be comparatively low;

(v)   Public authorities tend to regard other areas of criminality (e.g. drugs, violent crime) as more pressing areas of attention; and

(vi)   Other public policies such as competition and free trade agendas may appear to undermine the importance of policing intellectual property infringement.

For example, in Australia it has been suggested that police will not accept referrals for copyright and trade mark infringement matters unless substantial value and organised criminality are involved.[9]

IV. Legal Context

Depending on the legal system in each country, intellectual property rights may be enforced primarily through:

(i)   Civil action, with remedies including the award of damages, grant of injunctions, account of profits, and in some cases, delivery up or forfeiture of infringing material; or

(ii)   Criminal Prosecution, resulting in successful conviction in imprisonment and/or fines, and in some cases, forfeiture of the proceeds of crime.

However, while the civil and criminal jurisdictions are legally distinct, in practice a mixture of public and private enforcement measures is usually involved in the detection, investigation and prosecution of intellectual

---

[8] See IFPI website: http://www.ifpi.org/ (accessed 20 May 2004), particularly press item "European Commission shows 349% rise in pirate disc seizures: links with serious crime and terrorism" (26 July 2002).

[9] See IPCR 2000, at 250–251.

property infringement. In addition, intellectual property rights may also be protected through technological safeguards and business or consumer education.

In countries with stronger centralised systems of legislation, regulation and legal administration, a greater role for public authorities is to be expected. In China, for example, civil litigation in intellectual property matters is still relatively undeveloped, though this situation is changing.[10] By contrast, in Australia civil litigation is the most frequent form of intellectual property disputation, with criminal infringement prosecutions numbering only a few dozen cases per year.[11]

V. Economic Context

The information economy has become increasingly dominant over recent decades. In many countries, so-called "copyright-based" industries (involving the creation and distribution of copyright works) have overtaken more traditional industries such as mining and agriculture. For example, copyright-based industries contributed approximately A\$ 19 billion or 3.3% to Australia's Gross Domestic Product (GDP) in 1999–2000.[12] In the United States, the numbers are, of course, much greater – one estimate is that "core" copyright industries contributed over US\$ 535 billion to that country's economy in 2001.[13] Similar commercial importance attaches to the use of trade marks in relation to consumer goods, particularly on high value products such as fashion clothing and accessories, toys and games, and luxury items such as cosmetics and perfumes. These products are counterfeited in very high numbers around the world.

In some countries, intellectual property is such a substantial export sector that it takes on a more strategic aspect. For example, commenting on the Federal Appeals Court decision against the Napster file-sharing website in February 2001, Hilary Rosen of the Recording Industry Association of America (RIAA) stressed that "American intellectual property is our nation's greatest trade asset".[14] The seriousness with which the United States takes intellectual property protection is evident in its annual listings of various countries under the United States Trade Representative (USTR) "Special 301" decisions and associated watch lists.[15]

---

[10] See Clarke 1999; Sanqiang 2002.

[11] See Urbas 2000b.

[12] See Allen Consulting 2001.

[13] See Siwek 2002.

[14] "Hilary Rosen Press Conference Statement" (12 February 2001): http://www.riaa.com/news/newsletter/press2001/021201_2.asp (accessed 20 May 2004).

[15] See "Special 301" decisions on IIPA website: http://www.iipa.com/pdf/IIPA_USTR_2004_Special_301_DECISIONS_FINAL_050304.pdf (accessed 20 May 2004).

Intellectual property has also been identified as a major capital asset which determines whether companies can use the technology of their choice.[16] Indeed in some cases, intellectual property may be the principal or even sole capital asset of a business. This is particularly so in the case of businesses operating only in cyberspace, i.e. trading only or mainly through electronic or Internet commerce.[17]

VI. Policy Context

Intellectual property protection has to operate alongside various other policy priorities including:

(i)   Trade policy / International relations;
(ii) Consumer protection / Competition policy;
(iii) Demands on public enforcement resources; and
(iv) Perceptions of consumers and business regarding intellectual property piracy.

In some cases, polices designed to increase competition have been argued to weaken effective controls against copyright piracy. This has been particularly evident in countries such as Australia, where parallel importing restrictions have been relaxed in order to allow greater competition in the marketplace with the aim of reducing prices in some categories of goods, such as CDs.[18] Evidence of any significant increase in piracy following the relaxation of parallel importing restrictions has been difficult to establish.[19] Critics of these governmental reforms have also pointed out that promised price reductions have also been difficult to verify.

VII. Definitions and the TRIPS Agreement

Under the Trade-Related Aspects of Intellectual Property (TRIPS) Agreement administered by the World Trade Organisation (WTO), signatories are required to "provide for criminal procedures and penalties to be applied at least in cases of wilful trademark counterfeiting or copyright piracy on a commercial scale" (Article 61).[20]

"Pirated Copyright Goods" are defined (Art. 51, note 14) as "any goods which are copies made without the consent of the right holder or person duly authorized by the right holder in the country of production and which are made directly or indirectly from an article where the making of that copy

---

[16] See Wineburg 1991, 1.
[17] Consider companies such as Amazon.com or Yahoo! The risks of Internet commerce in the Asia–Pacific region are discussed in Smith and Urbas 2001.
[18] See IPCR 2000.
[19] See Urbas 2000b.
[20] See WTO website: http://www.wto.org/english/docs_e/legal_e/27-trips_01_e.htm (accessed 20 May 2004).

would have constituted an infringement of a copyright or a related right under the law of the country of importation."

"Counterfeit Trade Mark Goods" are defined (Art. 51, note 14) as "any goods, including packaging, bearing without authorization a trademark which is identical to the trademark validly registered in respect of such goods, or which cannot be distinguished in its essential aspects from such a trademark, and which thereby infringes the rights of the owner of the trademark in question under the law of the country of importation".

This paper follows the customary terminology in associating the term "piracy" with criminal copyright infringement, and "counterfeit" with criminal trade mark violation.

VIII. Impact of Intellectual Property Piracy

There is little doubt that intellectual property piracy has a significant impact on legitimate sales of products such as music recordings and computer software. Indeed, the increasing digitisation of information is opening up new avenues for infringers, as illustrated by the growth in music piracy associated with the digital copying of audio files. The International Federation of Phonographic Industries (IFPI) has reported that:[21]

"Music piracy poses a greater threat to the international music industry than at any other time in its history. Traffic in pirate recordings is not only proliferating worldwide – it is rapidly diversifying into new technologies and formats. Commercial pirate recordings today range from the traditional cassette to the manufactured CD, and from the CD-R disc replicated in a garage or laboratory to the audio file distributed on the internet. Adding to the threat of commercial piracy is the spread of CD burning, made possible by advances in digital copying technologies. The impact of this diversification goes far wider than the music industry – piracy stunts the growth of the information-based economy; erodes innovation and cultural creativity and increasingly impacts on the international reputations of countries that fail to protect intellectual property rights."

The impact of intellectual property piracy (and associated counterfeiting such as false labelling and/or packaging) is estimated annually by the International Intellectual Property Alliance (IIPA) in relation to five categories:

(i)   Music / Sound recordings;
(ii) Film / Motion pictures;
(iii) Business software applications;
(iv) Entertainment software; and
(v)   Books.

---

[21] International Federation of Phonographic Industries (IFPI), *Music Piracy Report* (June 2001): http://www.ifpi.org (accessed 20 May 2004); see also Grabosky and Smith 1998, especially Chapter 8.

Total losses through copyright piracy estimated by IIPA regularly exceed US $8 billion per year, and in 2003 exceeded US $10 billion. These estimates provide a basis for governmental responses, such as listing by the United States Trade Representative (USTR).[22] In addition, groups such as the Business Software Association (BSA) estimate losses and piracy trends for their industry sectors.[23]

C. Regional Piracy Levels

Estimated rates of piracy levels in the four main categories (excluding books) are reproduced in summary form below, for those countries in the Asia–Pacific region that have featured regularly in the USTR listings under 306 Monitoring, Priority Watch List and Watch List over the past six years (1998–2003).[24]

I. PR China

Piracy levels in the People's Republic of China (PR China) have been consistently high over recent years despite numerous governmental anti-piracy enforcement actions in which large numbers of infringing articles have been seized and destroyed and production operations dismantled (Figure 1). In China, criminal proceedings for copyright infringement are the norm, while civil litigation is of secondary importance.[25] It remains to be seen what effect China's accession to the World Trade Organisation (WTO) will have on piracy levels.[26]

---

[22] See "Special 301" decisions on IIPA website: http://www.iipa.com/pdf/IIPA_USTR_2004_Special_301_DECISIONS_FINAL_050304.pdf (accessed 20 May 2004).

[23] See Business Software Alliance (BSA) 2003.

[24] Some countries in the Asia–Pacific region, such as Australia and New Zealand, have not regularly appeared on the USTR listings due to comparatively lower piracy levels during the period under consideration; while some others with generally high piracy levels across the categories under consideration, such as Vietnam, are also not specifically considered due to the unavailability of statistics for some years.

[25] See Clarke 1999; Sanqiang 2002.

[26] China Daily 2002, "WTO entry boosts China's economy", at China.org (dated 18 November 2002): http://www.china.org.cn/english/49058.htm (accessed 20 May 2004). For an outline of regional membership of international intellectual property conventions, see Heath (n.d.); World Intellectual Property Organisation (WIPO), Intellectual Property Protection Treaties: http://www.wipo.int/treaties/ip/index.html (accessed 20 May 2004).

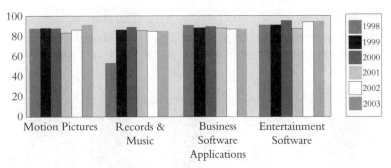

FIG. 1.   Piracy Levels (%) – PR China (1998–2003)
Source: International Intellectual Property Alliance (IIPA)

II. India

India has high levels of piracy in most categories, though music piracy appears to be at somewhat lower levels (Figure 2). It is interesting to note that high levels of software piracy persist despite amendments under the *Copyright Act 1994* (No. 38 of 1994) extending copyright protection to computer programs, and the introduction of the *Information Technology Act 2000* (No. 21 of 2000) which contains substantial penalties for specified computer-related offences.[27]

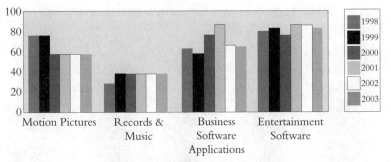

FIG 2.   Piracy Levels (%) – India (1998–2003)
Source: International Intellectual Property Alliance (IIPA)

Note: Levels for Entertainment Software in 2002 are not available (NA) so the previous year's figure has been used.

---

[27] See Carr 2000; Urbas 2001.

III. Indonesia

Indonesia appears to have very high piracy levels in all categories, with a particularly strong increase in music piracy over the period under consideration (Figure 3).

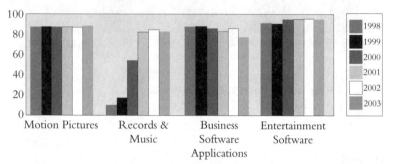

FIG 3.   **Piracy Levels (%) – Indonesia (1998–2003)**
Source: International Intellectual Property Alliance (IIPA)

Note: Levels for Business Software Applications in 1999 and Entertainment Software in 2001–2003 are not available (NA) so previous year's figures have been used.

IV. Malaysia

Malaysia appears to be experiencing high levels of piracy in all categories, though with some notable decreases in film, music and software piracy (Figure 4). Malaysia has been actively revising its technology and intellectual property laws over recent years.[28]

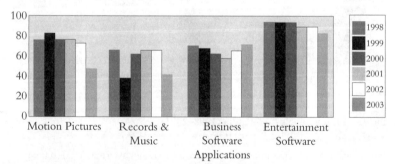

FIG 4.   **Piracy Levels (%) – Malaysia (1998–2003)**
Source: International Intellectual Property Alliance (IIPA)

Note: Levels for Entertainment Software in 2002 are not available (NA) so the previous year's figure has been used.

---

[28] See Urbas 2001.

V. Philippines

Music piracy levels in the Philippines appear to be lower than many other countries in the region, but on the increase. Piracy levels in other categories are high, particularly in entertainment software (Figure 5). This is despite the introduction of the new *Intellectual Property Code of the Philippines* (Republic Act No.8293, in force since 1 January 1998) containing substantial penalties for infringement, with increasing penalty ranges for second and subsequent offences.[29]

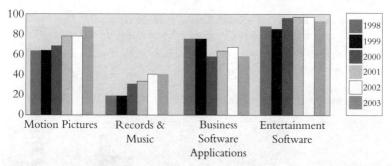

FIG 5.   **Piracy Levels (%) – Philippines (1998–2003)**
Source: International Intellectual Property Alliance (IIPA)

Note: Levels for Business Software Applications in 1999 and Entertainment Software in 2002 are not available (NA) so the previous year's figures have been used.

VI. South Korea

Overall piracy levels in South Korea are somewhat lower than in other countries in the region. This may be due to the fact that that South Korea's well-developed intellectual property laws have been consistently enforced by the Korean Intellectual Property Office (KIPO) over the period under consideration. The figures also indicate a significant recent decline in the Entertainment Software category (Figure 6 *over*).

VII. Taiwan

Piracy levels appear to be increasing in Taiwan, particularly in the categories of motion pictures and recorded music. However, as in South Korea, there is an apparent decline in Entertainment Software piracy (Figure 7 *over*).

---

[29] See Carr and Williams 2000; Urbas 2001.

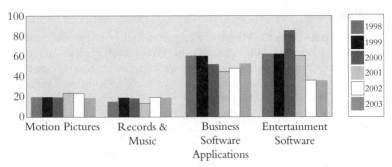

FIG 6. **Piracy Levels (%) – South Korea (1998–2003)**
Source: International Intellectual Property Alliance (IIPA)

Note: Levels for Business Software Applications in 1999 are not available (NA) so the previous year's figures have been used.

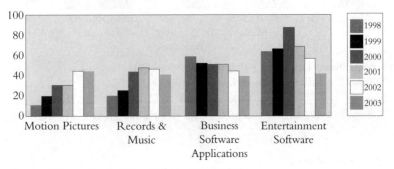

FIG 7. **Piracy Levels (%) – Taiwan (1998–2003)**
Source: International Intellectual Property Alliance (IIPA)

VIII. Thailand

Piracy levels in Business and Entertainment Software are high in Thailand, though these appear to be declining somewhat (Figure 8). A feature of Thailand's response to intellectual property infringement has been the creation of a specialised Intellectual Property Court in 1998, along with revision of its intellectual property legislation.[30]

D. Regional Enforcement Action

As noted earlier, a considerable amount of enforcement activity is conducted through co-operation between the public and private sectors, with key

---

[30] See Vechayanon 1998; Sayers 2001.

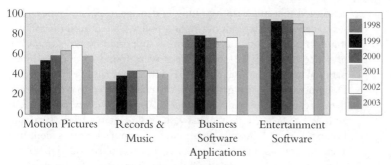

FIG 8.   **Piracy Levels (%) – Thailand (1998–2003)**
Source: International Intellectual Property Alliance (IIPA)

industry bodies taking an active role. This is observable also in the Asia-Pacific region. The following enforcement actions are highlighted in recent anti-piracy reports of the International Federation of Phonographic Industries (IFPI).[31]

I. PR China, Hong Kong SAR and Macao SAR

(i)   (2001) In the first eight months of 2001, Chinese authorities seized 29.86 million pirated VCDs and CDs. Between 1998 and 2000, China claims to have seized more than 54 million pirates CDs, most of which, it says, were seized while being smuggled into the country via Southern Chinese Waters. In August of 2001, over 16.4 million pirate VCDs were destroyed, underlining China's determination to wipe out illegal rackets and protect intellectual property rights in the region's thriving entertainment markets. The massive pulverizing, by 15 giant machines at a special ceremony at a sports centre in Guangdong province was the most significant event of its kind to date. Most of the discs were made in Hong Kong, Macao and the South East Asian region and were seized by Gongbei customs, adjacent to Macao Special Administrative Region.[32]

II. Indonesia

(i)   (January 2002) A major seizure of over one million suspected pirate discs was made when police conducted a search and seizure operation against 28 separate CD distributors at the Kota Kembang Building situated in Dalem Kaum, Bandung City in West Java. Prior to the operation police had cordoned off the building to be searched. This

---

[31] IFPI "Global anti-piracy watch": http://www.ifpi.org/site-content/antipiracy/piracy_watch_current.html (accessed 20 May 2004).

[32] IFPI "Global anti-piracy watch" no.2: http://www.ifpi.org/site-content/antipiracy/piracy_watch_02.html (accessed 20 May 2004).

action led to a street riot resulting in damage to police vehicles and several arrests. As a result of the riot, police waited until the following day, before entering the premises supported by an extra police presence. Around 80% of the discs were found to contain international and local music repertoire, and the remaining 20% movies. Documentary records gathered in the raids showed that on average, the 28 retailers were supplying over 280,000 CDs every week to East and West Java, Timor, Sulawasi, Kalimantan, Irian Jaya and Lombock areas. The suspected source of manufacture was identified as an underground plant near Jakarta airport. Police raided the plant, uncovering two concealed CD replication lines. There were no arrests and little product found at the plant as the occupants managed to flee the scene through a concealed route as the police were breaking through three sets of steel doors. At the conclusion of the raid the machinery was disabled and the warehouse sealed.[33]

(ii) (December 2001) Local police carried out a series of raids on six retail stores in a major shopping mall in Jakarta suspected of selling pirate music products. Around 50,000 pirate music products containing both local and international repertoire were seized. One shop owner was arrested on site and five others were summoned to appear for the police investigation. The next day, Indonesian state police raided a suspected underground CD replication facility at Tangerang, Jakarta. Workers at the plant resisted entry and managed to destroy a significant quantity of suspect CDs and stampers. However, over 2,000 pirate discs, infringing stampers and artwork were discovered. Documentation at the site revealed the vast majority were destined for the South East Asian marketplace. Workers at the site and the plant manager were arrested and the replication machinery was rendered inoperable.[34]

III. Malaysia

(i) (June 2001) Raids at residential premises in Penang, Malaysia uncovered a cassette manufacturing facility containing 98 recording decks and a few thousand cassettes and CDs. One Chinese male was arrested and charged with copyright offences.[35]

(ii) (July 2001) An illegal optical disc manufacturing facility located in an industrial estate in Mentakab, east of Kuala Lumpur was raided and two replication lines and a silkscreen printer located. Over 22,000

[33] IFPI "Global anti-piracy watch" no.2: http://www.ifpi.org/site-content/antipiracy/piracy_watch_02.html (accessed 20 May 2004).
[34] IFPI "Global anti-piracy watch" no.2: http://www.ifpi.org/site-content/antipiracy/piracy_watch_02.html (accessed 20 May 2004).
[35] IFPI "Global anti-piracy watch" no.1: http://www.ifpi.org/site-content/antipiracy/piracy_watch_01.html (accessed 20 May 2004).

VCDs containing international films, and nine stampers were found, along with three 750Kg bags of polycarbonate. The estimated value of the production machinery impounded on site was MYR 3.1 million (US$800,000 approx.). Two managers were arrested.[36]

(iii) (October 2001) Investigators with the Recording Industry of Malaysia raided two premises suspected of being used for a major pirate CD distribution network. Over 50,000 pirated optical discs, containing local and international music were recovered. Further investigation revealed the consortium involved had quickly restocked both premises. More raids were conducted netting a further 60,000 discs. One person was arrested.[37]

(iv) (March 2003) Personnel from the Malaysian Ministry of Domestic Trade and Consumer Affairs (MDTCA) raided a residential address suspected of being a storage facility for a notorious large-scale music piracy syndicate in March. IFPI has been targeting the manufacturing sources and supply chain network of the largest music piracy syndicate in South East Asia since 2000, resulting in several significant and notable operations including neutralisation of two licensed factories and several syndicate distribution centres, recovering over two million pirate music CDs. Following the raid, another major blow was struck when MDTCA and IFPI raiding personnel uncovered the syndicate's pre-mastering operation. Inside the premises, the team uncovered a state of the art computer system containing an extensive collection of MP3 files, remixed compilations, artwork for albums (including re-releases) and business records, as well as a vast number of inlays, sales records and other documentation relating to the syndicate's activities.[38]

(v) (March 2003) In a separate operation, MDTCA personnel carried out a raid on a two-line unlicensed replication facility that resulted in six arrests. In early 2003, the intelligence Division received non-specific information about the operation of an underground optical disc manufacturing factory active in the Klang Valley area. Following further investigation and covert surveillance to verify the information, the target address was identified. At time of entry both lines were pressing pornographic VCDs. Six people were arrested and charged under the Penal Code (in respect of the pornographic product) and Optical Disc Act for the operation of the unlicensed facility.

---

[36] IFPI "Global anti-piracy watch" no.1: http://www.ifpi.org/site-content/antipiracy/piracy_watch_01.html (accessed 20 May 2004).

[37] IFPI "Global anti-piracy watch" no.2: http://www.ifpi.org/site-content/antipiracy/piracy_watch_02.html (accessed 20 May 2004).

[38] IFPI "Global anti-piracy watch" no.4: http://www.ifpi.org/site-content/antipiracy/piracy_watch_current.html (accessed 20 May 2004).

IFPI personnel recovered evidence indicating that some personnel were previously employed by licensed factories.[39]

IV. Philippines / Singapore / Taiwan

(i)   (June / July 2001) Operation Rice was an investigation into the illegal production of back catalogue repertoire by a known entity, based in Singapore. The resulting product was being distributed as far afield as Canada and was found to have been produced at a factory in Taiwan. Raids on the Taiwan manufacturing facility uncovered masters, stampers and artwork along with customer orders and their details. The investigation spread to a number of different countries, including a suspect plant in the Philippines subsequently raided. Its records indicated that over 50,000 CDs had been produced at the facility.[40]

(ii) (2001) Authorities in the Philippines faced violent resistance from pirates during a number of raids on manufacturers or retailers of pirate product during the year. In April the Video Regulatory Board (VRB) conducted raids on retailers in the New Guadeloupe area of Metro Manila – a place notorious for the sale of pirate CDs. During the raid a violent struggle occurred and a policeman and three other traders were injured. In another operation at a similarly notorious shopping mall, traders threw teargas grenades; fortunately no one was injured. In January, Philippine authorities smashed a major CD-R piracy ring believed to be responsible for providing at least half of the pirate music and film products available in Metro Manila. Raids on nine locations involved over 500 armed police and military personnel, including sniper teams. The Philippine president also provided some of her own security people to escort IFPI operatives. The ringleader of the syndicate, a serving police officer, was apprehended. In the first-ever conviction for illegal replication by the Philippine courts, the court in Bulacan, Luzon convicted 12 pirates for illegal replication of music and video discs. The judge handed down fines totalling PhP1,200,000 (approx. US$23,000) and imprisoned the perpetrators for three months each.[41]

(iii) (August 2001) Investigations continued in Operation Rice, the major operation against the infringing production and distribution of back catalogue rock 'n' roll repertoire by a Singapore-based

[39] IFPI "Global anti-piracy watch" no.4: http://www.ifpi.org/site-content/ antipiracy/ piracy_watch_current.html (accessed 20 May 2004).

[40] IFPI "Global anti-piracy watch" no.1: http://www.ifpi.org/site-content/ antipiracy/piracy_watch_01.html (accessed 20 May 2004).

[41] IFPI "Global anti-piracy watch" no.4: http://www.ifpi.org/site-content/ antipiracy/piracy_watch_current.html (accessed 20 May 2004).

entity. Two raids in August 2001 saw Singapore police impound over 120,000 infringing discs. Master recordings and artwork were also seized, together with documents highlighting the target's involvement in the manufacture and distribution of the products throughout South East Asia. Eleven people were arrested and detained by the authorities, including those identified as being suspected of financing and managing the enterprise. The total value of the seizure was estimated to be Singapore $2.4 million (US$1.2 million).[42]

(iv)   (July 2001) After a number of pirate retailers were arrested in the Taipei night markets, information came to light regarding their suppliers and raids on suspect premises turned up a total of 130,500 pirate music CDs. Four people were arrested.[43]

(v)   (2001) Police raids on premises in Kaoshung City, Taiwan. The first raid uncovered 70,000 suspect pirate optical discs containing mainly pornographic material. Also found were illegal firearms, including Italian and German manufactured semi-automatic handguns. A second raid the following evening netted a quantity of illegal MP3 CDs and 1,500 computer software products. More illegal firearms were found and two people were arrested. A third target premises was raided and an illegal arms factory was found, housed with a CD burning laboratory. A Chinese male with a record of previous involvement in music piracy was arrested.[44]

(vi)   (2001) While a premises suspected of being a pirate disc packaging plant in Tainan City, Southern Taiwan was under prolonged observation, a lorry believed to be carrying pirate discs was seen entering and was stopped by the Southern Enforcement Unit of the Security Police. The lorry was later found to be carrying 20,000 pirated optical discs. The enforcement team then entered the premises. A packaging machine was operating and over 100,000 optical discs were found. After close examination, more than 90,000 were confirmed as being repertoire of members of IFPI Taiwan. Also recovered from the scene were around 200,000 inlays, 90,000 jewel boxes and other equipment. Five people on site and the lorry driver were arrested. A warrant for the arrest of the operator of the factory was issued. On the same date, information led to another raid, in Gueishan Shiang, Taoyuan County, North Taiwan where more

[42] IFPI "Global anti-piracy watch" no.2: http://www.ifpi.org/site-content/antipiracy/piracy_watch_02.html (accessed 20 May 2004).

[43] IFPI "Global anti-piracy watch" no.1: http://www.ifpi.org/site-content/antipiracy/piracy_watch_01.html (accessed 20 May 2004).

[44] IFPI "Global anti-piracy watch" no.1: http://www.ifpi.org/site-content/antipiracy/piracy_watch_01.html (accessed 20 May 2004).

than 80,000 discs were recovered. In total 28 warehouses and five packaging factories were hit in Taiwan in 2001.[45]

(vii) (August / November 2001) Between August and November 2001, a number of raids were made by government agencies that have had a significant impact on music pirates in Taiwan. Actions against five large-scale warehouses and two packaging centres resulted in the seizure of 500,000 pirate music CDs, the confiscation of packaging machinery and the arrest of 37 people.[46]

(viii) (December 2001) Following an October raid on a warehouse in Taipei, information was gathered regarding the existence of similar facilities in Taichung County. On 28 December, Taiwan Security Police raided four warehouses / distribution centres resulting in the seizure of over 200,000 pirate audio CDs of local and international artists. Two state-of-the-art packaging lines and related paraphernalia, along with vehicles used in distribution of product were also seized. Three Taiwanese were arrested and enquiries are continuing into the manufacturing source of the product.[47]

V. Thailand

(i) (April 2003) Thai police raided a suspected optical disc plant in Bangkok. Two machines in full operation were found producing counterfeit music CDs of works by popular international artists. Police seized thousands of discs, polycarbonate and stampers containing additional music titles. The plant operator was arrested and the machinery confiscated. Thailand has been earmarked as an IFPI top ten piracy country.[48]

E.   Conclusion – Strengths and Weaknesses of Public Intellectual Property Enforcement

Public enforcement of intellectual property rights can be highly effective if sufficient priority, resources and expertise are directed to the problem. An active role by customs, police and prosecution authorities serves to highlight the illegality of pirate or counterfeit activities, and can help to link investigations to other serious and organised crime activity. Moreover,

---

[45] IFPI "Global anti-piracy watch" no.2: http://www.ifpi.org/site-content/antipiracy/piracy_watch_02.html (accessed 20 May 2004).

[46] IFPI "Global anti-piracy watch" no.2: http://www.ifpi.org/site-content/antipiracy/piracy_watch_02.html (accessed 20 May 2004).

[47] IFPI "Global anti-piracy watch" no.2: http://www.ifpi.org/site-content/antipiracy/piracy_watch_02.html (accessed 20 May 2004).

[48] IFPI "Global anti-piracy watch" no.4: http://www.ifpi.org/site-content/antipiracy/piracy_watch_current.html (accessed 20 May 2004).

enforcement by public authorities spreads the burden of enforcement across the community, rather than leaving it solely up to intellectual property owners to protect their rights.

On the other hand, intellectual property enforcement can be low priority against terrorism, drugs, and traditional criminal activities. Police also often lack expertise in detecting or investigating infringing product, thus needing the active involvement of industry investigators to provide intelligence and technical assistance. Moreover, even if properly investigated, intellectual property infringements can be very difficult and expensive cases to prosecute to a criminal standard. It may also be argued that undue reliance on public authorities may reduce the incentive for industry to invest in its own intellectual property protection measures, such as technological protection.

Nonetheless, the clear pattern emerging in many parts of the world, including the Asia–Pacific region, is for continuing and strengthened interaction between public authorities and private interests, particularly industry bodies representing copyright owners in the film, music and software industries. The enforcement operations of police in conjunction with industry groups such as the International Federation of Phonographic Industries (IFPI) clearly illustrate the effectiveness of such public / private interaction.

F. References

Allen Consulting Group 2001, *The Economic Contribution of Australia's Copyright Industries*, Australian Copyright Council and Centre for Copyright Studies: http://www.copyright.org.au/PDF/Books/BCEPv03.pdf (accessed 20 May 2004).

Business Software Alliance (BSA) 2003, *Eighth Annual BSA Global Software Piracy Study*: http://global.bsa.org/globalstudy/2003_GSPS.pdf (accessed 20 May 2004).

Carr, I. 2000, "India joins the cyber-race: Information Technology Act 2000", *International Technology Law Review*, vol. 4, 121–30.

Carr, I. and Williams, K.S. 2000, "Securing the e-commerce environment: Enforcement measures and penalty levels in the computer misuse legislation of Britain, Malaysia and Singapore", *Computer Law and Security Report*, vol. 16, no. 5, 295–310.

Clarke, D. 1999, "Private enforcement of intellectual property rights in China", in: *Intellectual Property Rights in China: Evolving Business and Legal Frameworks*, vol. 10, no. 2, National Bureau of Research Analysis, Seattle.

Grabosky, P.N. and Smith, R.G. 1998, *Crime in the Digital Age: Controlling Telecommunications and Cyberspace Illegalities*, Transaction Publishers/ Federation Press, New Brunswick, New Jersey.

Heath, C. (n.d.), *Intellectual Property Rights in Asia: Projects, Programmes and Developments*, Max Planck Institute for Foreign and International Patent, Copyright and Competition Law, Munich, Germany: http://www. intellecprop.mpg.de/Online-Publikationen/Heath-Ipeaover.htm (accessed 20 May 2004).

Intellectual Property and Competition Review (IPCR) 2000, *Review of Intellectual Property Legislation under the Competition Principles Agreement*, Australian Government: http://ipcr.gov.au (accessed 20 May 2004).

International Federation of Phonographic Industries (IFPI), *Music Piracy, Organised Crime and Terrorism* (3rd edition, 2001): http://www.ifpi.org (accessed 20 May 2004).

International Intellectual Property Alliance (IIPA): http://www.IIPA.com (accessed 20 May 2004).

Sanqiang, Q. 2002, *Copyright in China*, Foreign Languages Press, Beijing.

Sayers, K. 2001, "Taming the Tiger: Towards a new intellectual property regime in Thailand", *Law Asia Journal* [2000/2001], 89–112.

Siwek, S.E. 2002, *Copyright Industries in the United States: 2002 Report*: http://www.iipa.com/pdf/2002_SIWEK_FULL.pdf (accessed 20 May 2004).

Smith, R.G. and Urbas, G. 2001, "Controlling Fraud on the Internet: A CAPA Perspective", Report for the Confederation of Australian and Pacific Accountants), *Research and Public Policy Series* No. 39, Australian Institute of Criminology, Canberra; available at CAPA website: http://www.capa.com.my (accessed 20 May 2004).

Urbas, G. 2000a, "Public Enforcement of Intellectual Property Rights", *Trends & Issues* No.177, Australian Institute of Criminology: available at http://www.aic.gov.au (accessed 20 May 2004).

Urbas, G. 2000b, "Parallel Importing and CD Piracy", in: *Review of Intellectual Property Legislation under the Competition Principles Agreement*, Intellectual Property & Competition Review (IPCR) Committee: available at http://ipcr.gov.au/ipcr (accessed 20 May 2004).

Urbas, G. 2001, "Cybercrime Legislation in the Asia–Pacific Region", *First Asia Cybercrime Summit*, HK University: available at http://www.aic.gov.au (accessed 20 May 2004).

Vechayanon, W. 1998, "Intellectual property rights enforcement and the role of Intellectual Property Court in Thailand", in *First Anniversary: The Central Intellectual Property and International Trade Court*, Thailand.

Williams, M. 2002, "Effective IP Enforcement: Strategic approaches to countering software piracy", *Computers and the Law: Journal for the Australian and New Zealand Societies for Computers and the Law*, March 2000, 32–38.

Wineburg, A. 1991, "Protecting the Capital Asset of the 1990s – Intellectual Property", in: Wineburg, A. (ed.), *Intellectual Property Protection in Asia*, Butterworth Legal Publishers, New Hampshire.

15
Recent Developments in Judicial Protection for Intellectual Property in China

LU GUOQIANG

A. In General

Judicial protection for intellectual property in China is growing and developing hand-in-hand with ongoing reforms and an increasingly open-door policy. Since the enactment and implementation of the Economic Contract Act of the People's Republic of China in December 1981, the People's courts have begun to accept cases relating to intellectual property. Over the past 20 years and especially in the past ten years, China's judges have made significant advances in the judicial protection of intellectual property.

From 1990 to 2000, China's courts on different levels have accepted 36,504 intellectual property disputes and concluded all but around 400 of these. Of these cases:

- 8 % related to trade mark disputes;
- 26% related to patent disputes;
- 12% related to copyright disputes;
- 16 % related to unfair competition and other IP disputes;
- 38% related to technology contract disputes.

Intellectual property cases differ from other cases requiring a high level of judicial professionalism as the issues are often complex and overseas influences considerable. Some notable foreign plaintiffs in recent years have included Walt Disney, Unilever and LEGO.

Some general trends in litigation in China have become apparent. First, the number of cases coming before the courts is increasing each year. Second, in those areas of the economy where culture and technology is relatively advanced, the number of intellectual property disputes is increasing and the percentage of patent and copyright cases is relatively high. Third, most intellectual property disputes relate to infringement of IP rights. Fourth, with the development of hi-tech industries such as information technology and biotechnology, new issues are constantly emerging. Fifth, cases involving foreign companies constitute a high percentage of all IP cases.

- Promulgation of Judicial Interpretations

In order to apply intellectual property and related procedural laws accurately and consistently, the Supreme People's Court has promulgated more than 30 judicial interpretations relating to IP, based on the trial outcomes of various intellectual property cases heard by all levels of the People's courts. Such judicial interpretations establish important guidelines in the application of law and procedures in intellectual property cases and ensure some consistency for the parties. The interpretations also aid courts when trying to resolve previously untried issues.

• Establishment of IP Tribunals

One of the key achievements has been the establishment by the Supreme Court of an intellectual property trial division, which oversees all IP trials in China. In August 1993, under the instruction of the Supreme Court, the Beijing People's Higher Court and Intermediate Court also set up an intellectual property trial division. The People's Higher Courts in Guangdong and Shanghai as well as a number of Intermediate Courts quickly followed suit. Several People's courts at the lowest level now also have special intellectual property trial divisions. Other courts have appointed panels of three judges for hearing intellectual property dispute cases.

• Promotion of the Courts' jurisdiction in IP cases and Increasing Social Awareness

The Supreme People's Court and other People's courts have undertaken several initiatives to promote the courts' jurisdiction over intellectual property cases. The Supreme Court has held two press conferences to introduce China's intellectual property trial system and report on several influential cases. In June 1998, CCTV broadcast live a copyright infringement case involving ten major studios, eliciting a strong response domestically and abroad. Other initiatives to promote the courts' work have been undertaken in the media with the aim of increasing public awareness of the need to protect IP.

B. Recent Developments

In order to comply with demands for intellectual property protection and standards resulting from WTO accession, China's legal system is in the process of revising its intellectual property laws. The amended Patent Act was formally implemented on 1 July 2001. The Copyright Act and the Trade Mark Act have recently been revised and were implemented on 27 October 2001 and 1 December 2001 respectively. At the same time Chinese courts have formulated a series of judicial interpretations. The main areas of recent development for China's intellectual property rights judicial protection are:

• Protection for Internet Copyright

Following the rapid development of dissemination of information over the internet, the number of disputed cases involving internet copyright has increased. Taking the Beijing City Intermediate Court as an example, during the two-year period 1999–2000, of the 24 internet dispute cases involving IP rights, 71% of these related to copyright. While copyright legislation was enacted early on in the course of development of an IPR legislative framework, it has been difficult to apply international standards to deal with protection of internet copyright. In order to deal with this new problem, on 22 November 2000 the Supreme People's Court formally issued the "Interpretations on Several Questions Concerning the Application of Law to Dispute Cases Involving Computer Internet Copyright". The Interpretations provide a legal overview for the correct application of existing copyright law to internet disputes. The most important aspects of the Interpretations deal with the jurisdiction of the Courts in internet dispute cases, the copyrighting of digital works, re-publication of copyright works on the internet, the legal responsibility of internet service providers (ISPs), remedies for copyright infringement on the internet, and determination of the level of civil liability, e.g., the calculation of damages.

As far as copyright of digital works is concerned, the Interpretations stipulate that when works are disseminated to the public over the internet, the methods of use of such digital works is covered under the Copyright Act.

As far as the legal responsibility of internet servers is concerned, the Interpretations state that if ISPs infringe on copyrights through internet use, or if they employ the internet to aid others in carrying out an infringing activity, then the courts may invoke copyright law and find collective responsibility for the infringement.

Should ISPs become aware of internet users using the internet to infringe the copyrights of others, or where copyright holders issue a clear warning (with accompanying evidence of ownership of copyright) to the ISP and the ISP does not remove the infringing content, then the courts shall impose collective responsibility on the ISP and the internet users.

If a copyright owner demands from an ISP providing a content service, information on infringing persons and if such information is withheld/refused for no proper reason, then the courts may find the ISP liable for infringement.

However, if a copyright holder discovers infringing information, issues a warning to the ISP and then demands information on the infringer without providing any corroborating identification of his own, then the ISP need not comply with the copyright holder's demands. If a copyright holder does, however, produce corroborating identification and the ISP still takes no action, the copyright holder may apply to the court for an order requiring the ISP to provide the information.

An alleged infringer may not sue an ISP for breach of contract over the removal of infringing content if the ISP removed such content based on a request from the copyright holder supported by evidence. A copyright holder may be liable for damage caused to an alleged infringer for such removal if the claim is subsequently not proved.

- Application of Injunctions

In compliance with its obligations under the TRIPs Agreement, China has introduced preliminary injunctions into its Patent Act and similar amendments to incorporate these are proposed for the Trade Mark and Copyright Acts.

As drafted in the Patent Act, injunctions may be granted to preclude actual or threatened conduct and may be used to preserve evidence. Accordingly, they are likely to be a very useful tool for IPR owners who previously could not control imminent infringement or preserve evidence or property before or during proceedings.

The Supreme People's Court has formulated the Several Rules Concerning the Application of Laws Regarding Stopping the Infringement of Patent Rights before Litigation on 5 June 2001 to guide courts in issuing injunctions. If the case for an injunction is proved by appropriate evidence and the applicant posting a bond, then the Court must issue the injunction. The injuncted party cannot post a "counter-bond" as a means for opposing enforcement of the injunction. The applicant will bear legal liability if it is subsequently proven, e.g., during trial, that the injunction was not warranted.

The regulations concerning injunctions within China's Patent Act similarly apply to the preservation of evidence where evidence of infringement may be destroyed or acquisition of such evidence is difficult or impossible without the order.

- Revised Patent Act and Rules

The Supreme People's Court has promulgated the Several Rules concerning the Application of Law When Trying Patent Cases on 19 June 2001. The rules apply to the application of the revised Patent Act. The questions of grounds for action, jurisdiction, compensation and limitation periods have been given detailed analysis in these Rules. It also includes several clear regulations concerning the new infringement provision in the revised Patent Act that includes offers for sale.

- The New Judicial Interpretation of the Trade Mark Act

In order to protect the legitimate rights and interests of trade mark registrants and other interested parties, such as licensees, the Interpretation of the Issues Relating to Application of Law to Preliminary Injunction of Infringement of Exclusive Right to Use Registered Trade Marks and to Evidence Preservation was issued by the Supreme People's Court on 25 December 2001. There are 17 sections in this Interpretation, which provides the concrete support for the courts to apply the preliminary injunction provisions promulgated in the Trade Mark Act and also provides powerful judicial guarantees to strengthen the protection of the exclusive right to use a registered trade mark.

A trade mark registrant and/or an interested party ('the applicant') may file an application with the People's Court requesting a preliminary injunction against infringement of the exclusive right to use a registered trade mark or an evidence preservation order.

Interested parties who may file an application include licensees of a registered trade mark and lawful heirs of the property right in a registered trade mark. An exclusive licensee may file the application with the People's Court alone; a sole exclusive licensee may only file the application on condition that the trade mark registrant forgoes his right to file the application.

When filing the application for preliminary injunction against the infringement of an exclusive right to use a trade mark, the applicant shall submit proof of the right, evidence attesting that the respondent is infringing or will imminently infringe the exclusive right to use the registered trade mark and also provide a guarantee against damage caused to the respondent in the event the injunction is subsequently overturned.

After the application is accepted by the People's Court and upon examination meeting the requirement of the relevant laws and regulations, the People's Court shall make an adjudication in writing within 48 hours and shall promptly notify the respondent of this adjudication within no more than five days from the date the adjudication was made. Any interested party who is not satisfied with the adjudication may make an application for reconsideration within ten days from the date of receipt of the adjudication.

If the applicant does not institute legal proceedings within 15 days after the People's Court issues a preliminary injunction or evidence preservation order, the People's Court shall cancel the order. If applicant does not institute legal proceedings or an unjustified application causes injury to the respondent, the respondent may institute legal proceedings in the People's Court requesting the applicant to pay compensation.

• Internet Domain Name Cases

Over the past two years, the number of civil disputes over domain names has steadily increased. These kinds of cases primarily involve either the registration of another party's well-known trade name or trade mark as a domain name or the registration of a domain name with the intention to sell it to the rightful owner and thus obtain an unfair advantage. The problem of how to resolve such cases and how to effectively apply the law has been tackled by the Supreme People's Court which drew on the unified experience of dealing with these cases at all levels of courts throughout the country. The Supreme People's Court formulated the "Interpretation of several questions concerning the adjudication of civil cases involving Internet domain names" on 26 June 2000.

When dealing with such cases of registration and/or use of domain names constituting infringement of trade mark or trade name rights or unfair competition, the courts should consider:

(1) Whether the rights and interests that the plaintiff has sought protection for are legal and effective;

(2) Whether the registered domain name or its major part constitutes a copy, imitation, translation or transliteration of the well-known trade mark of the plaintiff; or is the same as or similar to the registered trade mark or domain name of the plaintiff. Similarity must be judged according to whether it is likely to cause confusion amongst the relevant public;

(3) Whether the defendant both does not enjoy any other priority rights with regard to the domain name or its major part and does not have proper reasons to register or use the domain name;

(4) Whether there was bad faith with regard to the registration and use of the domain name by the defendant.

A finding of bad faith may be made if the courts believe that the defendant's behaviour falls into 1 of 4 categories:

(1) If a well-known trade mark has been registered as a domain name for the purposes of trade.

(2) If there existed the intention to sell, rent or sell back the domain name and thereby obtain an unfair advantage.

(3) If after having registered the domain name the registrant did not use it himself, but intentionally prevented the right holder from registering his trade mark name as a domain name.

(4) If for the purpose of trade the domain name used or registered is identical or similar to that of a registered trade mark holder and could thus create confusion about the products of the rights holder or mislead internet users to its website or other websites.

If there is other evidence to prove the defendant's bad faith, then the People's Court must act also accordingly.

By the end of March 2000, the Beijing and Shanghai courts have handled over 40 domain name disputes and reached verdicts on some of these. For example:

On 20 June 2000, Beijing City No. 2 Intermediate People's Court heard a case brought by Swedish Company Ikea against Beijing Internet Information Company Ltd (Cinet) claiming that the registration of the domain name "ikea.com.cn" constituted unfair competition. The court ruled that the "ikea.com.cn" domain name was not valid and ordered its use to cease within 10 days of the hearing. The court ruled that the appellant's "Ikea" trade mark ought to be recognised as a well-known trade mark and therefore that the defendant's behaviour constituted infringement of a trade mark and unfair competition. This case is significant in that it is the first case in the mainland where the courts recognised the right of a well-known trade mark. After the decision of the Beijing No. 2 Intermediate People's Court in this case, Cinet appealed to Beijing's Higher People's Court which rendered its final decision in November 2001. The appeal court upheld that the appellant's registration of ikea.com.cn constituted an act of unfair competition, but declined to recognise Ikea's trade mark as well-known because there was a lack of evidence to support "Ikea" as a distinguished brand at the time the appellant registered "ikea.com.cn". According to the relevant Chinese trade mark laws and regulations, the appellant's registration of the domain name did constitute unfair competition, but did not infringe the exclusive right to the use of a registered trade mark.

Shanghai's No. 2 Intermediate People's Court heard another case brought by Shanghai News Portal against Dream Multimedia Network Development Centre, Jinan, Shandong province. The court ruled that the plaintiff was the owner of eastday.com.cn and eastday.com. The defendant's registration of "eastdays.com.cn" and "eastdays.com" which was confusingly similar to the plaintiff's and the unauthorised use of the same net page design and link logo as those of the seven channels in plaintiff's website had resulted in confusion amongst ordinary users of the internet. Therefore it was held that Dream Multimedia actions amounted to unfair competition. It was ordered to cease using "eastdays.com.cn" and "eastdays.com" domain name, to pay the Shanghai News portal RMB 300,000 and to apologise for the infringement publicly through the media, including Xin Min Evening News.

On 9 October 2000, Shanghai City's No. 2 Intermediate People's Court heard a case brought by the U.S. company Procter & Gamble against Shanghai Chensi Ability Technology Development Company Limited. The court ruled that the defendant's registered domain name "Safeguard" was invalid, ordered an immediate end to its use and also ruled that the domain name be revoked within 15 days of the judgement. The court explained that the appellant's registered trade mark "Safeguard" enjoyed its reputation as a result of the fact that the general public was familiar with it as a registered trade mark. The degree to which the appellant's registered trade mark "Safeguard" was considered to be well-known and to have made an impression on consumers was deemed sufficient to prevent the defendant's domain name registration "safeguard.com.cn." from being a valid domain name and therefore any use of the domain name "safeguard.com.cn" constituted unfair competition. The defendant appealed. The Shanghai Supreme Court reached the final decision on 5 July 2001, dismissing the appeal and upholding the decision of the lower court. Furthermore, the court held that the trade mark "Safeguard" is a famous trade mark. This decision is the first final decision in respect of determination of a trade mark as well-known by courts.

• Judicial Review of Administrative Decisions

Establishing a modern judicial system is an important aspect for ensuring that all WTO provisions and regulations are implemented. The TRIPS Agreement clearly states that all administrative decisions made in the process of obtaining or maintaining intellectual property rights can be subject judicial or quasi-judicial review.

In China, judicial review refers to the judicial authority's examination of the actions of other government organisations, correction of the administrative body's behaviour through judicial remedies and provision of remedies to compensate entities or persons for their loss of rights or profit caused by administrative actions.

Before the Patent Act was revised, all grants, invalidations or renewals for utility designs and design patents were subject to final and binding administrative ruling. There was no right to appeal to the courts. The main reason for this is historical – when the Patent Act was first enacted, there existed difficulties in resolving patent disputes because the Administrative Procedural Law had not been promulgated. Additionally, revenues obtained from design patents and utility models per se were low and the issues involved were often not complicated. Judicial review of administrative decisions in relation to invention patents has always been available. The revised Patent Act now extends this to utility models and design patents.

The revised Trade Mark Act stipulates that administrative decisions in relation to trade marks will now also enjoy a right of appeal to the courts.

• The Application of WTO Regulations in Chinese Courts

One difficult question now faced by courts in China is how to apply the various WTO agreements. There are currently two main views held by academics:

The first view argues that the Courts may apply WTO agreements directly in deciding cases. The reason for this is that when China's legislature ratifies or enters into international treaties, this is a legitimate interpretation. Ratifying or entering into international treaties that are not the same as domestic legal regulations is also a form of revision and reinforcement. When China's participation in such international treaties becomes valid, it can begin to amalgamate them into its own domestic laws. When the WTO agreement and domestic laws conflict, the courts must allow the WTO regulations to take precedence.

The second view argues that since the WTO agreements are not the same in substance as most other international treaties, they are not directly applicable in domestic courts.

The Supreme People's Court has stated that once China has acceded to the World Trade Organisation, we must grant reciprocal rights to WTO members, and guarantee equal rights. Furthermore the People's Courts must understand and become familiar with the regulations of the World Trade Organisation. When dealing with cases involving foreign parties and the question of how to apply China's laws within the WTO regulations, the Supreme People's Court should issue corresponding regulations.

China's courts have achieved a great deal in increasing the enforcement and protection of intellectual property rights. In addition, great strides have been made in assessing damages and other penalties for infringement. In general, it can be said that China has made many efforts to comply with its

WTO obligations in the area of the judicial protection of intellectual property rights judicial protection under the TRIPs agreement. There is reason to believe that once China has acceded to the World Trade Organisation, the judicial protection for intellectual property rights in China will have taken a step to being strengthened and perfected.

16
The Enforcement of Intellectual Property Rights in Hong Kong

GABRIELA KENNEDY AND HENRY WHEARE

A. Introduction

Hong Kong's dramatic economic growth during the past 30 years has been matched by the development of an increasingly extensive and effective legal regime for the protection of intellectual property. The handover of Hong Kong to China has seen further improvements in this system.

A decade ago, Hong Kong used to be perceived as one of the world's counterfeiting black spots. In recent years this perception has changed largely due to the enactment of new intellectual property laws and consistent and thorough campaigns led by the Hong Kong Customs and Excise Department.

B. Intellectual Property Laws in Hong Kong

A member of the World Trade Organisation (WTO), Hong Kong has a sophisticated set of intellectual property laws which meet the standards set by the WTO Agreement in the Trade Related Aspects of Intellectual Property Rights (TRIPS) Agreement. The Basic Law of Hong Kong also provides in Arts. 139 and 140 that legal protection should be given to intellectual property rights in Hong Kong.

Although Hong Kong was returned to China in 1997, it retains an independent legal system. Hong Kong has independent legislation dealing with each of copyright, trade marks, patents and registered designs.[1]

C. Detection and Investigation of Infringements

I. Discovering Infringements – The First Steps

There are different ways in which a proprietor of an intellectual property right may become aware of an infringement of its rights in Hong Kong. These include:

---

[1] For a detailed discussion of the intellectual property regime in Hong Kong, see "*Intellectual Property Law in Asia*", Kluwer Law International, Heath Christopher ed 2003 pp 117–151.

(1) customer complaints about the quality of goods which, on investigation, turn out to be fake products;
(2) staff or business associates spotting fake products in the market; or,
(3) private investigators contacting the proprietor informing them of possible fake products on the market.

Having identified an infringement, it is important to find out as much information as possible concerning the infringement.

II. Private Investigators

If the information has come from a private investigator in the form of a "sighting report", the private investigators will either offer to provide further details concerning the infringement upon payment of a sighting fee or suggest a follow-up investigation to obtain more information. Sighting reports can be a valuable method of gaining information about counterfeit products, however, care must be taken not to pay too much for the information provided or to conduct too many investigations into what may be small-scale infringements.

No matter how the information has come to hand, private investigators are an essential tool to be used to conduct detailed investigations into potential infringements which have been identified either by sighting reports or the methods discussed above. This is not only because they will have developed appropriate cover stories and trading fronts over time, but also because in the event that the matter becomes litigious it is best that independent evidence can be given concerning the infringement.

III. Investigation – The Next Step

Almost all counterfeiters in Hong Kong will manufacture their infringing products in China. Therefore, while one of the main goals of any investigation is to identify the source of the products, investigations in Hong Kong should also concentrate on trying to identify:

(1) the main person or people behind the infringement;
(2) the markets into which the products are being sold; and,
(3) any assets of the infringers which may be attached against which court orders may be enforced.

The final point is very important. As it may not be possible to stop the actual production of infringing goods without taking action in China, the goal of taking action in Hong Kong must be to make it economically unjustifiable to use Hong Kong as a transit point for fake products. Any serious action will seek damages and payment of the court costs of the intellectual property right holder.

Investigators should not only provide details of the types of infringements that have been found but also provide asset checks as part of their investigations. At the basic level it is possible to conduct a company search to locate the infringer's office address as well as to ascertain the names and addresses of the company's directors. This information can be used to conduct land office searches to find out whether the infringers hold any real property in Hong Kong. In addition, investigators should attempt to ascertain which banks the infringers use, so that enforcement action can be taken against their bank accounts where necessary. Nowadays, many agents may provide a credit search report of the infringer with detailed information on its assets. Such credit search can be conducted against a Hong Kong company, a PRC company or an international company outside Hong Kong. The prices are different depending on the location of the infringer as well as the urgency of the request.

Investigators will usually visit infringers on the pretext of being business-men interested in purchasing the fake products. They will often do this after first establishing contact from a front company overseas. It is, however, important that the investigators do not engage in any illegal activities, such as breaking into premises, as this can seriously taint the evidence to be given in court.

D. Enforcing IP Rights in Hong Kong

Having obtained evidence concerning possible infringements, the next step is to take enforcement action. Enforcement of intellectual property rights in Hong Kong is generally effected by bringing civil actions for infringement in the High Court of Hong Kong.

In the case of trade mark and copyright infringement as well as false trade description, the Customs and Excise Department has the power to take criminal action against infringers. This power is not limited to actions at bor-der checkpoints. Customs and Excise regularly conducts raids on factories and premises all over Hong Kong.

Before considering the civil action process, the criminal action process is discussed.

I. Customs and Excise – Criminal Actions

Customs and Excise have powers under the Trade Descriptions Ordinance, the Copyright Ordinance and the Copyright Piracy Ordinance to search premises, seize goods and arrest and prosecute offenders in possession of infringing goods for the purpose of trade. Penalties for offences committed under the Trade Descriptions Ordinance and Copyright Ordinance can include fines of up to HK$500,000 and imprisonment for up to five years. Penalties for offences committed under the Copyright Ordinance can include fines of up to HK$50,000 or HK$1,000 for each infringing copy and imprisonment for up to four years. Penalties for offences which involve providing machines to make infringing copies can be up to HK$500,000 and

8 years imprisonment. The fines and penalties available under the Copyright Piracy Ordinance are higher, they range from HK$500,000 to HK$2,000,000 and imprisonment from 2 to 7 years.

The Customs and Excise Department also takes actions on its own initiative against infringers without the need of a formal complaint from rights owners. It will also take action where other law enforcement bodies, such as the police or the Independent Commission Against Corruption ("ICAC") have uncovered infringements during the course of their investigations.

If the formal complaint route is chosen, the procedure for bringing a matter to the attention of Customs and Excise is to contact the Intellectual Property Investigation Bureau of Customs and Excise and provide them with evidence of counterfeiting activities and of the rights which are being infringed.

Customs and Excise has complete discretion as to whether to take action and it is generally only in very clear instances of counterfeiting and when it is considered that the action will result in a successful prosecution that they will decide to take action. Customs and Excise will also consider the willingness of the rights holder to assist Customs and Excise in prosecuting the case.

The rights holder is required to provide a statement to Customs and Excise confirming the products are fake. In the case of copyright infringement, the rights owner also needs to provide an affidavit confirming the ownership and subsistence of copyright.

Customs and Excise places highest priority on fake products which may be harmful to public health, such as fake pharmaceuticals or food products. Quite high on the Customs and Excise's list are fake CDs, VCDs and DVDs partly because of the international attention that this problem has attracted.

The most noticeable difference between enforcement action through the civil courts and criminal actions is the time factor. Owing to the limited resources of Customs and Excise and because they must investigate the matter themselves, the procedure can take considerably longer than civil proceedings. For this reason most companies tend to favour civil proceedings as relief can be obtained far more quickly. In favour of Customs and Excise is the cost, in that the Government pays the bill as opposed to the rights owner. Added to this is the deterrent effect of a criminal prosecution. It is not uncommon however for a proprietor of intellectual property rights who has used Customs and Excise to follow up with civil proceedings in order to obtain damages and civil injunctions against the offenders.

Under the Trade Descriptions Ordinance and the Copyright Ordinance it is also possible as part of civil proceedings, to seek an order from the court that compels Customs and Excise to seize products entering or exiting Hong Kong and which infringe trade mark or copyright rights. When seeking such an order, the right owner may be required to put up security for damages caused by the order.

II. Civil Actions

Actions may be brought in Hong Kong to stop trade mark, copyright, registered design, patent and integrated circuit infringements under relevant Hong Kong intellectual property laws, namely, the Trade Mark Ordinance, the Copyright Ordinance, the Registered Designs Ordinance, the Patents Ordinance and the Integrated Circuits (Layout Design) Topography Ordinance respectively.

Where there is infringement of an unregistered trade mark, trade name and/or the get-up of products or business, it may be possible to bring an action for passing off under common law principles.

The essential characteristics in an action for passing off were identified by Lord Diplock in the landmark decision of *Erven Warnink BV v J Townend & Sons (Hull) Limited* [1979] AC 731 as: "a misrepresentation made by a trader in the course of his or her trade to the trader's prospective customers or the ultimate consumers of goods or services supplied by the trader that is calculated to injure the business or goodwill of another trader and which causes actual damages to a business or goodwill of the trader by whom the action is brought or will probably do so."

Goodwill, misrepresentation and damages have been described as the "classical trinity" in an action for passing off. The plaintiff needs to show the existence of goodwill or reputation associated with the distinctive names, marks, signs, or get-up used and relied on in the business. Goodwill is attached to the business and it includes every positive advantage acquired or arising out of the business. It is generally necessary to establish widespread use and reputation in Hong Kong, although reputation gained overseas "spilling over" into Hong Kong has been held to be sufficient.

Misrepresentation by the defendant must be capable of causing confusion to the ultimate consumers of the goods or services in question who would be led to believe that the defendant's goods or services are those of the plaintiff's or are associated with those of the plaintiff or authorised by the plaintiff.

The plaintiff should also be able to show that he has suffered damage as a result of the defendant's misrepresentation. The plaintiff can claim damages which represent the loss suffered, including compensation for lost business and lost goodwill. Where there is a market for the goods or services, damages may be based on the plaintiff's market price. Alternatively, the plaintiff can seek an account of profits from the defendant which represents the gain to the defendant through the use of the plaintiff's goodwill or reputation.

III. Remedies Available

The main remedies available for infringement of intellectual property rights in Hong Kong include an injunction restraining future infringement and compensation for past infringements (which can be ordered either in the form of damages or an account of profits).

IV. Procedures for Taking Actions

Most intellectual property cases are traditionally commenced in the High Court of Hong Kong which can accept claims of an unlimited amount. However, on 2 December 2003 the civil jurisdiction limit of the District Court was increased to HK$1 million. Accordingly, in cases where it may be difficult to obtain summary judgment and damages are likely to be less than HK$1 million, rights owners may consider it worthwhile to initiate proceedings in the District Court where cases are heard more quickly and where solicitors have rights of audience and the costs of proceedings are lower.

The basic steps and chronology when taking civil actions are as follows:

(1) a) Application for interlocutory relief and/or
     b) Letter before action
(2) Issue of Writ by the Plaintiff
(3) Filing of Statement of Claim by Plaintiff
(4) If appropriate, Judgment in Default of Defence
(5) If appropriate, Summary Judgment
(6) Filing of Defence (and counterclaim) by the Defendant
(7) Filing of Reply (and defence to counterclaim) by the Plaintiff
(8) Discovery of documents
(9) Exchange of Witness Statements
(10) Trial of the Action
(11) Appeal (if any).
(12) Assessment of damages
(13) Taxation (assessment) of costs
(14) Enforcement of Judgments and Orders

Other applications may be made by either party during the course of the action, such as for amendments to pleadings, further and better particulars, and further and better discovery.

V. Preliminary Measures and Interlocutory Relief

A number of pre-trial (or interlocutory) procedures are available to provide effective relief to rights holders at an early stage prior to a full trial and to ensure that any relief obtained at trial will be effective.

1. What are preliminary measures?

Litigation is a long process and expensive. In practice only a small proportion of cases go to trial.[2] Often it is the threat of litigation that allows disputes to be resolved.[3] Litigation is meant to be a means to an end not an end in itself.

---

[2] "99 cases out of 100 [go] no further", per Lord Denning in *Fellowes & Son v. Fisher* [1976] QB 122.

[3] Legislation restricts making unjustified (or indeed any) threats of litigation for infringement of certain intellectual property rights. Litigation is then a necessary evil.

Those with deep pockets may be able to face the pressures and uncertainties of litigation, but few litigants are willing to suffer the process to trial unless substantial damages or matters of principle are at stake.[4]

Preliminary measures assist in resolving issues by providing effective relief at an early stage or at least by ensuring that any relief obtained at trial will be effective. Common law judges (or strictly speaking judges of the courts of equity) have long recognised the usefulness of preliminary measures under the inherent jurisdiction of the court, originating in England under the equitable remedies of the High Court of Chancery and now recognised by statute.[5]

Preliminary measures are protective in nature and are intended to make the trial or disposal of the proceedings more effective. They fall into five broad categories:

(1) **Orders to prevent irreparable damage**, such as injunctions to prevent threatened or further infringement until trial.

(2) **Orders to preserve property**, such as in admiralty actions orders to sell perishable or deteriorating cargo and orders allowing access to premises to search for and detain infringing materials.

(3) **Orders to prevent dissipation of assets**, such as injunctions to freeze a defendant's bank account until trial.

(4) **Orders in aid of disclosure**, such as orders for disclosing the identity of infringers, discovery of documents and inspection of property.

(5) **Orders to prevent the defendant from escaping liability**, such as prohibition orders preventing a person leaving the jurisdiction.

Preliminary measures are particularly useful in intellectual property cases where the damage is often immediate and continuing but difficult to quantify; the source of infringement is frequently unknown; and there is a high risk of dissipation of goods or documents. In practice, interim or interlocutory injunctions, detention orders, search orders (Anton Piller), disclosure orders (Norwich Pharmacal) and freezing injunctions (Mareva) are common in intellectual property related actions.

2. *The TRIPS requirements*

Although rooted in the common law, the provision of preliminary remedies is now also recognised as an essential international requirement for enforcing intellectual property rights under the TRIPS Agreement.[6]

---

[4] "For one day in thy courts: is better than a thousand" (Psalm 84 verse 10).

[5] In the UK by the Supreme Court Act 1981 s 37(1) and Civil Procedure Rule 25; in Hong Kong by the High Court Ordinance s 21L(1) and Rules of the High Court Order 29 r 1.

[6] Agreement on Trade-Related Aspects of Intellectual Property Rights, Annex 1C of the Marrakesh Agreement Establishing the World Trade Organization signed in Marrakesh, Morocco on 15 April 1994.

Part III Section 3 of the TRIPS Agreement refers to "provisional measures" which has a more tentative ring than preliminary measures, recognising that such measures are generally intended to be interim in nature and not determinative of the proceedings (although in effect they often are). It is useful to set out the TRIPS requirements in full. Article 50 states:

"The judicial authorities shall have the authority to order prompt and effective provisional measures:

(a) to prevent an infringement of any intellectual property right from occurring, and in particular to prevent the entry into the channels of commerce in their jurisdiction of goods, including imported goods immediately after customs clearance;

(b) to preserve relevant evidence in regard to the alleged infringement.

The judicial authorities shall have the authority to adopt provisional measures *inaudita altera parte* where appropriate, in particular where any delay is likely to cause irreparable harm to the right holder, or where there is a demonstrable risk of evidence being destroyed.

The judicial authorities shall have the authority to require the applicant to provide any reasonably available evidence in order to satisfy themselves with a sufficient degree of certainty that the applicant is the right holder and that the applicant's right is being infringed or that such infringement is imminent, and to order the applicant to provide a security or equivalent assurance sufficient to protect the defendant and to prevent abuse.

Where provisional measures have been adopted *inaudita altera parte*, the parties affected shall be given notice, without delay after the execution of the measures at the latest. A review, including a right to be heard, shall take place upon request of the defendant with a view to deciding, within a reasonable period after the notification of the measures, whether these measures shall be modified, revoked or confirmed.

The applicant may be required to supply other information necessary for the identification of the goods concerned by the authority that will execute the provisional measures.

Without prejudice to paragraph 4, provisional measures taken on the basis of paragraphs 1 and 2 shall, upon request by the defendant, be revoked or otherwise cease to have effect, if proceedings leading to a decision on the merits of the case are not initiated within a reasonable period, to be determined by the judicial authority ordering the measures where a Member's law so permits or, in the absence of such a determination, not to exceed 20 working days or 31 calendar days, whichever is the longer.

Where the provisional measures are revoked or where they lapse due to any act or omission by the applicant, or where it is subsequently found that there has been no infringement or threat of infringement of an intellectual property right, the judicial authorities shall have the authority to order the applicant, upon request of the defendant, to provide the defendant appropriate compensation for any injury caused by these measures.

To the extent that any provisional measure can be ordered as a result of administrative procedures, such procedures shall conform to principles equivalent in substance to those set forth in this Section."

The TRIPS requirements envisage interim injunctions and orders for the preservation of evidence, which may be taken *ex parte* ("without hearing the other party") where delay may lead to irreparable harm or a demonstrable risk that evidence may be destroyed. These measures are already well established under common law regimes.

Separate provisions of TRIPS deals with cross-border detention of goods by customs authorities prior to being put into circulation.[7] These measures were not clearly provided for under the common law. Although customs officers in Hong Kong have the right to seize goods suspected of infringing trade marks or copyright, they have discretion whether or not to do so depending on the likelihood of securing a criminal conviction. The new cross-border provisions[8] only require reasonable grounds for suspecting infringement and the customs authority must take action upon the application of the rights owner.

3. Preliminary injunctions

In Hong Kong, under the High Court Ordinance and Rules of the High Court, a judge of the Court of First Instance may by order (whether interlocutory or final) grant an injunction in all cases in which it appears to be just or convenient to do so.[9] RHC Order 29 rule 1(1) states:

> "An application for the grant of an injunction may be made by any party to a cause or matter before or after the trial of the cause or matter, whether or not a claim for the injunction was included in that party's writ, originating summons, counterclaim or third party notice, as the case may be."

The court thus has jurisdiction to grant an injunction at any stage, or prior to the commencement, of proceedings, but there must be a cause of action. The cause of action may be in respect of an actual or threatened (*quia timet*) infringement. In the latter case the threat must be certain or very imminent. An injunction is either an order of the court that a person shall refrain from carrying out a specific act, or an order requiring a person to perform an act (other than the payment of money). The first of these categories of injunction is called a "prohibitory" injunction and the second is called a "mandatory" injunction.

The award of an injunction is always discretionary. An interlocutory injunction may be sought prior to trial where damages alone would not be an adequate remedy and the justice of the case requires. Normally the court will only consider granting prohibitory interlocutory injunctions and, in the absence of special circumstances or unless the case is clear or there is no arguable defence, will not grant an interlocutory mandatory injunction.

---

[7] Part III Section 4 Articles 51–60.

[8] Intellectual Property (World Trade Organization Amendments) Ordinance 1996, Part III (copyright) and IIIA (trade mark).

[9] High Court Ordinance s 21L(1) and RHC O.29, r.1. Similar powers are given to District Judges under the District Courts Ordinance and Rules of the District Court.

4. American Cyanamid guidelines

Guidelines adopted for interlocutory prohibitory injunctions are set out in the leading English case of *American Cyanamid Co. v Ethicon Ltd* [1975] AC 396 which has been applied many times in Hong Kong.[10] As indicated these are in the nature of guidelines and not principles of universal application as a number of judges in subsequent cases have been keen to point out.[11]

However, the *American Cyanamid* decision marked a change in the approach to granting interim injunctions. Previously this had relied much more on the merits of the plaintiff's case. This had involved assessing on affidavit evidence whether the plaintiff had a more than 50% chance of success. In most cases this cannot be done on the basis of evidence filed at the interlocutory stage and the following test was developed:

(1) **Is there is a serious question to be tried?**

If there is no serious issue to be tried, no interlocutory injunction will be granted. The plaintiff's prospects of success may be investigated to a limited extent but only to determine that they really exist. They are not to be weighed against any prospects of failure.[12] The standard falls short of a *prima facie* case and the chances of success (unless negligible) are not relevant.[13] The court may conversely also consider whether there is any real arguable defence.

(2) **Are damages an adequate remedy and is the other party able to pay?**

An injunction may only be granted if damages would not adequately compensate the plaintiff but would adequately compensate the defendant and the plaintiff is in a position to pay such damages. A plaintiff is thus required to give a cross-undertaking in damages to the defendant and in the event the injunction is discharged the plaintiff undertakes to compensate the defendant for any damage caused by the injunction.

Conversely, no injunction is granted where the plaintiff would be adequately compensated by damages and the defendant is in position to pay them under a cross-undertaking. In appropriate cases the undertaking may be fortified by a bond or payment into court. The defendant

---

[10] Applied, e.g. in *Attorney-General in and for the United Kingdom v. South China Morning Post Ltd* [1988] 1 HKLR 143, CA.

[11] "The *American Cyanamid* case contains no principle of universal application. The only such principle is the statutory power of the court to grant injunctions when it is just and convenient to do so", per Kerr LJ in *Cambridge Nutrition Ltd v. BBC* [1990] 3 All ER 523 at 534; "There are no fixed rules as to when an injunction should or should not be granted. The relief must be kept flexible", per Laddie J in *Series 5 Software v. Clarke* [1996] 1 All ER 853.

[12] *Swatch AG v. Captoon Industries Ltd* [1995] 2 HKC 444, CA.

[13] *Mothercare v. Robson Books* [1979] FSR 466.

may also be ordered to pay a notional royalty into a joint bank account held by the solicitors pending trial[14] or to keep an account of relevant income.[15]

(3) **If there is doubt as to the adequacy of damages as a remedy, where does the balance of convenience lie?** (sometimes referred to as the "balance of justice"[16])

There is no exhaustive list of what may be taken into account in assessing the balance of convenience. The relative effects of granting or not granting an injunction are to be assessed, including the significance of the relevant businesses and the public interest (a life saving drug may preclude an injunction[17]).

(4) **Where other factors are evenly balanced, what will preserve the status quo?**

An injunction is more likely to be granted when the alleged infringing business is not yet established. A question arises as to when the status quo is to be judged.

(5) **Does the court have a clear view of the relative strengths of the parties' cases?** If so, this is also a factor to take into account. Indeed, where there is no real dispute on the facts, the court will not even need to consider the adequacy of damages, the balance of convenience or the status quo.

5. Ex parte *applications*

An application for an injunction may be made *ex parte*, without issuing a summons or giving notice to the other side, either in the event of urgency when delay may cause irreparable injury or the nature of the case requires secrecy to be maintained. Examples of the latter include Anton Piller and Mareva injunctions where there is a real likelihood that evidence or assets may be destroyed or removed from the jurisdiction if the defendant were given notice of the application.

In each case, because the application is *ex parte*, there is a duty to give full disclosure. If anything, the affidavits should err on the side of excessive disclosure and the court is the judge of relevance. The defendant also has the automatic right to apply to discharge such an order.

---

[14] *Coco v. A.N Clark (Engineers) Ltd* [1969] RPC 41.

[15] *Warren v. Mendy* [1989] 1 WLR 853.

[16] Per Sir John Donaldson MR in *Francome v. Mirror Newspapers Ltd* [1984] 1 WLR 892.

[17] *Roussel-Uclaf v. Searle (GD) & Co* [1977] FSR 125.

6. *Mareva (freezing) injunction*

A Mareva[18] injunction, with its companion the Anton Piller order, is one of the law's two nuclear weapons.[19] It is an interlocutory injunction obtained *ex parte*. It restrains a party to any proceedings from removing from the jurisdiction of the court, or otherwise dealing with, assets located within that jurisdiction or, in certain circumstances, outside the jurisdiction. The Mareva injunction has the effect of "freezing" assets so that an existing judgment or an anticipated judgment may be satisfied from those assets. In England, following the Woolf reforms, it is now known as a freezing injunction.

A Mareva injunction is a right *in personam*, not *in rem*. It does not therefore create any property or security over the frozen assets. Breach of the order is a contempt of court, but if the defendant becomes bankrupt or goes into liquidation, the plaintiff is in the same position as other unsecured creditors.

The jurisdiction to grant a Mareva injunction is exercisable in any case where it appears just and convenient to the court to grant the injunction and:

(1) there is at least a good arguable case that the plaintiff is entitled to judgment for a sum of money from the defendant; and
(2) there is a real risk that the defendant will remove assets from the jurisdiction or dispose of them so that any judgment or award will remain unsatisfied.

The plaintiff does not have to show an intention to dispose of assets specifically as a reaction to the litigation. Also, he need not show that the risk of dissipation, hiding or removal of assets is more likely than not.[20] The court also need not expect proof of previous defaults or specific instances of commercial malpractice. The court may simply consider the evidence as a whole and draw inferences.

There are various examples of cases where the court has found sufficient evidence of a real risk of dissipation of assets. Relevant considerations include:

(1) Events which put the reliability of the defendant in doubt.
(2) The involvement of foreign companies whose structure invites comments—these might include the involvement of Panamanian or Liberian companies where it is often hard to determine who has the true ownership or control of the companies.
(3) The defendant's evasiveness in disclosing its assets.
(4) The defendant's failure to provide evidence of financial substance.

---

[18] Laid down by the English Court of Appeal in *Mareva Compania Naviera SA v. International Bulkcarriers SA* 2 Lloyd's Rep 50; [1980] 1 All ER 213, CA.

[19] Per Donaldson LJ in Bank Mellat *v.* Nikpour (Mohammed Ebrahim) [1985] FSR 87 CA.

[20] *Third Chandris Shipping Corporation v. Unimarine SA* [1979] 1 QB 645.

(5) The defendant's use of nominee companies and overseas connections enabling it to hide assets.[21]

In exceptional circumstances where a defendant has assets abroad, and its assets within the jurisdiction are insufficient to satisfy the potential judgment, the court will grant a Mareva injunction preventing the defendant from dissipating any assets, wherever they are located. However, the effect of such an injunction differs substantially from a "domestic" Mareva injunction in that third parties who are abroad will not be affected by the order. In addition, the court must act carefully to avoid any conflict of jurisdiction between itself and the court of the jurisdiction where the assets are situated.[22]

7. *Anton Piller order*

The Anton Piller[23] order is the second "nuclear weapon" of civil litigation. It has been described as a "civil search warrant". In England, following the Woolf reforms, it is now known as a search order. The name gives some indication of the nature of the order, but it is a little misleading because it is not an order to search but to allow to search.

The essence of an Anton Piller order is that, in addition to the usual prohibitory injunction, it requires the defendant or other person in apparent control of specified premises to permit the plaintiff and his solicitor to enter those premises, to allow them to search for offending articles and documents, to deliver up offending articles into the custody of the plaintiff's solicitors, to allow them to copy relevant documents and to provide information on sources of supply and destination of suspected infringements. Where documents are stored in a computer, the order may require them to be printed out in readable form.[24] If locked in a cupboard, the defendant may be required to provide the key.[25]

"It does not authorise the plaintiff's solicitors or anyone else to enter the premises against the defendant's will. It does not authorise the breaking down of any doors nor the slipping in by the back door, nor getting in by an open door or window. It only authorises entry and inspection with the permission of the defendant."[26] If the defendant does not give permission, he is liable for contempt of court.

---

[21] *Adams v. Cape Industries plc* [1991] 1 All ER 929 and *Trustor AB v. Smallbone and others* [2001] 2 BCLC 436.

[22] *Derby & Co Ltd v. Weldon* [1990] Ch 13; *Derby & Co Ltd v. Weldon* (Nos 3 & 4) [1990] Ch 65.

[23] Laid down by the English Court of Appeal in *Anton Piller KG v. Manufacturing Processes Ltd* [1976] 1 All ER 779, although recognised by the lower courts in earlier cases such as *EMI Ltd v. Pandit* [1975] 1 WLR 302.

[24] *Gates v. Swift* [1982] RPC 339.

[25] *Hazel Grove Music Co v. Elster Enterprises* [1983] FSR 379.

[26] Per Lord Denning in *Anton Piller KG v. Manufacturing Processes Ltd* [1976] 1 All ER 779 at 782.

Ormrod LJ set out three essential pre-conditions: [27]

(1) There must be an extremely strong *prima facie* case.
(2) The damage, potential or actual, must be very serious for the applicant.
(3) There must be clear evidence that the defendants have in their possession incriminating documents or items, and that there is a real possibility that they may destroy such material before any application *inter partes* can be made.

8. *A strong* prima facie *case*

This test is different from and more onerous than the test of a "good arguable case" for Mareva injunctions or a "serious question to be tried" which applies in the case of interlocutory injunctions generally. Suspicion of a good cause of action is not enough.

9. *Serious damage likely*

This requirement has two parts. First, the loss or damage caused by the alleged wrongful actions of the defendant must be serious and there must be evidence to show that. Second, if the material believed to be in the defendant's hands is destroyed, prejudice to the plaintiff's chances of success at trial must be serious.

10. *Likelihood of disposal of evidence*

The court must be satisfied that the defendant is in possession of documents or things that there is a "real possibility" that evidence or infringing material will be destroyed.[28] Such evidence is generally very difficult to obtain and it has been common for the court to infer the probability of disappearance or destruction of evidence where it is clearly established on the evidence before the court that the defendant is acting in an underhand manner.

A mere possibility that evidence will be destroyed is not enough to justify the order. It is not always appropriate to assume that a defendant will refuse to comply with an order requiring him to preserve or deliver up documents. Even evidence of breach of confidence may not be enough to satisfy the court that the defendant will flagrantly breach an order.

11. *Plaintiff's undertakings*

An undertaking is required stating that the order will be served by a solicitor of the High Court. In England, an independent supervising solicitor with experience of such orders must be appointed and this is sometimes a requirement in Hong Kong.

---

[27] *Anton Piller KG v. Manufacturing Processes Ltd* [1976] 1 All ER 779 at 784.
[28] *In Booker McConnell v. Plascow plc* [1985] RPC 425 at 441, Dillon LJ contrasted this with the "extravagant fears which seem to afflict all plaintiffs who have complaints of breach of confidence, breach of copyright or passing off."

Copies of the affidavits and exhibits read to the court at the *ex parte* application and any skeleton argument must be served on the defendant, together with the *inter partes* summons.

An undertaking is required assuring the court that any material obtained pursuant to the order will not be used other than for the purposes of the proceedings. Leave of the court may be obtained to allow the information obtained as a result of the Anton Piller order to be used against third parties implicated in the same infringement (such as suppliers or customers of the defendant business).

An undertaking in damages, including where necessary fortification, is required.

12. *Undertakings by the plaintiff's solicitors*

The plaintiff's solicitors are required to give the following undertakings:

(1) to inform the defendant of his right to seek legal advice before complying with the order, provided that such advice is sought and obtained immediately;

(2) to make a detailed record of the material taken pursuant to the terms of the order before the material is removed from the defendant's premises;

(3) to make copies of any documentary material taken pursuant to the terms of the order and to return the original material to its owner within a relatively short period of time;

(4) in cases where the ownership of material is in dispute and the circumstances require that it should, pending trial, be kept from the defendant, to deliver such material to the solicitors for the defendant (as soon as they are on the record) on their undertaking for its safe custody and production, if required, in court; and

(5) to retain all articles and documents delivered up in the plaintiff's solicitors' safe custody or under their control.

The above requirements follow guidelines laid down by Sir Donald Nicholls V-C in the English case of *Universal Thermosensors Ltd v Hibben* [1992] 3 All ER 256, which resulted in new practice directions for Anton Piller orders and Mareva injunctions being issued in England[29] and Hong Kong.[30] These include standard forms of orders and sets out the requirements of such orders in detail. Any departure from the standard form orders must be properly justified.

---

[29] Practice Direction (Mareva Injunctions and Anton Piller Orders [1994] 1 WLR 1233, now replaced by Civil Procedure Rules 1998 Part 25 Practice Direction (Interim Injunctions).

[30] Hong Kong High Court Practice Direction No. 11.2 "Mareva Injunctions and Anton Piller Orders".

The decision in *Universal Thermosensors* was considered by the Hong Kong Court of Appeal in *Tamco Electrical & Electronics (Hong Kong) Ltd v Ng Chun Fai & Others* [1994] 1 HKLR 178 holding *inter alia* that:

(1) An applicant's solicitors and counsel in an *ex parte* application come under a duty to assist the judge so as to ensure as far as possible that the court does not make an order which perpetrates an injustice against the absent party.

(2) No order should be made unless necessary in the interests of justice; nor in terms wider than necessary to achieve the legitimate object of the order; nor unless there is real reason to believe that without such an order the respondent would disobey an injunction for the preservation of the evidence the destruction of which would defeat the ends of justice.

In the United Kingdom, due to abuses that have occurred in execution of Anton Piller Orders, courts have been less willing to grant Anton Piller Orders. In Hong Kong, however, courts continue to grant Anton Piller Orders which are proved to be very powerful and effective tools in the hands of rights owners, especially where combined with raid actions in China.

13. Order for Preservation of Property (Order 29)

Where the plaintiff is aware of certain property that it wishes to have preserved, but it is not possible to satisfy the requirements for an Anton Piller Order, an application may be made under Order 29 of the High Court Rules for an order for the delivery up and detention of specific property which is relevant to the action and which is in the other party's possession or control, pending the full hearing of the action. This Order is more limited than the Anton Piller Order as it relates only to specified goods and does not permit the plaintiff to conduct a search of the Defendant's premises.

VI. Pre-action Alternative to Interlocutory Proceedings

Where it appears that an infringer is not aware that they are infringing the rights of the intellectual property holder, such as the case of small retailers, one method which can prove to be quite effective in eliminating infringements is a personal visit to the infringer's premises by representatives of the rights holder accompanied by their lawyers. This procedure involves explaining the rights of the proprietor of the intellectual property and requiring immediate delivery up of infringing materials together with a request that the infringer sign an undertaking to cease infringement. If the infringer does not comply with these requests, court action may be commenced.

The principal benefit of this approach is that the matter can be settled quickly and without the expense and time involved in taking legal proceedings. An important factor to take into account is that the infringer might be a future customer of the intellectual property right holder and an informal approach may not irrevocably sever ties with the infringer.

1. *Letter Before Action*

The Letter Before Action, which is also known as a "cease and desist" letter or warning letter, is generally the first step which is taken against an infringer, unless it has been decided to seek an Anton Piller Order or Mareva injunction where secrecy is required.

The Letter Before Action sets out a rights owner's intellectual property rights, the fact that the rights owner has evidence that the infringer has infringed those rights and a demand that the infringer should sign an undertaking in the following terms:

(1) The infringer admits the rights of the rights owner and that he has infringed those rights; and
(2) Undertakes: (i) to cease the infringing acts;
             (ii) to provide the names of customers and suppliers;
             (iii) to provide a full account of the sales and purchases;
             (iv) to deliver up or destroy on oath the infringing goods in their possession or control;
             (v) to pay compensation (the amount of which will depend on the extent and flagrancy of the infringement).

In the event that the infringer is not prepared to sign the undertaking or if he should fail to respond to the Letter Before Action within the given period, court action can be commenced against him.

Should the infringer sign the undertaking and subsequently breach any of the terms, he can be sued for breach of undertaking as well as for infringement of intellectual property rights. In such a case the damages will be assessed by reference to the position that the rights owner would have been in had the infringer complied with all of the terms of the undertaking.

Where the legal position of a right holder is not clear cut, it can be useful to obtain undertakings from infringers so as to strengthen any future infringement proceedings.

Care should be exercised when using cease and desist letters given groundless threats provisions in the Trade Mark Ordinance, the Registered Designs Ordinance and the Patents Ordinance. These provisions entitle persons aggrieved by the threats of proceedings to commence a groundless threat action against the maker of a threat. Such an action may be defended by showing that the threat is justified. Groundless threats are not available if proceedings are commenced within 28 days of the making of the alleged threat (trade mark matters) or if the letter/threat is addressed to the manufacturer of a product or user of a process (patent matters) or to the importer or manufacturer of a product (registered design matters).

A threat includes any statement (oral or written) that leads the recipient reasonably to believe that infringement proceedings may be commenced. A threat may be made by way of letter, circular, advertisement, warning notice or otherwise. It is not necessary for the threat to have been communicated either directly or through an agent to the person threatened for it to be actionable, so long as another person was threatened by it. A threat may still be actionable even if it was made in good faith and in the honest belief that the claimed infringement was valid.

The upshot of all this is that cease and desist letters as well as notices, circulars or advertisements need to be carefully checked before they are published, circulated or sent out, to ensure that they do not constitute an *"actionable"* threat. This is of paramount importance since even the slight insinuations may constitute an actionable threat, and the consequences for the maker of the threat can be severe.

A safe option is "to sue first, negotiated afterwards". This is especially desirable in cases where the plaintiff has a strong position on infringement, as it is possible to bring an infringement action before making any threats. After proceedings have been issued, the plaintiff can always enter into settlement negotiations with the infringer.

Saying this, depending on the nature of infringement, there are different ways in which cease and desist letters can be worded to avoid threats actions. For instance, in patent infringement action, the letter can be worded in such a way as to notify the suspected infringer that the plaintiff actually owns the patent right.

VII. Writ of Summons

To issue proceedings, a Writ of Summons is filed with the High Court and served on the Defendant. The Writ of Summons will either include an Indorsement of Claim, briefly setting out the plaintiff's claim against the defendant, or a Statement of Claim setting out in full the plaintiff's claims.

The Writ acts as an official notice that proceedings have been instituted against the defendant. The plaintiff must arrange to serve a sealed copy of the writ on the defendant. The method of service differs depending upon whether service is to be effected upon an individual, a limited company, a partnership or some other type of organisation. Generally, service can be effected personally or by post. Service by registered post or by leaving the Writ in the defendant's letterbox is also allowed. However, if the defendant claims not to have received the Writ, the court may find that service by registered post or leaving in the letterbox has not been properly effected.

When serving the writ, the plaintiff must enclose an acknowledgment of service form which is a standard court document. When the defendant receives the writ, he must complete the acknowledgment of service form and return it to the court within 14 days and indicate whether he intends to defend the action. In cases where the defendant is an individual and the writ is served on him by sending a copy of the writ by registered post to his usual or last known address, the date of service is deemed to be the seventh day after the date on which the writ was sent to the address in question unless the contrary is shown.

VIII. Statement of Claim

The Statement of Claim sets out in detail the plaintiff's claim against the defendant and the relief which he is seeking. The Statement of Claim must state the core facts the plaintiff relies on in support of the action. It will include details of the plaintiff's intellectual property rights and the alleged acts of infringement committed by the defendant.

The statement of claim may be included in the writ, but it is equally permissible to serve it as a separate document, either with the writ or at any time up to 14 days after the filing of the acknowledgment of service.

IX. Judgment in Default of Defence

If the defendant does not file a Defence within 14 days of service of the Statement of Claim (or where the Statement of Claim is served with the writ 28 days from service of the writ), the plaintiff is entitled to apply to the court for Judgment in default of defence. The plaintiff will need to file an affidavit/affirmation to confirm that service has been properly effected. The application for judgment in default of defence in intellectual property cases which will include claims for injunctions is made by summons to be heard by a judge. If the plaintiff is successful in his application for default judgment, then he will usually receive only nominal fixed costs in respect of the proceedings.

Because failure to file a Defence is a technical default, no evidence or proof of the plaintiff's claim is required. If the defendant does not appear on the summons or cannot give a good explanation for failing to file, a defence judgment will be entered for the plaintiff. If the defendant does appear and gives a good explanation the judge, the judge will usually allow more time to file a defence.

X. Summary Judgment

The court may grant summary judgment, i.e. judgment without a full trial, at any stage before trial if it is satisfied that the defendant has no credible defence to the plaintiff's claim. The plaintiff can make an application for summary judgment in most types of actions at any time after the defendant has given notice of intention to defend. The plaintiff will issue a summons supported by an affidavit/affirmation, which verifies the facts on which the claim is based and states the belief of the deponent (the person swearing the affidavit) that there is no credible defence.

If a private investigator has been engaged, the private investigator will need to give affidavit evidence of infringement. The defendant may file evidence in reply setting out its defence.

The court will grant summary judgment only in the most clear and straightforward cases. At the hearing, the master/judge may make any of the following orders:

- judgment for the plaintiff
  (i) If it is clear that the defendant's alleged defence is nothing more than "moonshine" (to use the court's words in one leading case);

- unconditional leave to defend
  (i) If the master is satisfied that the defendant has raised triable issues.

- conditional leave to defend
  (i) If the master doubts the good faith of the defendant or believes that the defence raised may be a sham, leave can be given to the defendant to defend the action but subject to conditions. The most common condition is for the defendant to pay all or part of the sum claimed into court before being allowed to defend the action.

If the defendant is given leave to defend, the master will give directions as to the further conduct of the action.

In intellectual property cases, summary judgment applications are generally made in trade mark and copyright cases where it is a relatively simple matter to prove infringement.

Where a defendant has been convicted in a criminal trial for intellectual property infringement, as a general rule the court will grant summary judgment in a civil case.

XI. Defence

If the defendant intends to contest the proceedings he must, unless he obtains an extension of time, file a Defence. If the statement of claim is endorsed on the writ, the defendant must serve a defence within 28 days of service of the writ. If the statement of claim is not served with the writ, the defence must be served within 14 days of service of the statement of claim.

The defendant must consider each and every allegation contained in the statement of claim and should address them in the defence. In the Defence, the defendant will set out his reasons for disputing the plaintiff's claim which he may deny in full or in part. The defendant may also choose to file a counterclaim with his defence if he has a claim against the plaintiff. This could include, for example, a claim that a patent is invalid. The plaintiff would then have to file a defence to counterclaim, failing which the defendant could enter judgment on the counterclaim.

XII. Reply (and Defence to Counterclaim)

Where there are matters in the Defence to which the plaintiff wishes to reply, or a counterclaim has been made by the defendant, the plaintiff will file a Reply and Defence to Counterclaim.

A reply should be served to plead specifically any matter which makes the defence of the other party unmaintainable, to plead specifically any matter which raises new issues of fact, or to admit part of the defence (to save costs).

XIII. Discovery

The next stage in proceedings is discovery. In discovery both parties are required to disclose all documents and records which are relevant to the action.

There is a strict obligation imposed on both parties not to misuse any documents obtained on discovery other than for the purposes of the action. The documents cannot, for example, be used in different proceedings against the defendant.

Where confidential information may need to be disclosed, a party can ask the court to limit disclosure, by for example not allowing the other party to take copies.

XIV. Witness Statements

Witness statements are exchanged prior to trial so that each side may see the evidence the other side intends to lead. All necessary evidence must be disclosed in the statement. Evidence not disclosed in this way may, at the trial, be ruled inadmissible.

It is now the practice of the court to order that the witness statement shall stand as the evidence in chief of the witness.

XV. Trial

Most civil trials in the Court of First Instance are before a single judge without a jury. Each party must be represented by a barrister (counsel) and solicitor or must appear "in person".

At trial of the action, the court will hear the evidence and legal submissions of the parties and make findings of facts as to whether infringement has occurred and then findings of law based on those findings of fact. The court will hand down a written judgment.

The procedure at trial is for the plaintiff to first open its case by making a statement setting out the facts it will prove and the law to support its case that the defendant has infringed its rights. The plaintiff will then call its witnesses to prove the facts. Except where a witness has died, cannot be found or is overseas and has a good reason for not coming to Hong Kong, witnesses are required to give oral evidence to the court and to be cross-examined by the other party.

Witnesses may be "examined-in-chief" by counsel for the party which called them who will ask questions based upon that witness's evidence. However, the general rule now is for witnesses' statements to stand as evidence-in-chief. The witnesses are open to cross-examination by counsel for the other side. A witness may be re-examined if counsel wishes to ask the witness questions arising from the cross-examination which were not addressed in the original statement or examination-in-chief.

Experts give evidence in the same way as normal witnesses but are entitled to give "opinion evidence".

After the plaintiff has given all its evidence the defendant will give its evidence. The defendant may decide to give no evidence and rely instead on points of law.

At the end of the trial, the plaintiff will make legal submissions on the evidence the court has heard. The defendant will then make submissions. The plaintiff has a final right of reply.

The judge will then make a decision or reserve his decision for later.

Unless there is a good reason to the contrary, once a trial is commenced, the court will hear all evidence and legal submissions without adjourning.

XVI. Appeal

If either side is not satisfied with a judgment or any interlocutory order, an appeal may be made to a higher court. There are two appellate courts in Hong Kong. The Court of Appeal and the Court of Final Appeal. With the handover of Hong Kong to China, the Court of Final Appeal was established locally to replace the Privy Council as Hong Kong's highest appellate court. There is an automatic right of appeal to the Court of Appeal. Leave must be granted by either the Court of Appeal or the Court of Final Appeal for appeals to the Court of Final Appeal.

Upon appeal after trial of an action, the appellate courts will generally only consider if the trial judge has made a mistake of law. The appellate courts will not interfere with the findings of facts of the trial judge unless it is shown that there was no evidence to support those findings.

XVII. Assessment of Damages

In intellectual property cases, the trial will usually focus solely on whether infringement has occurred or not. If the court finds in favour of the plaintiff, there will be an order for assessment of damages or an account of profits. The plaintiff must elect one or the other. Assessments and accounts are usually conducted before a master (a lower level judge).

In an assessment of damages, the plaintiff puts forward its claim as to the damage it has suffered by the infringement. This can include lost sales, lost future sales because of forced reduction in price and lost goodwill.

The defendant is required to disclose all its dealings in infringing products for the assessment. If the defendant refuses to disclose its records to show how many products it has dealt with, the court will accept any reasonable submission made by the plaintiff as to the amount of damages. This is because the defendant has shown bad faith in failing to disclose its records and the court will assume it has something to hide.

In an account of profits, a defendant is required to prepare a statement showing the profits it has made from its infringing activities. Because the defendant is allowed to deduct general business expenses from any profit made, this statement usually shows no profit has been made. For this reason, most plaintiffs will elect an assessment of damages. Damages will be ordered even where the defendant has made no profit.

XVIII. Taxation of Costs

The court will also make an award of the costs of the action and it is a rule of thumb that the successful party is awarded his costs. Where the parties cannot agree on a figure, they will apply to have them assessed or "taxed" by the court. This is a procedure where the party with the costs order in their favour will prepare a schedule of the lawyer's fees and other costs incurred in the conduct of the action. A master will conduct a hearing to assess these costs and order the other party to pay the amount determined after the hearing.

XIX. Enforcement of Judgments and Orders

1. Enforcement of injunctions

The court will enforce a final or interlocutory injunction ordering a defendant to do an act or not do an act by contempt proceedings. An undertaking given in a court order may also be enforced in the same way as an injunction.

Where the plaintiff considers that the defendant has not complied with an order, the plaintiff must apply to the court to have the order enforced. If the court agrees that the defendant has not complied with its order, the court will fine or imprison the defendant or, where the defendant is a limited company, one of the directors.

The court will very rarely find a party in contempt on its own motion, that is, without an application by one of the parties.

2. Enforcement of monetary awards

There are four principal methods which are used for enforcing monetary awards for damages or costs against a defendant.

3. Charging Order

A Charging Order has the effect of preventing the defendant from selling the property until the debt is paid. A charging order may be made over land, stocks and shares, unit trusts and funds in court. A charging order on land is registered at the Lands Office and a charging order on shares is registered at the Companies Registry. If the defendant does not pay the debt, the plaintiff may apply to the court to sell the property.

4. Writ of Fi-Fa

The Writ of Fi-Fa or Execution Order is a writ issued by the court to a bailiff, instructing him to enter the defendant's property and to seize the defendant's goods to the value of the claim. The defendant will then have a set amount of time to discharge the claim in default of which the goods seized will be sold to settle the debt. The bailiff sells the property and uses the proceeds to pay the debt, interest, bailiff fees and costs to the plaintiff. The writ can be issued as soon as the judgment or the order is entered. There is no need for the judgment or order to have been served on the defendant or any demand made of him.

5. *Garnishee order*

Where a plaintiff knows that the defendant holds a bank account or accounts and is aware of their details he can apply for a Garnishee order which will require the Bank to pay the defendant's debt to the plaintiff from the defendant's account or accounts with them.

6. *Prohibition order*

A prohibition order is an order prohibiting a person from leaving Hong Kong until a court award is paid. Prohibition orders are granted for a period of one month and are renewable. They can be a very effective means for forcing a debtor to pay.

XX. Settlement

The majority of cases before the courts will settle. Litigation is a long and expensive process. Often it is the threat of litigation that allows disputes to be resolved. Litigation is meant to be a means to an end not an end in itself. If the parties agree to settle a matter out of court it is advisable for a rights owner to insist that the defendant should consent to Judgment being entered against him which will be done by way of a Judgment by Consent. Such a judgment will include the relief sought in the Statement of Claim and can be enforced in the same way as any other judgment.

XXI. English Civil Procedure Rules and Report on Civil Justice Reform in Hong Kong

New Civil Procedure Rules were introduced in England following Lord Woolf's "Access to Justice" Report. A similar exercise is taking place in Hong Kong following the setting up of the Chief Justice's Working Party on "Civil Justice Reform".

On 3 March 2004 the Working Party appointed by the Chief Justice published its long-awaited Final Report on reform to Hong Kong's civil justice system (the Final Report). As anticipated, the Working Party has recommended that the reform should take the form of selective adoption of the changes implemented in England and Wales in 1999 (commonly known as the Woolf reforms) and integrate them into the existing Hong Kong legal framework. The Final Report addresses, amongst other things, the widely-held view that Hong Kong's existing system makes litigation far too expensive, too complex and too slow. A total of 150 recommendations have been put forward by the Working Party to the Chief Justice with the aim of remedying or at least reducing substantially these inherent problems.

The Chief Justice has accepted all the recommendations put forward by the Working Party in its Final Report. The next step will require the Department of Justice to start drafting the amendments to the High Court Rules, High Court Ordinance and other related legislation.